The Faculty Keystone
New Professor's Success Strategies

Dave Schippers, Sc.D.

Iron Dog LLC

Grand Rapids

Copyright © 2026 by Dave Schippers

All rights reserved.

Cover art created with Dall-E, ChatGPT.

Published in the United States by Iron Dog LLC

David Schippers.

the faculty keystone: new professor's success strategies

Includes bibliographical references and index.

ISBN 979-8-9922934-5-6

1. Higher education teaching, 2. Faculty development, 3. College pedagogy and andragogy, 4. Course design and curriculum development, 5. Assessment and evaluation in higher education, 6. Academic governance and accreditation, 7. Faculty professionalism and ethics, 8. Inclusive and student-centered teaching, 9. Educational psychology for faculty, 10. Technology and artificial intelligence in teaching, 11. Research–teaching integration, 12. Faculty mentorship and advising, 13. Academic career development and tenure, 14. Faculty well-being and resilience.

Table of Contents

Editor's Foreword 13
Chapter 1: Teaching and Learning Introduction 14
    Learning Outcomes 15
  Introduction to Faculty Training 15
  Developing the Right Mindset for Teaching: Understanding Andragogy vs. Pedagogy 17
  Growth Mindset in Teaching: A Cognitive Psychology Perspective 21
  Academic Rigor vs. Real-World Application 24
  Core Values of Higher Education Faculty 25
  Goals for New Faculty in Higher Education 33
  Conclusion and Next Steps 41
  Faculty Mindset Self-Assessment Tool 45
    Section A: Mindset & Identity 45
    Section B: Student-Centeredness & Inclusivity 45
    Section C: Growth Orientation & Professional Development 45
    Section D: Theory-to-Practice Integration 46
    Reflection Questions 46
Chapter 2: Foundations of Higher Education Teaching 47
  Overview of Higher Education Teaching 47
  The Evolution and Philosophical Foundations of Higher Education Teaching 48
  Understanding Adult Learners and Learning Theories: A Strategic Framework for Higher Education Faculty 51
    Critical Characteristics of Adult Learners 51
    Transformative Learning Theory and the Professional Identity Shift 52
  Faculty Self-Reflection: Psychological Safety, Emotional Intelligence, and Jungian Insights 53
    Psychological Safety: Creating Space for Engagement and Failure 53
    Emotional Intelligence: The Foundation of Safe Classrooms 54
    Jungian Psychology: Confronting the Unconscious Educator 54
    Reflection Prompts for Faculty Self-Exploration 56
    Conclusion: The Inner Work of Teaching 56
  Comparative Analysis of Core Learning Models 56
    Constructivist vs. Instructivist Models 56
    Behaviorism, Cognitivism, and Constructivism: A Comparative Lens [28] 57

- Differences Between Undergraduate and Graduate-Level Teaching 57
  - The Role of the Professor: Mentor, Facilitator, and Evaluator 62
- The Mentor Professor: Leading Academic and Professional Growth 62
- Higher Education Policies and Academic Governance 66
- Teaching Across Institutional Contexts: Adapting Approaches to Diverse Academic Environments 70
  - Institutional Missions and Core Expectations 70
  - Faculty Roles and Student Demographics 71
- Adapting to Institutional Mission and Student Demographics 72
  - Institutional Mission as a Driver of Teaching Practice 72
  - Aligning Course Design with Student Demographics 72
  - Pedagogical Calibration: Rigor, Accessibility, and Mentorship 73
- Working Within Resource Constraints 73
  - Resource Realities Across Institution Types 73
  - Strategies for Creative Adaptation 74
  - Leveraging Institutional Supports 74
  - Advocacy and Resource Stewardship 74
- Regional Accreditation Differences 75
  - Overview of Regional Accrediting Bodies 75
  - Differences in Emphasis and Faculty Implications 75
  - Faculty Roles in Accreditation Alignment 76
  - Risks of Misalignment 76
- Navigating Union Environments and Collective Bargaining Impacts 77
  - Key Areas Defined by Union Contracts 77
  - Protections Provided by Union Agreements 77
  - Obligations Under Union Agreements 78
  - Non-Union Environments: Flexibility with Fewer Safeguards 78
  - Practical Guidance for New Faculty 78
- Managing Teaching Loads Across Institution Types 79
  - Teaching Loads by Institution Type 79
  - Time Management and Workload Strategies 79
  - Balancing Quality and Sustainability 80
- Chapter 3: Course Design and Curriculum Development 82

- Backward Course Design: Setting Objectives First ... 82
- Aligning Course Content with Learning Outcomes ... 86
- Creating an Effective Syllabus: Structure, Policies, and Expectations ... 90
- Understanding Accreditation Requirements and Curriculum Alignment ... 94
- Developing Engaging and Inclusive Course Materials ... 98
- Cross-Disciplinary Pedagogies: Teaching Beyond Disciplinary Boundaries ... 102
  - Translating Concepts Across Disciplinary Languages ... 102
  - Managing Diverse Knowledge Bases Within Single Courses ... 103
  - Faculty Role in Balancing Knowledge Gaps ... 104
  - Leveraging Student Strengths in the Classroom ... 104
  - Creating a Supportive Learning Climate ... 104
  - Team-Based Interdisciplinary Project Design ... 105
  - Purpose of Interdisciplinary Team Projects ... 105
  - Structuring Effective Projects ... 105
  - Faculty Role in Guiding Collaboration ... 106
  - Assessment of Team Projects ... 106
  - Example in Practice ... 106
  - Assessment of Interdisciplinary Learning Outcomes ... 107
  - Facilitating Dialogue Between Different Academic Cultures ... 109
  - Resource Sharing Across Departments ... 110
  - Navigating Different Grading Standards and Expectations ... 112

Chapter 4: Effective Teaching Strategies ... 116
- Active Learning Techniques: Engaging Students in Deep Learning ... 116
- Lecture Design and Delivery Strategies ... 121
  - 1. Constructivism: Socratic Questioning as a Process of Knowledge Construction ... 124
  - 2. Scaffolding Thinking: Vygotsky's Zone of Proximal Development (ZPD) ... 125
  - 3. Beyond Cognition: Critical Pedagogy and the Politics of Questioning ... 126
  - 4. Socratic Questioning Within the Active vs. Passive Learning Debate ... 126
  - 5. Reframing the Instructor's Role: From Expert to Critical Co-Learner ... 127
  - 6. Practical Strategies for Deep Implementation ... 127
- Hybrid, Online, and In-Person Teaching Strategies ... 128
- Encouraging Student-Driven Learning and Autonomy ... 132

    Faculty Collaboration and Team Teaching Strategies 135

    Interdisciplinary Team Teaching Approaches 137

    Managing Different Teaching Philosophies Within Collaborative Settings 139

    Assessment Strategies for Team-Taught Courses 140

    Communication Protocols Between Co-Instructors 142

    Conflict Resolution When Teaching Partners Disagree 144

    Coordinating Grading and Feedback Across Multiple Instructors 145

    Crisis Management and Emergency Remote Teaching 147

    Student Communication During Disruptions 148

    Technology Triage and Backup Systems 150

    Maintaining Academic Rigor During Crisis Transitions 152

    Supporting Student Mental Health During Disruptions 153

    Managing Reduced Resources and Access Limitations 154

    Legal and Accessibility Considerations 156

    Post-Crisis Transition Back to Normal Operations 157

  Community Engagement and Experiential Learning Integration 159

    Community Partnership Development and Maintenance 161

    Risk Management for Off-Campus Learning Experiences 162

    Assessment of Experiential Learning Outcomes 164

    Balancing Academic Objectives with Community Needs 166

    Cultural Competency for Community Engagement 167

    Legal and Ethical Considerations for Community Partnerships 169

    Reflection and Integration Strategies for Experiential Learning 170

Chapter 5: Classroom Management and Student Engagement 173

  Creating a Positive and Inclusive Classroom Culture 173

  Managing Discussions and Handling Difficult Topics 177

  Conflict Resolution and Dealing with Disruptive Students 181

  Encouraging Participation and Addressing Classroom Anxiety 185

  Using Technology for Student Engagement 188

Chapter 6: Assessment and Feedback 193

  Designing Effective Assessments: Formative vs. Summative 193

  Developing Fair and Transparent Grading Rubrics 197

- Providing Meaningful Feedback to Students 201
- Academic Integrity and Handling Plagiarism Cases 205
- Alternative Assessments and Competency-Based Grading: Rethinking Traditional Evaluation Models 208
- Redefining Assessment in the Age of AI: Proving Workplace-Ready Skills 213
  - Why Redefine Assessment? 213
  - What AI Can Simulate vs. What Humans Must Demonstrate 214
  - The New Assessment Imperative: Proof of Professional Competence 214
  - Designing AI-Resilient Assessments: A Strategic Framework 214
  - Authentic Performance Tasks 214
  - Iterative Feedback Loops 215
  - Reasoning Documentation (Process Transparency) 215
  - Collaborative Demonstration 215
  - Cross-Context Adaptability 216
  - Discipline-Specific Examples: Proving Critical Skills 216
  - Cybersecurity 216
  - Business and Management 217
  - Health Sciences 217
  - Humanities and Communication 217
  - Experiential Learning as Assessment Validation 218
  - Sample AI-Resilient Assessment Rubric 218
  - Conclusion: From Knowledge Recall to Capability Proof 218

Chapter 7: Leveraging Technology in Teaching 220
- Learning Management Systems (LMS) Like Blackboard, Canvas, and Moodle 220
- Integrating Multimedia and Interactive Content: Enhancing Engagement and Learning in Higher Education 224
- Using AI Tools for Personalized Learning and Feedback: Transforming Higher Education . 228
- Best Practices for Hybrid and Online Instruction: Creating Effective Digital Learning Environments 233
- Digital Accessibility and Universal Design for Learning (UDL): Creating Inclusive Learning Environments 237
- Technology Integration Beyond Tools 241
  - Evaluating Emerging Educational Technologies 241

    Leading Technology Adoption Within Departments 242

    Training Colleagues on New Pedagogical Technologies 244

    Balancing Innovation with Proven Practices 246

    Managing Technology Equity Issues Among Students... 247

    Data Privacy and Security in Educational Technology 249

    Long-Term Technology Planning for Courses 250

Chapter 8: Research, Scholarship, and Teaching Integration 253

  Balancing Teaching, Research, and Service: Navigating the Multifaceted Role of a College Professor 253

  Incorporating Research into Teaching: Bridging Scholarship and Pedagogy for Enhanced Learning 257

  Encouraging Student Research and Collaboration: Fostering Inquiry and Academic Engagement 261

  Writing for Academic Publication and Professional Development: Establishing a Scholarly Identity 265

  Mentorship and Guiding Students Through Academic Research: Cultivating the Next Generation of Scholars 268

  Research-Practice Integration Models 272

    Discipline-Specific Research-Teaching Integration Strategies 272

    Undergraduate vs. Graduate Research Mentorship Models 274

    Managing Research Supervision Workload 276

    Intellectual Property Considerations in Student Research 277

    Publication Ethics When Working with Students 279

    Grant Writing That Includes Teaching Components 281

    Measuring Impact of Research-Integrated Teaching 282

Chapter 9: Student Inclusivity in Higher Education 286

  Understanding Diverse Student Backgrounds: Cultivating Inclusive and Equitable Learning Environments 286

  Creating Culturally Responsive Teaching Materials: Enhancing Equity, Engagement, and Representation in Higher Education 290

  Addressing Bias in Teaching and Grading: Ensuring Fairness, Equity, and Student Success 294

  Supporting Students with Disabilities and Learning Differences: Building Inclusive and Accessible Higher Education 298

  Building an Inclusive and Supportive Learning Environment: Cultivating Equity, Engagement, and Belonging in Higher Education 302

    Incorporating Global Perspectives into Curriculum 307

    Managing Cultural Differences in Learning Styles 309

    Cross-Cultural Communication Strategies 311

    Understanding Visa and Immigration Impacts on Student Experience 312

    Religious Accommodation in Academic Settings 314

    Language Support Strategies for Non-Native English Speakers 315

Chapter 10: Communication and Professionalism 319

    Professional Communication with Students and Colleagues: Fostering Clarity, Respect, and Academic Integrity 319

    Setting Boundaries and Managing Workload Effectively: Strategies for Sustainable Academic Success 323

    Ethics in Higher Education and Avoiding Conflicts of Interest: Upholding Integrity, Fairness, and Professionalism 335

Chapter 11: Teaching Evaluations and Continuous Improvement 341

    Understanding Student Evaluations and Faculty Reviews: Leveraging Feedback for Teaching Excellence 341

    Self-Assessment and Reflective Teaching Practices: Cultivating a Growth-Oriented Approach to Teaching Excellence 346

    Peer Observations and Collaborative Teaching Improvement: Enhancing Instruction through Collegial Feedback and Shared Learning 350

    Using Data Analytics for Course Improvement: Leveraging Evidence-Based Insights to Enhance Teaching and Learning 354

    Staying Current with Educational Trends and Pedagogical Research: Advancing Teaching Excellence through Lifelong Learning 358

    Faculty Peer Review and Collaborative Improvement 362

        Structured Peer Review Protocols Beyond Observation 362

        Cross-Disciplinary Teaching Consultation Models 363

        Faculty Learning Communities and Teaching Circles 365

        Collaborative Curriculum Development Processes 366

        Peer Mentorship Programs for Teaching Improvement 368

        Group Problem-Solving for Teaching Challenges 370

Chapter 12: Continuous Improvement 373

    Understanding Traditional Tenure and Promotion Processes and Promotional Opportunities 373

    Building a Strong Teaching Portfolio: Showcasing Excellence, Growth, and Impact in Higher Education 377

Documenting Teaching Effectiveness: A Comprehensive Approach to Measuring and Showcasing Instructional Impact 382

Leadership Opportunities Within Academia: Pathways for Faculty Growth and Institutional Impact 386

Networking and Professional Development for Faculty: Expanding Influence, Knowledge, and Career Growth 390

Faculty Leadership and Institutional Change 394

    Leading Curriculum Reform Initiatives 395

    Building Consensus Among Faculty Peers 396

    Transparency 397

    Shared Ownership 397

    Navigating Institutional Politics and Hierarchies 398

    Managing Resistance to Pedagogical Innovation 399

    Advocating for Teaching Resources and Support 401

    Mentoring Junior Faculty in Teaching Excellence 403

    Contributing to Institutional Teaching Culture 404

Chapter 13: Mentorship and Student Support Services 408

The Role of Faculty in Academic Advising and Mentorship: Guiding Students Toward Academic and Professional Success 408

Identifying Students at Risk and Offering Support: A Faculty Guide to Early Intervention and Student Success 412

Navigating Campus Student Services: Maximizing Institutional Resources for Student Success 416

Encouraging Professional Development and Career Readiness in Students: The Faculty's Role in Bridging Academia and the Workforce 420

Supporting Students in Research, Internships, and Career Placements: A Faculty Guide to Professional and Academic Development 425

Chapter 14: Academic Conduct, Integrity, and Proper Attribution 430

Understanding Academic Integrity in Higher Education 430

    Definition and Importance of Academic Honesty 430

    Role of Faculty in Upholding Academic Integrity 431

Plagiarism and Proper Attribution 433

Ethical Use of AI and Emerging Technologies 436

Preventing Academic Dishonesty 440

- Handling Academic Misconduct Cases ... 442
- Cultivating a Culture of Integrity ... 446

Chapter 15: Faculty Well-Being and Psychological Resilience ... 452
- The Unique Psychological Landscape of Higher Education ... 452
- Chronic Stressors in Academic Life ... 453
  - Job Market Pressures ... 453
  - Funding Uncertainties ... 453
  - Publication Demands ... 453
  - Workload Imbalances ... 454
  - Variation Across Institution Types ... 454
- Seasonal Patterns of Academic Stress ... 455
  - Semester Cycles ... 455
  - Conference Seasons ... 455
  - Job Market Timing ... 455
  - Accreditation and Reporting Cycles ... 456
- Recognizing Early Warning Signs of Burnout and Compassion Fatigue ... 456
  - Emotional Indicators ... 456
  - Cognitive Indicators ... 456
  - Physical Indicators ... 457
  - Behavioral Indicators ... 457
  - Burnout vs. Compassion Fatigue ... 457
- Imposter Syndrome in Academic Contexts ... 457
  - Defining Imposter Syndrome and Its Prevalence in Academia ... 458
  - Strategies for Reframing Self-Doubt and Building Authentic Confidence ... 459
  - Creating Supportive Peer Networks for Mutual Validation ... 460
  - Role of Senior Faculty ... 461
  - Long-Term Cultural Impact ... 461
- Managing Rejection and Professional Setbacks ... 462
  - The Psychology of Academic Rejection ... 462
- Developing Resilience Through Reframing and Growth Mindset ... 463
  - Reframing as a Developmental Tool ... 463
  - The Growth Mindset in Academia ... 463

    Practical Applications of Reframing 463

    Benefits of Reframing and Growth-Oriented Thinking 464

Work-Life Integration and Boundary Setting 464

    The Myth of Work-Life Balance in Academia 464

    Creating Sustainable Work Rhythms and Honoring Rest Periods 465

    Designing Work Rhythms Around Energy, Not Just Time 465

    The Role of Rest in Sustained Productivity 466

    Embedding Rest Into Academic Life 466

    Preventing Burnout Through Rhythmic Integration 466

    Managing the "Always-On" Culture of Academic Life 467

    Strategies for Protecting Personal Time and Relationships 468

Building Psychological Safety in Academic Environments 470

    Creating Emotionally Safe Classrooms for Both Students and Faculty 470

    Student Bullying of Faculty for Better Grades 471

    Addressing Toxic Department Cultures and Microaggressions 473

    Developing Assertiveness Skills for Academic Conflicts 474

    Self-Advocacy Strategies in Hierarchical Academic Structures 476

References 478

About the Author 497

Editor's Foreword

Higher education faculty training often ranges from minimal onboarding to a sole focus on Learning Management Systems (LMS) training. Yet, teaching in a college setting requires far more than just technical proficiency. Many business professionals, while highly skilled in their trades and disciplines, are not automatically equipped with the pedagogical expertise needed to translate their knowledge into effective teaching.

This book serves as a guide for educators who want to master the art of teaching at the college level. Unlike corporate training, which often focuses on job-specific tasks, higher education fosters a more profound

Figure EF.1. Nastrodavus [219].

intellectual engagement—combining theoretical knowledge, practical application, and critical thinking development. The true impact of higher education is in its ability to help students not just perform tasks but also learn how to learn, preparing them to navigate complex problems beyond their immediate job roles.

Teaching in higher education is not an easy endeavor. It demands commitment, continuous development, and a willingness to refine one's approach based on evolving pedagogical research, technological advancements, and diverse student needs. Faculty members who undertake this challenge deserve recognition for their dedication to shaping the next generation of professionals, researchers, and thought leaders.

This book is designed as a roadmap for both new and seasoned faculty members looking to enhance their teaching impact in a rapidly evolving academic landscape. It offers practical strategies, research-backed insights, and guidance on developing effective courses, engaging students, integrating technology, and upholding academic integrity.

To those embarking on this journey: kudos to you for your commitment to education and your willingness to give back by guiding and mentoring future generations. Higher education thrives when faculty members embrace lifelong learning, just as they encourage their students to do. This book will help you navigate that path with confidence and purpose.

-Nastrodavus

Chapter 1: Teaching and Learning Introduction

Higher education is more than just the transfer of knowledge; it is a transformative experience shaping students' intellectual, personal, and professional growth. Faculty members serve as the architects of this transformation, bridging gaps between knowledge acquisition and critical thinking, between theory and application, and between academic theory and real-world relevance. However, effective teaching in higher education demands more than subject matter expertise—it requires an understanding of pedagogy, student engagement strategies, and the evolving landscape of academic instruction.

Figure 1.1. Teaching and Learning [219].

For new faculty members, transitioning into academia can be both exciting and challenging. Whether coming from industry or research backgrounds, educators must develop a mindset that prioritizes student success, fosters inclusive learning environments, and continuously refines teaching methodologies. The purpose of this chapter is to provide a foundational framework for new faculty, equipping them with the core principles of effective teaching and learning in higher education.

This chapter begins by exploring the essential mindset, values, and goals that define successful faculty members. It discusses the transition from industry to academia, emphasizing the shift from practitioner to educator and the importance of balancing theory with practical application. Faculty members will also be introduced to the significance of growth mindsets, continuous professional development, and the role of feedback in refining teaching strategies.

In addition, this chapter examines the balance between academic rigor and real-world application, guiding faculty on how to align industry knowledge with academic expectations while fostering student engagement through active learning techniques. The core values of higher education faculty—including commitment to student success, intellectual curiosity, collaboration, and ethical professionalism—are also outlined to help faculty navigate their responsibilities as educators, mentors, and scholars.

Finally, this chapter sets forth clear goals for new faculty members, outlining strategies for enhancing student learning outcomes, developing effective teaching strategies, building a sustainable academic career, and balancing teaching, research, and service responsibilities. By understanding these core principles, faculty members will be better enabled to navigate the challenges and opportunities of academic life, ultimately contributing to a more dynamic, inclusive, and impactful educational experiences for focused students.

As you embark on your journey as an educator, remember that teaching is an evolving practice—one requiring continuous reflection, adaptation, and engagement with students, colleagues, and the broader academic community. This chapter serves as your guide to laying the groundwork for excellence in teaching and learning, setting the stage for deeper exploration of pedagogical strategies, course design, and faculty development in the chapters that follow.

Learning Outcomes

By the end of this chapter, readers will be able to:

1. **Articulate the mindset shift** required to move from industry practice to effective academic teaching.
2. **Differentiate** between pedagogical and andragogical approaches in higher education.
3. **Describe core values** of effective college faculty, including student-centeredness, inclusivity, intellectual curiosity, and ethical responsibility.
4. **Identify strategies** for balancing theory with real-world application in the classroom.
5. **Explain the role of a growth mindset** in teaching, reflection, and professional development.
6. **Recognize the foundational responsibilities** of faculty beyond content delivery—including mentorship, feedback integration, and lifelong learning.

Introduction to Faculty Training

Transitioning from industry to academia represents a significant shift in professional identity, requiring a recalibration of mindset, expectations, and instructional methodologies. Faculty training serves as the foundational bridge that equips new educators with the pedagogical frameworks, classroom management strategies, and assessment techniques necessary to foster meaningful student engagement. This transition program is designed to introduce industry professionals to the core principles of academic teaching, providing both theoretical insights and practical tools to ensure a smooth and effective entry into the world of higher education.

Faculty training encompasses essential elements such as curriculum enhancement and design, student engagement strategies, assessment and evaluation techniques, and the use of technology in modern classrooms. Beyond these technical aspects, training also delves into the philosophy of education, the psychology of learning, and the ethical responsibilities of educators. This holistic approach ensures that new faculty members not only convey their subject matter expertise but also inspire intellectual curiosity and critical thinking among students.

Importance of Faculty Roles in Shaping Student Success

Faculty members serve as the cornerstone of higher education, playing an important role in shaping student success both within and beyond the classroom. Unlike industry roles, where productivity and efficiency are often primary goals, teaching focuses on facilitating learning, guiding intellectual growth, and mentoring students toward personal and professional development.

The influence of a faculty member extends beyond lectures and assignments; it includes fostering environments where guided students can develop analytical reasoning, problem-solving skills, and ethical judgment. Instructors are instrumental in nurturing a growth mindset among students, helping them overcome challenges, and instilling resilience in their academic journeys. Effective educators recognize that their impact goes beyond content delivery—they are mentors, advisors, and catalysts for lifelong learning.

Furthermore, faculty members contribute to institutional success by engaging in research, participating in curriculum development, and collaborating with colleagues to enhance academic offerings. Their role in higher education is multifaceted, requiring a balance between instruction, scholarship, and service to the academic community.

Differences Between Industry Experience and Academic Instruction

For professionals transitioning from industry into academia, one of the most critical adjustments is the shift from application-based expertise to instructional methodology. While industry professionals excel in applying knowledge to real-world problems, academic teaching requires them to break down complex concepts into digestible learning modules that cater to diverse student populations and groups with varying levels of prior skills and knowledge.

In industry settings, learning often occurs informally through hands-on experience, mentorship, and professional development. In academia, however, structured learning environments emphasize scaffolding knowledge, sequential curriculum design, and student-centered learning strategies. Faculty members must understand pedagogical principles such as active learning, formative assessment, and differentiated instruction to ensure that students not only absorb information but also apply and critique it effectively.

Another key distinction lies in the assessment of success. In industry, performance metrics are typically tied to efficiency, profitability, and innovation. In academia, success is measured through student learning outcomes, mastery of subject material, and the ability to cultivate critical thinking skills. Faculty members must adapt their approach to evaluation by designing fair and effective assessments that measure comprehension, synthesis, and application of knowledge rather than just output or results.

Finally, the dynamics of interaction differ significantly between industry and academia. In the workplace, collaboration often involves peers with comparable levels of expertise, whereas in the classroom, faculty must engage with students who possess varying degrees of familiarity with the subject matter. This necessitates the development of strong communication skills, patience, and the ability to adjust teaching styles to accommodate different learning preferences.

Conclusion

The journey into higher education teaching is both rewarding and transformative. As industry professionals embark on this new path, it is essential to embrace a mindset prioritizing student learning, uphold values promoting academic excellence and integrity, and set clear goals aligning with institutional expectations and personal teaching philosophies. Understanding the role of faculty in shaping student success, recognizing the differences between industry practice and academic instruction, and undergoing comprehensive faculty training will lay the foundation for a fulfilling and impactful teaching career.

Developing the Right Mindset for Teaching: Understanding Andragogy vs. Pedagogy

Transitioning into higher education as a faculty member demands more than content expertise; it requires a deliberate recalibration of mindset from subject-matter expert to educational facilitator. Teaching is not a transactional act of information delivery—it is a strategic process of cultivating cognitive engagement, critical thinking, and long-term professional competency.

To frame this shift, educators should understand three core frameworks:

- **Pedagogy** (teacher-directed learning)
- **Andragogy** (adult learning principles)
- **Heutagogy** (self-determined, lifelong learning)

Together, these models form a **continuum of learner autonomy and professional development.**

Pedagogy, derived from traditional child-focused education models, centers on instructor-directed learning. Here, learners are assumed to be dependent on the teacher for structure, motivation, and knowledge sequencing. Pedagogical approaches emphasize foundational knowledge acquisition, often through structured lessons, rote memorization, and assessment-driven instruction.

Andragogy, as articulated by Malcolm Knowles, is the science of adult learning [1]. Unlike younger learners, adult students—whether in undergraduate or graduate environments—process professional learning differently. Adult learners:

- Bring prior professional and life experiences into the classroom.
- Are problem-centered, seeking learning that is immediately applicable.
- Require autonomy in their learning, preferring facilitative guidance over directive instruction.
- Are intrinsically motivated by relevance to their professional or personal objectives.

For faculty members, particularly those transitioning from industry or research domains, integrating andragogical principles into teaching practice is non-negotiable. Professional learners demand relevance, context, and co-ownership of their educational experience. Instructors who attempt to apply rigid, instructor-centered pedagogical methods to adult learners risk disengagement and learning inefficacy.

Strategic Shifts in Teaching Mindset:

- Move from "information authority" to "learning facilitator."
- Prioritize application over memorization, leveraging real-world problem-solving scenarios.
- Design instruction that acknowledges and utilizes learner experience as a foundational asset.
- Balance structured learning objectives with flexibility for self-directed inquiry.

Heutagogy, often described as the study of self-determined learning, extends beyond andragogy by placing full ownership of the learning experience in the hands of the learner [2]. In heutagogical environments, learners:

- Define their own learning goals and outcomes based on evolving personal and professional needs.
- Use prior experience not just as a foundation, but as a springboard for identifying emergent areas of growth.
- Engage in reflective practice, continuously evaluating and adjusting their learning strategies.
- Value adaptability and capability development over mere competency, aiming to build the capacity to learn in uncertain or novel situations.
- View instructors not as guides but as partners who help create flexible learning ecosystems rather than prescribed pathways.

Comparative Framework: Pedagogy vs. Andragogy vs. Heutagogy

Dimension	Pedagogy (Child-Centered)	Andragogy (Adult-Centered)	Heutagogy (Self-Determined Learning)
Learner Role	Dependent on instructor	Collaborative partner in learning	Autonomous architect of learning
Instructor Role	Knowledge authority and director	Facilitator and guide	Learning environment designer and co-learner
Learning Focus	Foundational knowledge acquisition	Problem-solving and application	Capability development and adaptive problem-solving
Experience Use	Minimal or not required	Central to learning	Central, with reflection to drive new learning paths
Motivation	Primarily external	Primarily internal	Intrinsically driven by evolving personal/professional goals
Content Relevance	Often abstract or generalized	Directly applicable to professional needs	Learner-defined, driven by emergent needs

Dimension	Pedagogy (Child-Centered)	Andragogy (Adult-Centered)	Heutagogy (Self-Determined Learning)
Outcome	Knowledge retention and reproduction	Competency development	Capability development and reflective adaptability

In today's rapidly evolving professional landscape, faculty are no longer mere transmitters of knowledge. They are ecosystem designers, capability builders, and co-learners. Embracing andragogy and progressing towards heutagogy positions educators not as the endpoint of knowledge, but as facilitators of lifelong, self-directed learning.

Developing the right mindset for teaching, therefore, is not just a pedagogical strategy—it is a leadership imperative.

The question is not whether you will adapt.

It is whether you will lead that adaptation—for your students and yourself.

Transitioning from Industry to Academia

Successfully transitioning from industry to academia involves more than simply transferring subject matter expertise—it requires a fundamental shift in perspective, approach, and pedagogy. Industry professionals entering the academic realm must be prepared to shift from a results-driven, efficiency-focused mentality to one centered on fostering intellectual curiosity, critical thinking, and lifelong learning. This transition is an opportunity to inspire and guide students while contributing to the broader academic community.

Shifting from Practitioner to Educator

Industry professionals are accustomed to problem-solving, innovation, and applying their expertise in real-world contexts. In contrast, educators must focus on facilitating student learning, structuring knowledge, and guiding intellectual development. This shift requires faculty members to:

- Adapt their expertise to diverse student needs and learning levels.
- Develop lesson plans and instructional strategies that scaffold complex concepts.
- Cultivate a classroom culture that encourages curiosity and independent thinking.
- Emphasize mentoring and guidance rather than direct problem-solving.

The transition to teaching necessitates a deep understanding of how students absorb, process, and apply knowledge. Rather than merely delivering information, faculty members must develop strategies that engage students, encourage participation, and foster analytical skills.

Understanding the Learning Process from a Student's Perspective

Effective educators recognize learning is not passive but an active process and iterative journey. Students originate from diverse backgrounds with inherently different levels of preparedness, motivation, and prior knowledge. Faculty members must cultivate empathy and adaptability by:

- Acknowledging different learning styles and cognitive processes.
- Implementing interactive and student-centered learning techniques.
- Encouraging reflection, discussion, and knowledge application.
- Utilizing formative assessments for gauging student understanding and comprehension to adjust teaching approaches accordingly.

Understanding how students learn allows faculty to create dynamic and effective learning environments where students feel empowered to engage with course material and develop intellectual autonomy.

The Balance Between Theory and Practice

One of the most significant contributions that industry professionals bring to academia is their practical experience. However, striking a balance between theory and real-world application is crucial. While students benefit from practical insights, they also require a strong theoretical foundation to enhance critical thinking skills and conceptual understanding.

To achieve this balance, faculty members should:

- Connect theoretical concepts to real-world applications through case studies, simulations, and industry examples.
- Encourage students to engage in problem-solving activities that blend academic knowledge with practical application.
- Foster interdisciplinary thinking by linking classroom learning to broader industry challenges.
- Guide students in applying academic frameworks to workplace scenarios.

By integrating both theory and practice, faculty members ensure that students gain the analytical, strategic, and problem-solving skills needed to thrive in both academic and professional settings.

Conclusion

Successfully transitioning from industry to academia requires adopting a student-centered mindset, refining instructional approaches, and balancing theoretical knowledge with real-world experience. Faculty members must embrace the role of an educator, fostering intellectual growth and critical thinking while guiding students through structured learning experiences. By shifting their perspective, understanding student learning processes, and effectively integrating theory with practice, new faculty can establish themselves as impactful and inspiring educators in higher education.

Growth Mindset in Teaching: A Cognitive Psychology Perspective

In higher education, the implementation of a growth mindset among faculty is not merely a pedagogical preference—it is a strategic imperative. Building on Carol Dweck's original framework, recent cognitive psychology research underscores that an instructor's beliefs about intelligence and ability profoundly shape their teaching efficacy and student outcomes [3].

Critically, a growth mindset positions intelligence and ability as dynamic, improvable traits. Faculty adopting this orientation prioritize effort, strategic adaptation, and learning from setbacks as integral to professional development. In contrast, a **fixed or constrained mindset** frames intelligence as static—where faculty may resist feedback, view teaching challenges as threats to competence, and avoid pedagogical experimentation due to perceived personal limitations.

Key Contrasts: Growth Mindset vs. Fixed Mindset in Teaching Practice

Dimension	Growth Mindset Perspective	Fixed Mindset Perspective
View of Intelligence	Expandable through effort and strategy	Fixed and predetermined
Response to Feedback	Seen as constructive; integrated for improvement	Viewed as criticism; often resisted or ignored
Pedagogical Adaptation	Experimentation is essential for skill growth	New methods viewed as risky or unnecessary
Student Potential	All students can improve with support and effort	Student ability viewed as innate and limited
Professional Development	Sought regularly to refine instructional skills	Deprioritized; existing expertise seen as sufficient

This cognitive framework explains why growth mindset-oriented faculty are statistically more likely to:

- Engage in continuous professional development.
- Integrate feedback from students and peers as operational data, not personal critique.
- Embrace instructional innovations, including active learning and adaptive assessment technologies.
- Cultivate a culture where student challenges are reframed as opportunities, not failures [4].

Conversely, **faculty entrenched in a fixed mindset** demonstrate:

- Resistance to change in instructional methods, often defaulting to traditional lecture formats.

- A defensive posture when confronted with poor student performance, attributing failures to student deficiencies rather than pedagogical approach.
- Limited engagement in reflective practice, which cognitive psychologists now identify as critical to teaching excellence [5].

Cognitive Psychology Insights

Emerging research from educational neuroscience further validates these distinctions. Neural plasticity studies confirm that both student and instructor cognition adapt in response to challenge and deliberate practice. Fixed mindset approaches inadvertently constrain this plasticity by creating environments where failure is penalized rather than leveraged as a learning input [6].

Moreover, cognitive load theory indicates that instructors modeling a growth mindset reduce extraneous cognitive load for students by fostering an environment where iterative learning is normalized. In contrast, fixed mindset instructors may inadvertently increase student cognitive strain by emphasizing performance outcomes over mastery processes [7].

Strategic Recommendations for Faculty Leadership:

- Integrate mindset evaluation tools within faculty development programs to assess and evolve teaching beliefs.
- Embed reflective pedagogical practice as a performance metric in instructional design and faculty assessment processes.
- Establish peer coaching frameworks that operationalize feedback as a growth mechanism.
- Leverage adaptive learning technologies that promote data-driven instruction aligned with growth principles.

Adopting a growth mindset in teaching transcends individual preference; it is a validated cognitive strategy for optimizing instructional performance and student outcomes. Institutions prioritizing this psychological shift position their faculty not only as content experts but as agile, reflective practitioners prepared for the evolving landscape of higher education. Faculty leaders must confront and mitigate fixed mindset behaviors, framing adaptability and continuous learning as professional mandates, not options.

Continuous Learning and Professional Development

A growth mindset in teaching necessitates a commitment to lifelong learning and professional improvement. Faculty members must continually expand their knowledge base, refine their instructional strategies, and remain current with educational research and innovations. This can be achieved by:

- Engaging in faculty development programs, workshops, and conferences.
- Participating in interdisciplinary collaborations to broaden teaching perspectives.
- Actively seeking out new pedagogical methodologies and technological tools.

- Reflecting on teaching practices and adapting strategies based on student outcomes.

By embracing an attitude of continuous learning, faculty members not only enhance their teaching effectiveness but also operate as role models for students, demonstrating the value of intellectual curiosity and adaptability.

Adapting to Diverse Learning Styles and Student Needs

Higher education institutions attract students from various backgrounds, each with unique learning styles, strengths, and challenges. Faculty members must recognize and accommodate these differences by employing diverse instructional techniques, such as:

- Utilizing multimodal teaching approaches, including visual, auditory, and kinesthetic methods.
- Encouraging active learning through discussions, group work, and hands-on experiences.
- Providing varied assessment methods to gauge student comprehension effectively.
- Offering personalized support and fostering an inclusive learning environment.

By tailoring instruction for the needs of diverse learners, faculty members can create an equitable and engaging educational experience that maximizes student success.

Embracing Feedback from Students, Peers, and Administrators

Constructive feedback is a vital tool for professional growth. Faculty members should actively seek input from students, colleagues, and administrators to refine their teaching strategies and improve classroom experiences. Effective ways to integrate feedback include:

- Conducting mid-semester and end-of-course evaluations to gauge student perceptions.
- Engaging in peer reviews and collaborative teaching observations.
- Participating in faculty mentoring programs to gain insights from experienced educators.
- Reflecting on student performance data and adjusting teaching methodologies accordingly.

By valuing and incorporating feedback, faculty members demonstrate a commitment to excellence in teaching and contribute to continuous improvement in higher education.

Conclusion

Developing a growth mindset in teaching requires faculty members to embrace lifelong learning, adapt to the evolving requirements and needs of students, and integrate constructive feedback into their pedagogical practices. By fostering intellectual curiosity, refining instructional strategies, and maintaining an openness to change, educators can create effective learning environments, empowering students for success in academia and beyond.

Academic Rigor vs. Real-World Application

One of the greatest challenges that faculty members with industry experience face is bridging the gap between academic rigor and real-world application. While industry settings prioritize efficiency, innovation, and immediate results, academic institutions emphasize theoretical foundations, analytical thinking, and long-term intellectual development. Striking a balance between these two paradigms enables faculty members to provide students with both the conceptual knowledge required for academic success and the practical skills necessary for professional excellence.

Aligning Industry Knowledge with Academic Expectations

Industry professionals deliver a wealth of practical and real-world experience to the classroom, offering invaluable insights into practical applications of theoretical concepts. However, academia requires a structured approach that ensures students build foundational knowledge before engaging in complex problem-solving. Faculty members can achieve this balance by:

- Designing courses that integrate both theory and practical case studies.
- Using real-world examples to contextualize academic concepts.
- Encouraging students to explore industry trends within an academic framework.
- Aligning course objectives with accreditation standards and institutional learning goals.

By carefully blending industry expertise with rigorous academic methodologies, faculty members can create enriching educational experiences that prepare students for both scholarly inquiry and professional practice.

Teaching Critical Thinking, Problem-Solving, and Adaptability

Higher education institutions aim to develop students into critical thinkers and adaptable problem-solvers. While industry professionals often rely on their expertise to make quick decisions, academic instruction necessitates guiding students through structured analytical processes. Faculty members should focus on:

- Encouraging students to question assumptions and explore multiple perspectives.
- Designing assignments that challenge students to apply knowledge creatively.
- Implementing problem-based learning techniques that require critical analysis.
- Providing opportunities for students to engage in research and experimentation.

By fostering these essential skills, faculty members help students develop intellectual agility and resilience, preparing them to navigate complex professional landscapes.

Encouraging Student Engagement Through Active Learning

Passive learning, where students simply absorb information from lectures, is often ineffective in fostering deep understanding. Instead, active learning strategies encourage students to interact with course material, collaborate with peers, and apply concepts in meaningful ways. Faculty members can enhance student engagement by:

- Incorporating interactive discussions, debates, and group projects.
- Utilizing hands-on simulations, role-playing exercises, and case studies.
- Encouraging reflection and self-assessment to deepen learning.
- Integrating technology and digital tools to facilitate dynamic learning experiences.

Active learning fosters a sense of curiosity and intellectual ownership among students, allowing them to engage more deeply with course content while developing essential communication and collaboration skills.

Conclusion

Balancing academic rigor with real-world application is essential for preparing students to succeed in both scholarly pursuits and professional careers. Faculty members must strategically integrate theoretical foundations with practical insights, cultivate critical thinking and problem-solving skills, and employ active learning methodologies to enhance student engagement. By embracing this holistic approach, educators can create transformative learning experiences that empower students to become innovative thinkers and adaptive professionals in an ever-evolving global landscape.

Core Values of Higher Education Faculty

Faculty members in higher education play a vital role not only in educating students but also in shaping the ethical and intellectual foundation of their institutions. The core values that define higher education faculty go beyond subject expertise—they encompass a commitment to student success, intellectual curiosity, collaboration, and ethical professionalism. These values serve as guiding principles that influence teaching practices, mentoring relationships, research endeavors, and institutional contributions.

A faculty member's role extends beyond delivering lectures; it involves mentoring students, engaging in scholarly inquiry, participating in institutional governance, and contributing to a broader academic community. To uphold the integrity of higher education, faculty members must prioritize ethical decision-making, foster inclusivity, and remain dedicated to continuous learning and professional growth.

In this section, we explore the fundamental values that define excellence in academia, including:

- **Commitment to Student Success:** Understanding diverse student backgrounds, fostering an inclusive learning environment, and encouraging academic integrity.
- **Scholarship and Intellectual Curiosity:** Promoting evidence-based learning, engaging in research, and contributing to institutional knowledge.
- **Collaboration and Collegiality:** Working effectively with faculty peers, administrators, and support staff while mentoring students and junior colleagues.

- **Ethics and Professionalism in Academia:** Upholding institutional policies, navigating faculty responsibilities, and maintaining appropriate boundaries between professional and academic roles.

By embracing these values, faculty members not only enhance their own effectiveness but also contribute to a vibrant and intellectually rich academic environment. These principles form the foundation for meaningful teaching, impactful research, and service to both students and the broader academic community.

Commitment to Student Success

A faculty member's foremost responsibility is fostering student success by creating an environment that promotes intellectual growth, inclusivity, and academic integrity. This commitment extends beyond delivering course material—it encompasses mentorship, support, and the cultivation of skills that enable students to thrive in their academic and professional careers.

Understanding Diverse Student Backgrounds and Learning Needs

Students come from a variety of cultural, socioeconomic, and educational backgrounds, each bringing unique perspectives and challenges to the learning environment. Faculty members must recognize and accommodate these differences to ensure equitable access to education. Key strategies include:

- **Recognizing Individual Differences:** Understanding that students possess varied learning styles, abilities, and levels of preparedness.
- **Employing Differentiated Instruction:** Utilizing a range of teaching methodologies, such as visual, auditory, and kinesthetic approaches, to cater to diverse learners.
- **Providing Additional Support:** Offering office hours, tutoring resources, and mentorship opportunities to assist students who need additional guidance.
- **Encouraging Student Engagement:** Creating an interactive classroom where students feel comfortable asking questions, participating in discussions, and sharing their viewpoints.

By prioritizing an understanding of student diversity, faculty members can create meaningful learning experiences that empower students to succeed academically and professionally.

Fostering an Inclusive and Supportive Classroom Environment

An inclusive classroom environment ensures that every student feels respected, valued, and capable of achieving their full potential. Faculty members play a crucial role in fostering inclusivity by:

- **Promoting Equity:** Ensuring that all students have access to the same opportunities for success, regardless of their background or circumstances.

- **Encouraging Open Dialogue:** Facilitating discussions that respect differing viewpoints while fostering critical thinking and respectful discourse.

- **Addressing Bias and Barriers to Learning:** Identifying and mitigating unconscious biases that may affect student outcomes, including implicit cultural or gender biases.

- **Incorporating Diverse Perspectives:** Integrating course materials that reflect a wide range of cultural, historical, and social perspectives to broaden students' understanding.

- **Creating a Safe Learning Space:** Encouraging students to express themselves without fear of discrimination, judgment, or marginalization.

By embedding inclusivity into their teaching practices, faculty members contribute to a supportive and engaging academic environment where students feel encouraged to learn and grow.

Encouraging Academic Integrity and Ethical Decision-Making

Academic integrity forms the foundation of a reputable and effective educational institution. Faculty members have a responsibility to instill ethical principles in students by:

- **Setting Clear Expectations:** Clearly defining policies regarding plagiarism, cheating, and proper citation practices to ensure students understand academic integrity requirements.

- **Modeling Ethical Behavior:** Demonstrating integrity through fair grading practices, transparent communication, and adherence to institutional policies.

- **Designing Integrity-Focused Assessments:** Crafting assignments and examinations that encourage original thought, discourage dishonesty, and emphasize the application of knowledge.

- **Addressing Violations Constructively:** Providing opportunities for students to learn from mistakes while enforcing consequences that uphold institutional academic standards.

- **Encouraging Ethical Discussions:** Integrating case studies and discussions on ethical dilemmas in professional and academic settings to prepare students for decision-making in their careers.

By reinforcing academic integrity, faculty members cultivate an ethical academic community that upholds the values of honesty, accountability, and respect for intellectual property.

Conclusion

A faculty member's dedication to student success is rooted in understanding diverse learning needs, fostering an inclusive environment, and promoting academic integrity. These core values guide educators in shaping not only students' academic achievements but also their personal and professional development. By committing to these principles, faculty members contribute to a culture of learning that is ethical, inclusive, and transformative, ensuring that students are well-prepared to meet the challenges of an ever-evolving world.

Scholarship and Intellectual Curiosity

Higher education thrives on a foundation of scholarship and intellectual curiosity, shaping the academic landscape through rigorous inquiry, evidence-based learning, and a commitment to the continuous expansion of knowledge. Faculty members play a crucial role in cultivating these values, inspiring students and peers alike to embrace the pursuit of learning and critical exploration.

Encouraging Evidence-Based Learning and Research

The hallmark of effective teaching in higher education is the integration of evidence-based learning practices. Faculty members must guide students toward a deeper understanding of how knowledge is constructed, verified, and applied in their respective disciplines. This can be achieved by:

- **Promoting research literacy:** Encouraging students to critically evaluate sources, distinguish between reliable and unreliable information, and apply scholarly methodologies to their work.

- **Incorporating current research into teaching:** Using up-to-date studies, case analyses, and peer-reviewed literature to illustrate key concepts and demonstrate how knowledge evolves.

- **Fostering a research-oriented mindset:** Encouraging students to engage in inquiry-based learning, conduct independent research projects, and contribute to the academic discourse within their fields.

- **Teaching critical analysis:** Guiding students to challenge assumptions, ask meaningful questions, and draw evidence-based conclusions to enhance their academic rigor.

By fostering an environment that prioritizes scholarly inquiry, faculty members empower students to approach learning with curiosity, rigor, and an appreciation for academic integrity.

Modeling Lifelong Learning and Professional Growth

Faculty members serve as intellectual role models, demonstrating the importance of continuous education and self-improvement. Lifelong learning is not just a concept to be taught but a practice to be embodied. Faculty members can model this principle through:

- **Engaging in professional development:** Participating in academic conferences, workshops, and continuing education programs to stay abreast of new developments in their disciplines.

- **Conducting research and publishing findings:** Contributing to the body of knowledge in their fields by engaging in scholarly research and disseminating their work through journals, books, and academic presentations.

- **Collaborating across disciplines:** Engaging in interdisciplinary initiatives that foster innovative approaches to problem-solving and knowledge creation.

- **Demonstrating adaptability:** Embracing new teaching methodologies, technological advancements, and shifts in educational paradigms to enhance the learning experience.

When faculty members exemplify lifelong learning, they reinforce the value of intellectual curiosity and inspire students to approach their own educational and professional journeys with a similar mindset.

Contributing to Institutional Knowledge and Thought Leadership

As stewards of higher education, faculty members have a responsibility to contribute to the intellectual growth of their institutions. Thought leadership involves advancing knowledge, shaping academic discourse, and influencing educational policies that foster innovation. This contribution can take many forms, including:

- **Mentoring junior faculty and students:** Providing guidance and support to emerging scholars, fostering their academic and professional development.

- **Serving on academic committees:** Participating in curriculum design, accreditation efforts, and institutional governance to shape the direction of higher education.

- **Advocating for educational improvements:** Engaging in discourse on best practices, equity in education, and innovative pedagogical strategies to improve teaching and learning outcomes.

- **Representing the institution in public discourse:** Publishing opinion pieces, speaking at conferences, and engaging with industry partners to extend the influence of the institution beyond the classroom.

By actively engaging in these activities, faculty members solidify their roles as leaders in higher education, shaping the future of their disciplines and institutions while reinforcing the importance of academic scholarship.

Conclusion

Scholarship and intellectual curiosity are the driving forces behind meaningful academic engagement and institutional excellence. Faculty members must encourage evidence-based learning, model lifelong intellectual growth, and contribute to the broader academic community. Through these efforts, educators not only enhance their students' learning experiences but also uphold the core values that define higher education as a transformative and enduring pursuit.

Collaboration and Collegiality

Higher education is fundamentally a collective endeavor that thrives on collaboration and collegiality. Faculty members play an essential role in fostering a cooperative academic environment where knowledge is shared, innovation is encouraged, and institutional goals are advanced through collective effort. Effective collaboration strengthens teaching, research, and administrative processes, ultimately benefiting students, faculty, and the broader academic community.

Working with Faculty Peers, Administrators, and Support Staff

Successful institutions are built on the foundation of effective teamwork among faculty, administrators, and support staff. Faculty members must actively engage in meaningful professional relationships that contribute to a productive and dynamic academic environment. Key aspects of this collaboration include:

- **Participating in shared governance:** Engaging in faculty senate meetings, curriculum committees, and academic planning discussions to contribute to institutional decision-making.

- **Coordinating with support staff:** Working alongside librarians, instructional designers, and academic advisors to enhance student learning experiences and streamline administrative functions.

- **Building positive relationships with administrators:** Maintaining open and constructive communication with department chairs, deans, and institutional leaders to align academic initiatives with institutional goals.

- **Engaging in professional development:** Attending faculty development programs, workshops, and peer mentoring sessions to continuously refine teaching and research skills.

By embracing collaboration with faculty peers and institutional leaders, educators contribute to an ecosystem where shared knowledge and coordinated efforts drive academic excellence.

Mentoring Students and Junior Faculty Members

One of the most significant responsibilities of higher education faculty is mentoring the next generation of scholars, practitioners, and educators. Faculty members serve as role models, providing guidance, encouragement, and expertise to students and junior faculty members as they navigate their academic and professional journeys. Effective mentoring includes:

- **Providing academic and career guidance:** Helping students identify academic pathways, career opportunities, and research interests that align with their personal and professional goals.

- **Offering constructive feedback:** Encouraging students and junior faculty to refine their work through iterative improvement and scholarly engagement.

- **Creating opportunities for research and professional development:** Inviting students to participate in research projects, conference presentations, and co-authored publications.
- **Fostering a supportive and inclusive mentorship culture:** Ensuring that all mentees receive equitable access to guidance and opportunities, regardless of background or academic experience.

Through active mentoring, faculty members contribute to a cycle of knowledge-sharing that strengthens the intellectual fabric of their institutions and disciplines.

Engaging in Interdisciplinary Collaboration and Innovation

Higher education institutions are increasingly recognizing the importance of interdisciplinary collaboration in addressing complex societal challenges. Faculty members can enhance the impact of their teaching and research by working across disciplinary boundaries to develop innovative approaches and solutions. Strategies for fostering interdisciplinary collaboration include:

- **Developing cross-disciplinary courses and programs:** Designing curriculum initiatives that integrate multiple fields of study to provide students with a more holistic learning experience.
- **Engaging in collaborative research initiatives:** Partnering with faculty from diverse disciplines to pursue grant-funded projects, joint publications, and interdisciplinary conferences.
- **Participating in cross-departmental initiatives:** Contributing to university-wide efforts such as sustainability programs, diversity and inclusion initiatives, and public engagement projects.
- **Leveraging technology for collaborative learning:** Utilizing digital platforms and virtual tools to connect with researchers, educators, and students across institutions and geographical boundaries.

By embracing interdisciplinary collaboration, faculty members expand the reach and impact of their scholarship, fostering innovative solutions and advancing the collective mission of higher education.

Conclusion

Collaboration and collegiality are at the heart of a thriving academic institution. Faculty members must actively engage with peers, administrators, and support staff to create a cohesive educational environment. Additionally, through mentoring students and junior faculty and embracing interdisciplinary collaboration, educators ensure that knowledge continues to evolve and adapt to the challenges of an ever-changing world. By prioritizing these core values, faculty members contribute to a culture of excellence that benefits both their institutions and the broader academic community.

Ethics and Professionalism in Academia

Ethics and professionalism serve as the foundation of higher education, ensuring that faculty members uphold the integrity of their institutions and foster an academic environment built on trust, fairness, and accountability. Faculty members must navigate complex responsibilities while adhering to ethical guidelines that govern grading, mentoring, curriculum development, institutional policies, and professional boundaries.

Understanding Faculty Responsibilities in Grading, Mentoring, and Curriculum Development

Faculty members play a pivotal role in shaping student outcomes through fair grading, meaningful mentorship, and thoughtful curriculum design. These responsibilities require adherence to ethical standards that promote equity and academic excellence. Key aspects include:

- **Maintaining Fair and Transparent Grading Practices:** Faculty should develop clear grading rubrics, provide constructive feedback, and ensure consistency in assessment methods to promote student success and fairness.

- **Mentoring with Integrity:** Effective faculty mentors provide guidance, support, and encouragement while fostering students' intellectual and professional development. Ethical mentoring involves respecting student autonomy, offering unbiased advice, and creating an inclusive learning environment.

- **Developing Curriculum with Academic Rigor:** Faculty members must ensure that course materials reflect the latest research, align with institutional goals, and prepare students for professional challenges while maintaining academic integrity.

By fulfilling these responsibilities with diligence and ethical mindfulness, faculty members contribute to a robust academic culture that values fairness, excellence, and integrity.

Upholding Institutional Policies and Accreditation Standards

Accreditation and institutional policies serve as the backbone of academic credibility, ensuring that faculty members operate within a framework of recognized educational standards [8]. Adherence to these guidelines guarantees that students receive a high-quality education while protecting the institution's reputation and compliance with regulatory bodies. Faculty members can uphold these standards by:

- **Understanding Institutional Policies:** Familiarizing themselves with academic integrity codes, faculty handbooks, and institutional expectations regarding teaching, research, and service.

- **Aligning Courses with Accreditation Standards:** Ensuring that syllabi, learning objectives, and assessments meet accreditation criteria set forth by regional and national accrediting agencies.

- **Participating in Institutional Assessments:** Engaging in program reviews, student evaluations, and faculty development initiatives to maintain the highest academic standards.

Commitment to institutional policies and accreditation ensures that faculty members contribute to a sustainable academic environment that fosters credibility, accountability, and continuous improvement.

Managing Boundaries Between Professional and Academic Roles

Faculty members often navigate multiple roles that include educator, researcher, mentor, and institutional representative. Maintaining clear professional boundaries is essential to fostering an ethical, respectful, and productive academic environment. Strategies for managing these boundaries include:

- **Defining Clear Instructor-Student Relationships:** Faculty should maintain professionalism in their interactions, avoid favoritism, and ensure that relationships remain focused on academic development.

- **Balancing Research and Teaching Commitments:** Faculty members must manage time effectively to fulfill both instructional and research responsibilities without compromising either.

- **Avoiding Conflicts of Interest:** Faculty should disclose any potential conflicts that may arise from personal, financial, or professional relationships that could influence academic decisions.

- **Maintaining Confidentiality:** Respecting student privacy in matters such as grades, advising sessions, and academic performance records aligns with ethical best practices and institutional policies.

By establishing clear boundaries, faculty members create an ethical and professional learning environment that fosters trust, respect, and integrity within the academic community.

Conclusion

Ethics and professionalism are integral to the role of faculty members in higher education. By upholding fair grading and mentoring practices, adhering to institutional policies and accreditation standards, and maintaining clear professional boundaries, faculty contribute to a culture of accountability and excellence. These core values ensure that higher education remains a space of integrity, equity, and continuous growth, reinforcing its mission of knowledge dissemination and societal advancement.

Goals for New Faculty in Higher Education

As new faculty members navigate their roles in higher education, establishing clear goals is essential for professional growth, effective teaching, and meaningful contributions to the academic community. The transition into academia requires balancing multiple responsibilities, including fostering student success, engaging in research, and participating in institutional service. By setting intentional goals, faculty members can develop a sustainable career path while enhancing their impact on students and colleagues.

This section explores key objectives that new faculty should prioritize, including:

- **Enhancing Student Learning Outcomes:** Aligning teaching methods with course objectives, utilizing assessment and feedback effectively, and encouraging critical thinking.

- **Developing Effective Teaching Strategies:** Exploring diverse instructional methods, integrating technology, and structuring courses for engagement and accessibility.

- **Building a Sustainable Academic Career:** Understanding tenure and promotion, engaging in research and publications, and forming industry partnerships.

- **Balancing Teaching, Research, and Service:** Implementing time management strategies, setting priorities for career advancement, and navigating faculty expectations.

By focusing on these goals, faculty members can create a dynamic and fulfilling academic career that not only supports their own growth but also contributes to the success of their students and the institution. This section provides actionable strategies and best practices to help new faculty establish a strong foundation in teaching, research, and professional service, ensuring long-term success in the academic landscape.

Enhancing Student Learning Outcomes

One of the fundamental goals for new faculty members in higher education is to enhance student learning outcomes through well-structured teaching methodologies, effective assessments, and a commitment to fostering critical thinking. By aligning teaching methods with course objectives, utilizing assessment and feedback, and encouraging analytical engagement, faculty can create meaningful learning experiences that prepare students for both academic and professional success.

Aligning Teaching Methods with Course Objectives

Effective teaching begins with intentional course design that ensures instructional strategies align with clearly defined learning objectives. Faculty members should:

- **Develop course syllabi that integrate learning goals** with instructional activities and assessments.

- **Utilize diverse teaching approaches**, including lectures, discussions, problem-based learning, and experiential exercises to accommodate different learning styles.

- **Incorporate active learning strategies** such as case studies, debates, simulations, and group projects to deepen student engagement.

- **Regularly revisit and refine course materials** to ensure alignment with evolving disciplinary standards and student needs.

By intentionally structuring their courses to align with learning outcomes, faculty members create a coherent and engaging educational experience that reinforces key concepts and skills.

Using Assessment and Feedback to Improve Learning Experiences

Assessment and feedback play a crucial role in shaping student learning and guiding instructional improvement. Faculty members should employ assessment strategies that not only measure student achievement but also foster growth and understanding. Best practices include:

- **Using formative assessments** such as quizzes, reflections, and in-class activities to gauge student comprehension and adjust instruction accordingly.
- **Incorporating summative assessments** like exams, research projects, and presentations to evaluate overall mastery of course content.
- **Providing timely and constructive feedback** that offers clear insights into student performance while encouraging improvement.
- **Utilizing peer and self-assessments** to promote self-regulated learning and critical reflection on academic progress.

When used effectively, assessments serve as both a measurement tool and a learning opportunity, allowing students to refine their skills and deepen their understanding of course material.

Encouraging Critical Thinking and Knowledge Application

Higher education is not just about the acquisition of knowledge; it is about fostering the ability to think critically and apply information in meaningful ways. Faculty members should:

- **Pose open-ended questions** and encourage students to analyze, interpret, and evaluate information rather than passively absorbing it.
- **Incorporate problem-solving activities** that require students to apply concepts to real-world scenarios, reinforcing practical understanding.
- **Promote interdisciplinary connections** by integrating insights from various fields and perspectives.
- **Encourage research and inquiry-based learning**, allowing students to develop independent thought and investigative skills.
- **Foster a classroom culture that values intellectual curiosity**, debate, and respectful discourse to enhance analytical abilities.

By emphasizing critical thinking and application, faculty members equip students with the skills necessary for navigating complex problems, making informed decisions, and contributing meaningfully to their fields.

Conclusion

Enhancing student learning outcomes is a central goal for new faculty members in higher education. By aligning teaching methods with course objectives, using assessments and feedback effectively, and fostering critical thinking and application, educators create a dynamic and enriching learning environment. These efforts not only support academic success but also cultivate lifelong learners who are prepared to tackle the challenges of their respective professions.

Developing Effective Teaching Strategies

Effective teaching is a dynamic and ever-evolving practice that requires faculty members to employ a diverse range of instructional strategies to accommodate different learning styles, maximize student engagement, and enhance the overall educational experience. By exploring various teaching methodologies, integrating digital tools, and structuring courses for accessibility, new faculty members can create a learning environment that fosters comprehension, critical thinking, and active participation.

Exploring Different Instructional Methods

A well-rounded educator understands the value of diverse teaching methods and applies them strategically to facilitate student learning. Some effective instructional approaches include:

- **Lectures:** Providing structured and comprehensive content delivery, ensuring clarity in explanations and engagement through storytelling, analogies, and real-world applications.

- **Case Studies:** Encouraging students to analyze real-life scenarios, apply theoretical concepts, and develop problem-solving skills by working through practical challenges.

- **Discussions:** Fostering interactive learning through structured debates, Socratic questioning, and peer-led dialogues that enhance comprehension and critical analysis.

- **Hands-on Activities:** Incorporating experiential learning techniques, such as simulations, lab exercises, and role-playing, to reinforce theoretical knowledge with practical applications.

By combining multiple instructional strategies, faculty members can cater to different learning styles and ensure a more engaging and effective educational experience for students.

Utilizing Technology and Digital Tools for Learning Enhancement

In an era where digital transformation is reshaping education, faculty members must harness the power of technology to enhance teaching effectiveness and student learning outcomes. Key technological tools and practices include:

- **Learning Management Systems (LMS):** Utilizing platforms like Blackboard, Canvas, or Moodle to organize course content, facilitate discussions, and provide digital assessments.

- **Multimedia Integration:** Incorporating videos, podcasts, infographics, and interactive simulations to cater to diverse learning preferences and enhance content retention.

- **Collaborative Online Tools:** Leveraging digital platforms such as Google Workspace, Microsoft Teams, and Padlet to facilitate group projects, peer reviews, and shared learning experiences.
- **Adaptive Learning Technologies:** Implementing AI-driven platforms that personalize learning paths based on individual student progress, strengths, and areas for improvement.

By effectively integrating digital tools into their teaching strategies, faculty members can create more engaging, interactive, and personalized learning experiences that meet the evolving needs of students.

Structuring Courses for Engagement and Accessibility

Course design plays a pivotal role in student success, and structuring courses for engagement and accessibility ensures that all students can effectively participate and achieve their learning objectives. Faculty members should consider the following best practices:

- **Clear Learning Objectives:** Establishing well-defined course goals and aligning them with instructional strategies and assessment methods to provide a structured learning experience.
- **Scaffolded Learning:** Designing a curriculum that builds knowledge progressively, helping students develop competencies step by step with guided support.
- **Universal Design for Learning (UDL):** Implementing inclusive teaching strategies that accommodate diverse learners, including those with disabilities, by offering multiple means of engagement, representation, and assessment [9].
- **Flexible Learning Opportunities:** Providing asynchronous content, recorded lectures, and self-paced modules to support students with varying schedules and learning preferences.
- **Frequent Checkpoints and Feedback:** Embedding formative assessments, discussion forums, and feedback loops to gauge student understanding and adjust instructional approaches accordingly.

By prioritizing engagement and accessibility, faculty members can create an inclusive and dynamic learning environment that supports student success and fosters academic excellence.

Conclusion

Developing effective teaching strategies is a key goal for new faculty members in higher education. By exploring various instructional methods, utilizing technology to enhance learning, and designing courses that prioritize engagement and accessibility, educators can create impactful learning experiences that empower students. Through continuous reflection and innovation in their teaching practices, faculty members can contribute to a more dynamic, inclusive, and effective higher education landscape.

Building a Sustainable Academic Career

A career in academia is both intellectually rewarding and professionally demanding. To build a sustainable academic career, new faculty members must strategically navigate tenure and promotion processes, actively engage in research and industry collaborations, and cultivate a strong network of mentors and academic peers. By taking a proactive approach to professional development, faculty members can ensure long-term success and fulfillment in their academic journey.

Understanding Tenure, Promotion, and Professional Development Paths

Academic careers are structured around clear milestones that guide faculty members from early-stage appointments to senior academic leadership roles. It is essential for new faculty to understand the tenure and promotion process within their institution, which typically includes:

- **Tenure-track Expectations:** Understanding the institutional benchmarks for research, teaching effectiveness, and service contributions that lead to tenure [10].

- **Promotion Criteria:** Advancing from assistant professor to associate professor, and eventually to full professor, requires consistent excellence in teaching, scholarship, and service [11].

- **Professional Development Opportunities:** Engaging in faculty development workshops, teaching enhancement programs, and leadership training initiatives to refine pedagogical and research skills [12].

- **Annual Review and Evaluation:** Actively participating in self-assessment and institutional evaluations to monitor career progress and align professional activities with institutional goals [13].

By staying informed about tenure and promotion policies and engaging in continuous professional growth, faculty members can create a stable and fulfilling career trajectory in higher education.

Engaging in Research, Publication, and Industry Partnerships

Scholarship is a critical component of an academic career, and faculty members must actively contribute to their field through research and publication. Successful engagement in research includes:

- **Developing a Research Agenda:** Identifying key areas of interest and formulating a long-term research strategy aligned with disciplinary needs and institutional priorities.

- **Publishing in Peer-Reviewed Journals:** Contributing original research to scholarly publications to establish credibility and advance knowledge in the field.

- **Securing Research Grants and Funding:** Seeking external funding through government agencies, foundations, and industry partnerships to support research projects and institutional initiatives.

- **Collaborating with Industry Partners:** Engaging with corporations, nonprofits, and government agencies to apply academic research to real-world problems, creating opportunities for knowledge transfer and professional impact.

- **Presenting at Conferences and Symposia:** Actively participating in academic conferences to share research findings, engage with peers, and gain recognition within the academic community.

A strong commitment to research and publication not only enhances faculty credibility but also contributes to the overall reputation of their institution and field of study.

Seeking Mentorship and Networking Opportunities Within Academia

Building a network of mentors and academic peers is essential for professional growth and career longevity. Faculty members should actively seek mentorship and networking opportunities through the following strategies:

- **Identifying Mentors:** Connecting with senior faculty members who can provide career guidance, research collaboration opportunities, and institutional insights.

- **Participating in Faculty Mentorship Programs:** Engaging in formal and informal mentoring relationships within academic institutions and professional organizations.

- **Attending Academic Conferences and Workshops:** Expanding professional networks through active participation in disciplinary conferences, workshops, and academic events.

- **Engaging in Cross-Disciplinary Collaboration:** Seeking opportunities to collaborate with faculty from other departments and institutions to foster interdisciplinary research and expand professional perspectives.

- **Joining Professional Associations:** Becoming an active member of organizations such as the American Association of University Professors (AAUP), discipline-specific societies, and academic consortiums.

By cultivating a strong academic network, faculty members can gain valuable support, guidance, and professional opportunities that contribute to long-term career success.

Conclusion

Building a sustainable academic career requires faculty members to navigate the tenure and promotion process effectively, remain actively engaged in research and scholarly publication, and establish meaningful professional relationships within the academic community. By understanding institutional expectations, developing a robust research portfolio, and seeking mentorship opportunities, faculty members can position themselves for long-term success and fulfillment in higher education. Through intentional planning and continuous professional development, faculty can contribute meaningfully to their discipline while achieving their personal and career goals.

Balancing Teaching, Research, and Service

One of the greatest challenges new faculty members face is balancing the triad of responsibilities that define academic careers: teaching, research, and service. Each of these areas plays a crucial role in shaping a well-rounded faculty member, but successfully managing them requires strategic time management, clear prioritization, and a comprehensive understanding of institutional expectations. Faculty who effectively navigate these demands can build sustainable and fulfilling careers in higher education.

Time Management Strategies for New Faculty

New faculty members often find themselves overwhelmed by the competing demands of course preparation, research obligations, and service commitments. Effective time management is essential to achieving balance and avoiding burnout. Key strategies include:

- **Establishing a structured schedule:** Allocating specific blocks of time for teaching, research, and service ensures that each area receives appropriate attention.

- **Prioritizing high-impact activities:** Focusing on tasks that contribute most significantly to career advancement and student success helps maximize efficiency.

- **Setting realistic goals:** Breaking down long-term objectives into manageable milestones allows for steady progress without unnecessary stress.

- **Using productivity tools:** Digital calendars, task management apps, and workflow automation tools can streamline administrative tasks and improve efficiency.

- **Protecting research time:** Designating uninterrupted periods for research and writing prevents teaching and administrative duties from consuming all available time.

By proactively managing their time, faculty members can create a balanced workload that allows them to excel in teaching, research, and service without sacrificing well-being.

Setting Priorities for Career Advancement and Institutional Contributions

A successful academic career requires careful prioritization of responsibilities to align individual goals with institutional expectations. Faculty members should focus on:

- **Clarifying institutional expectations:** Understanding tenure and promotion requirements helps faculty set strategic career goals.

- **Building a strong teaching portfolio:** Demonstrating excellence in course design, student engagement, and assessment fosters a reputation for instructional effectiveness.

- **Developing a focused research agenda:** Establishing a clear research trajectory ensures that scholarly contributions are impactful and aligned with professional aspirations.

- **Engaging in meaningful service roles:** Selecting service commitments that align with personal expertise and institutional needs enhances professional reputation and influence.

- **Balancing short-term and long-term goals:** Maintaining a steady trajectory of scholarly activity, instructional innovation, and service contributions ensures continuous career development.

By setting clear priorities, faculty members can advance their careers while contributing meaningfully to their academic institutions.

Navigating Administrative Responsibilities and Faculty Expectations

Administrative responsibilities are an integral part of faculty life, encompassing tasks such as committee work, student advising, and institutional governance. Successfully managing these duties requires:

- **Understanding faculty governance structures:** Becoming familiar with department policies, faculty senate roles, and institutional decision-making processes helps faculty engage effectively in academic administration.

- **Developing strong communication skills:** Effective collaboration with colleagues, administrators, and students fosters a positive academic environment.

- **Leveraging administrative support resources:** Utilizing institutional resources such as faculty development centers, teaching and learning support services, and research offices enhances efficiency.

- **Maintaining work-life balance:** Setting boundaries and recognizing when to decline additional commitments helps prevent professional overload.

- **Engaging in professional development:** Participating in leadership training, faculty mentorship programs, and academic networking opportunities prepares faculty for administrative advancement.

By navigating administrative expectations strategically, faculty members can contribute to institutional growth while maintaining focus on their teaching and research.

Conclusion

Balancing teaching, research, and service is a core challenge for faculty members in higher education. By implementing effective time management strategies, setting clear career priorities, and navigating administrative responsibilities with intention, faculty can achieve sustainable success. A deliberate and thoughtful approach to balancing these responsibilities not only enhances individual career satisfaction but also strengthens the overall academic environment, benefiting students, colleagues, and institutions alike.

Conclusion and Next Steps

The journey toward becoming an effective educator in higher education is one of continuous growth, reflection, and adaptation. This chapter has laid the groundwork for understanding the essential principles of teaching and learning, equipping new faculty members with the foundational knowledge they need to thrive in academia. However, learning to teach effectively is not a static process—it is a lifelong endeavor that requires faculty to remain open to new ideas, pedagogical innovations, and evolving student needs.

Faculty members must embrace ongoing professional development, engage with institutional resources, and seek mentorship opportunities that will support their growth as educators. By staying informed about best teaching practices, incorporating feedback from students and peers, and continuously refining instructional approaches, faculty can enhance both their teaching effectiveness and their students' learning experiences.

This section will summarize the key takeaways from this chapter and provide guidance on next steps for faculty members who are committed to excellence in higher education. It will also highlight the importance of institutional support systems, faculty development programs, and collaborative learning communities that can aid faculty in their professional journey. As faculty move forward, they should actively engage in discussions, seek out professional learning opportunities, and remain committed to fostering a dynamic and inclusive learning environment for their students.

By building on the insights from this chapter and integrating these principles into their teaching philosophy, faculty members can develop a strong foundation for a rewarding and impactful career in higher education.

Summary of Key Takeaways

Teaching in higher education is a complex and multifaceted endeavor that extends beyond the dissemination of knowledge. New faculty members must embrace the role of educators, mentors, and academic leaders, balancing instruction with research and service. The transition from industry to academia requires a shift in mindset, focusing on fostering intellectual curiosity, critical thinking, and student-centered learning. By integrating diverse teaching strategies, maintaining academic rigor, and leveraging technology, faculty members can create an enriching and engaging educational experience for students at all levels.

Key takeaways from this chapter include:

- The importance of transitioning from a practitioner's perspective to an educator's mindset.
- The role of academic rigor in balancing theoretical foundations with real-world applications.
- Strategies for fostering student engagement through active learning and critical thinking exercises.
- The necessity of inclusivity, ethics, and professionalism in shaping a positive learning environment.
- Effective time management techniques for balancing teaching, research, and service responsibilities.

- Building a sustainable academic career through mentorship, networking, and continuous professional development.

Encouragement for Ongoing Professional Development

Higher education is a dynamic and evolving field that requires continuous learning and adaptation. Faculty members should embrace a growth mindset, recognizing that teaching effectiveness improves over time through self-reflection, student feedback, and professional development.

Strategies for ongoing professional development include:

- **Attending Teaching Workshops and Conferences:** Engage in faculty development programs offered by institutions and professional organizations.
- **Seeking Peer Observations and Mentorship:** Collaborate with experienced educators to refine teaching methodologies and classroom management skills.
- **Engaging in Scholarship of Teaching and Learning (SoTL):** Conduct research on pedagogical strategies and contribute to the academic community.
- **Utilizing Student Feedback:** Regularly analyze student evaluations to identify areas for improvement and innovation in course delivery.
- **Staying Current with Educational Technology:** Explore new digital tools, learning management systems, and online instructional strategies to enhance student engagement.

By prioritizing professional growth, faculty members not only enhance their effectiveness as educators but also contribute to the advancement of higher education as a discipline.

Institutional Support Resources (Faculty Development Programs, Mentoring Opportunities)

Most institutions provide a wealth of resources to support faculty development and success. New faculty members should familiarize themselves with the available support structures and actively engage in institutional programs.

Common faculty support resources include:

- **Faculty Development Centers:** Many colleges and universities have dedicated centers that offer teaching workshops, training sessions, and one-on-one coaching for new faculty members.
- **Mentorship Programs:** Connecting with senior faculty members can provide guidance on navigating institutional culture, tenure requirements, and best teaching practices.
- **Teaching and Learning Committees:** Participate in committees focused on improving instructional quality and curriculum design.

- **Funding for Research and Teaching Innovation:** Seek institutional grants and funding opportunities to support pedagogical innovation and research endeavors.
- **Online Teaching Resources:** Leverage institutional subscriptions to digital libraries, teaching repositories, and instructional design resources.

By actively engaging with institutional support systems, faculty members can enhance their teaching effectiveness, expand their professional networks, and build a sustainable academic career.

Q&A and Discussion

As new faculty members embark on their teaching journeys, they may encounter challenges that require reflection, discussion, and collaborative problem-solving. Engaging in discussions with colleagues, attending faculty roundtables, and participating in professional teaching forums can provide valuable insights and strategies for overcoming obstacles in the classroom.

To facilitate ongoing growth and dialogue, consider:

- **Joining Faculty Learning Communities (FLCs):** Collaborate with peers to share best practices and teaching experiences.
- **Engaging in Online Academic Forums:** Platforms like the Chronicle of Higher Education, Inside Higher Ed, and discipline-specific teaching networks offer spaces for faculty discussions.
- **Hosting Q&A Sessions with Experienced Faculty:** Organize faculty panels where senior educators share advice and answer questions from new faculty members.
- **Participating in Reflective Teaching Practices:** Keep a teaching journal to document challenges, successes, and areas for future improvement.

By fostering a culture of inquiry and continuous learning, faculty members can develop their teaching philosophy, refine instructional techniques, and contribute to the broader academic community.

Final Thoughts

Becoming an effective educator in higher education is a journey that requires dedication, adaptability, and a commitment to student success. New faculty members should approach teaching with an open mind, embracing opportunities for growth and professional development. By leveraging institutional resources, engaging in peer collaboration, and continuously refining their teaching strategies, faculty members can create impactful learning experiences that inspire and empower students.

This chapter serves as a foundation for new educators, providing essential insights into the core principles of teaching and learning in higher education. As faculty continue to develop their expertise, they will play a vital role in shaping the future of education, fostering intellectual curiosity, and preparing students to navigate an ever-evolving world.

The next chapters will delve deeper into specific teaching methodologies, assessment techniques, classroom management strategies, and the integration of technology in higher education. Faculty members are encouraged to remain engaged, seek mentorship, and embrace the rewarding challenge of shaping the next generation of scholars and professionals.

Faculty Mindset Self-Assessment Tool

Purpose: To help new or transitioning faculty reflect on their current teaching orientation and align it with the values and practices essential for success in higher education.

Instructions: Rate yourself on a scale from 1 (Strongly Disagree) to 5 (Strongly Agree) for each of the following statements. Use the reflection prompts to identify areas of strength and opportunity.

Section A: Mindset & Identity

Statement	1	2	3	4	5
I see teaching as a partnership in learning, not just a delivery of expertise.	☐	☐	☐	☐	☐
I am open to evolving my teaching methods based on student feedback.	☐	☐	☐	☐	☐
I recognize the need to transition from a results-driven mindset to one that fosters intellectual growth.	☐	☐	☐	☐	☐
I view mistakes in teaching as opportunities for reflection and growth.	☐	☐	☐	☐	☐

Section B: Student-Centeredness & Inclusivity

Statement	1	2	3	4	5
I design learning experiences that consider diverse backgrounds and needs.	☐	☐	☐	☐	☐
I prioritize student success as a primary outcome of my teaching.	☐	☐	☐	☐	☐
I actively work to create an inclusive and psychologically safe classroom.	☐	☐	☐	☐	☐

Section C: Growth Orientation & Professional Development

Statement	1	2	3	4	5
I am committed to continuous learning about pedagogy and student development.	☐	☐	☐	☐	☐
I reflect regularly on what worked and what didn't in my teaching.	☐	☐	☐	☐	☐
I seek out professional development opportunities related to teaching.	☐	☐	☐	☐	☐

Section D: Theory-to-Practice Integration

Statement	1	2	3	4	5
I help students apply theoretical concepts to real-world scenarios.	☐	☐	☐	☐	☐
I use case studies, simulations, or problem-based learning in my instruction.	☐	☐	☐	☐	☐
I regularly update course content to reflect current industry trends.	☐	☐	☐	☐	☐

Reflection Questions

1. What areas did you score yourself highest in? Lowest?
2. How do your responses reflect your current strengths as an educator?
3. Which area(s) do you want to focus on over the next 6–12 months?
4. What professional development resources or mentorship might support that goal?

Chapter 2: Foundations of Higher Education Teaching

Higher education teaching is a dynamic and evolving discipline that extends far beyond the delivery of content. College professors play a multifaceted role as educators, mentors, and scholars, shaping students' intellectual development and professional growth. Teaching in higher education requires mastery of subject matter, instructional strategies, and student engagement techniques while adapting to technological advancements, diverse learning needs, and shifting educational paradigms.

This chapter explores the historical evolution, pedagogical foundations, and core competencies necessary for effective higher education instruction. It examines

Figure 2.1. Higher Education Teaching [219].

the philosophical underpinnings of modern teaching practices, from classical Socratic dialogue to contemporary learning theories that drive student-centered education. Additionally, it outlines the essential skills faculty must cultivate—including subject matter expertise, instructional design, assessment strategies, classroom management, and technological integration.

Through a combination of traditional methodologies and innovative approaches, faculty members can create learning environments, fostering critical thinking, knowledge application, and lifelong learning. By embracing mentorship and adaptability, professors can empower students to navigate a complex and interconnected world.

Overview of Higher Education Teaching

Higher education teaching is an intricate and evolving discipline that extends beyond the mere dissemination of information. It encompasses a broad spectrum of pedagogical strategies, mentorship responsibilities, and scholarly engagement designed to foster critical thinking, knowledge application, and lifelong learning. A college professor's role is multidimensional, requiring expertise in subject matter, instructional methodologies, student engagement, and institutional governance. As the landscape of education continues to evolve and transform with technological advancements, shifting student expectations, demographics, and evolving workforce demands, effective teaching necessitates a dynamic, student-centered approach that blends traditional academic rigor with innovative learning strategies.

The Evolution and Philosophical Foundations of Higher Education Teaching

The traditions of higher education teaching trace their origins to classical antiquity, where Socratic dialogue and rhetorical training formed the bedrock of intellectual discourse. Medieval universities institutionalized higher education through structured curricula in philosophy, theology, medicine, and law. By the Enlightenment era, the emphasis shifted toward empirical inquiry, specialization, and academic freedom, shaping modern higher education's commitment to research, critical thinking, and the dissemination of knowledge [14].

In contemporary academia, teaching is influenced by a variety of learning theories, including:

- **Behaviorism** (Pavlov, Skinner) – Emphasizing reinforcement, structured curricula, and observable learning outcomes.

- **Cognitivism** (Piaget, Vygotsky) – Focusing on mental processes, scaffolding, and the role of prior knowledge.

- **Constructivism** (Dewey, Bruner) – Advocating for experiential learning, student agency, and contextual learning environments.

- **Humanism** (Maslow, Rogers) – Prioritizing student autonomy, motivation, and holistic development.

Modern pedagogy integrates elements from these theories to create an adaptive and responsive teaching environment engineered to the diverse needs of learners [15].

The Core Competencies of Effective Higher Education Teaching

Higher education teaching requires faculty to develop and refine several key competencies that contribute to student success, institutional growth, and professional excellence.

1. Subject Matter Expertise and Scholarly Engagement

At the heart of higher education teaching is deep domain knowledge. However, expertise alone does not constitute effective teaching; rather, faculty members must possess the ability to articulate complex concepts, draw interdisciplinary connections, and engage students in meaningful discussions. Professors are expected to remain at the forefront of their fields by conducting research, publishing scholarly work, and participating in professional associations. This dual role—educator and scholar—ensures that faculty members bring cutting-edge insights into the classroom while maintaining credibility as thought leaders in their disciplines [16].

2. Pedagogical Mastery and Instructional Design

Instructional effectiveness relies on a strategic blend of pedagogical techniques designed to accommodate diverse learning styles and educational backgrounds. Professors must employ a range of teaching methodologies, including:

- **Lecture-Based Learning** – Traditionally dominant but evolving to incorporate active engagement techniques.

- **Discussion and Socratic Seminars** – Encouraging critical inquiry, debate, and student-driven learning.
- **Experiential and Problem-Based Learning** – Applying knowledge through case studies, simulations, and real-world scenarios.
- **Flipped Classrooms and Hybrid Learning** – Leveraging digital resources to supplement in-person instruction.
- **Competency-Based Education (CBE)** – Enables students to advance through learning based on demonstrated mastery rather than time-based measures.

An effective professor also understands **curriculum development**, aligning course objectives with institutional goals, accreditation standards, and industry expectations. Designing a robust syllabus, mapping learning outcomes, and implementing iterative course improvements based on student feedback and assessment data are integral to instructional success [17].

3. Assessment Strategies and Student Feedback

Assessment in higher education extends beyond grading; it serves as a mechanism for measuring comprehension, fostering intellectual development, and refining teaching strategies [18]. Professors employ a variety of assessment techniques, including:

- **Formative Assessments** – Low-stakes evaluations such as quizzes, reflections, and class discussions to monitor progress.
- **Summative Assessments** – High-stakes evaluations like exams, research papers, and final projects to gauge overall competency.
- **Authentic Assessments** – Case studies, portfolios, and presentations that simulate real-world applications of knowledge.
- **Self and Peer Assessments** – Encouraging metacognition and collaborative evaluation.

Effective feedback is **timely, constructive, and personalized**, guiding students toward deeper understanding while fostering a growth mindset.

4. Classroom Management and Inclusive Teaching Practices

Creating a productive and equitable learning environment requires intentional classroom management strategies. Professors must:

- **Foster Student Engagement** – Utilizing interactive discussions, real-world applications, and digital tools to sustain interest.
- **Manage Diverse Classrooms** – Acknowledging cultural differences, learning disabilities, and neurodiversity while ensuring an inclusive atmosphere.
- **Navigate Student Challenges** – Addressing academic misconduct, classroom disruptions, and mental health concerns with professionalism and empathy.

- **Promote Academic Integrity** – Instilling ethical scholarship practices and critical inquiry as foundational principles.

An inclusive approach prioritizes universal design for learning (UDL) concepts, ensuring course materials and assessments accommodate and address diverse student needs.

5. Adaptability, Innovation, and Technological Integration

The modern educator must remain adaptable in the face of technological disruption and changing student expectations. Online learning platforms, artificial intelligence, and data-driven instructional tools have redefined traditional teaching methodologies [19]. Professors can enhance their courses through:

- **Learning Management Systems (LMS)** – Platforms such as Blackboard, Canvas, and Moodle for content delivery and assessments.
- **Adaptive Learning Technologies** – AI-powered tools that personalize student learning experiences.
- **Open Educational Resources (OERs)** – Cost-effective materials that expand access to knowledge.
- **Virtual Reality (VR) and Augmented Reality (AR)** – Immersive technologies for interactive simulations and experiential learning.
- **Data Analytics for Learning Outcomes** – Using performance data to tailor instruction and identify at-risk students.

Faculty who embrace innovation can improve student engagement, retention, and overall learning outcomes [20].

Mentorship and the Transformational Role of the College Professor

Higher education teaching is not solely about imparting knowledge; it is about shaping intellectual identities, professional aspirations, and personal growth. Professors serve as guides, advisors, and role models, mentoring students through their academic and professional journeys.

Key Aspects of Academic Mentorship

1. **Career and Research Guidance** – Helping students navigate graduate programs, research opportunities, and career pathways.
2. **Fostering Critical Thinking** – Encouraging students to question assumptions, construct arguments, and engage in intellectual discourse.
3. **Building a Professional Network** – Connecting students with industry professionals, conferences, and scholarly communities.
4. **Providing Emotional and Academic Support** – Recognizing student challenges and offering resources for success.

5. **Encouraging Lifelong Learning** – Instilling a growth mindset that extends beyond the classroom.

A successful mentor does not merely advise students but empowers students to become self-directed learners and contributors to their disciplines [21].

Conclusion: The Art and Science of Higher Education Teaching

Teaching in higher education is a delicate combination of art and a science, requiring a balance of expertise, pedagogy, mentorship, and adaptability. Professors are tasked with cultivating intellectual curiosity, academic integrity, and practical application of knowledge, ensuring that students emerge as critical thinkers, ethical professionals, and lifelong learners.

As education continues to evolve, higher education faculty must remain committed to continuous improvement, innovation, and student-centered teaching, ensuring the next generation of scholars and professionals is enabled to meet the challenges of an increasingly complex and interconnected world.

Ultimately, the impact of a professor extends far beyond the confines of the classroom—it shapes institutions, industries, and society at large. By embracing the full spectrum of teaching, mentorship, and scholarly engagement, educators fulfill the profound responsibility of advancing knowledge, empowering learners, and transforming the future.

Understanding Adult Learners and Learning Theories: A Strategic Framework for Higher Education Faculty

Teaching in higher education, particularly to adult learners, demands a shift from content dissemination to transformational learning facilitation. Faculty—especially those transitioning from industry—must recognize that their learners are not passive recipients but active participants bringing professional identities, cognitive frameworks, and practical needs into the classroom. To design effective, adaptive learning environments, educators must critically engage with foundational learning theories and instructional models, choosing approaches that address not only knowledge acquisition but also identity transformation and capability development.

Critical Characteristics of Adult Learners

Adult learners (nontraditional students) approach education differently from younger, school-age students due to distinct cognitive, motivational, and experiential factors:

- **Autonomy and Self-Direction:** Adults prefer control over their learning processes.
- **Professional Identity:** Learning is evaluated based on its perceived relevance to current or future professional roles.
- **Experience as Asset:** Prior work and life experience shape understanding and influence knowledge acquisition.
- **Relevance and Pragmatism:** Content must have immediate, practical application to sustain engagement.

- **Cognitive Load Management:** Balancing education with careers and family introduces constraints not present in traditional student populations.
- **Respect and Peer Recognition:** Adult learners require acknowledgment of their experiences and value collaboration over hierarchical instruction.

These attributes necessitate instructional approaches that move beyond traditional teacher-centered models.

Transformative Learning Theory and the Professional Identity Shift

While many learning theories address how adults acquire knowledge, **Transformative Learning Theory (TLT)**—developed by Jack Mezirow—goes further. TLT focuses on how adults fundamentally change the way they see themselves, their roles, and the world around them. This theory is particularly relevant to industry professionals transitioning into higher education, where the shift from technical expert to educator often disrupts long-held professional identities [22].

Key Concepts in Transformative Learning Theory:

- **Disorienting Dilemmas**
  Transitioning into academia itself can serve as a disorienting dilemma—a situation that challenges previous assumptions and forces critical self-reflection. For example, a professional used to decision-making authority may struggle with the more facilitative, student-centered role required in teaching.
- **Critical Reflection**
  Through structured reflection, individuals examine their beliefs about expertise, authority, and success. They begin questioning assumptions such as:
    - "Does knowing a subject well automatically make me a good teacher?"
    - "Is control in the classroom equivalent to effectiveness?"
- **Perspective Transformation**
  Over time, this critical examination leads to new understandings of oneself—not as a content expert controlling knowledge transfer, but as a facilitator of learning, empowering students to construct their own knowledge.
- **Dialogue and Community**
  Transformative learning often occurs in dialogue with peers who validate, challenge, and refine the learner's new perspectives. Faculty mentorship, professional development cohorts, and reflective teaching circles can provide these spaces for dialogue.
- **Action and Rebuilding Identity**
  Finally, the process culminates in behavioral change. The individual adopts new teaching strategies, redefines their role as an educator, and rebuilds their professional identity around facilitation, reflection, and student empowerment.

Why Transformative Learning Matters for New Faculty

For faculty entering higher education from industry, this theory reframes professional development: not as acquiring new teaching skills alone, but as undergoing a personal transformation. Becoming an educator is not just a role change—it is an identity shift. Recognizing this allows institutions to:

- Design onboarding programs that address emotional and cognitive aspects of identity transition.
- Encourage reflective practices as core components of professional development.
- Support mentoring and dialogue communities where new faculty can safely explore their emerging educator identities.

Reflection Prompts:

- What assumptions from your previous profession might limit your effectiveness as a teacher?
- How do you currently define "expertise"? How might that definition shift as you transition into teaching?
- When have you experienced a professional situation that forced you to reevaluate your core beliefs about your role or identity?

Faculty Self-Reflection: Psychological Safety, Emotional Intelligence, and Jungian Insights

Teaching in higher education is not simply an intellectual exercise—it is a relational practice. Faculty members are not neutral transmitters of knowledge; they are emotional beings whose unconscious patterns, emotional responses, and inner conflicts shape the learning environment. While pedagogy focuses on how students learn, faculty must equally examine how they themselves influence that learning through their presence, reactions, and leadership.

Integrating concepts from psychological safety, emotional intelligence, and Jungian psychology offers a powerful framework for faculty self-reflection and personal transformation.

Psychological Safety: Creating Space for Engagement and Failure

Amy Edmondson defines **psychological safety** as "a climate in which people are comfortable expressing and being themselves" [22]. In higher education classrooms, this means students must feel safe to:

- Ask questions without fear of judgement.
- Offer imperfect answers without ridicule.
- Challenge assumptions without being penalized.

However, creating this environment is not just about instructional design—it's about modeling. Faculty themselves must:

- Demonstrate vulnerability (admitting uncertainty, modeling reflective practice).
- Frame failure as a learning opportunity.
- Actively protect student voice, especially from marginalized or quiet participants.

Psychological safety begins not with students, but with the professor's own emotional regulation and awareness.

Emotional Intelligence: The Foundation of Safe Classrooms

Emotional Intelligence (EI), as defined by Daniel Goleman, includes:

1. Self-awareness.
2. Self-regulation.
3. Empathy.
4. Social skills [23].

Faculty with high emotional intelligence can:

- Recognize when their frustration or anxiety is shaping classroom interactions.
- Pause before responding defensively to student challenges.
- Notice non-verbal cues of student disengagement or discomfort.
- Create moments of connection by responding empathetically to student struggles.

In practice, EI empowers educators to shift from unconscious reaction to conscious leadership, cultivating trust and psychological safety not as outcomes, but as ongoing practices.

Jungian Psychology: Confronting the Unconscious Educator

Carl Jung argued that much of human behavior is governed by unconscious drives—the "shadow" parts of ourselves we deny or suppress [24]. For educators, this shadow often manifests as:

- The need for control or perfection in the classroom.
- Defensive reactions when students challenge authority.
- Unacknowledged biases or emotional triggers from past professional experiences.

Shadow Work:
By engaging in reflective "shadow work," faculty can surface unconscious fears such as:

- "What if I'm not competent enough?"
- "Do my students respect me?"
- "Is my authority being questioned?"

Bringing these fears into conscious awareness allows educators to respond thoughtfully rather than reflexively.

Archetypal Patterns:
Jungian archetypes—universal behavioral patterns—can help faculty recognize dominant personas shaping their teaching [25]:

- **The Sage:** Values knowledge and expertise, but risks becoming disconnected from student needs.
- **The Warrior:** Enforces rules and discipline but may suppress student voice.
- **The Caregiver:** Prioritizes student well-being but risks overextension and emotional burnout.

Faculty are encouraged to identify which archetypes they embody most strongly and how these patterns serve or hinder their teaching effectiveness.

Individuation:
Jung's concept of individuation—the integration of fragmented aspects of self into a cohesive whole—frames faculty development as a process of personal transformation [26]:

- Moving from "I am a subject-matter expert" to "I am a reflective educator facilitating growth."
- Balancing authority with approachability, expertise with vulnerability.
- Seeing oneself not as static but as evolving, integrating both strengths and shadows.

This process is not linear, but cyclical—a continuous confrontation and integration of the known and unknown aspects of professional identity.

In my own life, individuation has not been theoretical. It's been transformational. Years of turbulence in professional and personal circles weren't random—they were signals. I wasn't broken. I was entangled.

Through individuation:

- I identified the narratives imposed upon me: the savior complex, the silence-for-acceptance, the servant-leader who must prove worth through sacrifice.
- I confronted the hidden shadow: the inner anger, the repressed creative force, the fear that revealing my abilities would result in attack rather than acceptance.
- I re-integrated those elements. My anger wasn't weakness—it was signal. My withdrawn creativity wasn't failure—it was potential restrained.

For me, individuation addressed critical issues:

- It transformed the need for external validation into internal clarity.
- It allowed me to understand resistance from others not as rejection, but as fear—fear of the clarity I carried disrupting their survival-based worldviews.
- Most importantly, it freed me from reactive leadership. I no longer lead to be seen. I lead because clarity requires action.

In an academic context, individuation means this:

- Educators must confront the conditioned roles they've assumed: the omniscient authority, the burned-out servant, the ego-driven expert.

- By individuating, faculty reclaim their core identity—not as content dispensers, but as human systems capable of guiding others through both knowledge and inner development.

Individuation has not made life easier for me. But it has made it honest.

And through that honesty, I've found strength, clarity, and purpose—far beyond what institutional systems ever taught me to expect.

Reflection Prompts for Faculty Self-Exploration

To support this inner work, faculty should engage with questions such as:

- **"What behaviors do I default to when I feel challenged as an instructor?"**
  (Do I become defensive? Withdraw? Overcompensate by exerting control?)
- **"Which parts of my professional identity feel in conflict, and how might they represent my 'shadow'?"**
  (Do I resist seeing myself as a 'teacher' because it challenges my identity as an expert?)
- **"How do my emotional responses shape the psychological climate in my classroom?"**
  (When I am anxious, do I inadvertently convey that students should fear mistakes?)

Conclusion: The Inner Work of Teaching

Becoming an effective educator is not solely about mastering teaching strategies—it is about mastering oneself. By cultivating psychological safety, developing emotional intelligence, and engaging in Jungian self-reflection, faculty members can:

- Create classrooms where students feel safe to learn.
- Interrupt unconscious behavioral patterns that hinder authentic connection.
- Transform their professional identity from isolated expert to integrated, reflective facilitator.

In doing so, educators not only foster student growth but embark on their own journey of individuation—becoming whole, adaptive, and resilient leaders in the evolving landscape of higher education.

Comparative Analysis of Core Learning Models

Constructivist vs. Instructivist Models

- **Instructivism** (often aligned with behaviorist and cognitivist models) assumes that knowledge is transmitted from instructor to learner in structured, controlled sequences. It values clear objectives, standardized assessments, and hierarchical knowledge transfer [27].

- **Constructivism**, in contrast, positions learners as constructors of knowledge through active engagement. Understanding is built, not received, through interaction with problems, peers, and reflective experiences [27].

Strategic Consideration:
Instructivist approaches may support foundational knowledge acquisition (essential for technical skills training), but constructivist models foster higher-order skills—critical thinking, meta-cognition, problem-solving, and adaptive instruction essential for professional environments.

Workplace Example:
A manufacturing firm conducting cybersecurity training might begin with instructivist methods for teaching compliance protocols but shift to constructivist case analyses for advanced incident response planning.

Behaviorism, Cognitivism, and Constructivism: A Comparative Lens [28]

Dimension	Behaviorism	Cognitivism	Constructivism
Learning Focus	Observable behaviors	Mental processes and structures	Knowledge construction via experience
Instructor Role	Controller of stimuli	Architect of knowledge structures	Facilitator of learning environments
Methodology	Repetition, reinforcement	Chunking, sequencing, modeling	Problem-solving, collaboration, reflection
Knowledge View	Objective, fixed	Organized schema	Subjective, contextual, evolving

Differences Between Undergraduate and Graduate-Level Teaching

Higher education teaching is not a monolithic endeavor; it varies significantly based on the academic level of the students being taught. Teaching at the undergraduate level differs substantially from graduate-level instruction in terms of student expectations, cognitive development, instructional strategies, assessment methodologies, and faculty-student dynamics. While both levels require a commitment to fostering intellectual growth, undergraduate education focuses on foundational knowledge and skill-building, whereas graduate education emphasizes advanced inquiry, research, and specialization.

Faculty members transitioning between these levels must be prepared to adjust their pedagogical approach, engagement strategies, and assessment techniques to align with the distinct needs and expectations of each student group. Recognizing these differences enhances teaching effectiveness and contributes to a richer learning experience for students.

1. Learning Objectives and Educational Outcomes

One of the most fundamental differences between undergraduate and graduate education is the intended learning outcomes at each level.

Undergraduate Education: Broad Knowledge and Skill Development

- Undergraduate programs are designed to deliver students a broad, multi-faceted education while introducing them to foundational concepts in their chosen fields.

- Learning objectives often emphasize conceptual understanding, memorization of key theories, fundamental skills, and critical thinking.

- Professors at the undergraduate level are responsible for helping students develop analytical, communication, problem-solving and logical analysis skills, fostering an appreciation for interdisciplinary connections.

- Many undergraduate courses include general education requirements, exposing students to subjects beyond their major to cultivate well-rounded knowledge and intellectual curiosity.

Graduate Education: Specialization and Independent Inquiry

- Graduate-level education is specialized, advanced, and research-intensive.

- Learning outcomes focus on deep expertise in a particular discipline, original research, methodological proficiency, and the development of scholarly or professional expertise.

- Unlike undergraduates, graduate students are expected to demonstrate meta-cognition, conduct independent research, and deliver new insights to their chosen professional field.

- Faculty members in graduate programs act as mentors and advisors, guiding students toward mastery of complex concepts and methodologies.

2. Cognitive and Intellectual Expectations

The cognitive demands placed on students at the undergraduate and graduate levels differ significantly. This distinction is often framed using Bloom's Taxonomy, aligning cognitive learning into six cascading levels:

1. **Remembering** (basic recall of facts and definitions)
2. **Understanding** (comprehension of concepts)
3. **Applying** (using knowledge in practical contexts)
4. **Analyzing** (breaking down ideas into components)
5. **Evaluating** (critical assessment and judgment)
6. **Creating** (synthesizing new knowledge or theories) [29]

Undergraduate Cognitive Development

- Undergraduate students primarily operate within the lower to mid-level cognitive domains (remembering, understanding, applying).

- Faculty must scaffold instruction by introducing fundamental theories, guiding structured discussions, and providing opportunities for application.

- Critical thinking is cultivated gradually, and students may require structured activities and significant faculty feedback to refine analytical skills.

Graduate Cognitive Development

- Graduate students are expected to engage in the higher cognitive domains (analyzing, evaluating, creating).
- Rather than passively absorbing information, they are expected to critically examine existing knowledge, develop original arguments, and produce scholarly or professional work.
- Faculty members must foster independent thought, encourage debate, and facilitate deep intellectual engagement.

3. Pedagogical Approaches and Classroom Dynamics

Teaching strategies must be adapted based on the level of student engagement, the complexity of the subject matter, and the desired learning outcomes.

Undergraduate Pedagogy: Structured and Instructor-Led

- **Instructor as a Guide:** Professors provide structured instruction, leading students through a carefully designed curriculum with clearly defined expectations.
- **Active Learning Integration:** While lectures remain a dominant method, flipped classrooms, case studies, and discussions enable students develop critical thinking skills.
- **Frequent Assessment and Feedback:** Assignments, quizzes, and structured exams are common to ensure comprehension and retention.
- **Skill Building and Conceptual Mastery:** Faculty focus on helping students develop foundational skills in writing, research, and critical analysis.
- **Diverse Learning Styles:** Professors must recognize that undergraduate students have varying degrees of preparedness and learning preferences, requiring a range of teaching methods.

Graduate Pedagogy: Research-Driven and Student-Led

- **Professor as a Mentor:** Faculty serve as facilitators and advisors rather than direct instructors, guiding students toward independent inquiry and research.
- **Seminar-Based Learning:** Graduate courses are often structured as discussion-driven seminars rather than lecture-heavy classes.
- **Case Studies and Problem-Solving:** Professors use real-world examples, advanced simulations, and peer-reviewed literature to develop analytical and evaluative skills.

- **Independent and Collaborative Research:** Students are required to conduct self-directed research, produce original work, and contribute to their academic or professional field.
- **Advanced Writing and Publication:** Many graduate courses focus on thesis or dissertation development, grant writing, and preparing for academic or professional publication.

4. Faculty-Student Relationships and Mentorship

The nature of faculty-student interactions evolves as students progress from undergraduate to graduate education.

Undergraduate Student Engagement

- Faculty members operate as instructors, guides, and role models, helping students navigate academic expectations, time management, and foundational research skills.
- The relationship is often hierarchical, with students expecting professors to provide direct guidance and structured learning experiences.
- Office hours and academic advising play a crucial component in supporting student learning.

Graduate Student Engagement

- The faculty-student dynamic shifts toward mentorship, collaboration, and professional networking.
- Professors serve as research advisors, career mentors, and professional contacts, helping students navigate academic publishing, conference presentations, grant writing, and job market preparation.
- Graduate students often assist faculty as teaching or research assistants, fostering a more collegial relationship with faculty.

5. Assessment, Evaluation, and Academic Rigor

Undergraduate Assessment

- Assessments focus on knowledge retention, comprehension, and the ability to apply concepts.
- Common assessment methods include:
    - Multiple-choice and short-answer exams
    - Research papers with guided prompts
    - Group projects and presentations
    - Reflective writing assignments

Graduate Assessment

- Graduate-level assessments prioritize original research, critical analysis, and scholarly writing.
- Common methods include:
    - **Thesis and dissertation work**
    - **Research-based term papers** requiring engagement with primary and secondary sources
    - **Peer-reviewed presentations** and conference participation
    - **Comprehensive exams** assessing mastery of an entire field
    - **Proposal writing and grant applications**

6. Career and Professional Preparation

Undergraduate Career Readiness

- Undergraduate education prepares students for entry-level careers, further education, or skill development.
- Professors often introduce industry standards, resume-building strategies, and foundational career competencies.
- Internships, co-ops, and capstone projects help bridge academia and professional work.

Graduate Career Readiness

- Graduate programs focus on producing scholars, researchers, industry leaders, and advanced practitioners.
- Faculty guide students in:
    - Academic publishing
    - Doctoral and postdoctoral research opportunities
    - Industry certifications and advanced credentials
    - Networking with professionals in specialized fields

Conclusion: Tailoring Teaching for Different Educational Levels

Undergraduate and graduate education differ not only in complexity but also in instructional approach, assessment, and student engagement. Faculty members must adapt their teaching strategies accordingly, providing structured guidance for undergraduates while fostering independence and specialization for graduate students.

By recognizing these distinctions, new college professors can create impactful, student-centered learning experiences, enabling students to succeed at every stage of their academic and professional journeys. Whether guiding students through foundational knowledge or mentoring them in advanced research, faculty play a transformative role in mentoring the next generation of scholars, professionals, and leaders.

The Role of the Professor: Mentor, Facilitator, and Evaluator

A professor in higher education serves far beyond the traditional role of delivering lectures and grading assignments. Faculty members shape the intellectual, professional, and personal development of students, acting as mentors, facilitators, and evaluators—three interconnected roles that collectively define the educational experience. Professors must inspire curiosity, cultivate analytical thinking, foster academic integrity, and challenge students to reach their highest potential.

Balancing these roles requires not only expertise in the subject matter but also pedagogical skill, emotional intelligence, and adaptability. An effective professor seamlessly transitions between mentorship, facilitation, and evaluation, ensuring that students receive guidance, develop autonomy in learning, and are held accountable for their academic progress. Understanding these dimensions allows new faculty to build engaging, rigorous, and student-centered learning environments.

The Mentor Professor: Leading Academic and Professional Growth

The Importance of Mentorship in Higher Education

Mentorship is one of the most profound and lasting contributions a professor can make to a student's life. Beyond transmitting knowledge, faculty members deliver guidance, encouragement, and career assistance to help students navigate their academic and professional journeys. Effective mentorship fosters intellectual confidence, self-efficacy, and a lifelong commitment to learning [30].

Mentorship Responsibilities of Professors

1. **Academic Advising and Intellectual Development**
    - Professors guide students in choosing courses, developing research interests, and refining critical thinking skills.
    - They encourage students to engage with complex ideas, ask deeper questions, and challenge assumptions.

2. **Career Guidance and Professional Networking**
    - Faculty introduce students to career opportunities, industry expectations, and academic research pathways.
    - They help students connect with internships, graduate programs, and professional organizations.

- Professors write letters of recommendation, review résumés, and prepare students for academic and professional interviews [31].

3. **Research and Scholarly Mentorship**
    - In graduate education, professors mentor students in thesis and dissertation development, guiding them through the research process.
    - Faculty provide insight into publishing, presenting at academic conferences, and securing research funding [31].

4. **Personal and Ethical Development**
    - Professors act as role models, instilling values of academic integrity, resilience, and ethical decision-making [32].
    - They provide support for students facing academic challenges, imposter syndrome, and work-life balance issues.

Key Traits of an Effective Mentor

- **Accessibility:** Professors must be approachable and available for student consultations.
- **Empathy:** Understanding students' struggles enables an supportive and encouraging learning environment.
- **Encouragement:** Motivating students to push their intellectual boundaries leads to deeper engagement.
- **Constructive Feedback:** Providing thoughtful and detailed feedback enhances learning and confidence.

By embracing mentorship, professors leave a lasting impact on students, shaping the next generation of scholars, professionals, and innovators.

The Professor as a Facilitator: Creating an Engaging Learning Environment

Shifting from Lecturer to Facilitator

Traditional higher education was built on a lecture-centric model, where professors transmitted knowledge, and students passively absorbed it [33]. While lectures still have their place, modern pedagogy emphasizes active learning, student engagement, and knowledge construction—requiring professors to transition into facilitators of learning rather than just conveyors of information.

Key Responsibilities of a Facilitator

1. **Encouraging Active and Collaborative Learning**
    - Effective facilitators design courses that emphasize interaction, discussion, and application of knowledge.

- o Strategies include:
    - Socratic questioning to deepen understanding.
    - Case studies that connect theory to real-world problems.
    - Flipped classrooms, where students engage with content before class to encourage discussion.
    - Problem-based learning (PBL) and simulations to develop practical skills.

2. **Adapting to Diverse Learning Styles**
   - o Professors must recognize that students learn differently—some thrive in discussion-based settings, while others need hands-on experience.
   - o Utilizing multimodal teaching strategies (visual, auditory, kinesthetic, and textual) ensures accessibility for all students [34].

3. **Encouraging Critical Thinking and Inquiry**
   - o A facilitator does not merely provide answers but guides students in asking the right questions.
   - o Encouraging debate, analysis, and reflection helps students develop intellectual independence.

4. **Utilizing Technology and Innovative Pedagogies**
   - o Effective facilitation integrates learning management systems (LMS), artificial intelligence tools, virtual simulations, and online collaboration platforms.
   - o Technology-enhanced instruction supports engagement in both online, hybrid and face-to-face courses [35].

5. **Creating an Inclusive Classroom Environment**
   - o An effective facilitator ensures that all students feel respected, valued, and heard.
   - o Encouraging diverse perspectives, integrating inclusive teaching strategies, and addressing biases cultivates a more equitable learning experience.

Traits of an Effective Facilitator

- **Adaptability:** Being responsive to student needs and adjusting teaching strategies accordingly.
- **Engagement:** Encouraging students to active participants in the learning process.
- **Humility:** Recognizing that learning is a collaborative process and that knowledge is ever-evolving.

- **Encouragement of Student Autonomy:** Empowering students to own their learning journey.

Through skillful facilitation, professors transform passive learning environments into dynamic, participatory spaces where students engage deeply with content.

The Professor as an Evaluator: Assessing Learning and Providing Constructive Feedback

The Role of Assessment in Higher Education

Assessment is not just about grading; it is a critical tool for measuring student learning, identifying strengths and weaknesses, and refining instructional approaches [36]. Professors, as evaluators, must design fair, rigorous, and meaningful assessments that align with learning objectives while providing students with constructive feedback that supports their academic growth.

Key Responsibilities of an Evaluator

1. **Designing Effective Assessments**
   - Assessments should align with course objectives and cognitive development.
   - Common assessment types include:
     - **Formative assessments** (quizzes, reflections, discussions) to gauge progress.
     - **Summative assessments** (exams, final projects, research papers) to measure mastery.
     - **Authentic assessments** (case studies, portfolios, presentations) that reflect real-world application [37].

2. **Ensuring Fairness and Transparency**
   - Clearly defined rubrics and grading criteria reduce subjectivity [38].
   - Offering opportunities for revision and feedback supports deeper learning.

3. **Providing Meaningful Feedback**
   - Feedback should be specific, timely, and actionable to guide student improvement.
   - Encouraging self-reflection through peer reviews, metacognitive activities, and revision opportunities fosters deeper engagement.

4. **Detecting and Addressing Academic Misconduct**
   - Professors must uphold academic integrity by teaching proper citation practices and research ethics.

- Utilizing plagiarism detection tools and discussing ethical scholarship prevents misconduct [39].

5. **Using Assessment Data to Improve Teaching**
    - Professors should analyze student performance to identify gaps in instruction, adjust content delivery, and refine teaching strategies.

Traits of an Effective Evaluator

- **Objectivity:** Ensuring assessments are unbiased and consistent.
- **Constructiveness:** Offering growth-oriented feedback that inspires improvement.
- **Accountability:** Upholding academic standards and rigor.
- **Reflection:** Using assessment data to enhance teaching practices.

Conclusion: Balancing Mentorship, Facilitation, and Evaluation

An effective college professor embodies all three roles simultaneously—they mentor students in academic and professional growth, facilitate engaging and interactive learning experiences, and evaluate performance with fairness and rigor. These roles are not isolated but interdependent, shaping the student experience and fostering deeper intellectual engagement.

By guiding, inspiring, and assessing students thoughtfully, professors cultivate a culture of inquiry, academic excellence, and lifelong learning—ultimately shaping the next generation of scholars and professionals.

Higher Education Policies and Academic Governance

Higher education operates within a structured framework of policies, governance systems, and institutional regulations that define academic standards, faculty responsibilities, student rights, and institutional decision-making processes [40]. Understanding these policies is essential for new faculty members, as they shape everything from curriculum development and assessment to faculty tenure, academic integrity, and institutional accreditation.

Academic governance in higher education is multi-tiered, balancing national regulations, institutional policies, faculty governance, and student engagement [41]. Professors must navigate this complex landscape to ensure compliance, uphold academic integrity, and contribute effectively to institutional decision-making. This section provides a comprehensive overview of higher education policies and governance structures, highlighting their impact on faculty roles and responsibilities.

1. Higher Education Policies: The Framework for Academic Operations

Higher education policies define the standards, rights, and responsibilities within academic institutions. These policies ensure consistency, fairness, and academic excellence, while also providing guidelines for student and faculty conduct.

Key Categories of Higher Education Policies

A. Academic Policies

Academic policies regulate the teaching, learning, and assessment processes within institutions. These policies ensure rigor, fairness, and quality control across courses and programs [42].

- **Curriculum Standards:** Policies outline degree requirements, general education mandates, and learning outcomes for each program.

- **Assessment and Grading Policies:** Faculty must adhere to institutional guidelines on grading scales, student appeals, and academic progress evaluations [43].

- **Academic Integrity and Misconduct:** Policies define plagiarism, cheating, and research ethics, ensuring that institutions maintain scholarly integrity.

- **Course Development and Approval Processes:** Faculty members participate in curriculum committees that review and approve new courses based on program alignment, accreditation standards, and student needs.

- **Student Accommodations:** Institutions establish policies for accessibility and inclusive learning, ensuring compliance with important legislative requirements such as the Americans with Disabilities Act (ADA) [44].

B. Faculty Policies

Faculty policies define hiring, promotion, tenure, and professional responsibilities. Understanding these policies is critical for new professors as they navigate career progression and institutional expectations.

- **Tenure and Promotion Guidelines:** Faculty members follow structured pathways for advancement based on teaching effectiveness, research contributions, and service to the institution [45].

- **Workload Expectations:** Policies define faculty workloads, balancing teaching hours, research expectations, committee work, and administrative duties.

- **Professional Conduct and Ethics:** Institutions establish codes of conduct to maintain professionalism, non-discrimination, and conflict resolution mechanisms.

- **Research and Grant Policies:** Faculty engaged in research must comply with funding regulations, intellectual property rights, and institutional review board (IRB) requirements for ethical research involving human subjects [46].

C. Student Policies

Student-related policies govern enrollment, academic progress, conduct, and support services. Professors play a key role in upholding these policies, ensuring fair application, and guiding students toward success.

- **Admissions and Enrollment Policies:** Define eligibility criteria for undergraduate and graduate programs.

- **Student Code of Conduct:** Outlines expectations for behavior, academic honesty, and community engagement.

- **Title IX and Anti-Discrimination Policies:** Federal policies mandate equity and inclusion, ensuring a safe learning environment free from harassment and discrimination [47].

- **Student Support Services:** Policies ensure students have access to advising, counseling, mental health services, and academic resources.

D. Institutional and Accreditation Policies

- **Accreditation Standards:** Institutions must comply with regional, national, or programmatic accreditation bodies to maintain legitimacy and funding.

- **Budgeting and Financial Aid Policies:** Faculty should understand how tuition policies, funding structures, and financial aid regulations impact students and academic programming.

- **Data Privacy and FERPA Compliance:** Policies such as the Family Educational Rights and Privacy Act (FERPA) define how student information is protected and shared [48].

2. Academic Governance: Structure and Decision-Making in Higher Education

Academic governance defines how decisions are made within institutions, who holds authority, and how faculty, administration, and students collaborate in institutional oversight. It is a shared governance model, meaning that faculty, administrators, and sometimes students participate in decision-making processes [49].

A. Shared Governance in Higher Education

Shared governance is the collaborative decision-making process between faculty, administration, and governing boards. It ensures that academic policies, institutional direction, and faculty concerns are balanced within university operations [50].

- **Faculty Role in Governance:** Faculty contribute through Faculty Senates, curriculum committees, and hiring committees. They provide expertise on academic policies, faculty hiring standards, and course development.

- **Administrative Leadership:** University presidents, provosts, and deans oversee institutional strategy, budgeting, and policy enforcement.

- **Governing Boards:** Boards of Trustees or Regents oversee financial sustainability, institutional mission, and compliance with accreditation standards.

B. Faculty Senates and Academic Committees

Faculty governance bodies, such as the Faculty Senate, ensure that professors have a voice in institutional decision-making [51]. These bodies oversee:

- **Curriculum and Academic Standards Committees:** Approve new courses, degree programs, and academic requirements.
- **Promotion and Tenure Committees:** Evaluate faculty performance for tenure and promotion.
- **Research and Ethics Committees:** Review faculty research proposals to ensure ethical compliance.

C. University Administration and Decision-Making

University leadership includes:

- **President/Chancellor:** Serves as the institution's chief executive officer, overseeing long-term strategy, external relations, and institutional reputation.
- **Provost/Vice President for Academic Affairs:** Oversees faculty, curriculum, and academic policies.
- **Deans and Department Chairs:** Manage specific colleges, schools, and academic departments, coordinating faculty and academic programs.

Professors interact regularly with department chairs and deans for course scheduling, funding requests, faculty evaluations, and policy discussions.

D. The Role of Accreditation Agencies

Accreditation agencies assess institutions based on academic rigor, student success metrics, and institutional governance [52]. Faculty contribute by:

- Participating in accreditation self-studies and external reviews.
- Aligning courses and assessments with accreditation requirements.
- Contributing to program evaluations and continuous improvement initiatives [53].

Common accrediting bodies include:

- **Regional Accreditation Agencies** (e.g., Higher Learning Commission, Middle States Commission on Higher Education).
- **Programmatic Accreditation Agencies** (e.g., AACSB for business schools, ABET for engineering programs).

3. The Impact of Policies and Governance on Faculty Responsibilities

New professors must navigate academic policies and governance structures while fulfilling teaching, research, and service expectations [54]. Key considerations include:

- **Compliance with institutional policies** on grading, assessment, and student conduct.
- **Participation in faculty governance** through committees and departmental meetings.

- **Understanding their rights and responsibilities** regarding tenure, promotion, and professional development.
- **Navigating institutional bureaucracy** for funding, course approvals, and curriculum changes.

By engaging in governance and staying informed about higher education policies, professors enhance academic integrity, contribute to institutional excellence, and advocate for faculty and student interests.

Teaching Across Institutional Contexts: Adapting Approaches to Diverse Academic Environments

Higher education encompasses a wide spectrum of institutional missions, student populations, and resource realities [55]. Faculty cannot assume that strategies effective in one context will translate seamlessly to another. A professor moving from a research-intensive university to a community college, or from a liberal arts college to a regional comprehensive university, will encounter new expectations that reshape the way teaching is approached. Understanding these institutional contexts is essential for aligning faculty practice with institutional priorities, accreditation requirements, and student needs.

Institutional Missions and Core Expectations

Each institution type operates under a distinct mission that informs its approach to teaching and learning:

- **R1 Universities** emphasize research productivity, external grant funding, and scholarly reputation. Teaching is important but often secondary to research. Faculty may face pressure to balance large undergraduate classes with mentoring doctoral candidates and advancing their own research agendas. Instructional approaches here often rely on scalable strategies, including the use of graduate teaching assistants, instructional technology, and structured course designs that can be delivered to hundreds of students.
- **Liberal Arts Colleges** prioritize holistic student development and emphasize teaching as the central faculty role. Faculty are expected to engage closely with students, foster critical thinking across disciplines, and mentor students both academically and personally. Courses are usually smaller, discussion-based, and designed to develop writing, reasoning, and integrative learning. Research remains valued, but its primary function is often to enhance pedagogy and create opportunities for undergraduates to participate in scholarly inquiry [56].
- **Community Colleges** focus on access, affordability, and workforce preparation. Faculty work with students who are highly diverse in background, academic preparation, and career goals. Teaching is almost exclusively the primary faculty responsibility, with heavy course loads and less institutional emphasis on research. Faculty must design courses that are accessible, flexible, and directly applicable to student goals, whether transferring to four-year institutions or entering the workforce [57].

Faculty Roles and Student Demographics

Faculty effectiveness is also shaped by the student populations they serve.

- At R1 universities, students may expect less individualized faculty attention at the undergraduate level, but they gain access to advanced labs, research projects, and professional networks. Graduate students at these institutions require advanced mentorship to transition into scholarly independence.
- Liberal arts students, often seeking close engagement, expect faculty to be available for intellectual dialogue outside class. Faculty must design courses that balance disciplinary rigor with broad exposure to humanistic and scientific perspectives.
- Community college students often balance full-time employment, caregiving responsibilities, and financial stressors. They may include first-generation college students and adult learners returning to education. Faculty must adopt strategies such as modular course design, clear scaffolding, and inclusive pedagogy to support persistence and success.

Pedagogical Implications

Adapting teaching methods requires faculty to understand not just *what* students need to learn but *how* they learn in each environment:

- Large R1 lectures benefit from active learning approaches that scale, such as think–pair–share, polling software, or breakout discussion sections led by graduate assistants [58].
- Liberal arts courses thrive when faculty adopt discussion-based formats, seminar-style teaching, and writing-intensive assignments that encourage depth of analysis [59].
- Community college classrooms often require practical, skills-based learning combined with flexible course formats such as evening, weekend, or hybrid delivery to meet student scheduling needs [60].

Workload and Institutional Priorities

Faculty workload also varies significantly. At R1 universities, teaching may account for a smaller share of faculty evaluation but must still demonstrate quality through student outcomes and accreditation reviews. At liberal arts institutions, teaching effectiveness is central to tenure and promotion. At community colleges, faculty success is measured almost entirely through teaching performance, student retention, and learning outcomes. Recognizing these variations helps faculty allocate time and energy appropriately across teaching, research, and service commitments.

Key Takeaway

Faculty who succeed across institutional types are those who recognize that effective teaching is not a single model but a context-driven practice. Aligning pedagogy with institutional mission, student demographics, and workload realities ensures that faculty can meet expectations while fostering meaningful student learning.

Adapting to Institutional Mission and Student Demographics

Faculty effectiveness depends on the ability to recognize how institutional mission and student demographics intersect to shape teaching expectations. A course that succeeds in one context may not translate directly into another. Professors who intentionally adapt to the realities of their institution enable learning cultures that are both rigorous and responsive to student needs.

Institutional Mission as a Driver of Teaching Practice

- **Research-Intensive (R1) Universities**: The institutional priority is advancing knowledge through research and scholarship. Faculty teaching often supports this mission by exposing undergraduates to disciplinary methods and preparing graduate students for independent research careers. While undergraduate courses may involve less direct interaction with faculty due to scale, students benefit from opportunities to engage in labs, independent studies, and honors programs. Faculty must design courses that introduce large groups of students to complex material efficiently, while also creating optional pathways for motivated students to participate in research.
- **Liberal Arts Colleges**: These institutions focus on cultivating broad intellectual capacities such as critical thinking, ethical reasoning, and cross-disciplinary exploration. Teaching is student-centered and intensive, with an expectation that faculty serve as both instructors and mentors. Courses are designed to foster inquiry and discussion, encouraging students to connect ideas across fields. Faculty often emphasize writing, speaking, and integrative projects that develop transferable skills suited to varied careers or graduate study.
- **Community Colleges**: The mission centers on access, affordability, and workforce readiness. Faculty prioritize practical learning outcomes that prepare students for immediate employment or transfer to four-year institutions. Course design emphasizes clarity, scaffolding, and skill application. Given the diverse demographics—ranging from recent high school graduates to working adults—flexibility in instructional delivery is critical. Online, hybrid, weekend, and evening classes are often essential for meeting student needs.

Aligning Course Design with Student Demographics

- **R1 Undergraduates**: Often highly prepared but seeking autonomy, these students benefit from structured large-lecture learning complemented by smaller discussion or lab sections. Assignments may be designed to scale (e.g., auto-graded quizzes, standardized rubrics) while still offering optional deeper engagement through research projects.
- **Liberal Arts Students**: Typically expect strong faculty accessibility and intellectual mentorship. Small seminar courses encourage debate, peer collaboration, and sustained writing projects. Faculty design assessments that prioritize analysis and synthesis rather than rote memorization, aligning with the institution's commitment to holistic intellectual development.
- **Community College Students**: Many juggle employment, caregiving, and financial challenges. Faculty must create courses that reduce barriers through modular design, clear learning objectives, and practical assessments that connect directly to career

pathways or transfer requirements. For example, a writing course may focus on professional communication formats alongside traditional essays, or a business course may integrate case studies drawn from local industries.

Pedagogical Calibration: Rigor, Accessibility, and Mentorship

Effective faculty practice requires balancing three interdependent dimensions:

- **Rigor**: Aligning learning outcomes with institutional mission ensures students are appropriately challenged. For example, advanced theoretical work may be emphasized at R1 universities, while applied problem-solving may be central at community colleges.
- **Accessibility**: Faculty must adapt delivery to ensure all students can succeed. This may include using open educational resources (OERs), integrating universal design for learning (UDL) principles, or offering flexible scheduling options.
- **Mentorship**: The faculty role in student development varies by context. At R1 institutions, mentorship often focuses on research pathways and graduate education. At liberal arts colleges, it emphasizes intellectual growth and personal development. At community colleges, mentorship frequently supports persistence, transfer readiness, and career alignment.

Key Takeaway

Faculty who adapt teaching to both institutional mission and student demographics can align their courses with broader institutional goals while meeting students where they are. This dual alignment—mission-driven and student-centered—ensures that teaching contributes to both institutional success and individual student achievement.

Working Within Resource Constraints

No institution offers unlimited instructional resources. Faculty must navigate the realities of budgets, staffing, and infrastructure when designing and delivering courses. Effective teaching often depends less on the abundance of resources and more on how creatively and strategically those resources are used.

Resource Realities Across Institution Types

- **Community Colleges**: These institutions often operate with lean budgets, high teaching loads, and limited support staff. Advanced laboratories, specialized software, or instructional designers may not be available. Faculty frequently take on multiple roles—advisor, curriculum developer, and sometimes even technology support. This requires resourceful approaches to course design, such as relying on low-cost materials, community partnerships, and adaptable teaching strategies that emphasize access and affordability.
- **Smaller Liberal Arts Colleges**: While class sizes are smaller and student-faculty engagement is high, budgets may not allow for the same level of technological or laboratory investment seen at larger universities. Faculty may need to integrate cross-

disciplinary resources, collaborate with colleagues to share equipment or expertise, and maximize the use of library holdings and open-access scholarship.
- **R1 Universities**: Despite larger budgets, resources are often directed toward research infrastructure rather than teaching. Faculty may find themselves with access to state-of-the-art laboratories but limited institutional investment in teaching centers, instructional support, or small-class innovations. In these contexts, faculty must advocate for teaching resources or leverage graduate assistants and online tools to enhance instructional quality.

Strategies for Creative Adaptation

Faculty can mitigate resource gaps through intentional instructional design:

- **Open Educational Resources (OERs)**: Freely available textbooks, modules, and multimedia can replace costly commercial materials. OERs also allow customization to local contexts, ensuring course content aligns with institutional mission and student demographics.
- **Simulations and Virtual Labs**: Low-cost or free digital platforms provide experiential learning opportunities when physical labs or equipment are unavailable. For example, virtual labs or business simulations allow students to practice complex skills without requiring expensive infrastructure.
- **Community-Embedded Learning**: Partnering with local businesses, nonprofits, or government agencies can provide authentic learning experiences that substitute for formal labs or costly projects. Service-learning and applied projects often yield meaningful engagement at minimal cost.
- **Cross-Institutional Collaboration**: Faculty can share resources, co-develop online modules, or engage in consortia to access expertise and materials beyond their home institution.

Leveraging Institutional Supports

Even under constraints, institutions typically offer some support structures. Faculty should proactively engage with:

- **Centers for Teaching and Learning (CTLs)**: These units often provide workshops, course design consultations, and small grants to support teaching innovation.
- **Instructional Technology Services**: Support for learning management systems, classroom technology, and media production can expand instructional possibilities without major financial investment.
- **Library Services**: Librarians can assist in integrating digital collections, databases, and open-access journals into course materials.

Advocacy and Resource Stewardship

Faculty play a role not only as users of resources but also as advocates for equitable allocation. Documenting student success outcomes tied to resource investments strengthens the case for increased teaching support. Likewise, faculty who adopt scalable, cost-effective practices (such as OER use or flipped classrooms) model stewardship that aligns with institutional missions of access and sustainability.

Key Takeaway

Resource constraints are universal, though they manifest differently across institutional types. Faculty who innovate within their means—by adopting OERs, leveraging community partnerships, and using available support structures—can sustain high-quality teaching despite limitations. The most effective educators view constraints not as barriers but as catalysts for creativity and intentional pedagogy.

Regional Accreditation Differences

Regional accreditation serves as the foundation for institutional legitimacy in U.S. higher education. While each accrediting body shares a common purpose—assuring quality, promoting accountability, and protecting students—differences in emphasis create unique contexts that shape faculty responsibilities. Professors must understand these nuances to design courses and assessments that align with institutional obligations while maintaining high standards of student learning.

Overview of Regional Accrediting Bodies

The United States is divided into regions, each served by accreditors recognized by the U.S. Department of Education and the Council for Higher Education Accreditation (CHEA) [61]. Key regional accreditors include:

- **Higher Learning Commission (HLC)** – Serves institutions across 19 states in the Midwest [61]. Known for emphasizing assessment of learning outcomes and institutional improvement processes.
- **Southern Association of Colleges and Schools Commission on Colleges (SACSCOC)** – Oversees institutions in the South. Strong focus on governance, mission integrity, and compliance with federal regulations, particularly financial aid and institutional stability.
- **Middle States Commission on Higher Education (MSCHE)** – Serves Mid-Atlantic states. Places emphasis on institutional effectiveness, strategic planning, and evidence-driven decision-making.
- **WASC Senior College and University Commission (WASC/WSCUC)** – Covers institutions in California, Hawaii, and Pacific territories. Recognized for emphasizing innovation, student success metrics, and continuous quality improvement [62].
- **New England Commission of Higher Education (NECHE)** and **Northwest Commission on Colleges and Universities (NWCCU)** – Smaller regional bodies with priorities aligned to their geographic and cultural contexts, often highlighting mission alignment and faculty qualifications [63].

Differences in Emphasis and Faculty Implications

While all accreditors require evidence of quality, specific focal points differ:

- **Assessment of Learning Outcomes (HLC, WASC, NWCCU)**: Faculty are expected to clearly articulate measurable learning objectives, collect evidence of student achievement, and use findings for continuous improvement. This means designing syllabi, assignments, and assessments that directly map to institutional and program-level outcomes.
- **Governance and Institutional Integrity (SACSCOC, NECHE)**: Faculty play a visible role in shared governance and must document participation in curriculum design, program review, and institutional decision-making. Transparency in faculty qualifications, hiring practices, and committee work becomes central.
- **Financial Stability and Federal Compliance (SACSCOC, MSCHE)**: Accreditation reviews often emphasize how institutions ensure fiscal responsibility and compliance with Title IV funding regulations. Faculty may encounter directives to monitor credit hours, instructional contact time, and reporting practices tied to federal aid compliance.
- **Innovation and Student Success (WASC, NWCCU)**: Institutions are evaluated on student persistence, graduation rates, and equity gaps. Faculty are expected to implement evidence-based pedagogies, track disaggregated student data, and contribute to initiatives that enhance student success across diverse populations.

Faculty Roles in Accreditation Alignment

Faculty contribute to accreditation compliance in several key ways:

- **Course Design**: Developing syllabi that explicitly state learning objectives aligned to program and institutional outcomes.
- **Assessment**: Using rubrics, embedded assignments, or standardized measures to collect evidence of learning, then participating in departmental assessment reporting cycles.
- **Program Review**: Contributing data, narratives, and reflective analysis to support cyclical program reviews required by accreditors.
- **Governance Participation**: Serving on committees related to curriculum, assessment, or institutional effectiveness, ensuring faculty voice in accreditation-related decision-making.
- **Continuous Improvement**: Engaging in reflective teaching practices and integrating student feedback, assessment results, and accreditation recommendations into course revisions.

Risks of Misalignment

Failure to adhere to accreditation expectations can have serious consequences for institutions, including probation, loss of accreditation, and ineligibility for federal student aid. At the faculty level, misalignment can lead to courses or programs being flagged for insufficient assessment, unclear outcomes, or lack of documentation. Awareness and proactive participation mitigate these risks.

Key Takeaway

Regional accreditation bodies share a common mission but differ in the weight they assign to learning outcomes, governance, financial stability, and student success. Faculty who understand these differences and align their teaching, assessment, and governance participation accordingly strengthen both institutional credibility and the quality of student learning.

Navigating Union Environments and Collective Bargaining Impacts

Faculty working in unionized environments must understand how collective bargaining agreements (CBAs) shape the conditions of their employment. These agreements are negotiated between faculty unions and institutional administrations, covering everything from teaching loads and class sizes to compensation, grievance procedures, and academic freedom. For professors—especially those new to unionized settings—familiarity with the CBA is not optional; it is essential for understanding both rights and responsibilities.

Key Areas Defined by Union Contracts

Union agreements vary by institution and state law, but they often address several core areas:

- **Workload and Course Loads**: CBAs typically set maximum teaching loads per semester or year, ensuring faculty are not overburdened. For example, a community college contract may establish a standard "5-5" load (five courses each semester), with restrictions on mandatory overload assignments.
- **Class Size Limits**: Many contracts include caps on student enrollment per course to protect instructional quality and faculty workload. Faculty may also receive additional compensation or support if enrollment exceeds the cap.
- **Office Hours and Student Availability**: Contracts often specify the minimum number of office hours per week, sometimes differentiating between in-person and online modalities. These requirements ensure student access while clarifying expectations for faculty availability.
- **Evaluation and Promotion**: CBAs outline processes for classroom observation, student evaluations, peer review, and tenure/promotion. This formal structure can provide transparency but may also impose rigid procedures that faculty must follow closely.
- **Academic Freedom**: Many agreements explicitly protect faculty autonomy in teaching and research, though the scope of this protection varies. Faculty should know what the contract guarantees and what limitations may apply.
- **Grievance Procedures**: CBAs establish formal pathways for resolving disputes, including appeals processes, mediation, or arbitration. This provides faculty with due process rights not always present in non-union institutions.

Protections Provided by Union Agreements

Union contracts generally strengthen faculty positions by:

- Preventing arbitrary workload increases.
- Protecting faculty from sudden policy changes imposed by administration.
- Ensuring clear salary scales, promotion criteria, and benefits.

- Guaranteeing due process in disciplinary actions.

These protections create stability and predictability, which is especially valuable in institutions with shifting enrollments or budgetary pressures.

Obligations Under Union Agreements

Alongside protections, faculty also assume obligations, such as:

- Adhering to required office hour schedules.
- Participating in union-mandated committees or governance activities.
- Following detailed procedures for assessment, reporting, or student evaluation submission.
- Respecting limits on outside employment or consulting when stipulated.

Failure to meet these obligations can place faculty in violation of the contract and subject them to institutional discipline.

Non-Union Environments: Flexibility with Fewer Safeguards

At institutions without faculty unions, working conditions may be less rigid but also less secure. Faculty may have greater flexibility in setting office hours, managing class sizes, or negotiating teaching loads individually. However, without contractual protections, they are more vulnerable to administrative changes, larger workloads without compensation, or unclear evaluation procedures. In such contexts, faculty must rely on institutional handbooks, administrative policies, or informal norms to guide expectations—none of which carry the legal enforceability of a union contract [64].

Practical Guidance for New Faculty

- **Read the Contract Thoroughly**: Faculty should review not only workload provisions but also sections on evaluation, professional conduct, and grievance rights.
- **Consult Union Representatives**: Union stewards or representatives can clarify ambiguous clauses and provide guidance on rights and obligations.
- **Document Compliance**: Keeping records of office hours, evaluations, and committee service helps demonstrate adherence to contractual requirements.
- **Stay Informed**: Contracts are renegotiated periodically, and changes can significantly impact faculty roles. Attending union meetings or reviewing updates ensures faculty remain current.

Key Takeaway

Union environments shape faculty work in structured and enforceable ways. Collective bargaining agreements provide vital protections around workload, evaluation, and academic freedom, but they also impose formal obligations. In contrast, non-union institutions offer more flexibility but fewer safeguards. Faculty success depends on understanding the specific context of their institution and aligning their practices with both contractual requirements and professional standards.

Managing Teaching Loads Across Institution Types

Teaching load is one of the most significant variables shaping the daily experience of faculty. While research expectations, advising, and service duties differ across institutional types, the number of courses and students assigned each semester determines how faculty allocate their time and energy. Understanding these differences allows professors to develop realistic strategies for workload management, course preparation, and student engagement.

Teaching Loads by Institution Type

- **Research 1 (R1) Universities**: Faculty often carry a "2-2 load" (two courses per semester) or lighter, particularly for tenure-track and research-active professors. In some cases, faculty may teach a single course per term, especially when supported by external grant funding or administrative release [65]. However, this reduced teaching load is offset by high research expectations, including publishing in top-tier journals, securing grants, and supervising doctoral students. Graduate instruction often requires intensive mentoring of individual students and research groups, which can be more time-consuming than formal classroom teaching.
- **Liberal Arts Colleges**: Faculty typically teach three or four courses per semester, resulting in a "3-3" or "4-4" load [66]. These courses are usually small and discussion-based, requiring significant preparation and direct engagement with students. In addition, advising, mentoring, and participation in faculty governance play major roles in faculty evaluation. Research is valued but usually framed as *scholarship in support of teaching*, with expectations that faculty integrate research into the classroom and involve undergraduates in scholarly inquiry.
- **Community Colleges**: Faculty often carry the heaviest course responsibilities, with "4-4" or "5-5" loads, sometimes equating to 150+ students per semester [67]. Unlike R1 or liberal arts settings, community colleges rarely provide teaching assistants, placing the full burden of grading, course management, and student support on faculty. Service and research obligations are minimal, but advising and student support often consume additional time, especially given the diverse needs of students balancing school, work, and family responsibilities.

Time Management and Workload Strategies

Because teaching is structured differently across institutions, faculty must adopt context-specific strategies:

- **At R1 Institutions**: Efficiency in teaching preparation is key. Faculty may use standardized rubrics, delegate grading to teaching assistants, and leverage learning management systems (LMS) for managing large courses. Since classroom instruction represents a smaller percentage of total workload, the challenge is to maintain impactful

teaching while balancing the competing demands of research productivity and grant writing.
- **At Liberal Arts Colleges**: Faculty must balance course preparation for multiple smaller classes with heavy advising responsibilities. Strategies include designing assignments that encourage peer feedback, staggering due dates to distribute grading, and integrating research into teaching to serve dual purposes. Building strong relationships with students is both expected and necessary for tenure and promotion, making time management in office hours and advising essential.
- **At Community Colleges**: Faculty must prioritize sustainable teaching practices to handle heavy course loads. Using modular course designs, automated LMS features (e.g., quizzes, discussion forums), and streamlined grading practices (e.g., checklists and rubrics) helps reduce administrative burden. Flexibility is also critical, as students' complex life circumstances often require faculty to adjust deadlines or provide additional support.

Balancing Quality and Sustainability

Regardless of institution type, faculty must strike a balance between delivering high-quality instruction and maintaining personal sustainability. Over-preparing lectures or over-grading assignments can quickly lead to burnout, particularly in high-load environments. Effective faculty adopt strategies such as:

- **Reusing and updating course materials** across semesters rather than creating new content from scratch.
- **Designing scalable assignments** (e.g., short reflection papers, group projects, or peer reviews) that provide meaningful feedback without overwhelming grading time.
- **Integrating technology** for communication, assessment, and feedback management.
- **Aligning effort with institutional priorities**—investing deeply in teaching when it is the central evaluative criterion, or balancing teaching efficiency with research when publications drive promotion.

Key Takeaway

Teaching loads differ dramatically across institutional types, shaping how faculty manage time, balance responsibilities, and interact with students. At R1 universities, the challenge lies in delivering impactful instruction while meeting demanding research goals. At liberal arts colleges, faculty balance intensive teaching and advising with modest research expectations. At community colleges, sustainability in teaching practices is crucial to managing heavy loads without sacrificing student support. Success depends on aligning time management strategies with institutional priorities while preserving both instructional quality and faculty well-being.

Conclusion: The Professor's Role in Higher Education Governance

A strong understanding of higher education policies and academic governance is essential for new faculty members to thrive in academic institutions. Professors must not only adhere to policies but also actively engage in governance, advocate for academic excellence, and contribute to institutional decision-making.

By balancing compliance with policy, participation in governance, and commitment to student success, faculty members play key roles in shaping higher education institutions, fostering academic integrity, and ensuring the success of students and programs. Ultimately, effective governance and well-structured policies create a sustainable, fair, and high-quality academic environment that benefits all stakeholders.

Higher education teaching is both an art and a science, requiring a balance of expertise, pedagogical skill, and student-centered engagement. Professors are responsible for imparting knowledge and skills, but also for mentoring students, fostering intellectual curiosity, and preparing them for real-world applications of their learning.

As the landscape of higher education evolves, faculty must remain committed to continuous improvement, embracing new teaching methodologies, technological advancements, and inclusive practices. The integration of diverse pedagogical strategies, effective assessment techniques, and personalized mentorship enhances student success and institutional excellence.

Ultimately, the impact of a college professor extends far beyond the classroom, shaping future scholars, professionals, and leaders. By refining their teaching practices and remaining adaptable to the ever-changing demands of higher education, faculty members contribute to a learning environment that is innovative, inclusive, and transformative.

Chapter 3: Course Design and Curriculum Development

Effective course design is the backbone of successful teaching in higher education. A well-structured course goes beyond content delivery, strategically aligning learning objectives, assessments, and instructional activities to create a meaningful and engaging student experience. Faculty members must approach course development with intentionality, ensuring that students gain both foundational knowledge and practical application of knowledge and skills they learn in real-world contexts.

Figure 3.1. Course Design and Creation [219].

This chapter explores key principles of course design, including backward course design, which emphasizes defining learning objectives first, aligning assessments, and then structuring instructional strategies accordingly. The process of curriculum development also involves ensuring course alignment with institutional standards, accreditation requirements, and evolving industry expectations. Furthermore, this chapter highlights best practices for developing a syllabus, incorporating inclusive course materials, and leveraging instructional technology to enhance student engagement.

By adopting a structured and student-centered approach to course design, faculty can create courses that foster critical thinking, practical application, and lifelong learning. The goal is not just to teach but to design learning experiences empowering students to succeed academically and professionally.

Backward Course Design: Setting Objectives First

Effective course design is intentional, structured, and student-centered, ensuring that learning experiences align with desired outcomes. One of the most widely used and research-supported approaches in curriculum development is backward course design, a methodology that emphasizes setting learning objectives first and then designing assessments and instructional activities that support those goals [68]. Unlike traditional course planning, which often begins with content selection or textbook choices, backward design ensures all aspects of a course is purposefully designed with what students should ultimately know, understand, and demonstrate by the end of the course.

Backward course design, popularized by Grant Wiggins and Jay McTighe in Understanding by Design (UbD), shifts faculty focus from teaching as content delivery to teaching as a process of facilitating meaningful learning [69]. This model enhances coherence, rigor, and assessment alignment, making it a fundamental strategy for higher education instructors [70].

1. Understanding the Backward Design Model

The backward design approach follows a three-step process, where faculty first establish learning objectives, then determine how they will measure success, and finally design learning experiences that lead students toward achieving the stated outcomes.

The Three Stages of Backward Course Design

1. **Identify Desired Learning Outcomes (What Should Students Learn?)**
   - Define what students should comprehend, understand, and demonstrate at the end of the course.
   - Align learning outcomes with programmatic, institutional, and accreditation standards.
   - Use frameworks like Bloom's Taxonomy or the DOK (Depth of Knowledge) model to ensure objectives promote higher-order thinking and application.

2. **Determine Acceptable Evidence (How Will Learning Be Assessed?)**
   - Develop assessments and performance tasks that measure whether students have met the learning objectives.
   - Include a balance of formative and summative assessments, such as:
     - Exams and quizzes to evaluate conceptual understanding.
     - Essays and research projects to assess critical thinking and argumentation.
     - Presentations, case studies, and portfolios for real-world application.
     - Peer evaluations and reflections to measure metacognitive growth.

3. **Plan Learning Activities (How Will Students Reach These Goals?)**
   - Select readings, discussions, case studies, and experiential learning opportunities that reinforce learning objectives.
   - Ensure alignment between activities and assessments so that students practice the skills they will be evaluated on.
   - Integrate active learning strategies, such as collaborative projects, flipped classrooms, and hands-on applications.

Backward design ensures that every instructional element serves a clear purpose—supporting student learning rather than simply covering content.

2. Step One: Defining Learning Objectives First

Why Start with Learning Objectives?

Many course designs fail when they begin with content selection instead of defining what students should achieve. Without clearly articulated goals, courses often become content-heavy but learning-light, resulting in students memorizing material without developing deep understanding or application skills.

By beginning with student learning outcomes (SLOs), professors ensure:

- Instruction is purposeful, with all activities leading to a specific learning goal.
- Assessments are meaningful, accurately measuring student comprehension and skill development.
- Students gain transferable skills, preparing them for application of knowledge and skills in the real world.

Characteristics of Strong Learning Objectives

When setting learning objectives, faculty should ensure they are:

1. **Specific** – Clearly defined so that students and faculty know what success looks like.
2. **Measurable** – Capable of being assessed through direct or indirect methods.
3. **Achievable** – Realistic given the course level and timeframe.
4. **Relevant** – Connected to broader program goals and real-world applications.
5. **Time-bound** – Achievable within the course duration.

A helpful tool for writing objectives is Bloom's Taxonomy, which classifies cognitive skills from basic to advanced [71]:

- **Remember** – Recall facts and concepts (e.g., "Define key cybersecurity threats.")
- **Understand** – Explain ideas in one's own words (e.g., "Summarize the main principles of encryption.")
- **Apply** – Use knowledge in a new situation (e.g., "Develop a risk assessment framework.")
- **Analyze** – Break down concepts (e.g., "Differentiate between symmetric and asymmetric cryptography.")
- **Evaluate** – Make judgments based on criteria (e.g., "Assess the security vulnerabilities in a cloud computing environment.")
- **Create** – Develop new theories or solutions (e.g., "Design a cybersecurity policy for a financial institution.")

By structuring objectives around higher-order thinking, faculty can ensure deeper learning and skill mastery [72].

3. Step Two: Designing Assessments to Align with Objectives

Once objectives are established, professors must determine how they will measure student progress and mastery. Effective assessment follows the principle of alignment, meaning that the way students are assessed should reflect the type of learning required in the objectives.

For example:

- If the objective is "Analyze financial statements to assess company performance", an essay or case study analysis would be a better assessment than a multiple-choice quiz.
- If the objective is "Design an experiment to test a hypothesis", a lab report or research proposal aligns better than a standardized test.

Types of Assessments in Backward Course Design

1. **Formative Assessments (Low-Stakes, Ongoing Feedback)**
    - Discussions, reflections, quizzes, peer reviews.
    - Provide insight into student understanding before high-stakes assessments.
2. **Summative Assessments (Higher-Stakes Evaluations of Mastery)**
    - Final exams, research papers, presentations.
    - Demonstrate how well students met the course objectives.
3. **Authentic Assessments (Real-World Applications of Learning)**
    - Case studies, simulations, portfolios, industry projects.
    - Help students connect classroom learning to professional settings.

Aligning assessments with learning outcomes ensures coherence in the learning experience and allows for meaningful measurement of student progress [72].

4. Step Three: Designing Learning Activities That Support Objectives

The final step in backward course design is selecting instructional methods and learning activities that help students achieve the stated objectives. Every lecture, discussion, and assignment should be purposefully integrated into the course plan.

Key Considerations for Planning Learning Activities

1. **Active Learning Strategies**
    - Problem-based learning, debates, flipped classroom models.
    - Encourage engagement and application rather than passive reception.

2. **Scaffolded Learning**
   - Gradual progression from basic to advanced skills.
   - Use sequenced assignments where students build toward higher-order application.

3. **Real-World Relevance**
   - Case studies, industry guest speakers, service-learning opportunities.
   - Help students comprehend the value of their education for professional and personal success.

4. **Technology Integration**
   - Online discussion boards, simulations, AI-enhanced learning tools.
   - Enhances engagement and caters to different learning preferences.

By carefully designing activities that directly align with learning objectives, professors create a structured yet flexible environment where students can thrive [73].

Conclusion: The Power of Backward Course Design

Backward course design is a deliberate, student-centered approach that ensures coherence between learning objectives, assessments, and instructional strategies. By beginning with the end in mind, faculty members craft courses that foster deep, meaningful, and transferable learning.

Key Takeaways for Faculty:

Set learning objectives first to define the course's purpose.
Design assessments that align with objectives, ensuring fair and effective measurement of student learning.
Plan instructional activities that directly support student success, creating engaging and impactful learning experiences.

By using backward design, faculty create courses that are rigorous, relevant, and rewarding, ensuring that students not only learn theory and knowledge but also demonstrate the knowledge in real-world contexts [74].

Aligning Course Content with Learning Outcomes

Effective course design in higher education institutions is not solely about selecting content and instructional materials; it requires intentional alignment between course content and learning outcomes to ensure that students gain the knowledge, skills, and competencies they need. This alignment serves as the backbone of a well-structured course, providing a logical progression of learning experiences that reinforce key concepts and foster deeper understanding.

When course content is properly aligned with learning outcomes, every reading, lecture, discussion, and assessment contributes meaningfully to student learning. This cohesive design prevents content overload, reduces redundancy, and ensures that students engage with material that directly supports the course's educational objectives [75]. Professors who adopt this approach help students see the importance of theory and knowledge, but also how it applies to their academic and professional goals.

1. The Importance of Course Alignment

Alignment is essential for clarity, consistency, and effectiveness in teaching and learning [76]. When course content is carefully mapped to learning outcomes, students:

- Understand what is expected of them and how different elements of the course contribute to their learning.
- See the connections between theory and practice, making it easier to synthesize their knowledge in real-world scenarios.
- Engage in deep learning rather than surface memorization, as instructional materials are purposefully chosen to reinforce critical concepts.

For faculty, proper alignment:

- Ensures instructional coherence, allowing for better pacing and sequencing of content.
- Supports fair and meaningful assessment, ensuring that evaluations accurately measure what students are expected to learn.
- Meets accreditation and institutional standards, as many accrediting bodies require evidence of alignment between course design and student learning outcomes.

Without clear alignment, students often struggle to see the purpose of course materials and activities, leading to disengagement, frustration, and gaps in knowledge [77].

2. Key Components of Course Alignment

Alignment occurs at multiple levels within a course. The primary goal is to connect learning outcomes, assessments, instructional content, and activities in a meaningful way.

A. Learning Outcomes as the Foundation

Learning outcomes identify student comprehension, knowledge, and skills to be demonstrated by the end of a course. These outcomes guide the selection of course content and must be:

Clear and specific – Well-defined expectations help students focus on essential concepts.
Measurable – Outcomes should be assessable through exams, projects, discussions, or practical applications.
Appropriate for the course level – Undergraduate outcomes should emphasize foundational knowledge, while graduate-level outcomes should focus on critical analysis, research, and application.

Example Learning Outcomes by Course Level:

- **Undergraduate Course:** "Students will be able to describe and apply fundamental economic principles in real-world business scenarios."
- **Graduate Course:** "Students will critically analyze macroeconomic trends and develop policy recommendations based on empirical data."

B. Course Content Selection: Ensuring Relevance and Depth

Once learning outcomes are defined, professors must select readings, lectures, case studies, and instructional materials that align with those goals.

Strategies for Content Alignment:

1. **Ensure that each topic directly supports one or more learning outcomes.**
    - If an outcome focuses on data analysis, students should engage with datasets, statistical tools, and research articles rather than just theoretical discussions.
    - If an outcome emphasizes ethical decision-making, include case studies and debates, challenging students to apply ethical principles.

2. **Use a balance of foundational and advanced materials.**
    - Undergraduate courses should provide introductory texts, foundational theories, and practical examples to build core knowledge.
    - Graduate courses should incorporate peer-reviewed research, case studies, and discipline-specific methodologies to deepen understanding.

3. **Incorporate multiple perspectives and interdisciplinary connections.**
    - Including diverse viewpoints and real-world applications enriches students' understanding and prepares them for complex problem-solving.

4. **Sequence content in a logical progression.**
    - Start with basic concepts and theories, then progress to complex applications and synthesis of ideas.
    - Scaffold learning by gradually increasing complexity to help students build confidence.

Example of Poor vs. Strong Content Alignment

- **Poor Alignment:** A finance course includes a guest lecture on corporate social responsibility without linking it to financial decision-making or risk analysis.
- **Strong Alignment:** The same guest lecture is integrated with a case study on how ESG (Environmental, Social, and Governance) factors impact investment strategies.

C. Assessment Alignment: Measuring Learning Effectively

Assessments must directly evaluate whether students have met the learning outcomes. If assessments are misaligned, students may be tested on content that does not reflect what they were expected to learn.

1. **Assessments must match the cognitive level of learning outcomes.**
   - If an outcome requires analysis, multiple-choice questions testing recall are insufficient. Instead, use essays, case studies, or data interpretation tasks.
   - If an outcome requires skill development, hands-on projects, portfolios, or simulations should be incorporated.

2. **Use a variety of assessments to provide a comprehensive measure of learning.**
   - Formative assessments (quizzes, reflections, discussions) gauge understanding throughout the course.
   - Summative assessments (final papers, exams, presentations) measure overall mastery of the subject.

3. **Ensure fair and transparent grading criteria.**
   - Use rubrics to communicate expectations and provide structured feedback.
   - Align grading weights with the significance of learning outcomes.

Example of Strong Assessment Alignment

- **Outcome:** "Students will evaluate the effectiveness of different leadership styles in organizational settings."
- **Aligned Assessment:** A case study analysis where students assess real-world leadership scenarios and propose recommendations.
- **Misaligned Assessment:** A multiple-choice exam that only asks students to identify leadership theories without application.

D. Instructional Strategies and Learning Activities

The final step in alignment is ensuring that learning activities support both content mastery and skill development.

Active learning techniques (debates, simulations, problem-solving exercises) enable students to demonstrate knowledge application in meaningful ways [78].
Collaborative learning (group projects, peer reviews) fosters deeper engagement and diverse perspectives [79].
Technology-enhanced learning (LMS platforms, AI-driven tutoring, interactive modules) supports different learning styles and accessibility needs [80].

For every learning activity, ask:

- Does this activity reinforce the learning outcome?
- Does it prepare students for their assessments?
- Does it scaffold learning in a way that builds upon prior knowledge?

Example of Strong Instructional Alignment

- **Outcome:** "Students will develop strategic marketing plans based on market research data."
- **Aligned Activity:** Students analyze consumer data sets and create a marketing strategy, receiving peer and instructor feedback.
- **Misaligned Activity:** Students read about marketing strategies but do not apply them in a practical setting.

3. Ensuring Continuous Alignment and Improvement

Even after designing a well-aligned course, faculty should continually assess and refine their approach based on student performance and feedback.

Methods for Evaluating Course Alignment:

Review student assessment data – Are students achieving learning outcomes as expected?
Collect student feedback – Do students find course materials relevant and useful?
Adjust content and activities – If misalignment is detected, refine instructional methods and assessments.
Consult faculty peers – Cross-review courses with colleagues to identify potential gaps or improvements.

Conclusion: The Impact of Alignment on Student Success

Aligning course content with learning outcomes is a fundamental aspect of effective teaching. When done well, it ensures students receive a cohesive, and meaningful learning experience, where every aspect of the course supports their academic and professional growth.

By focusing on intentional alignment, professors not only improve student learning but also enhance teaching effectiveness, institutional credibility, and overall course quality [81]. A well-aligned course is not simply a collection of topics—it is a structured journey that guides students toward mastery, critical thinking, and real-world application.

Creating an Effective Syllabus: Structure, Policies, and Expectations

A syllabus serves as the foundation of a well-organized course, functioning as both a contract and a roadmap that guides students through the academic journey. It sets the tone for the course, establishes expectations, and communicates essential details about learning objectives, course policies, grading criteria, and instructional methods. A well-designed syllabus fosters student engagement, clarifies academic responsibilities, and ensures alignment with institutional policies and accreditation standards [82].

For new college professors, creating an effective syllabus is a critical skill that enhances course organization, supports student learning, and promotes transparency. A strong syllabus should be clear, structured, accessible, and dynamic, balancing both rigor and flexibility to accommodate diverse student needs.

1. The Purpose and Role of the Syllabus

The syllabus is more than just a list of topics and assignments—it is a contract, a communication tool, a learning guide, and an organizational framework.

A. The Syllabus as a Contract

- Establishes mutual expectations between faculty and students.
- Defines grading policies, deadlines, academic integrity expectations, and course policies.
- Provides legal clarity in case of grade disputes or policy misunderstandings.

B. The Syllabus as a Learning Guide

- Helps students understand course goals and learning outcomes.
- Provides scaffolding for learning, showing how knowledge builds over time.
- Serves as a reference document for students to track assignments, due dates, and assessments.

C. The Syllabus as an Organizational Framework

- Helps faculty maintain course structure and pacing.
- Ensures alignment with institutional requirements, accreditation standards, and departmental guidelines.
- Serves as a tool for instructional design, integrating assessments, content, and activities cohesively.

A well-crafted syllabus enhances both student success and teaching effectiveness, reducing confusion and setting a positive, professional tone from the beginning [83].

2. Key Components of an Effective Syllabus

A comprehensive syllabus should include the following core sections:

A. Course Information and Instructor Details

Course Title, Number, and Credit Hours – Clearly identify the course, aligning with institutional records.
Semester and Year – Helps students track the course schedule within their academic plans.
Instructor Name and Contact Information – Email, office location, phone number, and preferred communication methods.

Office Hours and Availability – Specify in-person or virtual meeting times, and encourage engagement.

B. Course Description and Learning Objectives

Course Overview – Provide a brief yet engaging introduction explaining the subject matter, its significance, and what students can expect to learn.

Learning Outcomes – Clearly defined student learning objectives (SLOs) that articulate the skills and knowledge students will acquire.

Alignment with Institutional and Program Goals – Demonstrate how the course fits into broader degree requirements or career pathways.

Example of Well-Written Learning Outcomes:

- **Weak Outcome:** "Students will understand economic theories."
- **Strong Outcome:** "Students will analyze and apply Keynesian and classical economic models to assess real-world fiscal policies."

C. Course Schedule and Weekly Outline

A structured week-by-week (or module-based) outline listing:

- Topics covered.
- Required readings and multimedia materials.
- Assignments, assessments, and due dates.
  Flexibility clause: While schedules should be structured, including a disclaimer allows for **adjustments due to unforeseen circumstances**.

Example Course Schedule Snippet (Weeks 1–3):

Week	Topic	Readings	Assignments Due
1	Introduction to Microeconomics	Chapter 1 (Smith, 2022)	Syllabus Quiz
2	Supply & Demand Theories	Chapter 2 & Case Study	Discussion Post #1
3	Market Structures & Competition	Chapter 3 & Peer Articles	Quiz #1

D. Course Policies: Attendance, Late Work, Academic Integrity

Clearly outlined course policies help manage expectations and prevent disputes.

Attendance & Participation Policy:

- Define expectations for in-person vs. online participation.
- Address excused vs. unexcused absences and any penalty structure.

- Specify engagement expectations for asynchronous courses (e.g., discussion boards, peer reviews).

Late Work and Extensions:

- Clarify the policy on late submissions and if extensions are allowed.
- Specify penalties for late work (e.g., "Assignments submitted up to 24 hours late receive a 10% deduction per day").

Academic Integrity and Plagiarism Policy:

- Reinforce institutional policies on plagiarism, unauthorized collaboration, and exam misconduct.
- Provide links to university honor codes and plagiarism detection tools like Turnitin.
- Clarify penalties for academic dishonesty (e.g., failing grades, formal warnings).

Technology and Communication Expectations:

- Define policies for email etiquette, response times, and use of online platforms.
- Outline LMS (Canvas, Blackboard, Moodle) expectations for submissions, discussions, and announcements.
- Specify acceptable use of AI tools for coursework (if applicable).

3. Structuring a Student-Centered Syllabus

A student-centered syllabus is not just about listing rules—it is about creating a document that is accessible, engaging, and designed to support learning success.

A. Writing Style: Balance Formality and Accessibility

- Use clear, direct language that is welcoming rather than overly bureaucratic.
- Consider adding a "Welcome Statement" that sets a positive, inclusive tone.
- Provide FAQs or a quick-reference section for common questions.

B. Formatting for Readability

- Use headings, bullet points, tables, and bold text to improve navigability.
- Break up long sections to prevent information overload.
- Provide both a printable PDF and an interactive digital version for accessibility.

C. Including Support and Resources

- Provide links to campus resources (writing centers, mental health services, disability accommodations).

- Offer study tips and success strategies relevant to the course.

4. The Dynamic Syllabus: Adapting to Evolving Needs

A syllabus should be a living document that evolves with student feedback, institutional changes, and pedagogical advancements. Faculty should:

Periodically review and refine the syllabus based on student performance and engagement.
Use formative feedback (such as a mid-semester check-in) to assess whether students find policies and expectations clear.
Adapt policies and content when necessary, maintaining transparency with students about changes.

Conclusion: The Syllabus as a Foundation for Effective Teaching

A well-designed syllabus is a powerful tool for student success, instructional clarity, and academic integrity. It serves not just as a document of record but as an engagement tool that fosters a positive learning environment.

By focusing on clear structure, aligned policies, and student-centered design, faculty can create a syllabus that sets the stage for a productive, engaging, and academically rigorous semester. Ultimately, the syllabus is more than a contract—it is the first step in building a community of learners, setting expectations, and ensuring that both students and faculty have a roadmap for success.

Understanding Accreditation Requirements and Curriculum Alignment

Accreditation is the cornerstone of higher education, ensuring institutions and programs meet established standards of quality, academic rigor, and continuous improvement [84]. Professors, particularly those involved in curriculum development, must have a firm grasp of accreditation requirements and curriculum alignment to design courses that support institutional accreditation efforts while enhancing student learning outcomes.

Accreditation is not merely an administrative concern—it directly impacts program legitimacy, funding eligibility, student employability, and institutional reputation [85]. By aligning curriculum with accreditation requirements, faculty contribute to maintaining academic integrity, instructional effectiveness, and programmatic success.

1. The Role of Accreditation in Higher Education

A. What Is Accreditation?

Accreditation is a peer-reviewed process through which colleges and universities demonstrate compliance with educational standards established by accrediting bodies. These organizations evaluate institutions based on academic quality, faculty qualifications, student learning outcomes, governance structures, and financial stability.

There are two main types of accreditation:

1. **Institutional Accreditation** – Ensures an entire institution meets general quality standards.
    - Examples:
        - **Higher Learning Commission (HLC)**
        - **Middle States Commission on Higher Education (MSCHE)**
        - **Southern Association of Colleges and Schools Commission on Colleges (SACSCOC)**
        - **WASC Senior College and University Commission (WSCUC)**
2. **Programmatic Accreditation** – Focuses on specific academic programs, ensuring alignment with industry standards and professional licensure requirements.
    - Examples:
        - **AACSB (Association to Advance Collegiate Schools of Business) – Business programs**
        - **ABET (Accreditation Board for Engineering and Technology) – Engineering and computing**
        - **CCNE (Commission on Collegiate Nursing Education) – Nursing programs**
        - **CAEP (Council for the Accreditation of Educator Preparation) – Teacher education programs**

Accreditation ensures students obtain a high-quality education and degrees maintain credibility in academic and professional fields.

B. Why Accreditation Matters for Faculty

Professors play a direct role in maintaining accreditation compliance through:
Curriculum design that meets accreditation standards.
Assessment of student learning outcomes (SLOs) and continuous improvement efforts.
Ensuring faculty qualifications align with accreditation expectations.
Engagement in program review, self-study reports, and accreditation site visits.

Without proper alignment between curriculum and accreditation requirements, institutions risk losing accreditation, which can lead to funding cuts, student enrollment declines, and loss of credibility [86].

2. Curriculum Alignment: Ensuring Compliance with Accreditation Standards

A. What Is Curriculum Alignment?

Curriculum alignment is the process of structuring course content, learning objectives, instructional strategies, and assessments to ensure that academic programs:

- Meet institutional learning outcomes and accreditation standards.
- Provide students with relevant, high-quality educational experiences.
- Support degree progression, skill development, and career readiness [87].

Proper alignment ensures that courses are not just arbitrarily designed but are intentionally structured to support programmatic and institutional goals [88].

B. Key Components of Curriculum Alignment

1. Aligning Learning Outcomes with Accreditation Standards

Each accrediting body sets **core learning outcomes** that institutions must integrate into their curricula. Faculty must:
Map course objectives to program and institutional outcomes.
Ensure assessments measure key competencies required by accrediting agencies.
Regularly review and update outcomes to reflect industry changes and accreditation revisions.

Example of Learning Outcome Alignment

Accreditation Standard	Program Outcome	Course-Level Outcome	Assessment Method
AACSB: Critical Thinking in Business	Graduates will analyze business strategies.	Students will evaluate financial data to support business decisions.	Case study analysis & report.
ABET: Engineering Problem-Solving	Graduates will apply engineering principles to solve problems.	Students will design and test circuit systems.	Final design project & lab report.

2. Ensuring Course Sequencing Supports Degree Progression

Course alignment should support scaffolding, where students build on foundational knowledge before advancing to complex concepts. Faculty should ensure:
Introductory courses provide core knowledge and skills.
Mid-level courses expand analytical and application skills.
Capstone or thesis projects allow for synthesis and mastery of content.

Example of Course Progression in a Computer Science Program

Year	Course	Focus
1st	Introduction to Programming	Foundational coding skills

Year	Course	Focus
2nd	Data Structures & Algorithms	Problem-solving and efficiency
3rd	Software Engineering	Project-based learning & teamwork
4th	Capstone Project	Applied research & innovation

3. Integrating Assessment and Continuous Improvement

Accreditation requires ongoing assessment of student learning to demonstrate that educational programs achieve their goals [89]. Professors must:
Use both formative and summative assessments to measure student progress.
Collect and analyze data to highlight strengths and areas for improvement.
Adjust curriculum and teaching strategies based on assessment findings.

Example: Assessment Loop for Accreditation Compliance

1. **Define learning outcomes** → What should students learn?
2. **Implement assessments** → How will learning be measured?
3. **Analyze results** → What do student performance data reveal?
4. **Make improvements** → How can teaching and curriculum be refined?

Continuous improvement is not about compliance alone—it ensures programs remain current, rigorous, and responsive to student needs [90].

3. Best Practices for Faculty in Curriculum Alignment

Stay Informed About Accreditation Standards

- Read and review accreditation handbooks related to your discipline.
- Attend institutional workshops on curriculum development and accreditation.

Engage in Curriculum Mapping

- Use curriculum mapping tools to align courses with program objectives.
- Participate in faculty meetings where learning outcomes and assessments are reviewed.

Use Data to Drive Course Improvements

- Regularly assess student learning outcomes through exams, projects, and surveys.
- Adjust course content and teaching methods based on assessment findings.

Collaborate with Colleagues and Administrators

- Work with department chairs and curriculum committees to refine course offerings.

- Support accreditation self-study reports by providing course documentation and assessment data.

Promote Transparency and Communication
- Make course objectives clear to students so they understand their learning path.
- Provide feedback to administrators on challenges related to accreditation requirements.

Conclusion: Faculty's Role in Accreditation and Curriculum Excellence

Understanding accreditation requirements and curriculum alignment is critical for new college professors. Faculty must ensure that their courses:
Meet institutional and programmatic standards.
Provide students with meaningful, competency-based learning experiences.
Contribute to accreditation compliance and continuous program improvement.

A well-aligned curriculum strengthens academic programs, supports student success, and enhances institutional reputation. By engaging in thoughtful course design and systematic assessment, professors play an integral role in influencing the future of higher education, ensuring students graduate with the skills and knowledge necessary for academic, professional, and lifelong success.

Developing Engaging and Inclusive Course Materials

Effective course materials are the heart of an engaging and inclusive learning experience. Well-designed materials do more than simply convey information—they stimulate curiosity, promote active participation, and ensure accessibility for all learners. Developing course materials that are both engaging and inclusive requires intentionality in content selection, presentation, delivery modes, and assessment strategies.

Higher education environments are increasingly diverse, mingling learners from different backgrounds, learning styles, and abilities [91]. Professors must ensure that course materials reflect intellectual rigor while also enabling an inclusive environment where all students can engage equitably with content. This approach enhances student retention, comprehension, and overall success while reinforcing the role of education as a tool for empowerment and opportunity [92].

1. Understanding the Principles of Engaging Course Materials

A. Characteristics of Engaging Course Materials

Engaging course materials:
Capture student interest and encourage active learning.
Provide real-world relevance by connecting theory to application.
Incorporate multimedia and interactive elements to enhance comprehension.
Support different learning preferences through diverse instructional formats.
Encourage student participation and critical thinking.

Engagement increases when students feel a connection to the content—whether through personal relevance, interactive learning experiences, or real-world applications. Passive learning environments often lead to disengagement, while active, multimodal learning fosters deeper understanding [93].

B. Strategies to Foster Engagement

To develop engaging course materials, faculty should consider the following approaches:

1. **Active Learning Integration**
    - Use case studies, role-playing scenarios, problem-based learning, and debates to encourage participation.
    - Design scenario-based assignments that simulate real-world challenges.

2. **Multimedia and Digital Tools**
    - Incorporate videos, podcasts, interactive simulations, and gamified elements to support different modes of engagement.
    - Use visual aids (charts, infographics, mind maps) to clarify complex concepts.
    - Provide AI-enhanced tools (chatbots, adaptive learning platforms, virtual labs) to create personalized learning experiences.

3. **Storytelling and Real-World Applications**
    - Present narratives, historical case studies, or industry examples to make abstract concepts more tangible.
    - Invite guest speakers from relevant fields to bridge academic learning with practical knowledge.

4. **Scaffolding and Progressive Learning**
    - Break down complex ideas into smaller, digestible segments before moving into advanced content.
    - Use incremental assignments that build towards a final project or capstone experience.

5. **Student-Generated Content**
    - Encourage students to create presentations, blogs, videos, or wikis that contribute to the course knowledge base.
    - Promote collaborative learning through peer discussions and group projects.

2. Principles of Inclusive Course Materials

An inclusive classroom ensures all students, regardless of background or ability, have equal access to learning materials and opportunities. Inclusive course materials promote equity, representation, and accessibility while encouraging an environment where students feel valued and respected [94].

A. Why Inclusion Matters in Course Materials

Encourages diverse perspectives and helps students see themselves, as individuals reflected in the curriculum. Reduces barriers for individuals with disabilities, English language learners, and first-generation college students.
Creates a supportive learning environment where all students feel respected and included.

B. Strategies for Inclusive Course Material Development

1. **Ensure Diverse Representation in Content**
    - Use readings, case studies, and examples that feature diverse voices, cultures, and perspectives.
    - Avoid a single, dominant perspective—incorporate materials from scholars, authors, and experts from different ethnic, racial, gender, and socioeconomic backgrounds.
    - Encourage student contributions and perspectives to enrich discussions and content diversity.

2. **Design Materials for Accessibility (Universal Design for Learning – UDL)**
    - Ensure all course materials meet ADA (Americans with Disabilities Act) compliance and are accessible via screen readers.
    - Provide closed captions for videos, transcripts for audio materials, and alternative text for images.
    - Use accessible fonts, color-contrast-friendly materials, and digital formats compatible with assistive technologies.
    - Allows student engagement with content in multiple ways (e.g., text, audio, video, kinesthetic activities).

3. **Offer Flexibility in Learning and Assessment**
    - Incorporate multiple assessment formats (essays, videos, portfolios, projects) to cater to different learning styles.
    - Provide flexible deadlines and alternative assignment formats for students with different needs.
    - Allow students to demonstrate learning through personalized or project-based work that reflects their interests.

4. **Use Gender-Neutral and Inclusive Language**
   - Avoid stereotypes, assumptions, or exclusionary phrasing in course materials.
   - Use gender-neutral terms and pronoun inclusivity when referring to people in examples and case studies.
   - Encourage students to share their preferred pronouns and identities in a welcoming classroom environment.

5. **Address Bias and Challenge Assumptions in Course Content**
   - Regularly audit and update course materials to remove implicit biases.
   - Discuss how historical and cultural biases have shaped knowledge production in different fields.
   - Encourage critical discussions on power dynamics, privilege, and systemic inequities in academic disciplines.

3. Best Practices for Implementing Engaging and Inclusive Course Materials

Developing engaging and inclusive course materials requires ongoing reflection, adaptation, and collaboration. Faculty can implement the following best practices to ensure success:

Regularly Review and Update Course Content

- Course materials should evolve to reflect new research, societal changes, and technological advancements.
- Seek feedback from students, colleagues, and external experts to refine content inclusivity and engagement.

Leverage Institutional Resources

- Collaborate with university teaching and learning centers to access training on inclusive pedagogy.
- Utilize campus accessibility services and technology support teams to ensure ADA compliance.

Encourage Student Feedback and Co-Creation

- Conduct mid-semester surveys to gauge student perceptions of course materials.
- Involve students in course design discussions by integrating their perspectives and suggested resources.

Use Open Educational Resources (OERs) to Expand Access

- OERs provide free, high-quality academic materials that reduce financial barriers for students [95].

- Platforms like MERLOT, OpenStax, and the OER Commons offer diverse, accessible course content.

Monitor Engagement and Adapt as Needed

- Use learning analytics and student participation data to refine instructional materials and teaching methods.
- Adjust reading selections, assignments, and discussions based on student engagement levels.

4. The Impact of Engaging and Inclusive Course Materials on Student Success

Developing engaging and inclusive course materials leads to:
Higher student motivation and retention by fostering a dynamic learning environment.
Increased comprehension and deeper learning through active and multimodal instructional approaches.
A sense of belonging that enhances participation and reduces educational barriers.
Better academic performance and career readiness by equipping students with critical thinking, adaptability, and interdisciplinary knowledge.

Cross-Disciplinary Pedagogies: Teaching Beyond Disciplinary Boundaries

The twenty-first century workforce and society demand graduates who can think and act across disciplinary lines [96]. Challenges such as artificial intelligence ethics, global migration, sustainability, and health disparities highlight the insufficiency of single-discipline approaches. Employers and communities alike increasingly value professionals who can integrate diverse perspectives to craft solutions that are innovative, ethical, and practical [97]. For faculty, this requires designing teaching approaches that not only transmit disciplinary knowledge but also cultivate students' capacity to apply, translate, and connect knowledge across fields.

Cross-disciplinary pedagogy does not replace disciplinary depth; instead, it complements it by encouraging synthesis. Students learn to appreciate disciplinary rigor while also developing agility to apply methods and frameworks in new contexts. Effective educators guide students through the complexities of disciplinary integration, helping them identify overlaps, negotiate differences, and combine insights into coherent problem-solving strategies.

Translating Concepts Across Disciplinary Languages

One of the first hurdles in cross-disciplinary learning is language. Disciplines use unique vocabularies, conceptual frameworks, and even symbolic systems that can be opaque to outsiders. This creates barriers when students from different academic backgrounds must work together or when a professor introduces material from a field outside students' primary area of study.

Faculty can play the role of *translator*, ensuring disciplinary concepts are not only taught but also contextualized:

- **Defining Terminology Explicitly**: Acronyms, technical jargon, or specialized theories should be unpacked and connected to more familiar concepts. For example, when introducing "carbon sequestration" in a course on environmental policy, instructors might first explain it through everyday analogies, such as "storing carbon in the ground instead of releasing it into the air," before expanding into scientific detail.
- **Highlighting Disciplinary Assumptions**: Students benefit from seeing how disciplines prioritize different forms of evidence. In psychology, randomized experiments may be considered the "gold standard," while in anthropology, ethnographic fieldwork may hold greater authority. Making these assumptions explicit prevents confusion and promotes respect for varied approaches.
- **Modeling Translation in Real Time**: Faculty should demonstrate how to shift between languages. For instance, in a business-technology course, an instructor might explain the computer science concept of "algorithmic efficiency" in terms that align with business students' familiarity with cost-benefit analysis. By bridging the two, the professor shows how technical and managerial perspectives inform each other.
- **Encouraging Student Practice in Translation**: Assignments can require students to explain complex disciplinary concepts to a lay audience or to peers outside their field. This not only deepens understanding but also builds communication skills vital for interdisciplinary collaboration.

When translation is intentional, students move from being passive consumers of other disciplines' outputs to active participants in interdisciplinary dialogue. They begin to see disciplinary languages not as barriers but as complementary tools for understanding the same problem from different angles.

Managing Diverse Knowledge Bases Within Single Courses

Cross-disciplinary teaching requires navigating the reality that students come into the classroom with uneven levels of preparation, background knowledge, and disciplinary confidence. Unlike discipline-specific courses where most students share similar training, interdisciplinary environments combine learners from varied majors, professional experiences, and skill sets. This diversity can enrich the classroom but also create significant challenges if not carefully managed.

The Challenge of Uneven Preparation

In an interdisciplinary course, students' strengths often mirror the training of their home discipline:

- **Engineering students** may excel in quantitative modeling but struggle with open-ended writing or theoretical frameworks in the social sciences.
- **Business students** may be comfortable analyzing financial statements but find programming assignments or systems diagrams intimidating.
- **Health sciences students** may bring practical experience in patient care yet lack exposure to policy analysis or statistical modeling.

If left unaddressed, these imbalances can result in disengagement, over-reliance on certain team members, or uneven assessment outcomes.

Faculty Role in Balancing Knowledge Gaps

Effective instructors take deliberate steps to ensure that diverse backgrounds enhance rather than hinder learning:

- **Scaffolding**: Breaking complex concepts into smaller, structured steps allows students to build competence incrementally. For example, before asking all students to complete a data analysis project, the instructor might provide a tutorial on basic spreadsheet functions and statistical concepts.
- **Prerequisite Skill Checks**: Early diagnostic exercises—short quizzes, problem sets, or reflection assignments—help faculty gauge the readiness of students. These assessments reveal who needs additional support and prevent students from being blindsided by assignments requiring unfamiliar skills.
- **Targeted Supplemental Materials**: Assigning background readings, tutorials, or videos tailored to specific groups of students can fill gaps without slowing down the entire class. For instance, business students might complete a primer on coding logic, while computer science students review a brief guide to interpreting balance sheets.
- **Flexible Learning Pathways**: Faculty can provide multiple entry points into the same concept, such as offering both a technical explanation and a conceptual case study. This dual approach ensures students can engage from their own perspective while gradually expanding into less familiar territory.

Leveraging Student Strengths in the Classroom

Diverse knowledge bases are not merely obstacles—they can become assets when instructors design opportunities for peer-to-peer learning:

- **Interdisciplinary Teams**: Group projects can be structured to draw on each student's strengths. For example, in a sustainability project, environmental science students may provide technical data, political science students analyze policy implications, and communications students design outreach strategies.
- **Peer Teaching**: Faculty can assign rotating roles where students explain concepts from their field to classmates, reinforcing their own mastery while helping others.
- **Role-Based Assignments**: Structuring projects around roles (analyst, designer, communicator, evaluator) ensures that all contributions are valued while encouraging students to expand outside their comfort zones.

Creating a Supportive Learning Climate

Because cross-disciplinary classrooms expose students to areas where they may feel unprepared, psychological safety is critical. Faculty can:

- Normalize uneven preparation by acknowledging that no single student will master all domains.
- Emphasize learning *process* as much as content mastery, rewarding students for effort in unfamiliar areas.
- Encourage growth mindsets by highlighting stories of professionals who successfully bridged disciplinary divides.

Key Takeaway

Managing diverse knowledge bases within a single course requires both structured scaffolding and intentional use of student strengths. By combining diagnostic tools, supplemental resources, peer teaching, and role-based collaboration, faculty can transform uneven preparation into an engine for integrative learning. Students not only gain new knowledge but also learn how to work effectively across boundaries—an essential skill for interdisciplinary problem-solving.

Team-Based Interdisciplinary Project Design

Team-based projects are a cornerstone of cross-disciplinary pedagogy because they mirror the realities of professional collaboration in complex problem spaces. Rarely do organizations or industries rely on a single disciplinary lens; instead, solutions emerge from the interplay of technical expertise, strategic thinking, and social awareness. By engaging students in interdisciplinary teams, faculty provide opportunities for them to practice not only disciplinary application but also communication, negotiation, and integration of diverse perspectives.

Purpose of Interdisciplinary Team Projects

The goal is not simply to divide work according to disciplinary strengths but to foster **integration**. Students should learn how different fields approach problems, where their perspectives overlap, and how to reconcile conflicts in methodology or values. This prepares them to:

- Navigate ambiguity and conflicting assumptions.
- Recognize the value of perspectives outside their own expertise.
- Develop solutions that are more comprehensive and innovative than any single-discipline approach.

Structuring Effective Projects

Faculty design is critical to prevent teams from defaulting into siloed work where students contribute separate pieces with minimal integration. Strong interdisciplinary projects share several features:

- **Clearly Defined Problem**: Projects should address issues complex enough to require multiple perspectives—such as designing an affordable telehealth system, developing an urban sustainability plan, or creating cybersecurity protocols for financial institutions.

- **Role Definition with Flexibility**: Assigning roles aligned to disciplinary strengths helps ensure contributions, but roles should also stretch students beyond their comfort zones. For example, engineering students might take primary responsibility for technical design but also engage with communication tasks.
- **Integration Points**: Faculty should build checkpoints where teams must synthesize perspectives. These may include interim reports requiring combined input, peer presentations where each member explains how their discipline connects to others, or reflective essays discussing integration challenges.
- **Scaffolded Collaboration**: Faculty can provide templates for team charters, guidelines for conflict resolution, and structured collaboration tools (e.g., shared project management platforms) to support equitable participation.

Faculty Role in Guiding Collaboration

Professors act as facilitators rather than directors in interdisciplinary projects. Key responsibilities include:

- **Mediating Misunderstandings**: Disciplinary cultures differ in language, evidence, and priorities. Faculty can help clarify when disagreements arise from these differences rather than from lack of effort.
- **Ensuring Equity of Voice**: Faculty should monitor team dynamics to prevent dominance by one discipline or student group. Strategies include requiring rotating team leadership, assigning balanced speaking roles in presentations, or incorporating peer evaluations.
- **Modeling Interdisciplinary Thinking**: Professors can draw from their own experiences collaborating across fields to demonstrate how integration enhances outcomes. Sharing real-world examples signals that interdisciplinary tensions are not obstacles but opportunities.

Assessment of Team Projects

Evaluation must reflect both disciplinary contribution and integrative outcomes. Effective assessment includes:

- **Individual Accountability**: Grading mechanisms that assess each student's unique disciplinary input, such as technical reports, market analyses, or policy briefs.
- **Team Integration**: Rubrics that reward synthesis, coherence, and creativity in the final product, ensuring teams are evaluated on how well they combined contributions.
- **Collaboration Process**: Peer evaluations, reflective journals, or process reports can measure how effectively teams communicated, negotiated, and resolved conflicts.

Example in Practice

In a healthcare innovation course:

- Nursing students provide insight into patient needs and regulatory requirements.
- Business students design a sustainable business model and assess market potential.

- Computer science students build a prototype of a telemedicine app.

The project culminates in a presentation to a panel of faculty from all three disciplines, who evaluate both disciplinary rigor and integration.

Key Takeaway

Team-based interdisciplinary projects provide authentic opportunities for learners to apply disciplinary knowledge while developing the skills of collaboration, communication, and integration. Faculty who intentionally design roles, scaffold collaboration, and assess both individual and collective outcomes enable students to practice the type of problem-solving demanded by today's interconnected world.

Assessment of Interdisciplinary Learning Outcomes

Assessment in interdisciplinary teaching must go beyond verifying whether students have mastered the content of a single field. It should capture the higher-order skills of integration, collaboration, and reflective practice that define successful cross-disciplinary learning. This requires faculty to shift from traditional exams and content-specific essays toward evaluation models that recognize the complexity of interdisciplinary problem-solving [98].

Why Traditional Assessment Falls Short

Conventional grading tools such as multiple-choice tests or discipline-specific term papers primarily measure mastery within a single knowledge base. While valuable, they fail to capture:

- How students combine disciplinary insights into a unified solution.
- The process of collaboration, negotiation, and communication across knowledge traditions.
- Students' awareness of how disciplinary assumptions influence the framing of problems and solutions.

Without targeted assessment strategies, students may complete interdisciplinary courses without fully developing or demonstrating the integrative skills those courses are designed to cultivate.

Key Dimensions for Interdisciplinary Assessment

Faculty designing rubrics for cross-disciplinary courses should evaluate outcomes across four critical dimensions:

1. **Integration of Concepts** – The degree to which students can synthesize theories, methods, and data from different disciplines into a coherent framework. Example criterion: "Student demonstrates ability to connect social science insights with technical models to produce a solution that is both feasible and contextually informed."
2. **Collaboration and Communication** – How effectively students work in interdisciplinary teams, respect diverse contributions, and communicate across

disciplinary boundaries. Example criterion: "Student articulates disciplinary perspectives clearly to non-experts and engages constructively with alternative viewpoints."
3. **Creativity and Innovation** – The originality of solutions and whether students generate outcomes that would not have been possible through a single-discipline approach. Example criterion: "Solution demonstrates novel integration of approaches, producing insights or products not typical of disciplinary work alone."
4. **Critical Reflection** – Students' ability to examine their own disciplinary assumptions, recognize limitations, and articulate how engagement with other fields has shaped their thinking. Example criterion: "Student provides evidence of questioning disciplinary assumptions and demonstrates growth in perspective-taking."

Assessment Tools and Strategies

Faculty can use a variety of methods to evaluate interdisciplinary learning outcomes:

- **Reflective Essays and Journals**: Students analyze how their thinking evolved through exposure to other disciplines, highlighting challenges and breakthroughs in integration.
- **Group Portfolios**: Teams compile project documentation—including research notes, design drafts, and decision logs—to show how contributions from different disciplines shaped the final product.
- **Oral Presentations and Panels**: Presenting projects to panels of faculty from multiple disciplines ensures evaluation from diverse perspectives and highlights integration quality.
- **Peer and Self-Evaluations**: Students assess collaboration within teams, providing insights into communication effectiveness and equitable participation.
- **Capstone Projects**: Large-scale projects can be structured to require multiple disciplinary contributions and evaluated on both disciplinary rigor and integrative innovation.

Designing Effective Rubrics

Rubrics should explicitly reward integration and collaboration rather than treating them as incidental [99]. For example, a project rubric might allocate points across:

- 30% disciplinary rigor (accuracy and depth of contributions).
- 30% integration quality (how well disciplines were combined).
- 20% teamwork and communication.
- 20% reflection and creativity.

Such structures communicate that success in interdisciplinary contexts depends on more than disciplinary mastery alone.

Key Takeaway

Assessing interdisciplinary learning requires deliberate design. Faculty must evaluate integration, collaboration, creativity, and reflection using tools such as essays, portfolios, and multidisciplinary panels. When assessment is aligned with these goals, students are rewarded not only for what they know but also for how effectively they work across boundaries to produce innovative, integrated solutions.

Facilitating Dialogue Between Different Academic Cultures

Cross-disciplinary classrooms are not only spaces of diverse content but also spaces of distinct academic cultures [99]. Each discipline brings with it assumptions about what constitutes valid knowledge, how evidence is used, and how arguments should be structured [100]. These cultural differences—sometimes subtle, sometimes stark—can create misunderstandings if left unaddressed [101]. Faculty hold critical roles in making these differences explicit and guiding students in respectful dialogue that allows disciplinary traditions to inform, rather than conflict with, one another [102].

Understanding Academic Cultures

Academic cultures are built on deep-rooted conventions and practices, such as:

- **What counts as evidence**: Historians may privilege primary sources, while chemists rely on experimental data, and sociologists use survey research or ethnographic fieldwork.
- **Argument construction**: In philosophy, arguments may be structured deductively through logical reasoning, whereas in business, arguments are often pragmatic, data-driven, and solution-focused.
- **Methodological priorities**: Quantitative approaches dominate economics and engineering, while qualitative or mixed methods often drive education, social work, and cultural studies.
- **Standards of rigor**: Mathematics demands proof, art history may require visual interpretation, and law emphasizes precedent and interpretation of statutes.

These cultural norms shape how practitioners in each discipline evaluate knowledge claims, communicate findings, and engage in scholarly debates.

Faculty Role in Making Differences Explicit

Faculty can help students avoid confusion or frustration by proactively addressing these cultural differences:

- **Contrast Methodologies**: Create activities where students examine how different disciplines study the same problem (e.g., climate change as measured by scientific modeling, policy analysis, and ethical reasoning).
- **Highlight Epistemological Assumptions**: Discuss why one discipline might favor empirical data while another values narrative or theoretical critique.
- **Model Comparative Thinking**: When introducing disciplinary material, explain not just *what* the method is but also *why* it is valued in that field. For example, explain why randomized control trials are considered strong evidence in public health but may not capture the lived experience data valued in anthropology.

Techniques for Fostering Dialogue

- **Structured Class Discussions**: Use debates, roundtables, or case studies where students must articulate disciplinary perspectives and respond to others.
- **Interdisciplinary Panels**: Invite faculty or professionals from multiple disciplines to present how they approach a common issue, followed by facilitated student discussion.
- **Collaborative Assignments**: Require students to compare and contrast approaches in writing or team projects, explicitly identifying strengths and limits of each disciplinary culture.
- **Dialogue Protocols**: Introduce ground rules for interdisciplinary discussion—such as listening first, clarifying terminology, and asking discipline-specific questions respectfully.

Preparing Students for Professional Environments

Professional practice increasingly requires collaboration across disciplinary cultures:

- In healthcare, doctors, nurses, social workers, and administrators must negotiate different perspectives on patient care.
- In technology, computer scientists, ethicists, and policymakers must balance technical feasibility, ethical responsibility, and legal compliance.
- In business, finance professionals, marketers, and engineers must align product design with consumer demand and financial viability.

Faculty who foster interdisciplinary dialogue prepare students for these environments, teaching them how to:

- Recognize disciplinary blind spots.
- Value contributions outside their own expertise.
- Engage in constructive negotiation when perspectives diverge.

Key Takeaway

Facilitating dialogue between academic cultures is not just about teaching content—it is about teaching students how to listen, translate, and integrate across traditions of knowledge. By making disciplinary differences explicit and modeling respect for diverse epistemologies, faculty empower students with needed skills to thrive in collaborative, real-world problem-solving.

Resource Sharing Across Departments

Cross-disciplinary teaching rarely fits neatly within the boundaries of a single department. Because the questions such courses address span multiple domains of knowledge, they often demand resources—technological, intellectual, and human—that exceed what one unit can provide. Effective interdisciplinary instruction depends on faculty and departments working together to share expertise, facilities, and materials, thereby maximizing institutional capacity while modeling collaboration for students.

Types of Shared Resources

- **Laboratories and Equipment**: A sustainability course might require both environmental science labs for testing soil samples and engineering labs for modeling renewable energy solutions. By sharing labs across departments, students gain access to facilities that no single program could fully support.
- **Databases and Digital Tools**: Business, social science, and health sciences faculty may all rely on specialized databases (e.g., market analytics platforms, census data, or epidemiological datasets). Shared access arrangements reduce duplication and broaden student exposure to professional tools.
- **Instructional Staff**: Teaching assistants, lab coordinators, or instructional designers can be assigned across departments to support cross-disciplinary courses, ensuring faculty are not overburdened when experimenting with new teaching approaches.
- **Learning Materials**: Departments can co-develop case studies, simulations, or problem sets tailored to interdisciplinary contexts. For example, a case on urban planning could include economic impact data from the business school and GIS maps from geography.

Faculty Collaboration Models

- **Co-Teaching**: Two or more professors from different disciplines lead a course together, demonstrating for students how experts negotiate perspectives and integrate knowledge in real time.
- **Guest Lectures**: Faculty invite colleagues from other departments to deliver targeted sessions, exposing students to multiple perspectives without requiring a full co-teaching arrangement.
- **Cross-Listing Courses**: A course can be offered under multiple departmental codes (e.g., sociology and political science), allowing students from different majors to enroll and ensuring resource investments benefit more than one program.
- **Joint Curriculum Development**: Faculty collaborate on designing syllabi, assignments, and assessments that intentionally blend disciplinary approaches.

Institutional Strategies for Supporting Resource Sharing

Resource sharing is especially critical in institutions with limited budgets, where duplication of labs, staff, or course offerings is unsustainable [103]. Strategies include:

- **Encouraging Open Educational Resources (OERs)**: Adoption of OERs reduces costs while providing adaptable materials that can be used across fields.
- **Creating Interdisciplinary Centers**: Many universities establish centers (e.g., centers for sustainability, public health, or data science) that pool resources from multiple departments to support teaching and research.
- **Budget Incentives**: Institutions may provide small grants or release time for faculty who collaborate across departments, reinforcing the value of resource pooling.

Pedagogical Benefits for Students

Resource sharing not only addresses logistical challenges but also strengthens student learning by:

- **Modeling Professional Practice**: In the workplace, professionals regularly collaborate across organizational units. Shared teaching resources replicate this environment, showing students how collaboration produces stronger results.
- **Broadening Access**: Students gain exposure to tools, facilities, and perspectives they would not encounter within their home discipline alone.
- **Reinforcing Interdisciplinary Thinking**: Shared resources signal that complex problems cannot be solved by isolated approaches, underscoring the integrative goals of cross-disciplinary pedagogy.

Key Takeaway

Resource sharing across departments transforms institutional limitations into opportunities for collaboration. By pooling facilities, staff, and instructional expertise, faculty create richer interdisciplinary experiences while modeling the collaborative practices expected in professional environments. Institutions that prioritize and incentivize resource sharing empower faculty to deliver courses that prepare students for the interconnected challenges of the modern world.

Navigating Different Grading Standards and Expectations

Evaluation in cross-disciplinary teaching is complex because grading traditions vary widely across academic fields [104]. What counts as "excellent work" in one discipline may not even register as acceptable in another [105]. Without clear communication and careful design, students can become confused, feel unfairly judged, or disengage when their strengths are undervalued [106]. Faculty must therefore approach assessment with intentionality, balancing disciplinary rigor with interdisciplinary integration [107].

Disciplinary Norms in Grading

- **Humanities**: Emphasize critical thinking, argumentation, originality of interpretation, and effective use of sources. A history paper, for example, may be graded heavily on the ability to construct a persuasive argument supported by primary and secondary documents.
- **Sciences**: Often prioritize accuracy, reproducibility, and adherence to established methods. Lab reports or problem sets may be graded on correctness, data interpretation, and clarity of procedure.
- **Professional Fields (e.g., Business, Nursing, Engineering)**: Focus on applied skills, functionality, and feasibility. A business plan is judged on financial soundness and market realism, while a nursing case study emphasizes accurate application of protocols and patient care standards.
- **Arts and Design**: May emphasize creativity, technique, and innovation, sometimes incorporating peer or external juried review.

These norms reflect disciplinary values, but when students from different fields come together, the weight of each standard must be negotiated and explained.

Clarifying Expectations for Students

Faculty must be transparent about grading criteria from the outset. This involves:

- **Explaining Disciplinary Standards**: Making explicit what each discipline values helps students understand why assignments are graded differently across courses.
- **Providing Exemplars**: Sharing sample projects or papers from different fields illustrates how disciplinary norms manifest in practice.
- **Harmonizing Standards When Possible**: While each discipline must maintain rigor, interdisciplinary courses should develop grading frameworks that integrate standards fairly. For example, in a joint business–computer science project, grading could balance both technical functionality and strategic market analysis.

Designing Transparent Rubrics

Rubrics are particularly effective for interdisciplinary evaluation. They should:

- **Balance Individual and Integrative Goals**: Criteria should reward both disciplinary excellence and the ability to connect across fields.
- **Use Weighted Categories**: For example, a project might allocate 40% for disciplinary rigor, 30% for interdisciplinary integration, 20% for teamwork and communication, and 10% for creativity.
- **Make Tradeoffs Explicit**: Students should know how much weight is given to each standard, reducing ambiguity and potential frustration.

Grading Team-Based Work

Team projects introduce additional complexity because contributions vary by discipline and by individual. To ensure fairness:

- **Recognize Individual Contributions**: Require discipline-specific deliverables (e.g., technical code modules, financial models, policy briefs) to assess each student's expertise.
- **Evaluate Collective Achievement**: Grade the final product as a whole on integration, creativity, and coherence.
- **Incorporate Peer Evaluation**: Students can assess one another's collaboration and effort, providing insight into contributions that may not be visible to faculty.
- **Use Process-Based Assessment**: Journals, logs, or progress reports help capture learning that occurs through dialogue and negotiation, not just in the final outcome.

Challenges and Faculty Considerations

- **Perceived Inequity**: Students may feel disadvantaged if their discipline's norms are undervalued. Faculty can mitigate this by ensuring each discipline's contribution is explicitly recognized in grading.
- **Overemphasis on One Discipline**: Without careful rubric design, projects may lean toward the standards of the dominant field. Faculty teams should co-develop rubrics to avoid imbalance.
- **Workload in Assessment**: Interdisciplinary rubrics require more detailed grading, but investing in upfront clarity reduces disputes and student dissatisfaction later.

Key Takeaway

Navigating different grading standards in cross-disciplinary teaching requires transparency, balance, and fairness. Faculty must clarify disciplinary expectations, harmonize grading where possible, and design rubrics that value both disciplinary rigor and integrative achievement. In team projects, assessment should capture both individual contributions and collective outcomes, preparing students for the collaborative evaluation they will encounter in professional practice.

Conclusion: Crafting Course Materials for an Inclusive and Engaging Learning Experience

Higher education instructors have the responsibility to design course materials that are both engaging and inclusive, ensuring that students receive high-quality, accessible, and thought-provoking educational experiences.

By integrating diverse perspectives, embracing multiple learning formats, ensuring accessibility, and fostering active engagement, faculty create courses that inspire students, empower diverse learners, and contribute to a more equitable academic environment.

Developing inclusive and engaging course materials is not just about meeting institutional expectations—it is about shaping the future of higher education to be more responsive, dynamic, and inclusive for all students.

Designing Courses for Meaningful Learning

Course design and curriculum development are integral to the effectiveness of higher education instruction. By prioritizing clear learning objectives, aligning assessments with desired outcomes, and incorporating engaging instructional strategies, faculty can create courses that are not only informative but transformative.

Backward course design ensures that every aspect of a course—from content selection to assessment—serves a specific purpose in advancing student learning. Additionally, aligning course content with accreditation standards and institutional goals strengthens academic programs and enhances student success. Faculty must also remain adaptable, continuously refining their courses based on student feedback, emerging research, and technological advancements.

Ultimately, the impact of well-designed courses extends beyond the classroom. Effective course design prepares students to think critically, apply knowledge in practical settings, and navigate complex academic and professional challenges. By embracing best practices in curriculum development, faculty engineer educational environments that are rigorous, inclusive, and student-focused—ensuring that learners leave their courses with the needed skills and confidence for lifelong success.

Chapter 4: Effective Teaching Strategies

Teaching, especially in higher education, requires a dynamic blend of instructional techniques, student engagement strategies, and adaptable learning models. Unlike traditional lecture-driven approaches, modern faculty must navigate diverse learning environments, leverage technology, and cultivate critical thinking among students. An effective college professor is more than just an expert in their industry but also a skilled facilitator of learning, capable of creating an inclusive, engaging, and intellectually stimulating classroom.

This chapter explores key teaching strategies that empower educators to enhance student learning outcomes and foster deeper engagement. From active learning techniques that promote critical thinking to the art of structuring and

Figure 4.1. Skilled Professor [219].

delivering impactful lectures, the strategies outlined here will equip faculty with practical methods for both in-person and online instruction. Additionally, this chapter examines Socratic questioning, hybrid and online teaching approaches, and techniques for encouraging student autonomy. By integrating these strategies into their pedagogical toolkit, faculty enable learning environments that not only educate but also inspire students to become self-driven learners and analytical thinkers.

Active Learning Techniques: Engaging Students in Deep Learning

Active learning is a student-centered instructional approach that moves beyond passive absorption of information and encourages engagement, critical thinking, and knowledge application. Unlike traditional lecture-based methods where students act as passive recipients, active learning strategies require students to participate, analyze, discuss, and apply concepts in real-time. Research has consistently demonstrated that active learning enhances comprehension, retention, and the ability to transfer knowledge to new contexts [108].

Among the most effective active learning techniques are case studies, debates, and role-playing, each of which fosters analytical thinking, collaboration, and deeper understanding of complex topics. When properly integrated into course design, these methods bridge the gap of theoretical concepts and practical application, enabling students to develop important higher-order thinking skills necessary for professional and academic success.

Case Studies: Applying Theory to Real-World Scenarios

What Are Case Studies?

Case studies present learners with real-world, discipline-specific problems or scenarios, requiring them to analyze, evaluate, and propose solutions. This technique is commonly used in business, law, medicine, social sciences, and STEM fields, where professionals must make decisions based on incomplete or complex data.

Why Are They Effective?

- **Encourages Critical Thinking** – Students must assess the situation, identify key issues, and develop well-reasoned solutions.

- **Promotes Problem-Solving Skills** – Case studies mirror the challenges professionals face, fostering strategic decision-making.

- **Enhances Engagement** – Real-world relevance makes learning more compelling and relatable.

- **Strengthens Communication and Collaboration** – Group case discussions require learners to explain their reasoning and defend their conclusions.

How to Implement Case Studies Effectively

1. **Choose Relevant and Challenging Cases**
    - Use authentic scenarios that require students to apply key concepts.
    - Select cases with multiple perspectives and possible solutions to encourage debate.
    - For introductory classes, provide structured cases with guiding questions; for advanced courses, use more ambiguous, open-ended cases.

2. **Encourage Structured Analysis**
    - Use frameworks such as SWOT Analysis (Strengths, Weaknesses, Opportunities, Threats) for business cases or ethical decision-making models for law and healthcare.
    - Have students identify the problem, assess possible solutions, and justify their recommendations with evidence.

3. **Incorporate Collaborative Discussions**
    - Assign small groups to analyze different aspects of a case and report findings to the class.
    - Utilize role-playing elements where students adopt stakeholder perspectives (e.g., business executive, policymaker, researcher).

4. **Encourage Reflection and Application**

- After completing a case study, ask students to reflect on how their understanding evolved.
- Have students apply the case study concepts to a different context or a problem in their own field.

By integrating case studies into coursework, faculty empower students to think like professionals, making learning dynamic, immersive, and relevant.

Debates: Developing Argumentation and Analytical Thinking

What Are Debates?

Debates are structured discussions where students take opposing viewpoints on a topic and defend their positions with logic and evidence. This method is particularly effective in humanities, business, law, ethics, and political science, where issues often have multiple interpretations.

Why Are Debates Effective?

- **Enhances Critical Thinking** – Students must evaluate arguments, counterarguments, and supporting evidence.
- **Develops Persuasive Communication Skills** – Public speaking and structured argumentation are essential skills in professional settings.
- **Encourages Active Engagement** – Debates make abstract concepts more tangible and thought-provoking.
- **Fosters Respectful Discourse** – Teaches students to engage in civil, evidence-based discussions rather than emotional rhetoric.

How to Implement Debates Effectively

1. **Select Controversial but Manageable Topics**
   - Choose topics that have diverse perspectives but are rooted in academic inquiry. Examples:
     - **Business:** "Should companies prioritize profit over social responsibility?"
     - **Technology:** "Should AI-generated content be regulated in academic research?"
     - **Ethics:** "Is it ever ethical to break the law for a moral reason?"

2. **Structure the Debate Format**
   - Assign students to teams (affirmative vs. negative) or allow them to choose their stance and defend it.

- Establish time limits for opening statements, rebuttals, cross-examination, and closing arguments.
- Encourage evidence-based reasoning by requiring citations and structured argument frameworks.

3. **Encourage Constructive Engagement**
    - Require students to anticipate and counter opposing arguments, reinforcing analytical depth.
    - Use a peer feedback system where students critique each other's arguments for clarity and effectiveness.
    - Incorporate a moderator role (faculty or student) to maintain fairness and focus.

4. **Debrief and Reflect**
    - After the debate, hold a class discussion on key takeaways—what arguments were most effective and why?
    - Ask students to reflect on whether their own views shifted as a result of engaging with opposing perspectives.

Debates push students beyond memorization, requiring them to analyze, argue, and articulate complex positions—an invaluable skill for academia and beyond.

Role-Playing: Immersive and Experiential Learning

What Is Role-Playing?

Role-playing involves students assuming specific roles within a simulated scenario, requiring them to think and act from a particular perspective. This technique is widely used in education, healthcare, business, history, and conflict resolution.

Why Is Role-Playing Effective?

- **Promotes Empathy and Perspective-Taking** – Encourages students to consider and understand multiple viewpoints by stepping into different roles.
- **Develops Decision-Making and Problem-Solving Skills** – Students must make real-time judgments within complex situations.
- **Enhances Engagement and Memory Retention** – Active participation increases long-term recall of concepts.
- **Encourages Creativity and Adaptability** – Role-playing requires quick thinking and flexibility in response to dynamic scenarios.

How to Implement Role-Playing Effectively

1. **Design Realistic Scenarios**

- Base role-play activities on historical events, ethical dilemmas, or professional challenges. Examples:
    - **Business:** A company faces a PR crisis—students take roles as executives, PR specialists, and customers.
    - **Healthcare:** A medical ethics board must decide on a controversial patient case.
    - **Law/Policy:** Students act as legislators debating a new bill.

2. **Assign Defined Roles and Objectives**
    - Provide students with background information, motivations, and constraints related to their assigned roles.
    - Encourage students to research their roles beforehand to enhance realism.

3. **Facilitate Interaction and Decision-Making**
    - Allow students to engage in negotiations, debates, or problem-solving discussions within their roles.
    - Use structured prompts to guide the discussion but allow flexibility for improvisation.

4. **Debrief and Reflect on the Experience**
    - After the activity, conduct a debriefing session where students analyze their choices, challenges, and insights.
    - Encourage them to connect the role-play experience to real-world professional scenarios.

Role-playing transforms learning into a dynamic, immersive process, allowing students to develop not just content knowledge, but also emotional intelligence, leadership, and adaptability.

Conclusion

Active learning techniques, such as case studies, debates, and role-playing, engage students at a deeper cognitive level, bridging theory and practice. These methods foster analytical and critical thinking, problem-solving, and ethical reasoning, equipping students with skills essential for both academic success and practical applications. By integrating active learning into the classroom, faculty move beyond passive instruction, creating dynamic learning experiences that cultivate engaged, critical thinkers.

Lecture Design and Delivery Strategies

Lecturing has been a cornerstone of higher education for centuries, but in the modern academic landscape, effective lecture design and delivery require more than simply presenting information. A well-structured lecture is a strategically designed learning experience that balances clarity, engagement, interactivity, and cognitive stimulation. Professors must move beyond passive information transfer and create dynamic, thought-provoking lectures that encourage student participation, critical thinking, and long-term retention of knowledge.

Effective lecture design and delivery demand careful consideration of content organization, instructional pacing, audience engagement, and multimodal teaching techniques. Professors who refine their lecturing skills enhance student comprehension, participation, and overall academic success.

1. The Role of Lectures in Higher Education

Lectures remain one of the most efficient and scalable methods of instruction, particularly in courses with large class sizes or content-heavy curricula. When designed effectively, lectures can:

Provide foundational knowledge and establish key concepts.
Guide students through complex theories and frameworks.
Model disciplinary thinking by demonstrating how experts approach problems.
Encourage intellectual curiosity and further inquiry.
Incorporate storytelling, examples, and case studies to make abstract concepts tangible.

However, traditional, passive lectures—where students passively listen without engagement—are often ineffective for deep learning. Cognitive load theory suggests that students retain more information when lectures are structured to prevent overload, incorporate active engagement, and integrate opportunities for processing and reflection [109].

Modern lecture design blends direct instruction with interactive learning techniques, making content more accessible, memorable, and applicable.

2. Key Principles of Effective Lecture Design

Designing an effective lecture requires a student-centered approach, where the instructor carefully structures content, incorporates active learning, and adapts to diverse learning styles.

A. Structuring the Lecture: The Three-Part Model

A well-structured lecture follows a three-part framework that aligns with how students process and retain information:

1. **Introduction (10–15%)** – Set the stage.
2. **Main Body (70–80%)** – Deliver content strategically.
3. **Conclusion (10–15%)** – Reinforce and consolidate learning.

1. Introduction: Capturing Attention and Providing Context

Set clear learning objectives – Outline what students will gain by the end of the lecture.
Provide a compelling hook – Start with a thought-provoking question, anecdote, real-world problem, or relevant statistic.
Connect to prior knowledge – Activate existing schemas to provide cognitive scaffolding.
Preview key concepts – Offer a roadmap for what students should expect.

2. Main Body: Delivering Content with Clarity and Engagement

Organize material logically – Use **chunking, thematic divisions, and signposting** to guide learners through complex information.
Alternate between explanation and engagement – Avoid long blocks of passive lecture; instead, intersperse discussions, polling, and active learning.
Use examples, case studies, and real-world applications – Help students see the relevance of abstract concepts.
Emphasize conceptual connections – Continuously relate new material to previous topics.

3. Conclusion: Reinforcing Learning and Encouraging Reflection

Summarize key takeaways – Recap the main points clearly and concisely.
Encourage student reflection – Ask students to articulate their learning or pose lingering questions.
Provide a preview of the next session – Help students see how the material fits into the larger course structure.
Assign follow-up tasks – Direct students toward further readings, exercises, or discussion prompts.

By following this structured approach, professors create cohesive, digestible lectures that enhance student retention and comprehension.

3. Strategies for Effective Lecture Delivery

A. Engaging Delivery Techniques

Delivery is just as important as content. Professors must convey enthusiasm, clarity, and confidence while maintaining student engagement.

Vary vocal tone and pacing – Avoid monotony by emphasizing key points and modulating speech.
Use purposeful movement and gestures – Enhance explanations with dynamic body language.
Make eye contact and read the room – Gauge student reactions and adjust accordingly.
Encourage real-time participation – Use questioning techniques, polls, and discussions.
Incorporate humor and storytelling – Make content more relatable and memorable.

B. Active Learning Techniques to Enhance Lectures

To prevent **passive absorption and cognitive fatigue**, instructors should integrate **active learning techniques** throughout the lecture.

1. **Think-Pair-Share** – Pose a question, have students discuss briefly in pairs, and then share responses.
2. **Live Polling & Quick Checks** – Use tools like Mentimeter, Poll Everywhere, or Kahoot! to assess understanding in real-time.
3. **Mini Case Studies & Problem-Solving** – Present short scenarios that students analyze and discuss.
4. **Pause and Reflect** – Every 10–15 minutes, allow students to write a summary, generate questions, or apply a concept.
5. **Concept Mapping** – Have students visually connect key ideas to reinforce relationships between concepts.

C. Using Technology to Enhance Lectures

Technology can elevate lectures by making them more interactive, multimodal, and student-centered.

Multimedia Integration – Incorporate **videos, animations, and infographics** to illustrate complex ideas.
Learning Management Systems (LMS) – Post slides, interactive notes, and supplementary resources on platforms like **Canvas, Blackboard, or Moodle**.
AI-Powered Tools – Use chatbots, adaptive learning platforms, and real-time analytics to personalize instruction.
Flipped Classroom Elements – Assign recorded lectures and use class time for active discussion and problem-solving.

A well-balanced use of technology enriches lectures without overwhelming students.

4. Avoiding Common Pitfalls in Lecture Design and Delivery

Information Overload – Avoid excessive detail; focus on core principles and high-impact takeaways.
Monotony – Keep students engaged with storytelling, real-world applications, and interactive elements.
Lack of Structure – Disorganized lectures confuse students; use clear outlines and signposting.
Neglecting Student Interaction – Ensure regular opportunities for participation, discussion, and self-reflection.
Failure to Assess Comprehension – Use formative assessments (quizzes, polls, discussions) to gauge understanding.

By addressing these challenges, professors maximize student engagement, retention, and overall learning outcomes.

5. Best Practices for Continuous Improvement in Lecture Design

Seek Student Feedback – Conduct mid-semester surveys to assess clarity, engagement, and pacing.
Analyze Student Performance – Adjust lectures based on assessment trends and comprehension gaps.
Attend Faculty Development Workshops – Engage in teaching and learning seminars to refine techniques.
Experiment with Different Approaches – Blend lecture, discussion, and experiential learning to find the optimal mix.

Great lectures evolve over time. Professors who remain reflective and adaptable continuously refine their techniques to better serve their students.

Conclusion: Elevating Lecture Design and Delivery for Student Success

An effective lecture is not merely a transmission of information—it is a carefully crafted learning experience that combines clear structure, engaging delivery, and interactive learning elements. Professors who master lecture design and delivery strategies foster deeper student engagement, improved comprehension, and long-term academic success.

By integrating strong organization, active learning techniques, and adaptive teaching methods, instructors transform lectures into dynamic, participatory, and impactful educational experiences that empower students to think critically, retain knowledge, and apply their learning in meaningful ways.

Socratic Questioning and the Promotion of Critical Thinking: A Constructivist and Critical Pedagogical Framework for Higher Education

At its core, Socratic questioning is not a mere technique—it is a profound instructional philosophy that reshapes the learning environment into a dialogic space where meaning is constructed, not transmitted. In contemporary higher education, where developing critical thinkers rather than content memorizers is paramount, Socratic questioning serves as both a method and a mindset. Its theoretical foundations and pedagogical applications stretch far beyond the ancient origins of Socratic dialogue, anchoring in modern constructivist theory, Vygotsky's sociocultural learning frameworks, and critical pedagogy.

Instructors employing Socratic questioning deliberately move away from the role of "knowledge authority" toward that of a facilitator, co-inquirer, and scaffold for learners navigating increasingly complex cognitive and ethical terrains. It is through this lens that Socratic questioning becomes both a tool for cognitive development and a mechanism for challenging entrenched power structures within educational discourse itself.

1. Constructivism: Socratic Questioning as a Process of Knowledge Construction

From a constructivist perspective, learning is not an act of reception but of construction. According to theorists such as Bruner, Piaget, and Vygotsky, learners build new cognitive structures by interacting with problems, negotiating meaning with peers, and reflecting on contradictions in their current understanding. Socratic questioning operationalizes these processes by:

- Exposing learners to conceptual conflict through guided inquiry.
- Eliciting articulation of tacit assumptions.
- Encouraging reflective dialogue where new understanding is negotiated, not imposed.

Each Socratic question functions as a cognitive tool, nudging students toward re-examining their frameworks and constructing new, more sophisticated models of understanding.

Practical Example:
In a course on environmental policy, instead of delivering a lecture on carbon markets, the instructor poses a layered series of questions:

- "What defines a market?"
- "Who benefits from commodifying carbon emissions?"
- "What assumptions underlie the notion of 'market efficiency' in solving environmental crises?"
- "Who might challenge these assumptions, and why?"

Here, knowledge is not given; it is interrogated and built, aligning perfectly with constructivist principles of active engagement and situated meaning-making.

2. Scaffolding Thinking: Vygotsky's Zone of Proximal Development (ZPD)

Vygotsky's sociocultural theory and concept of the Zone of Proximal Development (ZPD) offer deeper insight into how Socratic questioning should be calibrated. The ZPD represents the conceptual space where learners, with appropriate scaffolding, can perform tasks and engage in reasoning beyond their current independent capability.

Socratic questioning acts as this scaffold:

- Initial questions target what students can articulate easily (within their comfort zone).
- Successive questions incrementally challenge students, stretching their cognitive reach into the ZPD.
- Through dialogue, peer interaction, and instructor support, learners internalize reasoning strategies, eventually operating independently at higher cognitive levels.

Example Strategy:
A law professor teaching constitutional interpretation might:

- Begin with basic clarification questions (within the learner's independent ability).
- Introduce assumption-probing and counterargument analysis (operating within the ZPD).
- Fade direct guidance as students engage in structured debate, reasoning independently.

This dynamic aligns Socratic questioning directly with Vygotsky's model of cognitive apprenticeship, where guidance is systematically withdrawn as expertise develops.

3. Beyond Cognition: Critical Pedagogy and the Politics of Questioning

While constructivism addresses the cognitive dimension, critical pedagogy, as advanced by Paulo Freire and others, foregrounds the socio-political dimension of education. Freire criticized the "banking model" of education, where instructors deposit knowledge into passive students. Socratic questioning, when applied through a critical pedagogical lens, resists this model by:

- Democratizing the learning process: students' voices become central, not peripheral.
- Interrogating power structures: questions are directed not just at content but at systems of knowledge production and control.
- Emphasizing dialogue over monologue: understanding emerges through negotiated meaning rather than top-down transmission.

Critical Socratic Questioning Example:
In a business ethics course:

- "Whose interests are prioritized in your company's mission statement?"
- "Who defines ethical practice in your industry?"
- "How does corporate policy reinforce or resist systemic inequities?"

Here, the educator shifts from neutral facilitator to critical co-investigator, using questioning to surface and challenge structural inequities embedded in professional practice.

4. Socratic Questioning Within the Active vs. Passive Learning Debate

In the scholarly discourse surrounding active versus passive learning, Socratic questioning embodies the most robust form of active learning. Where passive learning relies on:

- Content delivery,
- Note-taking, and
- Memorization for assessments,

Socratic dialogue demands:

- Active cognitive engagement,
- Verbalization of reasoning,
- Collaborative knowledge construction, and
- Reflective questioning of both content and underlying frameworks.

Meta-analyses of educational research (Freeman et al., 2014) consistently demonstrate that active learning methods significantly outperform traditional lectures in developing problem-solving skills and long-term retention, particularly in adult learners [110]. Socratic questioning, in facilitating higher-order thinking, transcends even many active learning techniques by embedding metacognitive reflection within the learning process itself.

5. Reframing the Instructor's Role: From Expert to Critical Co-Learner

Socratic questioning necessitates that instructors reconceptualize their professional identity. No longer mere content experts, they become:

- Cognitive scaffolders, guiding students through their ZPDs.
- Constructivist facilitators, orchestrating environments where knowledge is negotiated, not delivered.
- Critical co-learners, who challenge their own assumptions alongside their students.

This shift in educator role is itself a form of professional transformative learning (Mezirow), where the instructor's identity evolves in response to reflective engagement with their teaching practice.

6. Practical Strategies for Deep Implementation

To operationalize this enriched approach:

- **Sequence questions strategically**, beginning within current cognitive comfort zones and progressing into conceptual challenges (ZPD).
- **Use silence intentionally**, allowing cognitive struggle within a safe space for intellectual risk-taking.
- **Encourage peer questioning**, shifting the dialogic center away from the instructor alone.
- **Link questions to power analysis**, embedding critical pedagogy within content discussions.
- **Adopt reflective practice**, asking students to journal their evolving thought processes.

Socratic questioning is not merely a tool for sharpening argumentation—it is a foundational methodology for cultivating reflective, autonomous, and socially conscious professionals. By embedding constructivist scaffolding, operating within students' ZPDs, and framing inquiry through a lens of critical pedagogy, instructors transform learning environments from spaces of content delivery to arenas of intellectual and societal transformation.

Ultimately, Socratic questioning is not a method for controlling dialogue. It is a philosophy for liberating thought. Its purpose is empower students to ask better ones and enhance their thinking.

The fundamental question, then, for faculty is not:
"How do I get my students to answer?"
But rather:
"How do I get my students to question—relentlessly, reflectively, and critically?"

Hybrid, Online, and In-Person Teaching Strategies

Higher education has evolved into a multimodal learning environment, offering students diverse formats for engaging with course content. Professors must be proficient in hybrid, online, and in-person teaching strategies to create engaging, effective, and adaptable learning experiences across different modalities. Each teaching format presents unique opportunities and challenges, requiring deliberate instructional design, technological integration, and student-centered pedagogy.

Successful faculty members do more than simply transfer content between platforms—they strategically tailor their teaching methods to maximize student engagement, learning outcomes, and accessibility in each environment.

1. The Core Differences Between Hybrid, Online, and In-Person Teaching

While all three modalities aim to deliver high-quality education, they differ in student interaction, content delivery, technological reliance, and instructional design.

Teaching Modality	Description	Key Considerations
In-Person Teaching	Traditional classroom instruction where faculty and students interact face-to-face.	Classroom management, lecture engagement, active learning, real-time discussions.
Online Teaching	Fully virtual instruction, either synchronous (live) or asynchronous (self-paced).	Course structure, student autonomy, digital literacy, interactive multimedia content.
Hybrid (Blended) Teaching	A combination of in-person and online learning components.	Balance between online flexibility and face-to-face engagement, seamless integration of materials.

Each modality requires a unique instructional approach, ensuring that students remain engaged, motivated, and supported regardless of the learning environment.

2. In-Person Teaching Strategies: Maximizing Classroom Engagement

A. Key Advantages of In-Person Instruction

Real-time interaction and immediate feedback.
Stronger social learning and peer collaboration.
Dynamic discussions and hands-on activities.

B. Effective In-Person Teaching Strategies

1. **Active Learning Integration**

- Use Socratic questioning, debates, case studies, and role-playing to keep students engaged.
- Incorporate think-pair-share exercises and group problem-solving.

2. **Lecture Optimization**
   - Break up lectures with interactive elements (polls, discussions, brief reflection activities).
   - Use storytelling and real-world examples to enhance relatability.

3. **Classroom Management Techniques**
   - Establish clear expectations for participation and conduct.
   - Foster an inclusive environment by encouraging diverse perspectives.

4. **Technology-Supported Learning**
   - Utilize presentation tools (Prezi, interactive PowerPoints, smartboards).
   - Integrate live polling apps (Mentimeter, Kahoot!) for engagement.

5. **Immediate Assessment and Feedback**
   - Use exit tickets, quick in-class quizzes, and peer evaluations to gauge understanding.
   - Provide real-time clarification of misconceptions.

When classroom engagement is prioritized, in-person learning becomes a dynamic and immersive experience rather than a passive content-delivery method.

3. Online Teaching Strategies: Designing Effective Virtual Learning

A. Types of Online Learning

Synchronous (Real-Time): Live virtual classes with immediate interaction.
Asynchronous (Self-Paced): Pre-recorded lectures, discussion forums, and independent learning.

B. Challenges of Online Learning and How to Address Them

Challenge	Solution
Student isolation and lack of engagement	Use discussion forums, breakout rooms, and collaborative tools (Google Docs, Miro, Padlet).
Technical difficulties	Provide tutorials, tech support resources, and multiple submission options.

Challenge	Solution
Maintaining academic integrity	Utilize proctored exams, plagiarism detection tools, and authentic assessments.
Instructor presence	Increase virtual office hours, personalized video messages, and timely responses in discussion boards.

C. Strategies for Effective Online Teaching

1. **Course Structure and Navigation**
    - Organize content in a logical, user-friendly format with clear learning modules.
    - Provide a syllabus walkthrough video to help students navigate the course.

2. **Engaging Content Delivery**
    - Use short, focused lecture videos (6–15 minutes per topic).
    - Integrate interactive media (simulations, quizzes, case studies).

3. **Fostering Student Interaction**
    - Require weekly discussion posts with peer responses to maintain engagement.
    - Use virtual whiteboards (Jamboard, Mural) for collaborative brainstorming.

4. **Assessment Strategies in Online Learning**
    - Emphasize project-based learning, open-book exams, and student portfolios.
    - Implement formative assessments like self-reflections and peer reviews.

5. **Instructor Presence and Student Support**
    - Send weekly announcements summarizing key concepts and upcoming tasks.
    - Provide flexible office hours across different time zones.

An effective online instructor does not simply post materials online—they actively facilitate discussions, provide regular feedback, and ensure student engagement throughout the course.

4. Hybrid (Blended) Teaching Strategies: Combining the Best of Both Worlds

Hybrid learning offers a flexible learning structure by integrating face-to-face and online components. Successful hybrid course design ensures seamless integration between modalities rather than treating online and in-person components as separate entities.

A. Common Hybrid Course Models

Flipped Classroom: Students review materials online, then engage in active learning during in-person sessions.

HyFlex Model: Students choose whether to attend in-person or online.
Rotational Model: Students alternate between in-person and online learning.

B. Strategies for Effective Hybrid Instruction

1. **Align Online and In-Person Components**
   - Ensure online activities prepare students for in-person discussions.
   - Use online tools to extend classroom learning (e.g., online simulations, peer collaboration).

2. **Leverage Technology for Seamless Integration**
   - Use Learning Management Systems (LMS) like Canvas, Blackboard, or Moodle to organize content.
   - Incorporate asynchronous discussion boards to maintain engagement between class sessions.

3. **Balance Flexibility with Accountability**
   - Set clear expectations for student participation in both environments.
   - Offer equivalent learning experiences for online and in-person students.

4. **Maximize Active Learning During Face-to-Face Time**
   - Focus on hands-on projects, debates, and peer discussions rather than lecture-heavy sessions.
   - Use online modules for knowledge acquisition and class time for application.

5. **Ensure Equity in Learning Access**
   - Provide recordings of in-person sessions for online students.
   - Design assessments that account for both synchronous and asynchronous learners.

Hybrid teaching requires careful course design to avoid redundancy while leveraging the strengths of both learning formats.

5. Choosing the Right Teaching Modality: A Strategic Approach

Faculty should select teaching strategies based on:
Course content complexity – Highly interactive subjects may benefit from hybrid or in-person learning.
Student demographics and accessibility needs – Some students prefer online flexibility, while others thrive in face-to-face environments.
Technology and institutional resources – Ensure students have adequate digital access and support.

Instructor strengths – Professors should choose a format that aligns with their teaching style and expertise.

No single modality is superior; the key is intentionality in design, delivery, and engagement.

Conclusion: Mastering Multimodal Teaching for 21st-Century Education

The modern professor must seamlessly navigate in-person, online, and hybrid instruction, creating dynamic, inclusive, and interactive learning environments. Each modality requires distinct pedagogical strategies, but all share a commitment to student engagement, accessibility, and meaningful learning experiences.

By mastering adaptive, technology-enhanced, and student-centered teaching methods, faculty prepare students for a flexible and interconnected academic and professional future—one where learning is not confined to the classroom but extends across digital and physical landscapes.

Encouraging Student-Driven Learning and Autonomy

Higher education goes beyond the transfer of knowledge. It is about empowering students to take own their learning. In a world that demands adaptability, critical thinking, and lifelong learning, college professors must cultivate student-driven learning and autonomy, enabling students with the skills, abilities and confidence to engage with material beyond the classroom.

Student-driven learning is an instructional approach where students actively participate in shaping their educational journey, making decisions about how, when, and what they learn within a structured academic framework. Rather than relying on passive consumption of knowledge, students develop self-regulation, intrinsic motivation, and intellectual curiosity, fostering a deeper, more meaningful engagement with their studies.

Professors who intentionally integrate autonomy-supportive strategies help students build the habits of independent inquiry, critical thinking, and self-directed problem-solving, which are essential for academic and professional success.

1. The Foundations of Student-Driven Learning

A. What is Student-Driven Learning?

Student-driven learning shifts the traditional professor-centered model toward a more student-centered framework, where learners:
Set their own learning goals within course expectations.
Make choices about content engagement, project topics, and problem-solving approaches.
Develop self-discipline and accountability.
Engage in metacognition—thinking about how they think and learn.

B. The Role of Autonomy in Higher Education

Autonomy is a key driver of intrinsic motivation, according to Self-Determination Theory [111]. When students feel they have control over their learning, they:
Develop greater persistence and resilience.

Engage in deeper learning rather than surface memorization.
Take responsibility for their academic progress and intellectual development [112].

The challenge for educators is to provide structured opportunities for autonomy that support freedom within a guided learning environment.

2. Strategies for Encouraging Student-Driven Learning and Autonomy

A. Foster an Inquiry-Based Learning Environment

Professors should move away from directive instruction and encourage students to engage in open-ended exploration, critical questioning, and research-based inquiry.

Use Socratic Questioning: Encourage students to develop their own arguments and reasoning through guided discussion.
Assign Problem-Based Learning (PBL) Tasks: Present students with real-world challenges requiring research, analysis, and creative problem-solving.
Encourage Open-Ended Exploration: Allow students to formulate their own questions and guide the direction of discussions and projects.

Example: In a political science class, rather than lecturing on policy-making, the professor could ask:
"If you were designing a policy to address climate change, what factors would you consider?"
This invites students **to critically engage** with real-world issues and develop their own perspectives.

B. Provide Opportunities for Choice and Personalized Learning

Students engage more when they feel a sense of control over their learning process. Offering choice in assignments, projects, and discussion topics increases motivation and investment in the subject matter.

Flexible Assignment Formats: Allow students to demonstrate learning in various ways—traditional papers, multimedia projects, presentations, or even podcasts.
Student-Selected Research Topics: Encourage students to explore areas that align with their academic and career interests.
Self-Paced Learning Modules: Use asynchronous resources, such as interactive readings or video lectures, where students can control the pace of engagement.

Example: In a business course, students could choose between:

- A case study analysis.
- A presentation on a disruptive industry trend.
- A simulation project where they create a startup business plan.

This flexibility empowers deep student engagement with material in ways aligning with their strengths and learning preferences.

C. Promote Self-Regulated Learning (SRL)

Self-regulated learning is the ability to set goals, monitor progress, and adjust strategies based on outcomes. Professors can teach students how to take control of the learning process by integrating goal-setting and reflection techniques.

- Encourage Learning Contracts: Students create a personal learning plan outlining their goals, strategies, and evaluation criteria.
- Use Reflective Journals: Ask students to track progress, challenges, and insights from their learning experiences.
- Implement Peer Accountability: Assign peer mentors or learning partners to foster collaborative self-regulation.

Example: In a research methods class, students could maintain a journal reflecting on their evolving research process, documenting challenges, breakthroughs, and adjustments in methodology.

When students actively reflect on their learning habits, they develop stronger metacognitive skills—the ability to plan, monitor, and evaluate their own learning strategies.

D. Use Technology to Support Independent Learning

Digital tools can enhance student autonomy by providing access to self-directed learning resources, collaborative platforms, and real-time feedback mechanisms.

- LMS (Canvas, Blackboard, Moodle): Organize content for self-paced exploration.
- AI-Driven Learning Tools (Coursera, EdX, ChatGPT, Perusall): Enable personalized learning experiences and adaptive assessments.
- Collaborative Tools (Google Docs, Padlet, Miro): Allow students to co-create knowledge and engage in peer-driven discussions.

Example: In a history course, students might engage with primary sources through an interactive digital archive, drawing their own conclusions before discussing with the class.

Technology should enhance, not replace student autonomy—offering tools for critical thinking, collaboration, and exploration.

E. Encourage Peer-Led Learning and Collaboration

Autonomous learning does not mean learning in isolation. Peer-led discussions and collaborative learning communities foster both intellectual independence and social engagement.

- Student-Led Seminars: Assign students to lead discussions on course topics, guiding peers through critical debates.
- Peer Teaching Activities: Allow students to create and present mini-lessons, reinforcing their understanding through teaching.
- Collaborative Learning Contracts: Have student teams define group expectations, roles, and accountability measures.

Example: In a literature class, students could take turns leading Socratic discussions, posing interpretive questions, and moderating debates on textual analysis.

This approach cultivates leadership skills, reinforces subject mastery, and fosters a collaborative learning culture.

3. Balancing Structure and Autonomy: The Role of the Professor

While student-driven learning emphasizes autonomy, professors still play a critical role as facilitators and mentors.

Set Clear Expectations: Define learning outcomes, assessment criteria, and engagement guidelines while allowing flexibility.
Provide Scaffolding: Offer guidance at the beginning, gradually shifting responsibility to students as they build confidence.
Foster a Growth Mindset: Encourage individuals to view challenges as powerful opportunities for intellectual growth instead of obstacles.

By providing structure while promoting independence, professors create an environment where students develop self-efficacy, intellectual agency, and lifelong learning skills.

4. The Long-Term Impact of Student-Driven Learning

Encouraging autonomy and student-driven learning has profound benefits:
Enhances lifelong learning skills, preparing students for graduate studies and careers.
Builds adaptability and problem-solving abilities in an ever-changing world.
Increases student engagement and retention by fostering deeper connections with material.
Develops self-motivated learners, capable of independent research and intellectual inquiry.

Students who take ownership of their learning become more confident, capable, and resilient thinkers, equipped to navigate the complexities of both academia and the professional world.

Faculty Collaboration and Team Teaching Strategies

Collaborative teaching models are increasingly shaping higher education practice as institutions expand interdisciplinary programs, integrate academic theory with professional application, and prioritize innovation in student learning. While excellence in individual instruction remains essential, faculty are now expected to work together in ways that maximize expertise, model professional collaboration, and create richer learning environments. Team teaching and co-teaching offer significant benefits but also present unique challenges. Without intentional planning, transparent communication, and structured coordination, collaborative teaching risks producing a fragmented student experience.

Co-Teaching Methodologies and Role Division Strategies

Faculty must select co-teaching methodologies aligned with course objectives, student needs, and their own strengths. Different models suit different contexts, and clear role division is central to success.

- **Parallel Teaching**: In this approach, the class is divided into two groups, each taught simultaneously by one instructor. This reduces class size for more personalized instruction and allows faculty to differentiate content based on student readiness levels. For example, in a data science course, one group might receive foundational instruction while the other engages in advanced applications. Coordination between instructors is critical to ensure that all groups cover comparable material and achieve common outcomes.
- **Station Teaching**: Students rotate through learning "stations," each facilitated by an instructor. This model works well for applied or skills-based courses where students benefit from multiple modes of engagement. In a teacher education program, one station might focus on classroom management scenarios, another on lesson plan design, and a third on reflective pedagogy. Faculty must carefully synchronize timing and objectives so the stations form a coherent whole rather than disconnected activities.
- **Team Teaching (Integrated Delivery)**: Instructors jointly deliver instruction in the same space, building on one another's contributions. This method models real-time collaboration, showing students how disciplinary perspectives intersect. It works especially well in interdisciplinary courses, such as a psychology–sociology course on human behavior, where instructors can debate interpretations and illustrate integrative problem-solving. However, it requires strong interpersonal dynamics and a shared teaching philosophy to avoid confusion or competition.
- **Lead-Support Model**: One instructor assumes primary responsibility for delivering content while the other provides supplemental support. This support may include clarifying difficult concepts, facilitating group discussions, monitoring student engagement, or addressing technology issues in large classes. This model is especially useful for faculty pairs where one has deeper subject matter expertise while the other contributes complementary strengths in pedagogy, technology, or applied practice.

Role Division and Coordination

Regardless of methodology, role division must be explicit and equitable. Ambiguity often leads to duplicated efforts or uneven faculty workloads. Effective coordination involves:

- **Course Design**: Agreeing on learning objectives, sequencing of topics, and assessment strategies before the course begins.
- **Lecture Preparation**: Assigning responsibility for creating lecture content, slides, or readings to avoid redundancy.
- **Classroom Leadership**: Determining who will lead particular sessions, who will facilitate discussions, and how instructors will interact during class.
- **Assignment Management**: Dividing responsibility for grading, feedback, and student communication to ensure consistency.
- **Logistics**: Clarifying responsibilities for tasks such as posting to the learning management system, managing attendance, and organizing office hours.

Faculty who engage in honest conversations about teaching philosophies, workload distribution, and expectations before the course begins are better positioned to deliver a seamless and engaging learning experience.

Key Takeaway

Co-teaching models offer diverse ways for faculty to collaborate effectively, from dividing students into smaller groups to delivering fully integrated lectures. Success depends less on the model chosen and more on the clarity of role division, planning, and communication between instructors. When executed thoughtfully, co-teaching enriches the classroom by blending faculty expertise and modeling collaboration for students.

Interdisciplinary Team Teaching Approaches

Team teaching across disciplines provides students with an authentic experience of how knowledge from different fields can be integrated to address complex, real-world problems. Unlike co-teaching within a single discipline, interdisciplinary team teaching exposes students to contrasting assumptions, methods, and vocabularies. The goal is not simply to present multiple perspectives but to actively demonstrate how those perspectives interact—sometimes reinforcing, sometimes challenging, but ultimately deepening understanding.

Value of Interdisciplinary Team Teaching

- **Authenticity**: Students experience how professionals from different fields collaborate on practical problems such as climate policy, urban development, or healthcare reform.
- **Breadth and Depth**: Students gain both disciplinary depth and the ability to apply knowledge across boundaries.
- **Preparation for the Workforce**: Employers increasingly value graduates who can bridge technical expertise, human context, and organizational strategy. Interdisciplinary teaching cultivates this flexibility.

Challenges and Risks

Without careful design, interdisciplinary courses risk becoming fragmented or overwhelming. Students may struggle to reconcile differing disciplinary approaches, or they may perceive one instructor's content as more important than another's. Faculty must intentionally structure the course to highlight connections rather than leaving students to synthesize on their own.

Strategies for Effective Interdisciplinary Team Teaching

- **Developing a Shared Framework for the Course**
  Faculty must begin with collective planning, identifying overarching themes or problems that serve as the backbone of the course. A shared framework ensures coherence by establishing:
    - Common learning objectives that reflect contributions from all disciplines.
    - A sequence of topics that builds logically rather than jumping between disconnected content.
    - Clear articulation of how each discipline contributes to the overarching problem or theme.
      For example, in a course on cybersecurity policy, computer scientists might cover

system vulnerabilities, legal scholars address regulatory frameworks, and political scientists analyze geopolitical implications—all anchored by the shared goal of understanding cyber defense strategy.

- **Designing Assignments that Integrate Knowledge**
Assignments should require students to use concepts from multiple fields rather than treating disciplines in isolation. Effective designs include:
    - **Case Studies**: Students analyze problems (e.g., opioid addiction) from biological, social, and policy perspectives.
    - **Group Projects**: Teams combine skills to produce integrated solutions, such as designing an urban sustainability plan informed by environmental science, economics, and public policy.
    - **Comparative Analyses**: Students write papers comparing how two disciplines would study the same problem, then propose a combined approach.
    These assignments encourage students not only to learn content but also to practice synthesis.
- **Modeling Professional Negotiation of Differences**
Faculty should not hide disciplinary disagreements but instead use them as teaching opportunities. By openly discussing how their fields prioritize evidence differently—or why their interpretations diverge—faculty demonstrate constructive negotiation across traditions of thought. Strategies include:
    - Holding structured debates between instructors during class.
    - Pausing after disagreements to explain to students why disciplines approach the issue differently.
    - Showing how disagreements can lead to stronger, more nuanced solutions.
    This modeling helps students see conflict as a productive force in interdisciplinary work rather than as a flaw.

Practical Example

In a **public health course co-taught by a biologist, sociologist, and policy expert**:

- The biologist explains disease mechanisms and medical interventions.
- The sociologist highlights social determinants of health, such as poverty or community networks.
- The policy expert examines regulatory and funding structures that enable or constrain interventions.
Assignments require students to design health campaigns that incorporate biological accuracy, social feasibility, and policy compliance, ensuring integration across perspectives.

Key Takeaway

Interdisciplinary team teaching succeeds when faculty move beyond parallel content delivery and instead create a shared framework, design integrative assignments, and model real-world collaboration. By doing so, they prepare students to navigate and integrate diverse forms of expertise—an essential skill in addressing today's most complex challenges.

Managing Different Teaching Philosophies Within Collaborative Settings

When faculty collaborate in teaching, they bring not only disciplinary expertise but also distinct pedagogical identities—the personal philosophies and practices that shape how they view learning, students, and the role of the classroom. Some instructors may value traditional lecture for its efficiency in covering content, while others emphasize active learning, student-led dialogue, or experiential projects. These differences can be a strength, offering students exposure to multiple ways of learning, but if left unmanaged, they can also cause tension, student confusion, or inconsistent course delivery.

The Opportunity and the Challenge

- **Enrichment**: Multiple teaching philosophies expose students to varied modes of learning, making the course more dynamic. For example, one professor might explain theoretical frameworks through lecture, while another leads applied simulations that bring those frameworks to life.
- **Risk of Tension**: Differences in teaching philosophy may lead to conflicting expectations around classroom management, assignment design, or standards of rigor. If these tensions play out in front of students without context, they can undermine credibility and create mixed signals about what the course values.

Strategies for Managing Teaching Philosophy Differences

- **Early Alignment**
  Before the semester begins, faculty should openly discuss their pedagogical approaches. Questions to explore include:
    - Do you see learning as primarily knowledge acquisition, skill development, or critical reflection?
    - How do you typically balance lecture, discussion, and experiential learning?
    - What role do you expect students to play in shaping classroom dialogue?
      This early dialogue helps identify areas of overlap as well as friction points. Where differences exist, faculty can decide whether to blend approaches or designate clear boundaries (e.g., one professor handles content-heavy lectures while another runs workshops).
- **Blended Approaches**
  Rather than treating philosophical differences as obstacles, faculty can use them to design a richer course structure. Examples include:
    - **Lecture + Problem-Solving**: One instructor presents foundational theories, followed by the other facilitating case-based problem-solving that applies those theories.
    - **Discussion + Reflection**: One professor leads student dialogue on competing perspectives, while the other guides reflective writing or journaling to consolidate insights.
    - **Experiential Learning + Conceptual Frameworks**: A practice-oriented instructor designs a simulation or field exercise, complemented by a colleague who interprets the experience through disciplinary theory.

This intentional blending helps students appreciate the strengths of each method and how they complement one another.
- **Student Transparency**
Faculty should explain openly to students why different teaching methods are being used. Transparency prevents confusion and reframes diversity in pedagogy as a deliberate design choice rather than inconsistency. Instructors might say:
  - "You'll notice that Professor A emphasizes theoretical context while Professor B focuses on applied practice. We want you to experience both, because real-world collaboration requires moving between theory and application."
  - "Our different teaching methods reflect the reality of interdisciplinary work, where professionals must adapt to multiple perspectives."

  By positioning differences as intentional and beneficial, faculty help students view pedagogical diversity as part of their learning.

Conflict Prevention and Resolution

Even with alignment, differences may surface during the semester. Faculty can mitigate conflict by:

- Setting ground rules for how to handle disagreements (e.g., addressing them privately before revising course policies).
- Observing each other's sessions to better understand how students engage with different styles.
- Gathering student feedback mid-semester to assess whether multiple teaching philosophies are creating confusion or enhancing learning.

Key Takeaway

Different teaching philosophies in collaborative settings need not be a liability. When faculty engage in early alignment, blend approaches strategically, and communicate transparently with students, they transform diversity of pedagogy into a strength. Students gain a richer, more authentic learning experience that mirrors the diversity of professional collaboration, while faculty model how to navigate differences constructively.

Assessment Strategies for Team-Taught Courses

Assessment in team-taught courses presents unique challenges. With multiple instructors contributing to course design and delivery, it is critical that evaluation feels coherent and consistent to students. Without intentional coordination, students may receive conflicting feedback, experience uneven grading standards, or become confused about what is expected of them. Faculty must therefore adopt structured strategies that balance disciplinary rigor with course-wide integration, ensuring fairness and clarity.

Principles of Effective Assessment in Collaborative Teaching

- **Coherence**: All assessments must align with the shared learning objectives of the course, not just the perspective of one instructor.
- **Transparency**: Students should understand how their work will be graded, particularly when different faculty members bring distinct disciplinary lenses.
- **Fairness**: Grading systems should prevent favoritism or inconsistency between instructors.
- **Integration**: Assessments should reflect not only disciplinary mastery but also the ability to synthesize across perspectives, especially in interdisciplinary settings.

Strategies for Assessment

- **Unified Rubrics**
  Faculty collaboratively design detailed rubrics that reflect both disciplinary and integrative goals. This ensures that regardless of who is grading, students are evaluated using the same standards. For example, a rubric for a sustainability project might allocate points for scientific accuracy, policy analysis, and communication effectiveness, reflecting the expertise of all instructors. Unified rubrics also serve as communication tools, making expectations clear to students and helping faculty calibrate grading.
- **Joint Assessment of Major Projects**
  For capstone assignments, group projects, or final papers, instructors can evaluate together. This may involve both faculty reading the same project and discussing their evaluations before assigning a grade, or sitting on a panel to assess oral presentations. Joint assessment not only ensures consistency but also models interdisciplinary dialogue, showing students how experts reconcile different standards.
- **Division of Grading by Expertise**
  In some cases, dividing grading responsibilities by area of expertise is most efficient. For example, in a business–computer science course, the business professor grades market analyses while the computer science professor grades technical prototypes. This division allows each instructor to apply disciplinary rigor while maintaining a shared framework that integrates both areas. To avoid fragmentation, faculty must still agree on an overarching grading structure so students see the project as a single, coherent effort.
- **Feedback Coordination**
  Students can become frustrated if they receive contradictory comments from different instructors. Faculty should therefore:
  - Share drafts of feedback before returning them to students.
  - Consolidate comments into a single document when possible.
  - Agree on tone and style of feedback to avoid confusion.
  - Use shared grading platforms or LMS tools to coordinate commentary.
    This ensures that students receive integrated guidance that reflects the collaboration among instructors.

Additional Practices to Enhance Consistency

- **Calibration Sessions**: Before major grading begins, faculty can grade a sample assignment together and compare results to ensure alignment.

- **Mid-Semester Adjustments**: Reviewing student performance halfway through the course allows faculty to identify inconsistencies and adjust rubrics or grading practices.
- **Student Involvement**: Sharing rubrics with students early and inviting questions promotes transparency and trust in the grading process.

Key Takeaway

Assessment in team-taught courses must reflect the collaborative nature of instruction. Unified rubrics, joint evaluation of major projects, division of grading by expertise, and coordinated feedback all contribute to a coherent student experience. When executed well, these strategies ensure fairness, transparency, and integration—reinforcing the value of collaborative teaching rather than undermining it.

Communication Protocols Between Co-Instructors

Successful team teaching relies as much on strong communication as it does on pedagogical expertise. Without clear protocols, even experienced faculty can fall into misalignment, resulting in duplication of work, inconsistent messages to students, or avoidable conflict. Establishing structured communication practices ensures that instructors operate as a unified team, delivering a seamless learning experience for students.

Why Communication Protocols Matter

- **Consistency for Students**: When instructors communicate regularly, students receive coherent expectations rather than contradictory instructions.
- **Efficiency for Faculty**: Clear protocols prevent wasted time and reduce the risk of tasks being overlooked or unnecessarily repeated.
- **Conflict Prevention**: Many disagreements arise not from philosophical differences but from unclear communication. Protocols provide mechanisms for resolving issues before they escalate.
- **Adaptability**: Strong communication structures allow faculty to adjust quickly when challenges arise mid-semester, such as shifts in student needs, scheduling conflicts, or unexpected events.

Core Communication Practices

- **Pre-Course Planning Meetings**
  Prior to the semester, co-instructors should meet to:
    - Define learning objectives and course outcomes.
    - Decide on course structure, sequencing of topics, and distribution of responsibilities.
    - Draft a unified syllabus that reflects shared expectations for assignments, grading, and classroom policies.
    - Establish how students will perceive the teaching partnership—for example, as equal collaborators or with one serving as lead instructor.

Documenting these agreements prevents confusion later and sets a foundation for collaborative trust.
- **Weekly Check-Ins**
Regular, short meetings help faculty stay aligned throughout the semester. These check-ins can cover:
  - Review of classroom dynamics, including student engagement and emerging challenges.
  - Progress updates on upcoming lectures, labs, or activities.
  - Coordination of grading responsibilities and turnaround times.
  - Adjustments to schedules or assignments as needed.
  Weekly meetings need not be lengthy—15–20 minutes is often sufficient—but they provide a structured space to keep the partnership coordinated.
- **Shared Documentation**
Collaborative tools allow faculty to work from a common source of truth. Effective practices include:
  - Maintaining a shared drive or LMS folder for syllabi, lecture notes, rubrics, and assignment instructions.
  - Using version control practices (e.g., naming conventions, date stamping) to prevent confusion over which documents are current.
  - Employing project management tools (e.g., Trello, Asana, or LMS task features) to track responsibilities and deadlines.
  Shared documentation enhances transparency and ensures both instructors can step in seamlessly if the other is unavailable.
- **Clear Decision-Making Processes**
Even with strong alignment, changes will arise during the semester. Faculty should agree in advance on:
  - Which decisions require joint approval (e.g., changing major assignment deadlines, altering grading weights).
  - Which decisions can be made independently by one instructor (e.g., adjusting in-class activities, managing individual student requests).
  - How to handle disagreements—whether by deferring to the lead instructor, alternating authority, or escalating to a department chair if needed.
  Documenting these processes reduces ambiguity and models professionalism for students.

Supplementary Practices

- **Student-Facing Communication Alignment**: Ensure announcements on LMS, emails, and verbal instructions are consistent and, when possible, co-signed by both instructors.
- **End-of-Semester Debriefs**: After the course ends, faculty should review what worked well, what communication gaps emerged, and what adjustments to protocols will strengthen future collaborations.
- **Conflict Containment**: Instructors should commit to resolving disagreements privately and presenting a unified front in front of students.

Key Takeaway

Communication protocols are the backbone of effective co-teaching. By investing in pre-course planning, maintaining weekly check-ins, using shared documentation, and agreeing on decision-making processes, faculty minimize conflict and maximize coherence. These practices not only improve instructional delivery but also model professional collaboration for students.

Conflict Resolution When Teaching Partners Disagree

Disagreements are an inevitable part of collaborative teaching. Faculty bring different disciplinary perspectives, teaching philosophies, and personal working styles, all of which can lead to friction. While such conflicts are natural, how they are handled directly affects both the student experience and the professional relationship between instructors. Left unmanaged, disagreements can confuse students, undermine confidence in the course, and strain faculty partnerships. Managed well, they can serve as opportunities to strengthen collaboration and even provide valuable lessons in professional communication for students.

Address Issues Early

Minor disagreements, if ignored, often grow into larger problems. Faculty should commit to addressing concerns as soon as they arise, rather than waiting until frustration builds. Early intervention:

- Prevents small misunderstandings (e.g., differing interpretations of an assignment rubric) from escalating.
- Allows quick adjustments before students are affected.
- Maintains trust by demonstrating openness and respect.
  Practical approaches include scheduling a private conversation immediately after a class where tension arises, or using weekly check-ins as a safe space to surface concerns.

Focus on Shared Goals

At the heart of every collaborative course is a shared mission: student learning and success. Faculty should reframe disagreements by asking:

- How does this decision affect students' ability to achieve learning outcomes?
- Will one approach create more clarity, fairness, or engagement for the class?
- How can both perspectives be incorporated to enhance student experience?
  By centering on shared goals, instructors can shift the conversation from personal preferences to professional priorities, reducing defensiveness and fostering compromise.

Use Mediation if Necessary

When conflicts persist despite faculty efforts, external mediation may be necessary. Options include:

- **Department Chairs or Program Directors**: These leaders can provide guidance, clarify institutional policies, or help faculty align expectations.

- **Centers for Teaching and Learning (CTLs)**: CTLs often offer workshops, consultation, or facilitated mediation to support faculty collaboration.
- **Union or Faculty Governance Structures**: In unionized settings, contractual provisions may outline procedures for conflict resolution.
  Mediation ensures disagreements are addressed constructively while preserving professional relationships and preventing disruption to students.

Model Professional Disagreement

Not all conflict needs to remain hidden. When handled thoughtfully, respectful disagreement in front of students can be a powerful teaching moment. For example:

- Two instructors might debate the relative strengths of quantitative vs. qualitative methods.
- Faculty could present alternative disciplinary interpretations of a case study, showing how different approaches yield different insights.
  This models for students that professional disagreement is normal, productive, and essential for interdisciplinary problem-solving. The key is for instructors to demonstrate mutual respect, active listening, and evidence-based argumentation so students learn collaboration does not mean uniformity.

Preventive Strategies

In addition to resolving conflicts as they occur, faculty can minimize disputes through:

- **Written Agreements**: Outlining role division, grading policies, and decision-making processes in writing.
- **Regular Debriefs**: Checking in on how the partnership is functioning beyond course logistics.
- **Clarifying Non-Negotiables**: Identifying early which elements of pedagogy or assessment each instructor considers essential.

Key Takeaway

Conflict between teaching partners is natural and, if managed well, can enhance collaboration. Addressing issues early, focusing on shared goals, seeking mediation when necessary, and modeling professional disagreement help ensure conflicts do not disrupt student learning. When faculty demonstrate constructive conflict resolution, they prepare students to navigate the realities of teamwork in professional environments.

Coordinating Grading and Feedback Across Multiple Instructors

One of the most common challenges in team-taught courses is ensuring consistency in grading and feedback. Students quickly notice when one instructor evaluates more leniently than another or when feedback from different instructors points them in contradictory directions. Such inconsistencies undermine student confidence in the fairness of the course, create confusion about expectations, and can negatively impact learning outcomes. Faculty must therefore adopt coordinated strategies that present a unified front, ensuring grading reflects shared standards rather than individual differences.

Agree on Standards Before Grading Begins

Faculty should meet early to establish clear, shared expectations for what constitutes high-quality work. This includes:

- **Defining criteria**: What specific elements will be evaluated (e.g., accuracy, originality, clarity, application)?
- **Setting thresholds**: What distinguishes an "A" from a "B" in both quantitative and qualitative assignments?
- **Identifying non-negotiables**: For example, all written assignments must meet minimum standards of citation and academic integrity, regardless of instructor.
  Documenting these agreements in a unified rubric ensures that grading is transparent and consistent across instructors.

Divide Responsibilities Thoughtfully

Instructors should play to their strengths while maintaining an integrated approach:

- A **technical specialist** might grade coding functionality, lab procedures, or quantitative analyses.
- A **communication-oriented instructor** could evaluate clarity of writing, argument structure, or presentation style.
- In interdisciplinary contexts, each faculty member can grade the sections of an assignment that align with their field, while also cross-checking for coherence.
  This division reduces workload duplication and allows each instructor to apply disciplinary expertise without losing sight of course-wide goals.

Cross-Review Samples to Calibrate Standards

Even with shared rubrics, interpretation of criteria can vary. To address this, instructors should:

- Grade a subset of the same assignments independently and then compare results.
- Discuss discrepancies to align grading philosophies.
- Adjust rubrics or provide clarifying notes for borderline cases.
  Calibration sessions build mutual understanding and ensure students are evaluated equitably, regardless of which instructor grades their work.

Deliver Unified Feedback

Students benefit most when feedback feels integrated rather than piecemeal. Faculty can achieve this by:

- **Consolidating comments**: Combining observations from both instructors into a single feedback document.
- **Co-signing feedback**: Even if only one instructor writes the comments, both names can appear to reinforce the sense of collaboration.
- **Using a shared digital platform**: Learning management systems (LMS) or collaborative grading tools allow instructors to leave joint comments and avoid duplication.
  This unified approach ensures that feedback reinforces, rather than contradicts, the messages students receive in class.

Additional Best Practices

- **Consistent Turnaround Times**: Faculty should agree on deadlines for returning graded work so students do not receive uneven treatment.
- **Communication with Students**: If instructors differ slightly in grading styles, they should be transparent with students about how integration will occur.
- **Continuous Review**: Mid-semester check-ins on grading practices allow for course corrections before inconsistencies accumulate.

Key Takeaway

Coordinating grading and feedback across multiple instructors requires shared standards, thoughtful division of responsibilities, calibration of grading practices, and unified communication with students. When done well, it ensures fairness, clarity, and coherence in the student experience. Faculty collaboration in assessment not only enriches learning but also models the professional integration of diverse perspectives.

Crisis Management and Emergency Remote Teaching

Emergencies such as pandemics, natural disasters, cyberattacks, or political unrest can disrupt higher education with little or no warning. Faculty who are unprepared for such transitions may find their courses stalled, students confused, and learning outcomes jeopardized. The COVID-19 pandemic underscored the necessity of institutional and faculty readiness to pivot quickly between in-person, hybrid, and fully online formats [113]. Today, the expectation is that higher education professionals can adapt rapidly while preserving instructional continuity, academic rigor, and student support. Effective crisis management requires not only technical agility but also strong communication, empathy, and attention to compliance and accessibility standards.

Rapid Course Conversion Protocols

The first step in crisis management is the ability to shift courses online efficiently and without unnecessary disruption. Faculty should develop clear, repeatable protocols that allow for smooth transitions regardless of the crisis.

- **Prioritize Essentials**
  Faculty should identify the core learning outcomes that students must achieve and focus instructional design around those essentials. Noncritical activities—such as extended

group projects, supplemental readings, or enrichment assignments—can be modified, postponed, or removed altogether. This ensures that even during disruption, the course maintains academic integrity by emphasizing its fundamental objectives.

- **Use Existing Platforms**
  In moments of crisis, consistency is more important than novelty. Faculty should rely on tools that students already know, such as the institution's LMS (Canvas, Blackboard, Moodle, etc.) and established videoconferencing platforms (Zoom, Teams, Webex). Introducing unfamiliar technology during a disruption adds confusion and raises barriers to participation. Leveraging institutional platforms also ensures alignment with IT support and compliance standards.

- **Simplify Delivery**
  Emergencies require streamlined approaches to reduce cognitive and logistical strain. Instead of long lectures, faculty should record shorter, focused segments that can be viewed asynchronously. Asynchronous discussion boards or low-bandwidth options help reach students with unstable internet. Assignments should be clear, simple to submit, and directly aligned with learning outcomes, minimizing additional stress for both students and faculty.

- **Document Processes**
  Preparation before a crisis greatly reduces response time. Faculty can maintain pre-built course shells, template syllabi, and repositories of digital resources (e.g., recorded lectures, question banks, rubrics). Having these materials ready allows courses to be converted rapidly without the pressure of creating content from scratch during an emergency. Documentation should also include contingency instructions for students—for example, a "Crisis Teaching Plan" included in the syllabus outlining how the course will proceed if in-person sessions are suspended.

Key Takeaway

Rapid course conversion is not about creating a perfect online experience overnight; it is about ensuring continuity and clarity while protecting essential learning outcomes. By prioritizing the core, using familiar tools, simplifying delivery, and preparing templates in advance, faculty can pivot smoothly when emergencies arise, preserving stability for students in uncertain times.

Student Communication During Disruptions

In times of crisis, communication becomes as important as course content. When students face uncertainty, they look to faculty for stability, clarity, and reassurance. Silence or delayed communication can heighten anxiety, foster misinformation, and erode trust. Faculty who establish consistent and empathetic communication protocols help maintain a sense of continuity, even when normal operations are interrupted.

Early Messaging

Faculty should communicate promptly, even if all the details of a course adjustment are not yet resolved. Early updates accomplish three key objectives:

- **Reassurance**: Students know their professor is actively managing the situation and has not abandoned the course.
- **Rumor Control**: Clear, authoritative messages prevent misinformation from spreading among students.
- **Expectation Setting**: Students understand that changes are forthcoming and can mentally prepare to adapt.
  For example, a brief message such as, *"Due to campus closure, our course will shift online next week. I will provide more details within 48 hours, but please check the LMS for updates,"* sets expectations and calms uncertainty.

Regular Updates

Crisis conditions are fluid, and course plans may evolve. Students benefit from a predictable rhythm of updates:

- **Weekly or Biweekly Announcements**: Posting updates at consistent intervals (e.g., every Monday morning) helps students organize their schedules and reduces the need for repeated inquiries.
- **Structured Format**: Updates should outline what has changed, what remains the same, and what students need to do next.
- **Transparency in Adjustments**: If deadlines, assignments, or grading policies change, explain the reasoning to maintain trust.

Multiple Communication Channels

Not all students will have equal access to a single communication medium during a disruption. Faculty should diversify delivery:

- **LMS Announcements**: Central hub for official course communication.
- **Email**: Ensures messages reach students directly, including those who may not log into the LMS frequently.
- **SMS or Text Alerts**: Useful in severe emergencies when internet access may be limited. Institutions often provide opt-in systems for this purpose.
  Faculty should reinforce that the LMS is the authoritative source for instructions, while other channels serve as redundancy.

Tone and Style of Communication

The way faculty communicate matters as much as the information itself. Tone should balance professionalism with empathy:

- **Professional**: Use clear, direct language to avoid ambiguity.
- **Supportive**: Acknowledge the challenges students may be facing. For example: *"I recognize many of you are juggling family responsibilities and technology issues. I will remain flexible while ensuring you meet the core learning goals."*

- **Consistent**: Avoid sudden changes in tone, which may confuse students about expectations.

Enhancing Student Engagement Through Communication

Beyond announcements, faculty can use communication to foster connection during disruptions:

- **Virtual Office Hours**: Scheduled times for Q&A help reduce student isolation.
- **Surveys or Polls**: Quick check-ins gauge student access to technology and overall well-being.
- **Encouragement**: Positive reinforcement helps students maintain motivation under stressful conditions.

Key Takeaway

Clear, frequent, and empathetic communication provides stability when external circumstances disrupt normal teaching. By sending early messages, maintaining predictable updates, using multiple channels, and striking a professional yet supportive tone, faculty enable special learning environments where students feel guided and supported despite uncertainty.

Technology Triage and Backup Systems

Technology is the backbone of emergency remote teaching, yet crises often expose disparities in access, reliability, and digital literacy. Faculty cannot assume that every student—or every instructor—will have high-speed internet, advanced hardware, or uninterrupted access to institutional systems. To maintain instructional continuity, faculty must adopt a triage mindset, focusing on the most essential and accessible technologies first, while preparing backups for when primary systems fail.

Baseline Tools

The first priority in technology triage is to use platforms and tools that are familiar, reliable, and low bandwidth. Introducing complex new systems during a crisis adds unnecessary barriers.

- **Use What Students Know**: Most institutions have a learning management system (LMS) and standard communication platforms already in place. Faculty should anchor instruction there rather than experimenting with new tools.
- **Low-Bandwidth Options**: Students with limited internet access may struggle with streaming video. Providing content in PDF, text-based forums, or audio-only files ensures broader accessibility.
- **Mobile Compatibility**: Many students rely on smartphones rather than laptops. Materials should be accessible on mobile devices to reduce inequities.

Backups for Core Activities

Even the most reliable systems fail under strain, especially during large-scale disruptions. Faculty should anticipate these failures and provide alternatives:

- **If Video Fails**: Replace live sessions with pre-recorded lectures, audio podcasts, or detailed written guides. Provide transcripts to ensure accessibility.
- **If LMS Fails**: Use email distribution lists, cloud storage (e.g., Google Drive, OneDrive), or even institutional websites as temporary repositories for materials.
- **If Communication Fails**: Establish an emergency contact method, such as SMS alerts or a secondary email list.
A **backup plan shared with students in advance** reduces panic and confusion if the primary system collapses.

Support Resources

Technology barriers are not solved by tools alone—students and faculty also need clear guidance on using them.

- **Troubleshooting Guides**: Provide short, step-by-step instructions for common tasks (e.g., uploading assignments, accessing discussion boards).
- **IT Help Desk Connections**: Share contact details for institutional tech support early and often. Encourage students to use official help desks rather than relying solely on peers.
- **Peer Support Networks**: Where IT resources are stretched, faculty can organize peer "tech buddies" who help classmates troubleshoot basic issues.

Contingency Planning

Faculty should not wait until a crisis to plan for outages. Effective contingency planning includes:

- **Documenting Procedures**: Add a "Technology Contingency Plan" to the syllabus that outlines what students should do if LMS access, video conferencing, or email fails.
- **Redundancy**: Store materials in multiple locations (e.g., LMS, cloud storage, and external drives) to prevent data loss.
- **Testing Alternatives**: Periodically test backup communication channels so students know how to access them.
- **Institutional Alignment**: Ensure personal contingency plans align with campus-wide emergency policies to prevent contradictory instructions.

Key Takeaway

Technology during crises should be treated like an emergency utility: reliable, simple, and supported by backups. By prioritizing familiar, low-bandwidth tools, preparing alternatives for system failures, providing clear support resources, and documenting contingency plans in advance, faculty ensure instructional continuity even when technology falters. This proactive approach reduces inequities and builds resilience in teaching and learning.

Maintaining Academic Rigor During Crisis Transitions

Emergencies disrupt normal teaching conditions, but they should not dilute the intellectual quality of higher education. Students benefit from flexibility during crises, yet they also need to know that academic expectations remain meaningful. When rigor collapses, students may disengage, perceive coursework as busywork, or fail to develop the competencies they need for long-term success. The key for faculty is to adapt assessments and delivery methods while preserving the integrity of learning outcomes.

Adjust Assessment, Not Standards

The goal is to measure the same learning outcomes, even if the tools for doing so must change. Faculty can:

- **Shift from Proctored Exams**: Online proctoring tools can be unreliable, intrusive, and inequitable. Instead, faculty can adopt:
    - **Open-Book Exams**: Focus on important skills such as analysis and synthesis rather than memorization.
    - **Project-Based Assignments**: Students design solutions, create reports, or build prototypes demonstrating applied learning.
    - **Reflective Assessments**: Journals or essays that ask students to connect course concepts to personal or societal experiences during the crisis.
- **Maintain Outcome Alignment**: Even as formats shift, faculty must ensure assessments still target critical outcomes such as problem-solving, writing, research, or technical mastery.

Transparency in Grading

During crises, students may fear that grading will become arbitrary or inconsistent. Clear, transparent grading practices help sustain trust and accountability:

- **Detailed Rubrics**: Provide explicit criteria for each assignment, showing students how their work will be evaluated.
- **Examples of Excellence**: Share sample projects, reports, or essays that illustrate what successful work looks like under the revised expectations.
- **Consistent Communication**: Reinforce that standards are unchanged, though methods of demonstrating achievement may differ.

Focus on Application

Crisis contexts provide authentic opportunities for applied learning. Faculty can design assignments that connect course content directly to real-world challenges:

- **Discipline-Specific Applications**:
    - Public health students might analyze pandemic response strategies.
    - Business students could create contingency plans for supply chain disruptions.

- - Computer science students might evaluate cybersecurity risks under remote work conditions.
  - **Personalized Relevance**: Encourage students to apply theories to their own experiences during the crisis, increasing motivation and engagement.
  - **Problem-Solving Orientation**: Frame assessments as tools for navigating real-world uncertainty, emphasizing adaptability and innovation.

Key Takeaway

Flexibility during crises should never mean abandoning rigor. By adjusting assessment formats rather than lowering standards, ensuring grading transparency, and emphasizing real-world application, faculty preserve the intellectual quality of their courses while meeting students where they are. This approach communicates that higher education remains meaningful—even under extraordinary circumstances—and prepares students to apply their learning to unpredictable challenges beyond the classroom.

Supporting Student Mental Health During Disruptions

Crises create not only logistical challenges but also emotional and psychological strain. Students may face anxiety, grief, financial instability, caregiving responsibilities, or social isolation. These factors directly impact the ability to focus, participate, and perform academically. Faculty are not expected to serve as counselors, but they play a vital role in acknowledging challenges, normalizing struggle, and connecting students to appropriate resources. A supportive learning environment helps students remain engaged while protecting their overall well-being.

Flexible Deadlines

Rigid schedules may be unrealistic when students are coping with disrupted lives. Flexibility communicates understanding without compromising academic integrity.

- **Extensions**: Allow students additional time to submit assignments if they face illness, family responsibilities, or technology issues.
- **Alternative Submissions**: Permit modified formats (e.g., audio reflections instead of essays, or shorter projects when full-length work is not feasible).
- **Clear Boundaries**: Flexibility should be balanced with structure. Faculty can set final cut-off points to maintain fairness and course progression.

Check-Ins

Regular check-ins allow faculty to monitor student well-being and identify issues early.

- **Surveys or Polls**: Quick, anonymous surveys can assess student stress levels, technology access, and overall workload.
- **Informal Communication**: Simple gestures—asking "How are you managing?" at the start of class—signal care and open lines of communication.

- **Office Hours for Support**: Virtual drop-in sessions provide opportunities for students to share challenges privately.
  Check-ins not only support individuals but also help faculty adjust course design to better meet collective needs.

Resource Referral

Faculty should serve as connectors to professional and institutional support systems:

- **Counseling Services**: Share contact details for campus mental health services early and often.
- **Peer Support Groups**: Direct students toward study groups, mentoring programs, or student-led wellness initiatives.
- **Wellness Resources**: Provide links to mindfulness apps, stress-management workshops, or online self-care guides.
  By repeatedly emphasizing these resources, faculty reduce stigma and remind students that support is available and encouraged.

Normalize Struggle

Students often feel isolated when they believe they are the only ones struggling. Faculty can counteract this by:

- **Acknowledging Reality**: Openly state that distraction, stress, and dips in productivity are expected during crises.
- **Sharing Encouragement**: Emphasize that persistence, not perfection, is the goal.
- **Modeling Empathy**: Faculty who admit that they, too, face challenges normalize struggle as part of the shared human experience.
  Normalization reduces shame and encourages students to seek help rather than withdrawing.

Key Takeaway

Supporting student mental health during crises does not mean lowering expectations—it means creating conditions where students can realistically succeed. Flexible deadlines, regular check-ins, resource referrals, and normalization of struggle all contribute to a climate of empathy and stability. Faculty who adopt these practices help students preserve not only their academic progress but also their personal resilience in the face of disruption.

Managing Reduced Resources and Access Limitations

Emergencies often expose inequities in access to educational resources. Students may lose reliable internet connections, face financial hardship, or lack access to hardware such as laptops and webcams. Institutions themselves may operate under strained budgets, limiting the availability of software licenses, lab access, or instructional support. Faculty must recognize these constraints and proactively design courses that remain equitable and effective under reduced-resource conditions.

Adapt Materials

High-cost or high-bandwidth materials may be unattainable for many students during crises. Faculty should shift toward **low-cost, flexible alternatives**:

- **Open Educational Resources (OERs)**: Freely available textbooks, articles, simulations, and videos provide quality content without financial barriers. OERs also allow faculty to tailor content to course needs.
- **Free or Freemium Software**: Instead of requiring costly licenses, instructors can recommend open-source tools (e.g., LibreOffice instead of Microsoft Office, R instead of proprietary statistics software).
- **Alternative Media Formats**: Replace video-heavy resources with audio recordings, slide decks, or written transcripts, all of which are more accessible in low-bandwidth settings.

Scale Activities

Complex assignments may become unrealistic when students have limited time, technology, or collaborative capacity. Faculty can scale activities without sacrificing learning outcomes:

- **Simplify Group Projects**: Instead of multi-phase, large-team projects, assign smaller, modular tasks that can be completed independently or in pairs.
- **Focus on Core Outcomes**: Prioritize assignments that directly align with essential learning goals and reduce "extras" that create additional burden without significant payoff.
- **Incremental Deliverables**: Break large assignments into smaller steps (e.g., proposal, draft, reflection) to maintain engagement while reducing overwhelm.

Accessibility First

Accessibility must be at the center of course design during emergencies, since crises often amplify disparities:

- **Offline Availability**: Ensure that lecture slides, readings, and assignments can be downloaded for offline use, allowing students to work without constant internet access.
- **Low-Bandwidth Alternatives**: Record audio-only versions of lectures or provide PDF summaries in place of streaming video.
- **Mobile Compatibility**: Design materials that are functional on smartphones, recognizing that many students rely on mobile devices when laptops are unavailable.
- **Universal Design for Learning (UDL)**: Provide materials in multiple formats (text, audio, visual) so students with disabilities or limited resources can access them equitably.

Faculty Adaptation to Limited Resources

Instructors may also face reduced resources, such as limited IT support or fewer teaching assistants. To cope:

- **Streamline Course Management**: Use the LMS for centralized communication and grading to avoid juggling multiple systems.
- **Leverage Peer Support**: Encourage students to help one another troubleshoot technical issues or share resources.
- **Prioritize Faculty Well-Being**: Faculty should recognize their own limits and focus on sustainable teaching practices rather than attempting to replicate every element of pre-crisis instruction.

Key Takeaway

Resource limitations during crises should not prevent meaningful learning. By adapting materials with OERs and free tools, scaling assignments to focus on essentials, and prioritizing accessibility, faculty can design courses that remain equitable and effective under constrained conditions. Thoughtful adaptation ensures that all students, regardless of circumstance, continue to progress toward their academic goals.

Legal and Accessibility Considerations

In emergencies, faculty often prioritize instructional continuity, but compliance with legal and accessibility standards must remain a central concern. Neglecting these obligations not only creates inequities but also exposes institutions and instructors to legal risks. Thoughtful planning ensures that rapid transitions to remote teaching do not inadvertently exclude students with disabilities, compromise privacy, or disadvantage those with limited access to technology.

Accessibility Standards

Accessibility is a legal and ethical requirement under the Americans with Disabilities Act (ADA), Section 504 of the Rehabilitation Act, and comparable global regulations [114]. Faculty should ensure that all course materials remain usable for students with diverse needs [115].

- **Captioning and Transcripts**: All recorded lectures and videos should include accurate captions. Audio-only materials should be accompanied by transcripts. Automated tools can assist, but faculty should review for accuracy.
- **Screen Reader Compatibility**: Documents should use accessible formatting (e.g., structured headings, alt-text for images, and properly tagged PDFs) so screen readers can interpret them.
- **Accessible Platforms**: Faculty should prioritize institution-approved platforms, which are more likely to meet ADA and WCAG (Web Content Accessibility Guidelines) standards.
By embedding accessibility from the outset, faculty avoid retrofitting materials after student needs arise.

Privacy Concerns

Rapid adoption of third-party tools during a crisis can create significant risks if privacy standards are overlooked. Faculty must remain vigilant about compliance with the Family Educational Rights and Privacy Act (FERPA) and institutional data protection practices and policies.

- **FERPA Compliance**: Do not share student data (e.g., grades, participation records) on platforms not vetted by the institution [116].
- **Third-Party Tools**: Avoid requiring students to create accounts on apps that collect personal data without proper privacy protections.
- **Recording Sessions**: Inform students if live classes are recorded, clarify how recordings will be used, and store files securely in institution-approved systems.
- **Cybersecurity Awareness**: Faculty should remind students about safe practices (e.g., using institutional email accounts, avoiding unverified links) to protect both student and institutional data.

Equity of Access

Accessibility is not limited to disability accommodation; it also includes equitable access to technology, learning resources, and support. Faculty should:

- **Offer Alternatives**: Provide low-bandwidth options (PDFs, audio recordings, text transcripts) for students without reliable internet.
- **Device Flexibility**: Ensure materials function on mobile devices, recognizing that many students may not have access to laptops during disruptions.
- **Reasonable Accommodations**: Continue to honor accommodations for extended testing time, alternative assignment formats, or assistive technologies. Collaborate with disability services offices to ensure compliance.
- **Financial Considerations**: Avoid requiring costly software, textbooks, or hardware upgrades that students cannot afford during a crisis.

Key Takeaway

Faculty must balance urgency with responsibility. Accessibility standards, privacy protections, and equity of access are not optional—they are essential to fair and legal instruction. By captioning media, ensuring screen-reader compatibility, safeguarding student data, and offering equitable alternatives, instructors protect both their students and their institutions. In doing so, they reinforce the principle that quality education must remain inclusive and legally compliant, even under crisis conditions.

Post-Crisis Transition Back to Normal Operations

The return to in-person or hybrid instruction after a crisis is not simply a matter of reopening classrooms. Emergencies leave behind disruptions in learning, student well-being, and faculty workflows. A thoughtful transition requires intentional planning to restore continuity, rebuild community, and strengthen preparedness for future disruptions. Faculty play a central role in guiding students through this recovery, ensuring that the post-crisis period does not widen achievement gaps or erode academic confidence.

Debrief with Students

The first step in transition is reflection. Faculty should invite students to share their experiences of the emergency phase.

- **Feedback Collection**: Use surveys, focus groups, or informal discussions to ask what instructional strategies were effective and what challenges they faced.
- **Transparency**: Communicate to students how their feedback will inform future teaching practices.
- **Acknowledgment**: Recognize the resilience students demonstrated, validating their contributions to maintaining academic continuity.
  This process gives students a sense of agency and signals that their voices matter in shaping recovery.

Bridge Learning Gaps

Emergencies often interrupt progress toward course outcomes. Faculty must identify and close these gaps to ensure students do not advance with weakened foundations.

- **Diagnostic Assessments**: Short quizzes or concept checks can reveal areas where mastery was disrupted.
- **Supplemental Modules**: Provide optional review sessions, online tutorials, or remedial assignments for skills students may have missed.
- **Targeted Interventions**: Collaborate with tutoring centers, writing labs, or peer mentors to support students individually.
  Closing these gaps ensures continuity of learning across semesters and programs, preventing long-term academic setbacks.

Rebuild Community

Crises can fracture the sense of academic and social belonging that supports student success. Faculty should actively work to re-establish community in the classroom.

- **Discussion and Reflection Activities**: Begin with structured conversations that allow students to process experiences together.
- **Collaborative Projects**: Design assignments that require teamwork, helping students reconnect academically and socially.
- **Classroom Rituals**: Reinstate familiar routines—such as group check-ins, peer feedback sessions, or weekly summaries—that reinforce stability.
  Restoring community strengthens engagement, motivation, and the peer networks students rely on for resilience.

Document Lessons Learned

Each crisis provides insight into institutional and instructional preparedness. Faculty should capture these lessons to build long-term resilience.

- **Personal Documentation**: Keep records of effective tools, assignments, and communication strategies used during the disruption.
- **Departmental Sharing**: Contribute to collective repositories or workshops where faculty share what worked across courses.
- **Institutional Preparedness**: Collaborate with administrators to create or refine policies for emergency teaching, ensuring smoother pivots in the future.
  Documenting lessons ensures that the struggles of one crisis become the foundation of readiness for the next.

Key Takeaway

Transitioning back to normal operations after a crisis requires more than resuming face-to-face instruction. Faculty must debrief with students, repair learning gaps, rebuild classroom community, and document lessons learned to strengthen future preparedness. By approaching post-crisis recovery with the same intentionality as crisis response, faculty safeguard not only academic continuity but also the resilience of the higher education community.

Community Engagement and Experiential Learning Integration

Higher education increasingly emphasizes the importance of connecting academic learning with real-world applications. Community engagement and experiential learning serve as powerful strategies for bridging classroom content with lived experiences, preparing students to become professionals and citizens who can apply their knowledge in meaningful contexts. These approaches not only deepen student learning but also foster mutually beneficial relationships between institutions and the communities they serve. To maximize impact, faculty must design, manage, and assess these experiences with intentionality, ensuring that academic objectives and community needs are aligned.

Service-Learning Course Design and Management

Service-learning differs from simple volunteerism or internships because it is explicitly tied to curricular goals and structured to achieve both academic and community outcomes. Designing such courses requires balancing rigor, sustainability, and reciprocity.

- **Integration with Curriculum**
  Service-learning projects should be embedded into the academic structure of the course, not treated as extracurricular activities. Faculty should map service activities directly onto course content, ensuring students see the relevance. For example:
    - Public health students might work with local clinics to conduct needs assessments, directly applying epidemiological methods.
    - Engineering students could collaborate with municipal agencies to design low-cost water filtration systems, linking classroom design principles to community problem-solving.
    - Business students might help nonprofit organizations with strategic planning, applying theories of management, finance, and marketing.

This intentional integration ensures service enhances—not distracts from—the academic mission of the course.

- **Clear Learning Outcomes**
Faculty must articulate what students are expected to learn beyond the technical performance of tasks. Outcomes should emphasize transferable skills, such as:
    - **Problem-Solving**: Applying disciplinary methods to ambiguous, real-world contexts.
    - **Leadership**: Taking initiative in organizing projects and motivating peers.
    - **Communication**: Translating disciplinary knowledge into language accessible to community partners.
    - **Civic Responsibility**: Understanding how professional expertise intersects with broader social needs.

    Clearly stated outcomes allow both faculty and students to measure growth in ways that extend beyond traditional academic benchmarks.

- **Structured Reflection**
Reflection is the link between theory and practice. Without it, students may fail to connect their service activities to disciplinary learning. Faculty should structure reflection into the course through:
    - **Journals** that prompt students to analyze experiences in light of course theories.
    - **Discussion Boards or Seminars** where students compare experiences and identify common themes.
    - **Debrief Sessions** that encourage students to reflect critically on the successes and challenges of their community engagement.

    Reflection should move beyond description to interpretation, synthesis, and critical evaluation, enabling deeper learning.

- **Sustainability**
Faculty must design service-learning components that are sustainable for both students and community partners:
    - Avoid projects that require more resources than students or partners can realistically provide.
    - Ensure that community partners are not overburdened with supervision responsibilities.
    - Build courses that can be offered repeatedly, with each cohort of students contributing to ongoing initiatives rather than starting from scratch.

    Sustainable design fosters continuity, strengthens partnerships, and creates long-term impact.

Key Takeaway

Service-learning courses succeed when they are intentionally integrated into the curriculum, built around clear learning outcomes, supported by structured reflection, and designed for long-term sustainability. Faculty who invest in these practices create opportunities where academic rigor and community engagement reinforce one another, producing graduates who are both knowledgeable in their fields and prepared to serve society.

Community Partnership Development and Maintenance

Community engagement in higher education depends on strong, reciprocal partnerships. These relationships cannot be transactional or one-sided—effective partnerships are built on mutual trust, shared goals, and sustained collaboration. Faculty who invest in developing and maintaining community relationships not only create richer student learning opportunities but also contribute meaningfully to the capacity and resilience of local organizations.

Alignment of Goals

The foundation of any successful partnership is a clear match between academic and community objectives.

- **Complementary Missions**: Faculty should seek partners whose organizational goals align naturally with course learning outcomes. For example, a social work program may partner with a homeless shelter to connect theory of social services with hands-on practice.
- **Needs Assessment**: Before committing, faculty should consult with community leaders to understand pressing needs. This prevents mismatches where academic priorities overshadow real community concerns.
- **Win-Win Structure**: Projects should be designed so both students and community organizations benefit—students gain experiential learning, while organizations gain meaningful contributions to their mission.

Clear Expectations

Misunderstandings often arise when roles and responsibilities are not defined in advance.

- **Memoranda of Understanding (MOUs)**: Formal agreements outline responsibilities, deliverables, timelines, and communication protocols. These documents provide accountability while signaling professionalism.
- **Defined Student Roles**: Partners should understand what students can and cannot do. For example, students in a health sciences program may assist with community education campaigns but should not perform clinical work beyond their training.
- **Faculty Responsibilities**: Faculty must remain engaged, ensuring that students meet expectations and that community partners receive adequate support.

Ongoing Communication

Partnerships thrive on consistent dialogue rather than one-time agreements.

- **Regular Check-Ins**: Scheduled meetings throughout the semester allow for monitoring progress, resolving challenges, and making adjustments.
- **Feedback Loops**: Faculty should invite community partners to provide feedback on student performance, project impact, and partnership effectiveness.

- **Shared Reflection**: End-of-project debriefs help both faculty and community partners reflect on successes, challenges, and opportunities for future collaboration.

Long-Term Commitment

Trust and impact deepen over time, making sustained partnerships especially valuable.

- **Continuity Across Semesters**: Faculty should design projects that build from one cohort of students to the next, creating cumulative benefits for the community.
- **Institutionalization**: Embedding partnerships into departmental or institutional strategy ensures continuity beyond the involvement of individual faculty members.
- **Scaling Impact**: Long-term partnerships open the door to more ambitious projects, including multi-year initiatives, research collaborations, or grant-funded programs that expand community benefits and enhance student learning.

Key Takeaway

Community partnerships are not short-term transactions but long-term collaborations built on alignment, clarity, communication, and commitment. When faculty nurture relationships with respect and reciprocity, they create opportunities that extend beyond the classroom, allowing students to apply their learning in authentic settings while strengthening the capacity of community organizations.

Risk Management for Off-Campus Learning Experiences

Experiential learning often requires students to engage in community settings, workplaces, or field environments that extend beyond the classroom. While these experiences offer rich educational value, they also introduce risks related to safety, liability, accessibility, and compliance. Faculty must proactively address these risks to protect students, uphold institutional responsibilities, and maintain the trust of community partners. Effective risk management balances opportunity with responsibility, ensuring that learning takes place in safe and supportive contexts.

Institutional Policies

Faculty must begin by understanding and complying with university policies governing off-campus learning.

- **Liability Waivers**: Many institutions require students to sign forms acknowledging risks and releasing the institution from certain liabilities. Faculty should coordinate with legal and risk management offices to use institution-approved documents.
- **Travel Policies**: If students are traveling to sites, whether locally or internationally, faculty must follow university travel procedures, including approval processes and emergency contact registration.

- **Insurance Coverage**: Confirm whether the institution provides insurance for students in community-based learning, and communicate clearly to students what coverage exists and what they are personally responsible for.
- **Compliance with Regulations**: Faculty must also remain aware of state or federal requirements related to internships, service learning, or workplace placements.

Site Vetting

Not every community site is appropriate for student involvement. Faculty are responsible for ensuring that placements meet minimum standards of safety and accessibility.

- **Safety Review**: Visit sites (or conduct virtual assessments) to evaluate physical safety, including facilities, equipment, and adherence to health standards.
- **Accessibility Considerations**: Ensure sites are compliant with ADA standards and can accommodate students with mobility or other needs.
- **Appropriateness of Activities**: Confirm that student tasks align with their training level and academic purpose. For example, nursing students may assist in patient education but should not perform unsupervised medical procedures.
- **Partner Capacity**: Evaluate whether the community partner has the staff and infrastructure to support students effectively.

Emergency Planning

Emergencies can occur even in well-vetted environments. Faculty must prepare students with clear guidance on how to respond.

- **Protocols**: Provide students with written instructions on what to do in case of injury, illness, harassment, or legal incidents during off-campus work.
- **Emergency Contacts**: Collect up-to-date student emergency information and ensure students know how to contact faculty, supervisors, and institutional support services.
- **Training Sessions**: Before beginning off-campus work, hold an orientation covering topics such as personal safety, conflict de-escalation, and reporting procedures.
- **Institutional Resources**: Align plans with campus offices (e.g., campus police, health services, legal counsel) so students know what support is available.

Faculty Oversight

Even though learning occurs outside the classroom, faculty remain ultimately responsible for student experiences.

- **Monitoring**: Check in regularly with both students and community partners to confirm progress and address concerns.
- **Site Visits**: When feasible, conduct periodic site visits to observe student engagement and reinforce alignment with course outcomes.

- **Documentation**: Require students to keep logs or journals documenting activities, challenges, and reflections. This not only supports assessment but also provides a record in case issues arise.
- **Responsibility for Alignment**: Ensure that off-campus experiences consistently advance learning outcomes, rather than devolving into unpaid labor disconnected from academic objectives.

Key Takeaway

Risk management in community-based learning is not about eliminating all risk but about ensuring preparedness, oversight, and compliance. By adhering to institutional policies, carefully vetting sites, preparing students for emergencies, and maintaining oversight, faculty safeguard students while maximizing the benefits of off-campus experiential education. Thoughtful risk management builds trust with students, families, institutions, and community partners, allowing experiential learning to flourish responsibly.

Assessment of Experiential Learning Outcomes

Assessing experiential learning requires approaches that go beyond conventional exams and essays. Because these experiences often take place in real-world contexts with variable conditions, the outcomes are multidimensional: students gain disciplinary knowledge, professional competencies, civic awareness, and personal growth. Effective assessment must therefore capture both the tangible outputs of student work and the intangible development of skills and attitudes. Faculty should employ multiple measures to evaluate how well students integrate theory with practice, contribute to community needs, and develop transferable competencies.

Performance-Based Assessment

Experiential learning is best evaluated through evidence of what students produce or accomplish in collaboration with community partners.

- **Projects and Deliverables**: Assess written reports, strategic plans, lesson plans, prototypes, or campaigns that students develop for community organizations.
- **Presentations**: Require students to present their findings or solutions to both academic and community audiences, which tests their ability to adapt communication across contexts.
- **Quality Criteria**: Evaluation should include accuracy, relevance, creativity, feasibility, and responsiveness to community partner needs.
This type of assessment mirrors professional evaluation, preparing students for expectations in the workplace.

Reflective Assignments

Because experiential learning emphasizes meaning-making, structured reflection is essential to assess how students connect practice with theory.

- **Journals**: Encourage ongoing reflection on challenges, successes, and insights during the experience.
- **Portfolios**: Collect artifacts such as project drafts, feedback from partners, and reflective essays to demonstrate both process and product.
- **Capstone Essays**: Ask students to synthesize their experience with academic concepts, identifying lessons learned and implications for future practice.
  Reflection assignments provide evidence of critical thinking, self-awareness, and intellectual integration—outcomes not visible in deliverables alone.

Community Feedback

Community partners serve as authentic evaluators of student contributions. Their perspectives provide a reality check that academic assessments alone cannot capture.

- **Partner Evaluations**: Structured forms or surveys allow partners to rate student professionalism, reliability, and quality of contributions.
- **Qualitative Feedback**: Open-ended comments provide rich insights into how students impacted the organization or community.
- **Reciprocal Dialogue**: Faculty should also share assessment results with partners, reinforcing the reciprocal nature of the relationship.
  Community feedback adds external validation to student work, enhancing accountability and authenticity.

Skill Development Measures

Experiential learning cultivates competencies that extend beyond disciplinary knowledge. Faculty should design rubrics that capture growth in:

- **Teamwork**: Ability to collaborate, resolve conflicts, and distribute responsibilities effectively.
- **Leadership**: Initiative-taking, decision-making, and the ability to guide group efforts.
- **Cultural Awareness**: Sensitivity to diverse perspectives, respect for community values, and ability to adapt behavior in multicultural settings.
- **Professional Communication**: Clarity, appropriateness of tone, and effectiveness in conveying information to varied audiences.
- **Problem-Solving**: Innovation, adaptability, and the ability to manage ambiguity in real-world contexts.
  Assessment of these skills often requires observation, peer evaluations, and rubrics that highlight behaviors as well as outcomes.

Multi-Modal Assessment Strategy

No single assessment captures the richness of experiential learning. Faculty should combine methods:

- A performance-based project to demonstrate applied knowledge.

- A reflective component to show meaning-making and integration.
- Community partner feedback to validate authenticity.
- Skill development rubrics to track professional and civic growth.
Together, the combination of methods provide a complete picture of student achievement.

Key Takeaway

Assessment of experiential learning must measure more than academic content—it must capture applied skills, reflective integration, professional growth, and community impact. By combining performance-based evaluations, reflective assignments, community partner input, and skill rubrics, faculty create a balanced and authentic assessment framework that validates the transformative power of experiential learning.

Balancing Academic Objectives with Community Needs

One of the greatest challenges in community-engaged learning is balancing the academic priorities of the course with the practical needs of community partners. Faculty must ensure that students meet disciplinary learning outcomes while also making meaningful contributions to the organizations and communities they serve. If either side is neglected, the partnership risks becoming exploitative, tokenistic, or unsustainable. Achieving balance requires negotiation, transparency, and a commitment to reciprocity.

Negotiated Project Scope

Effective projects begin with dialogue between faculty and community partners to clarify goals and establish realistic expectations.

- **Course Alignment**: Faculty should articulate the learning outcomes that students must achieve (e.g., applying research methods, practicing technical skills, or developing cultural competency).
- **Community Relevance**: Partners should identify pressing needs that align with those outcomes, such as creating marketing plans, analyzing survey data, or developing educational workshops.
- **Feasibility Check**: The scope should be achievable within the academic calendar, considering student skill levels, partner capacity, and available resources.
- **Iterative Adjustment**: Faculty should remain flexible, adapting project scope as the semester progresses and conditions evolve.

Avoiding Tokenism

Tokenistic engagement—where students perform symbolic acts of service without real impact—undermines both learning and community trust. Faculty can prevent this by:

- **Designing Substantive Contributions**: Ensure that projects address genuine community needs rather than serving as superficial exercises for students.

- **Respecting Community Expertise**: Recognize that community members bring valuable knowledge and should not be treated as passive recipients of student work.
- **Monitoring Quality**: Faculty must oversee student projects closely, ensuring that deliverables meet professional standards and do not burden partners with correcting incomplete or ineffective work.
- **Reflecting on Power Dynamics**: Encourage students to consider how privilege, institutional authority, or cultural assumptions may shape the engagement.

Mutual Benefit Framework

The most sustainable community-engaged projects are those that create reciprocal value for both students and partners.

- **Learning for Students**: Students gain practical experience, develop transferable skills, and connect theory to real-world practice.
- **Benefits for Communities**: Organizations receive useful deliverables, expanded capacity, or fresh perspectives that advance their mission.
- **Knowledge Exchange**: Students and community members both contribute expertise, creating a two-way flow of learning rather than a one-sided transfer.
- **Institutional Trust-Building**: When partnerships consistently deliver mutual benefit, community organizations are more likely to engage in long-term collaborations, opening opportunities for future projects and research.

Key Takeaway

Balancing academic objectives with community needs requires careful negotiation, avoidance of tokenism, and commitment to reciprocity. Faculty must design projects that advance student learning while producing tangible, meaningful benefits for community partners. When mutual benefit is prioritized, both students and communities grow, and the relationship between higher education and society is strengthened.

Cultural Competency for Community Engagement

Community engagement is not only about applying academic knowledge in real-world contexts; it is also about doing so with respect, humility, and awareness of cultural differences. Students and faculty often enter communities whose cultural, social, or economic realities differ significantly from their own. Without preparation, this can lead to misunderstandings, unintentional harm, or reinforcement of stereotypes. Cultural competency equips students to approach engagement ethically, value community voices, and build the important skills needed to work across differences in their professional and civic lives.

Pre-Engagement Training

Preparation before entering a community is critical. Faculty should incorporate structured training that emphasizes cultural humility and effective communication.

- **Workshops on Cultural Humility**: Move beyond cultural awareness to humility—the recognition that one can never fully master another culture, but can remain open, respectful, and willing to learn.
- **Communication Skills**: Train students in active listening, respectful questioning, and avoiding jargon or disciplinary language that may alienate community members.
- **Ethical Engagement**: Emphasize respect for community knowledge, consent in participation, and sensitivity to historical or social contexts that may affect relationships.
- **Scenario Practice**: Use role-playing or case studies to prepare students for navigating cultural misunderstandings before they occur in real settings.

Critical Reflection

Cultural competency develops not only through exposure but also through self-examination. Faculty should integrate opportunities and interactions for students to reflect critically on their assumptions.

- **Journals and Reflection Papers**: Prompt students to examine how their cultural identities shape their perceptions of the community.
- **Bias Awareness**: Encourage students to identify implicit biases and consider how these may influence their behavior or interpretations.
- **Dialogue Spaces**: Facilitate structured class discussions where students can share observations and respectfully challenge one another's perspectives.
- **Growth Mindset**: Reinforce that cultural competency is a lifelong process, not a skill mastered in a single course.

Inclusive Practices

For engagement to be meaningful, projects must respect and reflect the voices of the communities involved.

- **Community-Led Priorities**: Ensure projects are shaped by what the community identifies as needs, not by assumptions from faculty or students.
- **Representation**: Include community members in planning, decision-making, and evaluation processes whenever possible.
- **Respect for Identity**: Acknowledge and affirm the cultural, linguistic, religious, and socioeconomic diversity of community participants.
- **Avoiding Deficit Framing**: Present communities not as "problems to be solved" but as partners with valuable expertise and strengths.

Key Takeaway

Cultural competency is essential to ethical and effective community engagement. By preparing students with pre-engagement training, fostering critical self-reflection, and embedding inclusive practices into projects, faculty ensure that partnerships are built on respect and reciprocity. This not only enhances student learning but also strengthens trust between institutions and the communities they serve.

Legal and Ethical Considerations for Community Partnerships

While community engagement provides invaluable opportunities for experiential learning, it also introduces legal and ethical responsibilities that extend beyond classroom pedagogy. Faculty are accountable for ensuring that community-based projects operate within the bounds of institutional policies, relevant laws, and professional codes of ethics. Failure to address these considerations risks damaging community trust, exposing institutions to liability, and undermining the integrity of the student experience.

Legal Agreements

Formal agreements establish clear boundaries and expectations between institutions and community partners.

- **Memoranda of Understanding (MOUs)**: These documents define roles, responsibilities, and mutual obligations. For example, they may specify who supervises students on-site, what deliverables are expected, and who is responsible for providing necessary resources.
- **Contracts**: In cases where financial resources, research funding, or proprietary tools are involved, contracts may be required to address financial obligations, timelines, and deliverable ownership.
- **Liability Provisions**: Agreements should clarify responsibility in the event of accidents, damages, or misconduct. Institutions often require students to sign waivers, but faculty must ensure compliance with university risk management offices.
- **Intellectual Property (IP)**: Projects that generate research findings, creative works, or technical innovations should specify who owns the resulting IP. For example, if engineering students design a prototype for a nonprofit, ownership must be addressed before the project begins.

Ethical Standards

Ethical engagement demands respect for community members and avoidance of exploitation.

- **Non-Exploitation Principle**: Faculty should guard against projects where students benefit academically while the community receives little of value.
- **Respect for Dignity**: Ensure projects do not reinforce stereotypes, stigmatize vulnerable populations, or treat community members merely as "subjects" of study.
- **Transparency**: Be clear with communities about what students can realistically achieve within the scope of a semester-long project. Overpromising creates disappointment and erodes trust.
- **Reciprocity**: Build projects around genuine collaboration, ensuring that communities help shape goals and benefit tangibly from the partnership.

Privacy Concerns

Community-based projects often involve sensitive information, particularly in sectors like healthcare, education, or social services.

- **Data Protection**: Students handling personal or organizational data must be trained in confidentiality practices, including secure storage and restricted access.
- **FERPA and HIPAA Compliance**: In U.S. contexts, student records are protected by the Family Educational Rights and Privacy Act (FERPA), while patient information is protected by the Health Insurance Portability and Accountability Act (HIPAA). Faculty must ensure students understand and comply with these regulations [117].
- **Informed Consent**: If students gather data (e.g., interviews, surveys), they must obtain consent from participants, ensuring that individuals understand the purpose, use, and limits of their involvement.
- **Institutional Review Board (IRB)**: For projects involving research with human subjects, faculty must confirm whether IRB approval is required [118]. Even community projects framed as "classwork" may need oversight if data is collected systematically for publication or presentation.

Key Takeaway

Community engagement is not just an instructional practice—it carries legal and ethical obligations that safeguard students, institutions, and community partners. Faculty must secure clear agreements, uphold ethical standards, and protect privacy throughout the process. When managed responsibly, these safeguards not only prevent risk but also strengthen trust, ensuring partnerships are sustainable, equitable, and respectful.

Reflection and Integration Strategies for Experiential Learning

Experiential learning extends beyond simply participating in community-based or applied projects. The true educational value lies in how students interpret their experiences, connect them to academic theory, and apply the lessons to their personal and professional growth. Without structured opportunities for reflection and integration, students risk viewing their engagement as isolated activities rather than as part of a broader educational journey. Faculty must therefore design intentional processes that guide students in analyzing, synthesizing, and internalizing their learning.

Guided Reflection

Structured reflection helps students critically examine their experiences and link them directly to course concepts.

- **Reflective Journals**: Students can document weekly entries describing what they did, what they learned, and how it connects to course objectives. Prompts such as *"How did today's experience challenge or confirm the theory we studied in class?"* encourage depth of thought.
- **Discussion Prompts**: Class discussions or online forums allow students to compare experiences, exchange insights, and identify common themes.
- **Presentations**: Oral or multimedia presentations provide students with the chance to articulate their learning publicly, reinforcing communication skills while deepening their understanding.

Faculty should evaluate reflection not on personal opinion but on evidence of critical thinking, connection to course materials, and growth over time.

Integration into Coursework

Reflection becomes most powerful when woven into the curriculum, not treated as an afterthought.

- **Debrief Sessions**: Regular in-class or online debriefs allow faculty to highlight how student experiences align with disciplinary theories or professional practices.
- **Case Studies**: Transform student experiences into case studies that can be analyzed collectively, helping the class see how individual experiences reveal larger patterns or issues.
- **Peer Sharing Activities**: Structured peer feedback sessions allow students to learn from each other's diverse community engagements, broadening their perspectives.
  This integration ensures that experiential learning is fully embedded within the academic framework of the course.

Long-Term Reflection

The impact of experiential learning often extends beyond a single semester. Faculty can encourage students to carry lessons forward through:

- **Capstone Essays or Portfolios**: Students synthesize experiences from multiple semesters, drawing connections between academic training, community engagement, and personal growth.
- **Professional Identity Development**: Assignments can prompt students to consider how their engagement shapes their sense of professional responsibility, leadership, or civic identity.
- **Future Applications**: Encourage students to articulate how they will apply lessons learned to future courses, careers, or community involvement.
  Long-term reflection transforms immediate experiences into enduring lessons that inform students' academic trajectories and life choices.

Key Takeaway

Experiential learning without reflection is incomplete. By embedding guided reflection, curricular integration, and long-term reflection opportunities, faculty ensure that students move beyond "doing" to understanding and applying. Structured reflection allows students to connect theory with practice, develop critical and civic awareness, and strengthen professional identity. When combined with thoughtful course design, ethical safeguards, and community reciprocity, reflection transforms experiential learning into a powerful driver of personal and societal impact.

Conclusion: Shaping Independent Thinkers for the Future

The ultimate goal of higher education is for intellectual empowerment, stepping beyond simple knowledge transfer. By fostering student-driven learning and autonomy, professors help students transition from passive learners to critical thinkers, problem-solvers, and independent scholars.

Through structured choice, reflective practice, inquiry-based learning, and collaborative engagement, faculty can create transformative learning experiences that shape self-directed, motivated, and lifelong learners—ready to excel in academia, their careers, and beyond.

Elevating Teaching Through Strategic Instruction

Effective teaching is both an art and a science—requiring intentional planning, adaptability, and a comprehensive understanding of how students learn. The strategies outlined in this chapter emphasize the importance of fostering student engagement through active learning, leveraging technology, and creating an inclusive learning environment that accommodates diverse learners. By refining lecture delivery, implementing Socratic questioning, and embracing hybrid and online teaching methodologies, faculty can create learning spaces that are interactive, thought-provoking, and impactful.

As higher education continues to evolve, professors must remain committed to lifelong learning, continuously refining their teaching methods to align with changing student needs and technological advancements. The goal is not merely to transfer knowledge but to cultivate an environment where students develop critical thinking skills, intellectual curiosity, and the ability to apply their learning beyond the classroom. By mastering and integrating these effective teaching strategies, faculty contribute to a richer, more transformative educational experience—preparing students for academic, professional, and lifelong success.

Chapter 5: Classroom Management and Student Engagement

An effective college classroom is more than just a place for delivering content—it is an adaptive learning environment where students actively engage with course materials, collaborate with peers, and cultivate critical thinking skills. Classroom management and student engagement are integral to fostering a learning space that is respectful, inclusive, and intellectually stimulating. Professors must balance structure with flexibility, ensuring that students feel both supported and challenged in their academic journey.

This chapter explores key strategies for managing discussions, handling conflicts, encouraging participation, and integrating technology to enhance engagement. Professors must navigate diverse student needs, address classroom anxiety, and create equitable opportunities for learning. By establishing clear expectations, fostering respectful discourse, and leveraging innovative teaching methods, faculty can cultivate a classroom culture that promotes academic curiosity and lifelong learning.

Figure 5.1. Effective Classroom Management [219].

Creating a Positive and Inclusive Classroom Culture

A positive and inclusive classroom culture is the foundation of an effective learning environment—one where students feel valued, included, and empowered to participate fully. In higher education, where classrooms are increasingly diverse in terms of backgrounds, learning styles, and experiences, it is imperative that professors foster equity, belonging, and intellectual engagement for all students.

Building an inclusive classroom culture requires deliberate action in course design, instructional strategies, and interpersonal interactions. Faculty must create a space where all students feel safe to express their ideas, engage with challenging material, and contribute meaningfully to academic discourse. A culture of respect and belonging enhances student motivation, participation, and overall academic success, while also preparing learners for collaboration in an increasingly global and diverse workforce [118].

This section explores key strategies for fostering a classroom environment that is welcoming, intellectually stimulating, and inclusive, ensuring all learners—regardless of background, ability, or identity—can thrive.

1. The Pillars of a Positive and Inclusive Classroom

A successful classroom culture is built on three core foundational pillars:

Psychological Safety: Students feel comfortable taking intellectual risks without fear of embarrassment or discrimination.
Mutual Respect: Both students and faculty uphold a culture of active listening, open dialogue, and professional conduct.
Equitable Access and Participation: Learning opportunities, resources, and engagement strategies are designed to include all students, ensuring that diverse voices are heard.

A professor's role extends beyond content delivery—it includes shaping the social and intellectual climate of the classroom, encouraging curiosity, respectful discourse, and active learning.

2. Establishing a Welcoming and Inclusive Environment

A. Setting the Tone on Day One

First impressions set the stage for the entire course experience. Faculty should:
Introduce themselves warmly and invite student introductions.
Establish clear expectations for communication, collaboration, and participation.
Acknowledge the diversity in the classroom and emphasize inclusion as a shared responsibility.
Encourage a "growth mindset"—where mistakes are seen as part of learning, and all students are capable of success.

Example: Instead of a generic syllabus review, start with an interactive discussion:

- Ask students about their learning goals.
- Invite them to share what helps them feel engaged in a course.
- Incorporate an icebreaker activity that fosters connection.

By intentionally shaping an inviting classroom culture from the beginning, professors create a sense of community that enhances student engagement.

B. Establishing Clear and Inclusive Class Policies

Classroom policies should be transparent, fair, and accommodating of diverse needs. Faculty can promote inclusivity by:

Using clear and welcoming language in the syllabus (e.g., including a statement on diversity and inclusion).
Providing multiple ways to participate (verbal, written, online discussions, peer collaboration).
Offering flexibility in deadlines or assessment methods for students with differing needs.
Encouraging a "zero-tolerance policy" for discrimination, bias, or exclusionary behavior.

Example: Inclusive Syllabus Statement
"This course is committed to creating an inclusive environment where all students—regardless of

race, gender identity, disability status, or cultural background—feel respected and supported. If you encounter barriers to your learning, please reach out so we can discuss possible solutions."

This explicit commitment helps signal to students that their well-being and success matter.

3. Promoting Equitable Participation and Engagement

An inclusive classroom ensures that all students have a voice—not just the most vocal or confident ones.

A. Encouraging Diverse Participation

Use a variety of discussion formats (small groups, think-pair-share, online discussion boards).
Rotate speaking opportunities to prevent a few students from dominating conversations.
Use cold-calling strategically—frame questions as an invitation rather than a demand.
Allow students to submit questions or comments anonymously via digital tools.

Example: Instead of an open-ended "Does anyone have questions?" (which often results in silence), ask:

- *"What is one thing from today's lecture that challenged your thinking?"*
- *"Can someone provide a counterargument to the perspective we just discussed?"*

This method invites deeper thinking and encourages all students to contribute.

B. Culturally Responsive Teaching and Representation

Students engage more when they see themselves reflected in course content. Faculty can:

Use diverse examples, case studies, and scholarly perspectives in the curriculum.
Acknowledge multiple worldviews and challenge Eurocentric or dominant narratives.
Recognize and honor cultural differences in communication styles and learning preferences.
Invite guest speakers from underrepresented groups to provide broader perspectives.

Example: In a business ethics class, instead of only analyzing Western corporations, incorporate case studies from companies in Africa, Asia, and Latin America to demonstrate global perspectives.

4. Addressing Classroom Conflicts and Sensitive Topics

Diverse classrooms sometimes lead to differing opinions, misunderstandings, or tensions—especially when discussing controversial topics. Faculty must be prepared to facilitate difficult conversations with respect and fairness.

A. Strategies for Managing Sensitive Discussions

Set ground rules for discourse (e.g., "Critique ideas, not people").
Acknowledge multiple perspectives without reinforcing harmful rhetoric.
Guide discussions with open-ended questions rather than leading with personal opinions.
Encourage students to "pause and reflect" before responding impulsively.

Example: If a discussion on social justice policies becomes tense, a professor could pause the debate and ask:

"How can we frame this discussion in a way that prioritizes understanding rather than defensiveness?"

By modeling calm, balanced dialogue, professors help students develop critical thinking and respectful debate skills.

5. Supporting Diverse Learning Needs and Accessibility

To ensure all students can fully engage, faculty must consider neurodiverse learners, students with disabilities, and those facing external challenges (e.g., financial insecurity, caregiving responsibilities).

A. Strategies for Accessibility and Inclusion

- Offer lecture recordings or transcripts for students who may need review time.
- Provide alternative assessment formats (e.g., written papers instead of oral exams for students with speech anxiety) [119].
- Use Universal Design for Learning (UDL) to deliver multiple ways for students to engage with, and demonstrate knowledge [119].
- Collaborate with disability services to accommodate students' needs [119].

Example: Instead of requiring all students to give an in-class presentation, offer a choice between presenting live, recording a video, or submitting a detailed written analysis [119].

Small adjustments enhance equity and provide all students with a fair opportunity to succeed.

6. Encouraging a Growth Mindset and Sense of Belonging

A growth mindset—the belief intelligence, skills and abilities are developed through effort—improves student confidence and resilience [120]. Faculty can:

- Praise effort and progress, not just outcomes (e.g., "I can see your analytical thinking developing.").
- Normalize failure as part of learning—share examples of historical figures or personal academic struggles.
- Use formative assessments that provide feedback without penalizing mistakes.
- Encourage peer mentorship and study groups to reinforce a sense of belonging.

Example: If a student struggles with an assignment, rather than simply giving a low grade, provide constructive feedback and offer a revision opportunity:

- *"Your argument is strong, but could benefit from clearer evidence. Would you like to revise this with my feedback?"*

This promotes growth rather than discouragement, reinforcing that learning is a process.

Conclusion: Cultivating a Classroom Where All Students Thrive

Creating a positive and inclusive classroom culture requires intentionality, empathy, and adaptability. Professors play a pivotal role in fostering environments where students feel safe, valued, and motivated to learn.

By implementing equitable participation strategies, fostering open dialogue, integrating diverse perspectives, and supporting different learning needs, faculty can build transformative learning spaces, preparing students for academic success and for thoughtful, engaged citizenship in a diverse world.

Ultimately, inclusive classrooms are not just about policies—they are about fostering a culture of mutual respect, belonging, and intellectual empowerment.

Managing Discussions and Handling Difficult Topics

Classroom discussions are a cornerstone of higher education, fostering critical thinking, student engagement, and intellectual exploration. However, effectively managing discussions—particularly those involving controversial or sensitive topics—requires skillful facilitation, thoughtful preparation, and the ability to navigate diverse perspectives with respect and fairness.

Professors must create an environment where students feel empowered to express their ideas, engage in meaningful dialogue, and challenge assumptions without fear of judgment or hostility. At the same time, faculty must set boundaries, maintain academic rigor, and intervene when discussions become unproductive or disruptive.

This section explores strategies for managing discussions effectively, techniques for handling difficult topics, and approaches for fostering a classroom culture of respectful and open dialogue.

1. The Role of Classroom Discussions in Higher Education

A. Why Discussions Matter

Encourage Active Learning: Students interact more deeply with material when discussing, debating, and applying concepts.
Develop Critical Thinking: Exposure to multiple viewpoints sharpens students' analytical and reasoning skills.
Foster Civil Discourse: Learning to discuss controversial topics respectfully is an essential academic and professional skill.
Promote Diversity of Thought: Inclusive discussions challenge biases and broaden perspectives.

Well-managed discussions move beyond opinion-sharing—they cultivate analytical depth, evidence-based reasoning, and respectful engagement with complex ideas [121].

B. Common Challenges in Classroom Discussions

Dominant Voices vs. Silent Participants: Some students may monopolize discussions, while others hesitate to contribute.
Emotional or Heated Exchanges: Sensitive topics may provoke defensiveness, frustration, or

conflict.

Lack of Depth or Critical Engagement: Discussions may remain surface-level without proper scaffolding.

Disruptions or Off-Topic Tangents: Unstructured discussions can lose focus and academic value.

Professors must anticipate these challenges and develop strategies to steer discussions productively while maintaining a balanced and inclusive atmosphere.

2. Preparing for Successful Discussions

Effective discussions begin before class even starts. Professors must plan how to frame the conversation, establish expectations, and structure student participation.

A. Setting Ground Rules for Productive Discourse

Establishing clear guidelines at the start of the semester helps ensure respectful and structured discussions. Professors should:

Co-Create Discussion Norms with Students: Involve students in defining guidelines for respectful communication.

Emphasize Active Listening: Encourage students to listen to understand, not just to respond.

Clarify the Importance of Evidence-Based Arguments: Require students to support claims with logic, data, or scholarly sources.

Encourage Intellectual Humility: Normalize the idea that changing one's perspective based on new information is a strength, not a weakness.

Define the Role of the Instructor: Professors should facilitate, not dominate discussions—ensuring fairness, maintaining focus, and stepping in when needed.

Example Ground Rules:

- Engage with curiosity, not confrontation.
- Challenge ideas, not people.
- Use "I" statements to express personal perspectives.
- Support claims with evidence whenever possible.
- Allow space for all voices, not just the most vocal ones.

Making these guidelines explicit and visible (e.g., in the syllabus or on the board) reinforces expectations and minimizes misunderstandings.

B. Structuring Discussions for Maximum Engagement

Discussions are most effective when they follow a structured format, balancing spontaneity with focused inquiry.

1. Start with a Provocative Question or Case Study
    - Frame the discussion around a dilemma, ethical question, or real-world scenario.

- Example: *"Should artificial intelligence be used to replace human decision-making in criminal sentencing?"*

2. **Use a Structured Discussion Model**

    - Socratic Seminar: Students respond to open-ended, instructor-led questions, building on each other's ideas.

    - Debate Format: Assign students opposing perspectives, requiring evidence-based argumentation.

    - Think-Pair-Share: Students formulate individual thoughts, discussins with a partner, and then sharing with the class.

    - Fishbowl Discussion: A small group discusses a topic while others observe, then roles switch.

3. **Encourage Multimodal Participation**

    - Provide opportunities for written, verbal, and online participation (e.g., discussion boards, polls, or anonymous submissions).

    - Use live polling tools (Mentimeter, Padlet, Google Jamboard) to engage quieter students.

By designing discussions intentionally, faculty cultivate an environment where all individuals feel included and challenged.

3. Handling Difficult Topics with Confidence and Sensitivity

Difficult topics—such as race, gender, politics, ethics, and social justice—can ignite strong emotions and differing viewpoints. Professors must be prepared to navigate these discussions with fairness, balance, and sensitivity.

A. Strategies for Facilitating Sensitive Discussions

Acknowledge the Complexity of the Issue

- Set the expectation that there are no simple answers, and multiple perspectives exist.

- Example: *"This topic is complex, and reasonable people can disagree. Let's explore various viewpoints thoughtfully."*

Use Grounding Techniques to De-Escalate Tension

- If a discussion becomes heated, pause and have students write down their thoughts before continuing.

- Redirect with questions:

    - *"What evidence supports this viewpoint?"*

- *"What assumptions might be shaping our responses?"*

Encourage Self-Reflection and Civil Disagreement

- Teach students how to engage in disagreement without hostility.
- Example: *"Let's take a step back—can someone articulate the opposing argument fairly?"*

Monitor Nonverbal Cues and Emotional Responses

- If a student appears distressed, acknowledge emotions and provide an option to step out or process the discussion later.

Know When to Intervene

- If a comment is offensive or harmful, address it immediately but constructively:
  - *"I'd like to pause here. That statement may be interpreted differently by different people—let's examine why."*

By approaching difficult topics with thoughtfulness, structure, and respect, faculty model civil discourse and critical inquiry.

4. Navigating Common Discussion Challenges

Challenge	Solution
One or Two Students Dominate the Discussion	Politely invite others: *"I'd love to hear from someone who hasn't spoken yet."*
Students Hesitate to Speak	Use small-group discussions first to build confidence before opening to the class.
Discussion Becomes Too Heated	Pause, refocus, and encourage students to articulate opposing viewpoints respectfully.
Students Resort to Personal Attacks	Redirect: *"Let's focus on critiquing ideas, not individuals."*
Students Make Unsupported Claims	Encourage evidence-based reasoning: *"What source or experience informs that view?"*

Addressing challenges proactively and skillfully ensures discussions remain productive, respectful, and intellectually enriching.

5. Conclusion: Creating a Culture of Thoughtful Discourse

Discussions—when effectively structured and well-facilitated—are among the most powerful tools in higher education. They cultivate intellectual curiosity, strengthen critical thinking, and teach students the skills of civil debate and analysis.

By setting clear expectations, fostering respectful engagement, structuring discussions for inclusivity, and navigating difficult topics with care, professors create an academic environment where students feel confident exploring complex ideas.

Ultimately, the goal is not consensus but growth—helping students develop the ability to engage thoughtfully, challenge ideas critically, and contribute meaningfully to scholarly and societal conversations.

Conflict Resolution and Dealing with Disruptive Students

A well-managed classroom fosters engagement, respect, and intellectual curiosity, but even the most carefully structured learning environments can experience conflict and disruptive behavior. Whether it manifests as dominant voices overpowering discussions, passive disengagement, inappropriate remarks, or outright hostility, classroom disruptions can derail learning and create an uncomfortable environment for students and faculty alike.

Effective conflict resolution requires a proactive approach that establishes clear expectations, de-escalates tensions, and ensures that disruptions do not interfere with the integrity of the learning process. Faculty must navigate these challenges with fairness, professionalism, and emotional intelligence, balancing authority with empathy to maintain a positive, inclusive, and respectful classroom culture.

This section explores strategies for preventing, addressing, and resolving classroom conflicts, as well as approaches for handling disruptive student behavior with tact and authority.

1. Understanding Conflict and Disruptive Behavior in the Classroom

A. Common Sources of Conflict in Higher Education

Classroom conflicts can stem from a variety of sources, including:

 Differing Perspectives & Ideologies – Heated debates on controversial issues can escalate into personal conflicts.
 Group Dynamics & Power Struggles – Some students dominate discussions, while others feel marginalized.
 Miscommunication or Misinterpretation – Comments can be misunderstood, leading to unintended offense.
 Perceived Unfairness – Conflicts may arise over grading disputes, participation expectations, or faculty decisions.
 External Stressors – Personal, financial, or social stressors can manifest as behavioral disruptions in class.

Understanding why conflicts arise is essential for addressing them effectively and preventing future disruptions.

B. Types of Disruptive Student Behavior

Disruptive behaviors can range from minor distractions to serious classroom disturbances. These include:

Type of Disruption	Examples
Mild Disruptions	Whispering, texting, excessive side conversations, arriving late.
Moderate Disruptions	Dominating discussions, dismissive or sarcastic remarks, refusing to participate.
Severe Disruptions	Interrupting lectures, arguing aggressively, making offensive or inappropriate comments.
Critical Disruptions	Harassment, threats, or escalating behavior that compromises safety.

While mild disruptions can be managed with subtle redirection, moderate to severe conflicts require intervention to ensure a respectful and constructive learning environment.

2. Preventing Classroom Conflicts Through Proactive Management

Professors can prevent many conflicts before they arise by setting clear expectations, fostering mutual respect, and designing courses that minimize friction.

A. Establish Clear Expectations and Boundaries

Set Classroom Norms on Day One – Co-create guidelines for discussion, participation, and respectful conduct.
Define Consequences for Disruptions – Clearly outline in the syllabus how various levels of misconduct will be handled.
Address Expectations for Controversial Discussions – Encourage students to critique ideas, not individuals, and base arguments on evidence, not personal attacks.

Example Syllabus Statement:
"This class values diverse perspectives and rigorous debate. Disagreements should be articulated with respect, using logical reasoning rather than personal critique. Disruptions that hinder productive discussion will be addressed promptly."

B. Foster a Culture of Respect and Inclusion

Model Professionalism – Demonstrate active listening, open-mindedness, and respect in your interactions.
Ensure Equitable Participation – Rotate speaking opportunities so no single voice dominates.
Acknowledge Tension Without Escalation – If tension rises, pause the discussion, acknowledge different viewpoints, and redirect focus to constructive dialogue.

Example: If a student repeatedly interrupts others, instead of saying, *"You're dominating the conversation,"* reframe it as:
"Let's make sure everyone has an opportunity to contribute before we move forward."

A proactive approach to classroom management minimizes disruptions while creating an atmosphere where students feel safe to engage, disagree, and explore challenging ideas.

3. Addressing Disruptive Behavior in the Moment

When classroom conflicts or disruptions arise, faculty must respond swiftly and professionally, ensuring that interventions are measured, fair, and appropriate to the situation.

A. Using Non-Confrontational Redirection Techniques

Use Proximity & Nonverbal Cues – Move closer to disruptive students to signal awareness.
Pause & Ask Reflective Questions – Instead of reacting emotionally, ask:

- *"What do you think the impact of your comment is on this discussion?"*
- *"How does this perspective align with the course materials we've explored?"*
Restate Classroom Norms as a Gentle Reminder –
- *"Remember, our goal is to engage in productive discussion where all voices are heard."*

These techniques allow professors to maintain authority without escalating tensions.

B. Direct Intervention for More Serious Disruptions

For more persistent or confrontational behaviors, faculty should:

Remain Calm and Neutral – Avoid reacting with frustration; instead, address the issue firmly but professionally.
Privately Address the Student When Possible – Confronting a student publicly may escalate tensions; if feasible, request to speak after class.
Use "I" Statements to De-Escalate –

- Instead of *"You're being disruptive,"* say, *"I want to ensure that our classroom remains a space where everyone can contribute productively."*
Set Clear Consequences – If disruptions persist, outline next steps (e.g., a formal warning, a meeting with administration).

Example: If a student challenges the instructor aggressively, a measured response could be:
"I appreciate that you have strong opinions on this topic, and I want to make sure we discuss them in a way that benefits the entire class. Let's talk after class about how to approach this constructively."

Setting firm but respectful boundaries helps maintain control while reinforcing expectations.

4. Conflict Resolution: Restoring Classroom Harmony

When conflict arises—between students or between students and faculty—effective resolution requires a focus on dialogue, understanding, and accountability.

A. Mediation and Resolution Strategies

Encourage One-on-One Conversations – Have students meet outside of class to clarify misunderstandings.

Use Structured Mediation Techniques – If a conflict escalates, consider a mediated discussion where each party:

- Expresses their perspective.
- Listens actively without interrupting.
- Proposes possible resolutions.
  Refer to Institutional Support When Necessary – If conflicts involve harassment, discrimination, or threats, faculty should engage campus resources, such as:
- Student Affairs
- Office of Diversity & Inclusion
- Title IX or Conduct Offices

Example: In a case where two students engage in a heated argument, a professor could mediate by asking:
"Can each of you summarize the other's viewpoint before responding? Let's identify areas of agreement and disagreement."

This de-escalates tensions while promoting mutual understanding.

---

5. Handling Critical or Escalated Situations

In cases where a student becomes aggressive, threatening, or refuses to comply with classroom norms, immediate action may be required.

Do Not Engage in an Argument – Maintain a calm, authoritative tone and avoid escalating the confrontation.
Ask the Student to Leave if Necessary – If behavior disrupts the learning environment:

- *"I need to ask you to leave for today. We can discuss this further after class."*
  Involve Campus Security or Administration for Severe Threats – If a student's behavior is threatening or dangerous, follow institutional protocols.

Faculty should always document incidents, including steps taken, to ensure accountability and appropriate follow-up.

Conclusion: Cultivating a Respectful and Engaged Learning Environment

Effective conflict resolution and classroom management require a balance of proactive strategies, real-time interventions, and structured resolution techniques. By establishing clear expectations, fostering mutual respect, addressing disruptions with professionalism, and using mediation when necessary, professors can create a classroom climate where all students feel safe, valued, and engaged.

Ultimately, a well-managed classroom is not just about discipline—it is about creating an environment where intellectual challenge, productive debate, and respectful engagement flourish.

Encouraging Participation and Addressing Classroom Anxiety

Engaged participation is a cornerstone of impactful learning in higher education, fostering critical thinking, collaboration, and deeper comprehension. However, student participation is not always spontaneous—many learners experience classroom anxiety, fear of judgment, or hesitation to engage in discussions. Some may struggle with self-confidence, cultural barriers, learning differences, or past negative experiences in academic settings.

Professors must cultivate a learning environment where all students feel encouraged and empowered to contribute, ensuring that participation is inclusive, equitable, and meaningful. This requires strategic facilitation, structured opportunities for engagement, and proactive efforts to reduce anxiety that may hinder student involvement.

This section explores techniques for fostering participation, addressing classroom anxiety, and creating a culture of intellectual engagement that supports diverse learners.

1. The Importance of Participation in Higher Education

Participation is not just about speaking in class—it is about active engagement, intellectual curiosity, and student investment in learning. A participatory classroom benefits students by:

Enhancing comprehension – Actively engaging with course material deepens understanding and retention.
Developing critical thinking – Participation allows students to analyze, question, and challenge ideas.
Building communication skills – Expressing ideas verbally strengthens articulation, persuasion, and confidence.
Creating an inclusive learning community – A culture of participation fosters peer collaboration and knowledge exchange.

Yet, despite its benefits, participation does not come naturally to all students. Professors must cultivate an environment where individuals feel safe, supported, and motivated to engage.

2. Understanding Classroom Anxiety and Barriers to Participation

Classroom anxiety is a **significant obstacle to engagement**, often stemming from **psychological, social, or environmental factors** [122].

A. Common Causes of Participation Anxiety

Fear of Judgment or "Getting it Wrong" – Many students hesitate to speak due to fear of embarrassment, looking bad or making mistakes.
Social Anxiety or Introversion – Some students experience anxiety in public speaking or prefer to process information before responding.
Cultural and Language Barriers – Non-native speakers may worry about language proficiency or cultural differences in discussion norms.

Past Negative Experiences – Previous criticism, dismissiveness, or lack of encouragement can make students hesitant to engage.
Lack of Confidence in Knowledge – Some students may feel unprepared or underqualified to contribute.

Recognizing these barriers is the first step toward addressing participation challenges and fostering a more inclusive classroom culture.

3. Strategies for Encouraging Participation

Professors can increase student engagement by implementing structured, inclusive, and low-risk participation strategies that cater to different learning styles.

A. Establishing a Supportive Classroom Culture

Normalize Mistakes as Part of Learning – Frame participation as exploration, not performance.

- Example: *"We're here to experiment with ideas. Your contributions don't have to be perfect—just thoughtful."*
Acknowledge All Contributions Positively – Reinforce participation with affirmation and constructive feedback.
Emphasize a Growth Mindset – Encourage students to see challenges as learning opportunities rather than failures.
Use Inclusive Language – Avoid dismissive phrases like *"That's wrong"* and instead say:

- *"That's an interesting perspective. Let's explore it further."*

B. Providing Multiple Participation Pathways

Participation should not be limited to verbal discussion. Offering multiple ways to engage ensures that all students can contribute in a way that feels comfortable and meaningful.

Think-Pair-Share – Students reflect individually, work in pairs, then share insights with the full class.
Polls and Anonymous Responses – Tools like Mentimeter, Padlet, or Google Forms allow students to submit responses without fear of public scrutiny.
Small Group Discussions – Break students into smaller, lower-pressure groups before opening discussion to the full class.
Written Participation – Use discussion boards, reflection journals, or shared documents for text-based engagement.
Role-Based Participation – Assign specific roles (e.g., questioner, summarizer, devil's advocate) to give students a clear purpose in discussions.

Example: Instead of open-ended participation, a professor might say:
"In groups of three, discuss your responses to the case study. One person will summarize your group's key takeaways to the class."
This approach structures participation while minimizing individual anxiety.

C. Using Gentle Cold-Calling and Structured Turn-Taking

Some students will never voluntarily participate, but structured opportunities ensure that all voices are included.

Use Predictable, Non-Pressuring Cold-Calling – Instead of random cold-calling, give students time to prepare:

- Example: *"I'll ask a few people to share their thoughts. Take a moment to jot down a response."*
  Round-Robin Discussion – Have students contribute in sequence, ensuring everyone has a turn without pressure.
  Pass or Contribute Option – Allow students to say *"Pass for now"* if they are not ready to speak.
  Gradual Progression for Hesitant Students – Start with low-stakes participation (e.g., polls, written responses) before moving to verbal contributions.

4. Reducing Anxiety and Supporting Hesitant Students

A. Building Confidence Over Time

Start with Low-Stakes Participation – Use informal, ungraded participation activities before expecting full engagement.
Provide Advanced Notice for Discussion Topics – Let students prepare responses in advance to reduce pressure.
Validate Student Perspectives – Even if a response is partially incorrect, find something valuable:

- Example: *"That's an interesting approach. Can we build on that idea?"*

B. Accommodating Different Learning and Communication Styles

Allow Asynchronous Participation – Discussion boards, pre-recorded responses, or written reflections offer alternative engagement modes.
Pair Students with Trusted Peers – Partner hesitant students with a supportive classmate for peer discussions.
Encourage Private Office Hours for Concerns – Some students may need individual encouragement before feeling comfortable engaging in class.

C. Creating a Safe Space for Discussion

Reinforce That Learning is a Process, Not Perfection – Normalize incomplete ideas and evolving thoughts.
Intervene If Students Dismiss or Critique Peers Harshly – Encourage a supportive, constructive discussion tone.
Use Humor and Relatability to Lower Tension – A light, encouraging atmosphere reduces participation anxiety.

5. Addressing Persistent Non-Participation

If a student consistently avoids participation, professors should investigate possible causes and provide individualized support.

Check in Privately – Approach the student outside of class with curiosity, not criticism:

- Example: *"I've noticed you've been quiet in discussions. Is there anything I can do to make participation more comfortable for you?"*
  Offer Flexible Alternatives – Some students may need non-verbal participation options (e.g., written reflections, peer-led discussions).
  Encourage Gradual Involvement – Start with smaller contributions before expecting full engagement.

By recognizing that participation anxiety is real, professors can proactively support students without forcing them into discomfort.

6. Conclusion: Fostering a Culture of Engagement and Confidence

Encouraging participation is not about forcing students to speak—it's about creating conditions where they feel empowered to contribute. By normalizing mistakes, offering multiple participation formats, scaffolding engagement, and addressing anxiety with empathy, professors can transform hesitant learners into confident, engaged participants.

A classroom where all learners feel heard, respected, and supported in their contributions is one that fosters curiosity, deep learning, and intellectual growth—preparing students for success in academic and professional settings.

Using Technology for Student Engagement

Technology has transformed higher education, offering innovative ways to engage students, personalize learning, and create dynamic classroom experiences. However, simply integrating technology into a course is not enough—effective use of digital tools must be intentional, pedagogically sound, and aligned with learning objectives. Professors must strike a balance between technology usage to enhance engagement and ensuring it supports deep, meaningful learning rather than serving as a distraction.

When used strategically, technology can:
 Encourage active participation in both in-person and online settings.
 Foster collaboration and communication among students.
 Provide real-time feedback and adaptive learning opportunities.
 Enhance accessibility and accommodate diverse learning styles.
 Extend learning beyond the classroom through digital resources and interactive experiences.

This section explores effective strategies for using technology to engage students, best practices for implementation, and considerations for maintaining inclusivity and balance in digital learning environments.

1. The Role of Technology in Student Engagement

Technology enhances both synchronous and asynchronous learning by facilitating:

- Interactive discussions and real-time collaboration.
- Digital assessments and personalized feedback.
- Access to multimedia and real-world applications of course content.

By integrating digital tools purposefully, faculty can increase student motivation, improve participation, and create a more engaging and equitable learning environment.

2. Strategies for Enhancing Engagement with Technology

A. Interactive Learning and Real-Time Participation

Active learning techniques become more effective when paired with interactive technology. Digital tools can:
Encourage student participation through live polling, quizzes, and interactive presentations.
Facilitate real-time student feedback, allowing professors to adjust instruction dynamically.
Reduce participation anxiety, providing low-risk ways for students to engage.

Recommended Tools:

- Poll Everywhere, Mentimeter, Kahoot! – Conduct real-time polls, quizzes, and word clouds.
- Padlet, Miro, Jamboard – Enable collaborative brainstorming and visual idea mapping.
- Top Hat, Slido – Facilitate live student engagement during lectures.

Example: Instead of asking, *"Does everyone understand?"* (which often results in silence), a professor can use Poll Everywhere to anonymously check student comprehension with a quick quiz.

B. Digital Collaboration and Peer Engagement

Technology can facilitate peer-to-peer interaction, creating collaborative learning experiences even in large or asynchronous classes.

Use discussion boards and social annotation tools to encourage deep engagement with readings.
Incorporate collaborative documents for group projects and peer review activities.
Leverage video conferencing tools for virtual study groups and student-led discussions.

Recommended Tools:

- **Google Docs, Microsoft OneNote** – Support collaborative writing and peer feedback.
- **Hypothesis, Perusall** – Allow students to annotate readings together.

- **Zoom Breakout Rooms, Microsoft Teams** – Foster small-group discussions and virtual office hours.

Example: In an online literature course, students use Perusall to highlight and comment on passages, responding to classmates' interpretations before class discussion.

C. Gamification and Interactive Simulations

Game-based learning and simulations increase engagement by providing interactive, challenge-based learning experiences [123].

Gamify learning with point systems, leaderboards, or challenge-based assessments.
Use simulations to bring abstract concepts to life in science, business, and social sciences.
Incorporate scenario-based learning where learners apply theoretical knowledge in practical real-world contexts.

Recommended Tools:

- Kahoot!, Quizizz – Gamified quizzes that turn assessments into engaging challenges.
- H5P, ThingLink – Interactive multimedia content creation tools.
- Simulations (Harvard Business Publishing, Labster, PhET Interactive Simulations) – Subject-specific simulations for business, science, and engineering.

Example: In an economics class, students participate in a stock market simulation where they make real-time trading decisions based on global news.

D. Personalized Learning and Adaptive Technology

Technology allows for **personalized instruction**, adapting to each individual's pace and learning needs [124].

Offer self-paced modules with interactive content and guided practice.
Use AI-driven platforms, adjusting difficulty levels based on student performance.
Provide instant feedback on quizzes and assignments to reinforce learning.

Recommended Tools:

- **LMS Platforms (Canvas, Blackboard, Moodle)** – Deliver structured content with progress tracking.
- **EdX, Coursera for Campus** – Supplement courses with high-quality, self-paced learning materials.
- **Grammarly, Turnitin, ChatGPT** – AI-assisted tools for writing improvement and academic integrity.

Example: In a statistics class, students use an AI-powered learning platform that adjusts problem difficulty based on their previous quiz performance.

E. Virtual Reality (VR) and Augmented Reality (AR) for Immersive Learning

Emerging technologies like VR and AR create immersive experiences, allowing students to interact with complex concepts in a simulated environment [125].

Use virtual labs for hands-on scientific exploration without physical lab space.
Explore historical events through virtual field trips.
Integrate AR overlays to enhance real-world applications of learning.

Recommended Tools:

- **Google Expeditions VR, ClassVR** – Virtual field trips and immersive storytelling.
- **Labster** – Virtual labs for biology, chemistry, and physics.
- **Merge Cube, CoSpaces Edu** – Augmented reality for interactive learning.

Example: In a medical anatomy course, students use VR headsets to explore 3D human body models, interacting with organs in a fully immersive environment.

3. Best Practices for Using Technology in the Classroom

Align Technology with Learning Objectives – Ensure tools serve a clear pedagogical purpose.
Balance Technology and Traditional Teaching Methods – Avoid over-reliance on technical tools at the expense of critical discussion and human interaction.
Ensure Digital Accessibility – Provide alternatives for students with limited tech access, visual impairments, or learning disabilities.
Introduce Technology Gradually – Familiarize students with tools through guided demonstrations and small-scale implementation before full integration.
Collect Feedback on Tech Effectiveness – Regularly assess whether technology enhances or detracts from engagement and learning.

Example: Instead of fully replacing lectures with digital content, a professor might use an interactive quiz mid-lecture to reinforce key concepts while maintaining instructor presence.

4. Addressing Common Challenges with Classroom Technology

Challenge	Solution
Tech Disruptions & Glitches	Have a backup plan and alternative activities in case of failure.
Student Disengagement with Digital Tools	Ensure technology is interactive and not just passive consumption.

Challenge	Solution
Equity & Access Issues	Use low-bandwidth alternatives and ensure all learners have access to necessary devices.
Overuse Leading to Cognitive Overload	Implement technology in moderation to avoid overwhelming students.

By addressing these challenges proactively, professors ensure a smooth and effective integration of technology in learning.

5. Conclusion: Leveraging Technology for Meaningful Engagement

Technology is a powerful tool for enhancing student engagement, but its success depends on intentionality, balance, and accessibility. When used strategically, digital tools can:

- Make learning interactive and participatory.
- Support diverse learners through multimodal content.
- Extend learning beyond traditional classroom walls.

Ultimately, technology should not replace human connection in education—it should enhance it. Professors who thoughtfully integrate digital tools create a richer, more engaging, and inclusive learning experience, preparing students for an increasingly tech-driven world while preserving the critical elements of intellectual discourse, creativity, and inquiry.

Creating a Culture of Engagement and Respect

Classroom management and student engagement are not merely about maintaining order or increasing participation; they are about shaping a learning environment where individuals feel motivated, included, and intellectually empowered. A well-managed classroom fosters respect, collaboration, and critical inquiry, helping students develop both academically and professionally.

Effective classroom management requires proactive strategies, from setting clear expectations to addressing disruptive behavior with fairness and consistency. Student engagement, on the other hand, depends on creating opportunities for meaningful interaction, leveraging technology, and accommodating diverse learning needs. Professors who master these skills contribute to a vibrant academic culture where students are inspired to think deeply, engage actively, and take ownership of their learning.

By embracing these principles, faculty can transform their classrooms into spaces of exploration, dialogue, and academic excellence—preparing students not just for success in their coursework, but for lifelong intellectual growth and professional achievement.

Chapter 6: Assessment and Feedback

Assessment and feedback are critical components of effective teaching and learning. They serve as both a measure of student progress and a tool for continuous improvement, ensuring that students develop the important knowledge, skills, and critical thinking abilities required for academic and professional success.

This chapter explores the principles of designing meaningful assessments, aligning with learning objectives, differentiate between formative and summative evaluations, and provide fair and transparent grading criteria. This chapter also discusses the importance of timely and positive feedback, which not only enhances student learning but also fosters engagement, motivation, and self-regulation.

Figure 6.1. Assessment and Feedback Cycles [219].

Moreover, this chapter examines challenges such as academic integrity, plagiarism prevention, and alternative assessment strategies, including competency-based grading. By integrating these best practices, faculty can create an assessment framework that promotes fairness, inclusivity, and deep learning while maintaining academic rigor.

Designing Effective Assessments: Formative vs. Summative

Assessment is at the heart of effective pedagogy, serving as both a diagnostic instrument and a means of facilitating deeper learning. It shapes instructional strategies, drives student engagement, and provides critical insights into both individual and collective progress. However, not all assessments serve the same purpose, nor do they measure learning in the same way. In higher education, two dominant forms of assessment—formative and summative—play distinct yet interconnected roles in enhancing student outcomes.

While formative assessments focus on the process of learning, offering continuous feedback and opportunities for growth, summative assessments are more product-oriented, evaluating students' mastery at key checkpoints. An effective assessment strategy balances these two approaches, ensuring that learning is not only measured but also cultivated through intentional feedback loops and iterative improvements.

Formative Assessments: Fostering Growth Through Continuous Feedback

Defining Formative Assessment

Formative assessments refers are ongoing, diagnostic approaches designed to inform both instructors and students about progress toward learning objectives. Rather than serving as a final measure of achievement, formative assessments function as low-stakes checkpoints that help students develop competence over time while allowing instructors to tailor their teaching strategies.

The primary goal of a formative assessment is to identify strengths and weaknesses, adjust instruction dynamically, and promote a culture of reflective learning. This approach enables students to engage with their learning in a metacognitive way, meaning they are not just passive consumers of information but active participants in building their skills and knowledge.

Key Characteristics of Formative Assessments

1. **Continuous and Iterative:**
    - Formative assessments are not one-time events but occur throughout the learning process.
    - They allow students to refine their understanding incrementally rather than facing a high-stakes, pass-or-fail scenario at the end of a course.

2. **Low-Stakes and Developmental:**
    - Unlike summative assessments, formative assessments typically do not contribute heavily to final grades, reducing anxiety and encouraging experimentation.
    - They are designed to help students learn from mistakes without punitive consequences, making learning a safer and more exploratory process.

3. **Feedback-Rich:**
    - Formative assessments emphasize qualitative feedback over quantitative scoring, offering detailed insights into students' thought processes.
    - Effective feedback is specific, actionable, and timely, enabling students to make meaningful adjustments.

4. **Responsive to Individual Learning Needs:**
    - Formative assessments provide instructors with real-time data to adjust instruction, ensuring that misconceptions are addressed before they become entrenched.
    - They support differentiated instruction, where faculty can modify content delivery based on students' progress.

Examples of Formative Assessments in Higher Education

1. Interactive Quizzes and Polls:

- Short, non-graded quizzes or polling tools (e.g., Kahoot, Socrative, Google Forms) allow instructors to assess comprehension quickly.

2. Think-Pair-Share Activities:

- Students reflect individually first, then discuss their thoughts with a learning partner before sharing insights with the class. This helps reinforce learning through dialogue.

3. Reflective Writing and Journals:

- Encouraging students to document their learning process in journals fosters metacognition and deeper self-awareness.

4. Concept Mapping and Visual Representation:

- Asking students to create concept maps allows them to visually organize relationships between ideas, reinforcing critical thinking.

5. Peer Review and Collaborative Feedback:

- Structured peer assessments encourage individuals to engage with each other's work critically, honing both their evaluative and communicative skills.

6. Minute Papers and Exit Tickets:

- Short reflections at the end of a class session where students answer prompts like "What was the most important concept you learned today?"

By embedding formative assessments throughout a course, instructors create a culture of iterative learning, where students view assessments not as mere judgments of ability but as tools for intellectual refinement.

Summative Assessments: Measuring Achievement and Mastery

Defining Summative Assessment

While formative assessments are developmental, summative assessments serve an evaluative function—they measure student learning at the conclusion of an instructional period. Whether it is the end of a unit, semester, or degree program, summative assessments are designed to determine the extent that students have successfully met the designed learning objectives.

Summative assessments are often high-stakes and carry significant weight in grading. However, their purpose extends beyond grading; they provide evidence of competency, certify knowledge acquisition, and help institutions assess the effectiveness of curricula.

Key Characteristics of Summative Assessments

1. **Cumulative and Final:**
    - Summative assessments take place at the end of a learning cycle and assess overall achievement rather than ongoing progress.

- They require students to synthesize and apply the skills and knowledge acquired over an extended period.

2. **Standardized and Structured:**
    - These assessments typically adhere to formal grading rubrics to ensure fairness, reliability, and validity.
    - Clear assessment criteria enables students to comprehend expectations and enable faculty to evaluate performance consistently.

3. **Higher Stakes and Grade-Determining:**
    - Because summative assessments often contribute significantly to final grades, they can create pressure on students.
    - It is essential to ensure fairness and accessibility, offering multiple ways for students to demonstrate mastery.

4. **Less Immediate Feedback:**
    - Unlike formative assessments, summative assessments primarily serve an evaluative role rather than a developmental one.
    - Feedback is still important but is often provided after the assessment, making it less actionable for immediate improvement.

Examples of Summative Assessments in Higher Education

1. Final Exams:

- Comprehensive tests assessing cumulative knowledge over an entire course.

2. Research Papers and Term Papers:

- In-depth written assignments requiring synthesis of concepts, analysis, and original argumentation.

3. Capstone Projects and Theses:

- Extended research projects demonstrating mastery of interdisciplinary skills.

4. Standardized Certification Exams:

- Industry-recognized tests assessing competency in a professional field (e.g., CPA, PMP, GRE).

5. Performance-Based Assessments:

- Simulations, case studies, and live demonstrations to assess real-world application of skills.

Bridging the Gap: Balancing Formative and Summative Assessment

Rather than treating formative and summative assessments as opposing forces, effective teaching integrates both to maximize student learning outcomes.

Best Practices for Blending Formative and Summative Assessments

- **Scaffolded Learning:** Formative assessments should build toward summative assessments, providing students with opportunities to refine skills incrementally.

- **Authentic Assessment Strategies:** Move beyond rote memorization by using real-world applications, such as case studies and project-based evaluations.

- **Feedback-Rich Summative Assessments:** Even in summative assessments, offering rubric breakdowns and post-assessment reflections helps individuals comprehend their strengths and areas needing improvement.

- **Leveraging Technology:** Adaptive learning platforms and AI-driven assessment tools can deliver personalized learning paths, using formative insights to refine summative evaluations.

Conclusion: From Assessment to Advancement

A well-rounded assessment strategy does not merely measure learning—it enhances it. Formative assessments serve as compasses, guiding students along the learning journey, while summative assessments act as milestones, evaluating progress and certifying achievement. By thoughtfully integrating both, educators can foster deeper engagement, promote self-directed learning, and ultimately, cultivate academic excellence.

Developing Fair and Transparent Grading Rubrics

Assessment in higher education is not merely about assigning grades. Assessment is about ensuring clarity, consistency, and fairness in evaluating student performance. A well-structured grading rubric is a powerful tool that serves both instructors and students by providing explicit criteria for evaluation, eliminating ambiguity, and fostering a sense of equity in the grading process.

Rubrics are particularly important in subjective assessments, such as essays, research projects, presentations, and group work, where grading can be influenced by implicit biases, inconsistencies, or unarticulated expectations. When developed properly, grading rubrics enhance transparency, promote academic integrity, and serve as formative tools that help students understand and improve their work.

The Purpose and Benefits of Grading Rubrics

A grading rubric is a structured assessment tool, defining specific criteria and clear performance expectations for an assignment. It typically consists of a matrix that delineates:

- **Assessment Criteria**: Key components that will be evaluated (e.g., argument clarity, organization, use of evidence).

- **Performance Levels**: A scale indicating varying degrees of achievement (e.g., Excellent, Proficient, Needs Improvement).
- **Descriptors**: Detailed explanations of what each level of performance entails for each criterion.

Why Are Grading Rubrics Essential?

1. **Ensuring Fairness and Objectivity**
    - Without a rubric, grading can become inconsistent and subjective, influenced by an instructor's mood, implicit biases, or unclear expectations.
    - A well-designed rubric minimizes **grading discrepancies**, ensuring that every student is evaluated by the same standard.

2. **Enhancing Transparency for Students**
    - Clear rubrics demystify grading by explicitly communicating what is expected and how performance is measured.
    - They serve as guiding documents, helping students focus their efforts on essential learning outcomes rather than guessing what their instructor values most.

3. **Providing Constructive Feedback**
    - A rubric functions as more than just a grading tool; it also serves as a feedback mechanism by pinpointing strengths and areas for improvement.
    - By breaking down performance into clear categories, students receive targeted insights into how they can refine their work.

4. **Facilitating Consistency Across Multiple Graders**
    - In courses with multiple instructors, teaching assistants, or peer reviewers, rubrics ensure uniformity in evaluation across different graders.
    - They help establish grading reliability, reducing variability in scoring that could result from different interpretations of assignment quality.

5. **Encouraging Self-Reflection and Metacognition**
    - Students can use rubrics before submitting assignments to self-assess their work, fostering deeper engagement with the learning process.
    - When students understand the expectations, they take a more proactive approach to their academic growth.

Key Elements of an Effective Grading Rubric

A well-constructed rubric is more than a grading checklist—it is an instructional tool that should be clear, precise, and aligned with learning objectives. Below are the core components of an effective rubric:

1. Clearly Defined Criteria

Each rubric should include a comprehensive yet specific list of criteria that reflect the learning objectives of the assignment. Criteria should:

- Focus on critical skills and knowledge needed for success in the assignment.
- Use clear and discipline-specific language that students understand.
- Avoid vague terms such as "good" or "adequate" and instead use actionable descriptors like "provides a well-supported argument with multiple relevant examples."

Example of well-defined criteria:
Poorly defined: "Uses evidence effectively."
Clearly defined: "Integrates at least three credible sources that support the argument and properly cites them using APA format."

2. Distinct Performance Levels

A rubric should include gradations of performance, typically organized into four or five levels, ranging from exemplary work to inadequate performance. The levels should:

- Be clearly distinguishable from one another.
- Reflect consistent scaling (e.g., Excellent, Proficient, Developing, Needs Improvement).
- Avoid excessive granularity—having too many levels can make distinctions overly complex.

Example:

Criteria	Excellent (10 pts)	Proficient (8 pts)	Developing (6 pts)	Needs Improvement (4 pts)
Argument Clarity	Argument is well-developed, logical, and supported by strong evidence.	Argument is clear but lacks some supporting details.	Argument is present but underdeveloped.	Argument is unclear or lacks support.

3. Detailed Descriptors for Each Level

Each performance level should have specific descriptors that articulate the expectations for students.

- Avoid overly generic language (e.g., "good" or "bad").

- Provide qualitative distinctions between different levels of performance.
- Use objective, measurable terms rather than subjective opinions.

Example:

Poor Descriptor: "Essay is well-organized." (Vague—what does "well-organized" mean?)
Stronger Descriptor: "Essay follows a logical structure with clear transitions between sections and a well-articulated thesis."

4. Weighting and Point Distribution

If different components of an assignment hold varying importance, rubrics should include point distributions that reflect those priorities. For instance, if content knowledge is more critical than grammar, the rubric should assign a greater percentage of the total score to content-related criteria.

Example of weighted rubric sections:

- Argument and Analysis (40%)
- Use of Evidence (30%)
- Organization and Clarity (20%)
- Grammar and Formatting (10%)

This ensures that higher-order thinking skills (e.g., critical analysis) receive greater weight than surface-level mechanics.

Strategies for Implementing Fair and Transparent Rubrics

1. Involve Students in the Process

- Encourage students to review the rubric before submitting assignments and use it for self-assessment.
- Consider co-creating rubrics with students in certain cases, especially in advanced or project-based courses, to increase their investment in the grading process.

2. Use Rubrics for Peer Review and Revision

- Before submitting final assignments, students can use rubrics for structured peer assessments.
- This helps them internalize expectations while receiving constructive feedback from their peers.

3. Provide Rubrics with Assignment Instructions

- Attach rubrics before students begin their work to clarify expectations.

- Ensure that students understand how they will be assessed by discussing key components in class.

4. Be Consistent in Application

- If multiple graders are involved, conduct norming sessions to ensure that everyone applies the rubric consistently.
- Periodically re-evaluate and refine rubrics based on student performance and instructor experience.

Conclusion: Rubrics as Tools for Equity and Learning

Developing fair and transparent grading rubrics is essential to cultivating learning environments where individuals feel guided, valued, and fairly assessed. A well-designed rubric:
Clarifies expectations so learners understand requirements.
Minimizes subjectivity, ensuring consistent grading across different assignments and graders.
Encourages student learning and self-improvement by providing structured feedback.

By integrating clear, equitable, and transparent rubrics into their teaching, instructors not only create a more just assessment system but also cultivate a deeper, more reflective learning experience for their students.

Providing Meaningful Feedback to Students

Feedback is one of the most powerful instructional tools in higher education [126]. It has the potential to bridge the gap between a student's current performance and their learning goals, guiding them toward deeper understanding and skill development. However, not all feedback is equally effective—meaningful feedback goes beyond mere corrections or numeric scores; it provides constructive insights, fosters engagement, and encourages self-regulated learning.

The role of feedback in higher education extends beyond assessing correctness—it should promote critical thinking, encourage reflection, and inspire students to refine their work. When delivered effectively, feedback can motivate students, clarify expectations, and enhance overall academic performance. However, ineffective feedback—vague, untimely, or overly critical—can lead to confusion, frustration, and disengagement [127].

To ensure feedback is impactful, it must be timely, specific, actionable, balanced, and student-centered. This section explores key principles of meaningful feedback, effective delivery techniques, and strategies for fostering a feedback-rich learning environment.

The Core Principles of Meaningful Feedback

1. Timeliness: Delivering Feedback at the Right Moment

Feedback is most effective when provided as soon as possible after an assignment or assessment. Immediate or near-immediate feedback allows students to reflect while the learning experience is still fresh [128]. If feedback is delayed for weeks, students may have moved on mentally and be less likely to integrate it into their learning process [129].

Best Practices for Timely Feedback:

- Provide quick formative feedback on low-stakes assignments, even if summative grading occurs later.
- Use technology-enhanced tools (e.g., automated quizzes, AI-powered feedback systems) to offer instant feedback where applicable.
- Balance depth and efficiency—instructors should not feel pressured to provide excessive detail on every minor issue but should prioritize key areas that require improvement.

2. Specificity: Moving Beyond Generic Comments

Students cannot improve if they do not know exactly what they need to change. Meaningful feedback should highlight specific strengths and areas for growth rather than offering broad, non-specific comments such as "Good job" or "Needs improvement."

Best Practices for Specific Feedback:

Instead of: "Your thesis is unclear."
Try: "Your thesis presents an interesting idea, but it could be more specific. Consider explicitly stating your argument in the introduction and ensuring it is consistently supported throughout the essay."

Instead of: "Be more analytical."
Try: "In your literature review, you summarize key studies effectively, but you could add more critical analysis by comparing methodologies and evaluating how each study contributes to your research question."

3. Actionability: Providing Clear Steps for Improvement

The best feedback not only points out errors or weaknesses but also suggests concrete ways to improve. Without actionable insights, students may struggle to apply the feedback effectively.

Best Practices for Actionable Feedback:

- Frame feedback with guidance on how to correct issues, such as:
  "Your argument would be stronger if you integrated more evidence from primary sources. Try incorporating at least two direct citations in your next revision."
- Use examples or models to illustrate correct approaches.
- Offer questions that encourage critical thinking, e.g., "How might this claim change if you considered a counterargument?"

4. Balanced Approach: Combining Positive Reinforcement with Constructive Criticism

Effective feedback should balance encouragement and critique. Overly negative feedback can discourage students, while excessively positive feedback that lacks constructive insights can fail to promote improvement [130].

The Feedback Sandwich Approach (Praise - Critique - Recommendation):

1. Start with strengths: Identify what the student did well to reinforce effective learning habits.

2. Provide constructive critique: Address areas for improvement while maintaining a supportive tone.

3. Offer guidance for next steps: Suggest specific ways to refine their work.

Example:
"Your introduction effectively engages the reader with a thought-provoking question. However, your thesis statement could be clearer—try explicitly stating your argument in one concise sentence. Your use of evidence is strong, so consider reinforcing it with additional citations in paragraph three."

5. Student-Centered: Encouraging Engagement and Ownership

Feedback should not be a one-way directive but an interactive process that encourages students to reflect, ask questions, and take personal ownership of their learning.

Best Practices for Student-Centered Feedback:

- Encourage self-assessment by asking students to review their work before receiving feedback.

- Engage in dialogue-based feedback by prompting students with reflective questions:
  "What challenges did you encounter while writing this section?"
  "What strategies have you considered to improve your argument?"

- Use personalized language (e.g., "I noticed that…" or "One approach you might try is…") to foster a growth-oriented mindset rather than a punitive one.

Methods for Delivering Effective Feedback

Different contexts call for different feedback methods. Faculty should use a combination of approaches to meet diverse student needs.

1. Written Feedback: Structured and Reflective

- Use digital annotation tools (e.g., Google Docs comments, Canvas SpeedGrader) for real-time feedback.

- Provide summary comments at the end of assignments to reinforce key takeaways.

- Use rubrics with space for personalized comments to ensure clarity.

2. Audio and Video Feedback: Enhancing Personalization

- Recording personalized video feedback (e.g., using Loom, Kaltura, or Panopto) can make feedback feel more engaging.

- Audio feedback allows for more nuance in tone, reducing the likelihood of misinterpretation.

3. Peer Feedback: Fostering Collaborative Learning

- Incorporate structured peer review sessions where students use guided rubrics to evaluate each other's work.
- Encourage discussion-based feedback, where students explain their critiques rather than just writing comments.

4. Live Feedback: Immediate and Interactive

- Use one-on-one meetings or office hours for real-time discussion of feedback.
- Implement in-class feedback activities, such as interactive workshops where students refine work in real time.

Creating a Feedback-Rich Learning Environment

1. Set Clear Expectations for Feedback Use

- Provide students with guidance on how to interpret and apply feedback.
- Encourage revision policies that allow students to resubmit work based on feedback.

2. Normalize Feedback as a Growth Tool

- Promote a growth mindset by framing feedback as a natural part of the learning process rather than a judgment of ability.
- Use reflective assignments where students describe how they applied feedback in their revisions.

3. Foster a Two-Way Feedback Loop

- Solicit student feedback on instruction and assessment methods, ensuring that the feedback process itself evolves based on student needs.
- Use mid-semester feedback surveys to gauge students' perceptions of how feedback is helping them.

Conclusion: Feedback as a Catalyst for Learning

Providing meaningful feedback is more than a grading obligation—it is a fundamental pedagogical practice that supports students' intellectual growth and confidence. When feedback is specific, timely, actionable, balanced, and student-centered, it enables students to take ownership of learning and make continuous improvements.

A feedback-rich learning environment fosters engagement, resilience, and self-efficacy, preparing students not just for academic success, but for their lifelong learning and professional development [131]. By making feedback a dialogue rather than a monologue, instructors transform assessment from a passive judgment into an active tool for improvement.

Academic Integrity and Handling Plagiarism Cases

Academic integrity is a cornerstone of higher education, embodying the critical principles of trust, honesty, respect, fairness, and responsibility. It is the foundation upon which intellectual inquiry, scholarly research, and ethical teaching are built. For new college professors, maintaining academic integrity within their classrooms is not only about preventing dishonest practices but also about cultivating a culture of ethical scholarship and intellectual responsibility.

Plagiarism—one of the most common violations of academic integrity—poses a significant challenge in higher education [132]. Whether intentional or unintentional, plagiarism undermines the learning process, devalues academic credentials, and compromises the credibility of both students and institutions. Addressing plagiarism effectively requires a proactive, educational, and consistent approach, combining preventive measures, structured detection strategies, and fair disciplinary actions when violations occur.

This section explores the nature of academic integrity, the various forms of plagiarism, strategies for prevention, methods of detection, and best practices for handling plagiarism cases in a way that upholds fairness, promotes learning, and preserves academic credibility.

Understanding Academic Integrity and Plagiarism

Academic integrity extends beyond simply avoiding plagiarism or cheating; it encompasses ethical engagement with knowledge, respect for intellectual property and attribution, and accountability in scholarly work. Institutions typically define academic integrity policies that students are expected to follow, but it is the role of faculty to actively reinforce these values and ensure compliance.

Defining Plagiarism

Plagiarism is the unauthorized use or representation of another person's ideas, work, or words as one's own, without proper attribution. It can range from deliberate cheating to unintentional misrepresentation due to lack of knowledge about citation practices.

Plagiarism can take many forms, including:

1. **Direct Copying (Verbatim Plagiarism):** Word-for-word reproduction of another's work without citation.

2. **Patchwriting (Mosaic Plagiarism):** Rewriting a passage by making slight modifications while retaining the original structure and ideas.

3. **Self-Plagiarism (Duplicate Submission):** Submitting one's previous work for a different assignment or publication without disclosure.

4. **Unattributed Paraphrasing:** Summarizing or rewording another's work without citing the original source.

5. **Fabricated Citations:** Providing false or misleading references [133].

6. **Contract Cheating (Ghostwriting):** Submitting work that was written by someone else, such as a paid writer or a friend.

While some students intentionally plagiarize, others may unknowingly commit plagiarism due to lack of awareness about citation standards, paraphrasing techniques, or institutional policies. Thus, an effective response to plagiarism must incorporate both disciplinary measures and educational interventions.

Preventing Plagiarism Through Proactive Teaching Strategies

Prevention is the most effective strategy for maintaining academic integrity. Rather than solely focusing on punitive measures, faculty should emphasize academic integrity as a fundamental learning principle. The following strategies help create an environment where students understand the importance of ethical scholarship and are equipped with the skills to avoid plagiarism.

1. Clearly Define Academic Integrity Expectations

- Explicitly outline plagiarism policies in the syllabus, including definitions, examples, and potential consequences.
- Use orientation sessions, academic integrity pledges, or classroom discussions to reinforce ethical research practices.
- Emphasize that plagiarism is not just about cheating but about intellectual honesty and scholarly ethics.

2. Teach Proper Citation and Paraphrasing Skills

- Many students struggle with plagiarism due to lack of familiarity with citation conventions (APA, MLA, Chicago, etc.).
- Provide workshops, handouts, and practice exercises to teach proper source attribution.
- Use plagiarism detection tools as formative learning aids, showing students how to check and correct their work before submission.

3. Design Assessments That Minimize Opportunities for Plagiarism

- Use unique and evolving prompts rather than generic, easily searchable essay topics.
- Incorporate staged assignments, requiring drafts, outlines, and annotated bibliographies to track students' research progress.
- Include personal reflection components that require original thinking, such as case studies, problem-solving scenarios, or application-based projects.

4. Foster a Culture of Integrity

- Model academic integrity by citing sources in lectures, discussions, and instructional materials.

- Encourage open dialogue about ethical dilemmas in academia to engage students in discussions on integrity.

- Emphasize that scholarship is a process of building upon others' ideas, not copying them—attribution is a way of participating in academic conversations, not just a bureaucratic requirement.

Detecting Plagiarism: Tools and Best Practices

Despite preventive efforts, some students will still commit plagiarism, whether intentionally or inadvertently [134]. Effective detection involves a combination of technological tools, manual review, and a keen understanding of writing inconsistencies.

1. Utilizing Plagiarism Detection Software

- Turnitin, Grammarly, Copyscape, and Unicheck can flag similarities between student submissions and existing sources [135].

- Limitations: These tools identify textual overlap but cannot always detect paraphrased content, contract cheating, or AI-generated text [136].

2. Identifying Anomalies in Writing Style

- Sudden shifts in vocabulary, tone, or complexity may indicate sections copied from an external source.

- Mismatched formatting, varied citation styles, or inconsistent reference usage may suggest copy-pasting from multiple sources [136].

- If a student's writing drastically differs from their previous submissions, investigate whether they used external assistance [137].

3. Cross-Referencing Unusual or Suspicious Citations

- Check whether cited sources actually exist—fabricated references are a common form of academic dishonesty.

- If references appear inconsistent with the student's discipline or level of expertise, consider whether they are copied from another work.

Handling Plagiarism Cases: A Fair and Educational Approach

When plagiarism is detected, faculty must respond in a way that is fair, transparent, and aligned with institutional policies. The goal is not just to penalize but to educate students on academic integrity and prevent future violations.

Step 1: Investigate the Case Objectively

- Gather all relevant evidence, including plagiarism reports, student drafts, and original sources.
- Assess the nature and extent of plagiarism (e.g., minor citation errors vs. extensive copying).
- Determine whether the violation appears intentional or due to misunderstanding.

Step 2: Engage in a Constructive Dialogue with the Student

- Schedule a private meeting to discuss the findings and allow the student to explain.
- Maintain a neutral and non-accusatory tone, focusing on learning rather than punishment.
- Ask reflective questions, such as:
    - "Can you explain how you developed this section?"
    - "What challenges did you face in citing your sources?"
    - "Do you understand why this is considered plagiarism?"

Step 3: Apply Appropriate Consequences and Remediation

- **For unintentional plagiarism** (e.g., citation errors, paraphrasing issues):
    - Require students to revise and resubmit assignments with proper citations.
    - Assign academic integrity training or citation workshops.
- **For intentional plagiarism** (e.g., full-paper copying, contract cheating):
    - Follow institutional disciplinary procedures, which may include grade penalties, failing the assignment, or formal academic misconduct review.
- Document all cases to ensure consistency in handling future incidents.

Conclusion: Upholding Integrity, Promoting Ethical Scholarship

Academic integrity is not just a rule—it is a fundamental value that shapes the credibility of higher education. Faculty play a critical role in preventing plagiarism, educating students on ethical scholarship, and enforcing academic standards with fairness and transparency.

By fostering a proactive, supportive, and integrity-focused classroom environment, educators can help students not only avoid plagiarism but also develop the skills and ethical mindset necessary for responsible academic and professional success.

Alternative Assessments and Competency-Based Grading: Rethinking Traditional Evaluation Models

Assessment in higher education serves as more than just a means of assigning grades—it is a fundamental component of student learning, skill mastery, and academic development. While traditional assessment methods such as timed exams and standardized testing have long dominated higher education, there is increasing recognition that these methods do not always capture the depth of student understanding, practical skills, or real-world competencies.

As educational paradigms shift toward learner-centered approaches, alternative assessments and competency-based grading are gaining traction as more equitable, flexible, and meaningful methods of evaluating student achievement. These approaches focus on what students can demonstrate and apply rather than how well they perform in conventional testing scenarios.

This section explores alternative assessments and competency-based grading in detail, examining their philosophical foundations, implementation strategies, and benefits for both students and educators.

Alternative Assessments: Moving Beyond Traditional Testing

What Are Alternative Assessments?

Alternative assessments provide diverse and flexible ways for learners to demonstrate critical understanding, thinking, and skill applications. Unlike traditional assessments, which often emphasize rote memorization and recall, alternative assessments prioritize:

- Authentic learning experiences that connect theory to practice.
- Diverse methods of evaluation that account for different learning styles.
- Demonstration of higher-order thinking skills rather than just factual recall.

Key Characteristics of Alternative Assessments

1. Performance-Based – Students engage in real-world tasks rather than answering standardized questions.
2. Process-Oriented – Focuses on how students arrive at their answers, not just the final response.
3. Flexible and Inclusive – Allows multiple pathways to success, accommodating different learning styles and backgrounds.
4. Iterative and Reflective – Encourages students to revise, reflect, and improve their work based on feedback.
5. Contextualized in Real-World Applications – Students apply knowledge to authentic problems, bridging gaps between theory and practice.

Examples of Alternative Assessments

1. Project-Based Assessments

Students work on extended projects that require synthesis, creativity, and application of course concepts.

- Example: In an engineering course, students might design and prototype a renewable energy device.
- Example: In a marketing course, students might develop a full campaign for a real business.

2. Case Studies and Simulations

Students analyze real-world scenarios and propose evidence-based solutions.

- Example: In a business course, students analyze financial data and propose investment strategies.
- Example: In a healthcare program, students engage in patient care simulations.

3. Portfolios and Digital Showcases

Students compile a collection of work demonstrating their growth and expertise over time.

- Example: A graphic design student submits a digital portfolio of completed projects.
- Example: A computer science student presents a GitHub repository of coded projects.

4. Peer and Self-Assessments

Encourages metacognition by having students evaluate their own or their peers' work using structured rubrics.

- Example: In a writing course, students provide peer feedback on research papers.
- Example: In a leadership course, students write self-assessments reflecting on their growth as leaders.

5. Experiential Learning and Field-Based Assessments

Students engage in internships, service learning, or fieldwork, followed by critical reflections.

- Example: In a social work program, students complete field placements and reflect on casework.
- Example: In a biology course, students conduct field research and present findings.

By integrating alternative assessments, educators create more engaging, meaningful, and equitable learning experiences, aligning with students' real-world career aspirations and academic goals.

Competency-Based Grading: Evaluating Mastery Over Time

What Is Competency-Based Grading?

Competency-based grading (CBG) is an outcome-driven evaluation system that assesses students based on their demonstrated proficiency in specific skills, knowledge areas, and learning objectives. Unlike traditional grading models that rely on cumulative points or weighted averages, CBG ensures that students progress based on demonstrated mastery rather than completion of tasks.

Key Principles of Competency-Based Grading

1. **Focus on Mastery Rather Than Seat Time**
    - Students advance by proving competence, not by completing assignments for points.

2. **Explicit Learning Outcomes**
    - Each course or unit is broken into clear, measurable competencies that students must achieve.

3. **Multiple Attempts for Mastery**
    - Students can revise and improve work until they demonstrate proficiency.

4. **Elimination of Arbitrary Points and Curve-Based Grading**
    - Rather than ranking students against each other, grading is based on absolute criteria.

5. **Personalized Learning Pathways**
    - Students progress at individualized rates, allowing flexibility in learning.

Competency-Based Grading Scales

Rather than using traditional letter grades (A-F) or percentage scales (0-100%), competency-based grading often uses:

Level	Description
Exceeds Expectations (EE)	Demonstrates deep mastery, surpassing expected competencies.
Proficient (P)	Meets all required competencies with solid understanding.
Developing (D)	Shows partial mastery but needs further development.
Not Yet Proficient (NYP)	Does not yet meet competency; needs revision or additional learning.

This approach encourages students to improve rather than settle for a low grade, fostering a growth mindset and deeper engagement with learning.

Implementing Competency-Based Grading in Higher Education

1. Defining Course Competencies Clearly

- Break down learning goals into specific, assessable competencies.
- Example: Instead of grading an entire research paper holistically, assess specific competencies such as argumentation, evidence integration, clarity, and citation formatting separately.

2. Allowing for Multiple Demonstrations of Learning

- Provide learners with opportunities to update and resubmit work until they meet the required competencies.
- Example: A computer science student may refine their code over multiple iterations until it meets efficiency and security standards.

3. Using Rubrics to Guide Assessment

- Competency-based rubrics should clearly define expectations at each performance level.
- Example: A public speaking rubric might assess competencies such as content organization, verbal clarity, audience engagement, and non-verbal communication.

4. Shifting Mindsets from Grades to Learning Progress

- Encourage students to focus on growth rather than grades by promoting the idea that learning is an iterative process.
- Implement self-assessments and reflections to help students track their own progress.

5. Integrating Technology for Competency Tracking

- Use learning management systems (LMS) with competency-based tracking (e.g., Canvas, Moodle, Blackboard).
- Provide students with digital dashboards that show their progress on different competencies in real-time.

The Benefits of Alternative Assessments and Competency-Based Grading

For Students

Promotes real-world skill development rather than rote memorization.
Encourages self-paced learning, reducing pressure from arbitrary deadlines.
Fosters a growth mindset by allowing revisions and reattempts.
Enhances engagement and motivation through personalized learning.

For Instructors

Provides a more accurate measurement of student learning and skill application.
Reduces grading subjectivity by using explicit criteria.
Encourages innovative teaching strategies that connect theory with practice.
Helps identify individual student needs, supporting differentiated instruction.

Conclusion: Transforming Assessment for 21st-Century Learning

The shift toward alternative assessments and competency-based grading reflects a broader movement in higher education to cultivate more inclusive, skill-driven, and meaningful learning experiences [138]. By focusing on demonstrated mastery and authentic engagement, educators empower students to take ownership of their learning, preparing them not just for academic success, but for lifelong competence in their chosen fields.

Strengthening Learning Through Assessment and Feedback

Effective assessment and feedback are not merely about grading students; they are about guiding learning, reinforcing understanding, and encouraging growth. When thoughtfully designed, assessments provide valuable insights into student progress, while constructive feedback helps students refine their skills, enhance their critical thinking, and take ownership of their learning journey.

Faculty must strike a balance between rigor and support, ensuring that assessments challenge students without creating unnecessary barriers. Transparent grading rubrics, clear expectations, and diverse assessment methods contribute to a fair and inclusive learning environment. Additionally, leveraging alternative assessments and integrating technology can enhance engagement and better reflect students' competencies.

Ultimately, assessment is not just a measure of what students know—it is an opportunity to shape how they learn, apply knowledge, and develop lifelong learning habits. By prioritizing thoughtful assessment strategies and meaningful feedback, educators can cultivate a more effective, student-centered learning experience that drives academic excellence and professional preparedness.

Redefining Assessment in the Age of AI: Proving Workplace-Ready Skills

Why Redefine Assessment?

As artificial intelligence systems become increasingly adept at tasks like content generation, data analysis, and even basic decision-making, traditional higher education assessments—focused on recall and replication—risk obsolescence. Faculty must shift focus from "Can this learner produce content?" to "Can this learner demonstrate human judgment, adaptability, and professional reasoning?"

In the AI era, assessments must:

- Prioritize skills AI cannot easily replicate.
- Focus on human-centered decision-making and ethical reasoning.
- Provide authentic, practical demonstrations of applied knowledge.
- Validate students' readiness to navigate real-world complexity.

What AI Can Simulate vs. What Humans Must Demonstrate

AI-Capable Tasks	Human-Centric Skills Required
Summarizing reports	Synthesizing nuanced, contextual insights
Generating written content	Ethical reasoning and value-based judgment
Recommending strategies	Critical evaluation of risks, impacts, and trade-offs
Automated data analysis	Making decisions under uncertainty
Pattern recognition	Innovating and generating novel solutions

The New Assessment Imperative: Proof of Professional Competence

Instructors must now design assessments that focus on:

- Process as well as product: How a student thinks is as important as what they produce.
- Collaboration and communication: Students must work with others and convey complex ideas clearly.
- Ethics and adaptability: Learners must demonstrate responsible action in ambiguous contexts.
- Reasoning transparency: Documenting how decisions are made is key for AI-era credibility.

Designing AI-Resilient Assessments: A Strategic Framework

Authentic Performance Tasks

Definition:
Simulated or real-world tasks that replicate what professionals actually do in the workplace.

Why It Matters:
Unlike exams or essays, these tasks assess applied skills in context—where AI output lacks judgment or adaptability.

Implementation Examples:

- Role-play negotiation simulations in business courses.
- Case study crisis response in healthcare training.
- Design and prototype creation in engineering.

Faculty Tip:
Assess both the quality of the learner's final product and the learner's process for getting there.

Iterative Feedback Loops

Definition:
Assessments should be staged, providing opportunities for formative feedback before summative grading.

Why It Matters:
Professional growth is incremental. Assessments should mirror real-world feedback cycles.

Implementation Examples:

- Draft submissions with instructor and peer review.
- Agile-style "sprint reviews" in project-based courses.
- Revision-based grading policies.

Faculty Tip:
Emphasize the "learning journey" over one-time performance.

Reasoning Documentation (Process Transparency)

Definition:
Students must explain how and why they made decisions—not just what decisions they made.

Why It Matters:
AI can produce answers, but cannot transparently explain human decision processes.

Implementation Examples:

- Require reflective memos accompanying technical deliverables.
- Use decision rationale matrices in engineering and business assessments.
- Include justification narratives in nursing or clinical reports.

Faculty Tip:
Make process documentation a formal part of grading rubrics.

Collaborative Demonstration

Definition:
Students are assessed on their ability to collaborate, negotiate, and solve problems collectively.

Why It Matters:
Modern work environments demand teamwork, which AI cannot replicate.

Implementation Examples:

- Group design challenges in architecture or engineering.
- Collaborative policy briefs in public administration courses.
- Peer-reviewed project components.

Faculty Tip:
Assess both individual contributions and team dynamics.

Cross-Context Adaptability

Definition:
Assessments should evaluate the learner's ability to transfer knowledge across unfamiliar or novel contexts.

Why It Matters:
AI is powerful in narrow domains; human professionals must adapt knowledge to new challenges.

Implementation Examples:

- Applying core ethical frameworks to emerging technologies.
- Solving new case studies in different industries.
- Exploring hypothetical scenarios beyond course material.

Faculty Tip:
Use "What-if?" scenarios to assess adaptability.

Discipline-Specific Examples: Proving Critical Skills

Cybersecurity

Skill Assessed: Real-time judgment in threat prioritization.

Example Assessment:

- Conduct a simulated network penetration test.
- Deliver an executive risk assessment report.
- Participate in a live oral defense justifying actions and priorities.

Proof of Competence:

- Technical execution.
- Strategic communication.
- Justified, ethical decision-making under uncertainty.

Business and Management

Skill Assessed: Critical evaluation of AI-generated strategies.

Example Assessment:

- Use an AI tool to draft a business plan.
- Annotate flaws or ethical concerns in the AI's output.
- Collaboratively revise the plan using human judgment.

Proof of Competence:

- Human oversight of machine outputs.
- Strategic reasoning.
- Peer collaboration.

Health Sciences

Skill Assessed: Ethical decision-making in patient care.

Example Assessment:

- Participate in a simulated emergency room scenario.
- Submit both a clinical decision log and an ethical reflection journal.
- Conduct peer feedback sessions on teamwork performance.

Proof of Competence:

- Context-driven judgment.
- Team-based problem solving.
- Transparent decision rationale.

Humanities and Communication

Skill Assessed: Creative message design for public engagement.

Example Assessment:

- Produce a multimedia public service announcement (video, podcast).
- Submit a reflective journal detailing audience strategy.
- Provide annotated sources supporting claims.

Proof of Competence:

- Communication creativity.

- Strategic audience analysis.
- Research integrity.

Experiential Learning as Assessment Validation

Experiential learning activities are ideal for authentic assessment:

- Capstone projects
- Service-learning deliverables
- Simulations
- Internships

Assessment Focus:
Did the learner demonstrate:

- Effective collaboration?
- Problem-solving under ambiguity?
- Reflection and process improvement?
- Ethical, strategic reasoning?

Sample AI-Resilient Assessment Rubric

Dimension	Weight
Critical Judgment in Context	30%
Documentation of Process & Rationale	20%
Collaboration and Team Contribution	15%
Ethical and Strategic Reflection	15%
Final Deliverable Quality	20%

Conclusion: From Knowledge Recall to Capability Proof

In the AI education era:

- Content reproduction is irrelevant—AI can do it.
- Human judgment, creativity, and leadership become the true measures of learning.

Assessment must answer:

- Can this learner think critically under uncertainty?
- Can they collaborate ethically and effectively?
- Can they explain their decisions transparently?
- Can they innovate and adapt across contexts?

In short: Can they demonstrate workplace-ready skills AI cannot replicate?

By adopting these assessment practices, educators prepare learners not just to succeed in school—but to thrive as adaptive, ethical, and reflective professionals in the AI-augmented workplace.

Chapter 7: Leveraging Technology in Teaching

Technology is an integral part of higher education, transforming how instructors teach and how students engage with course content. From Learning Management Systems (LMS) to artificial intelligence-driven learning tools, the effective use of technology can expand student learning, foster collaboration, and improve instructional efficiency. However, incorporating technology into teaching requires intentional planning to ensure alignment with pedagogical goals and student needs.

This chapter explores key technological tools and strategies that faculty can use to enhance learning experiences. It examines the role of Learning Management Systems (such as Blackboard, Canvas, and Moodle), the use of multimedia and interactive content to increase engagement, the integration of AI tools for individualized learning and feedback, and best practices for hybrid and online instruction. Additionally, this chapter highlights the importance of digital accessibility and Universal Design for Learning (UDL) in creating inclusive learning environments.

Figure 7.1. Technology in Teaching [219].

By understanding and effectively leveraging these technologies, faculty can enhance student engagement, streamline course delivery, and prepare learners for the digital landscape of modern education.

Learning Management Systems (LMS) Like Blackboard, Canvas, and Moodle

In the modern academic landscape, Learning Management Systems (LMS) serve as the digital backbone of higher education, providing a centralized, structured, and interactive environment for course management, content delivery, assessment, and student engagement. These platforms—such as Blackboard, Canvas, and Moodle—have transformed traditional classroom dynamics, enabling faculty to extend learning beyond the physical classroom, facilitate blended and online instruction, and enhance student participation through digital tools.

For new college professors, effectively leveraging an LMS is not merely about digitizing course materials but about creating a seamless, interactive, and student-centered learning experience. This section explores the fundamental role of LMS platforms, key features, comparisons between Blackboard, Canvas, and Moodle, and best practices for optimizing LMS usage in college teaching.

The Role of Learning Management Systems in Higher Education

A Learning Management System (LMS) is a software application designed to create, manage, and deliver educational content. It acts as a virtual learning hub where faculty and learners interact, engage with course materials, submit assignments, communicate, and monitor academic progress.

Key Functions of an LMS:

1. **Course Content Management**
   - Organizes lectures, readings, videos, and resources in a structured manner.
   - Supports varied content formats, including PDFs, slides, recorded lectures, and interactive media.

2. **Assessment and Feedback Tools**
   - Facilitates quizzes, exams, discussion boards, peer reviews, and assignments.
   - Provides automated grading and detailed feedback mechanisms.

3. **Communication and Collaboration**
   - Integrates discussion forums, messaging systems, announcements, and virtual meeting tools.
   - Enhances student interaction through group projects and peer-to-peer collaboration tools.

4. **Progress Tracking and Analytics**
   - Monitors student engagement, participation, and academic performance.
   - Generates reports on course trends, attendance, and assessment outcomes.

5. **Integration with External Tools**
   - Connects with Google Drive, Microsoft Teams, Turnitin (plagiarism detection), and AI-based learning tools.
   - Offers API-based customization for faculty needing specialized functionalities.

By streamlining instructional delivery, student engagement, and administrative tasks, an LMS provides efficiency, flexibility, and scalability in college teaching.

Comparing Major LMS Platforms: Blackboard, Canvas, and Moodle

1. Blackboard: Feature-Rich with Enterprise-Level Capabilities

Blackboard has been a long-standing LMS solution, widely adopted by universities due to its robust tools for large-scale academic institutions. It offers:
Comprehensive assessment tools – Advanced quiz engines, self-assessments, and peer evaluations.
Customization and scalability – Flexible course structures for large and small class formats.
Integrated communication features – Email, chat, and announcement boards for faculty-student interaction.
Strong data analytics – In-depth student performance tracking for early intervention strategies.
Institution-wide integration – Seamless compatibility with library systems, student information systems (SIS), and third-party applications.

Challenges:

- Steeper learning curves for new learners due to extensive features.
- More expensive than open-source options like Moodle.

2. Canvas: Intuitive, Cloud-Based, and Mobile-Friendly

Canvas is known for its user-friendly interface and cloud-based accessibility, making it a popular choice among universities seeking a modern, streamlined LMS. It offers:
Drag-and-drop course design – Easy content creation and organization.
SpeedGrader tool – Efficient grading and annotation system for rapid feedback.
Mobile-first approach – Optimized for smartphone and tablet usage.
Integration with edtech tools – Google Docs, Zoom, Turnitin, and other platforms.
API support for personalized customization – Allows faculty to modify features and workflows.

Challenges:

- Limited advanced quiz options compared to Blackboard.
- Fewer built-in analytical tools—though external integrations can address this.

3. Moodle: Open-Source, Flexible, and Customizable

Moodle is an open-source LMS that provides high flexibility and customizability, making it a popular choice for institutions looking for cost-effective and adaptable solutions. It offers:
Highly customizable framework – Faculty and institutions can modify the source code to meet specific needs.
Scalability – Works for small colleges and large universities alike.
Robust plugin ecosystem – Supports a vast number of third-party add-ons for extended functionality.
Multi-language support – Ideal for institutions with diverse student populations.

Challenges:

- Requires more technical expertise for customization and maintenance.
- User interface can feel outdated compared to Canvas and Blackboard.

Best Practices for Using an LMS in College Teaching

To maximize the impact of an LMS, instructors must go beyond basic content uploads and actively engage students through thoughtful course design and interactive features.

1. Structure Courses for Clarity and Accessibility

Organize modules logically (e.g., weekly topics, units, or themes).
Use consistent naming conventions for files, assignments, and discussion boards.
Provide accessible content (e.g., captioned videos, screen reader-friendly PDFs).

2. Leverage Interactive and Collaborative Tools

Use discussion forums to encourage peer engagement.
Implement group assignments to foster teamwork.
Integrate video conferencing tools for virtual office hours and live Q&As.

3. Utilize Analytics to Support Student Success

Track student engagement and progress through built-in analytics.
Identify at-risk learners and intervene early with support.
Use adaptive learning features to personalize the learning experience.

4. Provide Timely and Meaningful Feedback

Use automated feedback for quizzes and assignments.
Offer video or audio feedback to add a personal touch.
Set up rubrics and grading criteria to ensure transparency.

5. Integrate with External EdTech Tools

Use Turnitin for plagiarism detection.
Incorporate Google Drive/Microsoft OneDrive for collaborative projects.
Connect with adaptive learning platforms for personalized instruction.

The Future of LMS: Emerging Trends and Innovations

As educational technology evolves, LMS platforms are becoming more adaptive, AI-driven, and student-centered. Emerging trends include:

Artificial Intelligence (AI) and Machine Learning

- AI-powered chatbots for student inquiries.
- Automated grading and feedback analysis.
- Personalized learning recommendations based on student performance.

Gamification and Immersive Learning

- Badges, leaderboards, and challenges to increase motivation.
- Virtual and augmented reality (VR/AR) integrations for simulated learning experiences.

Adaptive Learning Pathways

- LMS platforms that customize coursework based on student progress.
- Dynamic assessments that adjust difficulty levels in real-time.

Data-Driven Insights for Institutional Decision-Making

- Advanced predictive analytics to improve retention rates.
- Custom dashboards for faculty and administrators to track trends.

Conclusion: Maximizing LMS Potential in Higher Education

Learning Management Systems like Blackboard, Canvas, and Moodle have revolutionized instructional delivery, engagement, and assessment in higher education. However, the effectiveness of an LMS depends not on the technology itself, but on how educators leverage its capabilities to foster meaningful learning experiences.

By thoughtfully structuring courses, integrating interactive elements, utilizing analytics, and adapting to emerging trends, professors can create dynamic, inclusive, and student-centered learning environments that extend beyond the classroom, preparing students for success in an increasingly digital world.

Integrating Multimedia and Interactive Content: Enhancing Engagement and Learning in Higher Education

The integration of multimedia and interactive content into college teaching has revolutionized the way educators deliver instruction, engage students, and enhance learning outcomes. In an era where students are increasingly accustomed to digital interactions, leveraging multimedia tools and interactive elements is not just an enhancement—it is a necessity. When used effectively, multimedia can transform passive learning into an active and immersive experience, catering to diverse learning preferences and improving knowledge retention.

For new college professors, understanding how to thoughtfully integrated multimedia elements—such as videos, podcasts, animations, simulations, and interactive exercises—into their teaching strategies can significantly boost student motivation, comprehension, and engagement. This section explores the pedagogical benefits of multimedia, best practices for integration, and the various types of interactive content that can enrich higher education instruction.

The Pedagogical Benefits of Multimedia and Interactive Content

Multimedia refers to the combination of multiple forms of content, including images, text, video, audio, and interactive simulations, designed to create a dynamic learning experience. Interactive content involves two-way engagement, allowing learners to actively participate rather than passively consume information.

Key Advantages of Using Multimedia in Teaching

Enhances Comprehension and Retention

- Visual and auditory stimuli reinforce complex concepts and improve memory recall.
- Research shows that multimodal learning (engaging multiple senses) increases information retention [139].

Engages Diverse Learning Styles

- Supports visual learners (diagrams, infographics, videos), auditory learners (podcasts, recorded lectures), and kinesthetic learners (simulations, interactive labs).

Fosters Active Learning

- Interactive content requires student participation, promoting critical thinking and problem-solving.
- Encourages real-world application through simulations, gamification, and case-based learning.

Bridges Theory and Practice

- Real-world examples and interactive case studies help students connect abstract concepts to practical applications.
- Provides hands-on experiences in disciplines where physical access to materials may be limited (e.g., virtual labs for science students).

Increases Accessibility and Flexibility

- Multimedia content can be viewed asynchronously, allowing individuals to learn at their own pace.
- Captioning, transcripts, and screen reader compatibility enhance accessibility for individuals with disabilities.

By leveraging multimedia and interactive elements, professors move beyond traditional lecture-based teaching, creating a more engaging and inclusive learning environment.

Types of Multimedia and Interactive Content for Higher Education

Different forms of multimedia and interactivity serve distinct instructional purposes. Choosing the right tool depends on learning objectives, subject matter, and student needs.

1. Video-Based Learning: Enhancing Understanding Through Visual Engagement

- Lecture Recordings & Micro-Lectures: Bite-sized videos (5–10 minutes) allow students to review complex topics at their own pace.
- Concept Animations & Explainer Videos: Platforms like TED-Ed, Khan Academy, and Edpuzzle simplify abstract theories through visual storytelling.
- Virtual Field Trips & 360-Degree Videos: Tools like Google Expeditions and VR-enabled documentaries immerse students in distant locations and historical events.

Best Practices:

- Keep videos concise and focused (avoid information overload).
- Add embedded quizzes and discussion prompts to maintain engagement.
- Ensure closed captioning and transcripts for accessibility.

2. Audio-Based Learning: The Power of Spoken Word

- Podcasts & Audio Lectures: Recorded discussions with experts and faculty provide an alternative to reading-heavy materials.
- Student-Generated Podcasts: Encourages students to synthesize and articulate knowledge creatively.
- Text-to-Speech Tools: Assist students who prefer auditory learning or require accessibility accommodations.

Best Practices:

- Provide guiding questions to help students critically engage with podcast content.
- Use professional-quality recording tools to enhance clarity.
- Offer supplementary text materials to reinforce key concepts.

3. Infographics and Data Visualizations: Simplifying Complex Concepts

- Graphical Summaries: Mind maps, flowcharts, and infographics visually organize information, improving recall.
- Data Storytelling: Platforms like Tableau, Infogram, and Power BI allow students to interact with data sets.

Best Practices:

- Encourage students to create their own infographics as a learning activity.
- Use contrast and color coding to emphasize key points.

4. Interactive Simulations and Virtual Labs: Learning by Doing

- STEM Simulations: Tools like PhET Interactive Simulations, Labster, and Wolfram Alpha enable individuals to experiment with physics, chemistry, and engineering models.
- Business and Economics Simulations: Platforms like Harvard Business Publishing Simulations and Capsim help students apply market analysis and financial decision-making.
- Language Learning Simulations: AI-powered platforms like Duolingo and Rosetta Stone enhance language acquisition through interactive exercises.

Best Practices:

- Clearly define learning outcomes before assigning a simulation.
- Provide guiding questions or reflection prompts to encourage deeper thinking.

5. Gamification: Enhancing Motivation Through Play

- Game-Based Learning Platforms: Kahoot, Quizlet Live, and Socrative turn assessments into engaging, competitive activities.
- Point-Based Challenges: Awarding digital badges, leaderboards, and incentives motivates student participation.

Best Practices:

- Keep game-based learning aligned with course objectives.
- Encourage collaborative gameplay to enhance peer learning.

6. Discussion and Interactive Collaboration Tools

- Discussion Boards & Polling Tools: Platforms like Padlet, Flipgrid, and Piazza facilitate peer interaction and asynchronous discussions.
- Live Interactive Polling: Tools like Mentimeter and Poll Everywhere engage students in real time during lectures.

Best Practices:

- Design open-ended prompts that encourage critical discourse.
- Use anonymous polling to engage hesitant students.

Best Practices for Integrating Multimedia and Interactive Content into Teaching

1. Align Multimedia with Learning Objectives

- Use multimedia strategically—ensure that it enhances, rather than distracts from, learning.
- Design activities, requiring students to engage actively with the content (e.g., responding to video-based questions, analyzing data visualizations).

2. Ensure Accessibility and Inclusivity

- Provide alternative formats (captions, transcripts, colorblind-friendly visuals).
- Use screen reader-compatible materials to accommodate visually impaired students.

3. Balance Multimedia with Traditional Learning Methods

- Avoid overloading students with excessive multimedia, which can lead to cognitive fatigue.
- Combine digital tools with readings, discussions, and hands-on activities for a well-rounded experience.

4. Use Analytics to Track Student Engagement

- LMS analytics (Canvas, Blackboard, Moodle) can show which videos, simulations, or discussion boards students engage with most.
- Use student feedback surveys to evaluate which multimedia strategies are most effective.

Conclusion: Transforming Learning Through Multimedia and Interactivity

Integrating multimedia and interactive content into teaching is no longer an optional enhancement—it is an essential strategy for fostering student engagement, deepening understanding, and preparing students for a digital-first world. By thoughtfully incorporating videos, podcasts, simulations, gamification, and interactive tools, professors can cater to diverse learning styles, create dynamic learning environments, and ensure their teaching remains relevant and impactful.

The goal is to enhance pedagogical effectiveness, ensuring that multimedia content complements learning objectives, promotes active engagement, and empowers students to take control of their educational journey.

Using AI Tools for Personalized Learning and Feedback: Transforming Higher Education

The integration of artificial intelligence (AI) in higher education is revolutionizing how instructors design courses, assess student performance, and provide feedback. AI-driven tools offer personalized learning experiences that adapt to individual student needs, enhancing both engagement and academic achievement. By leveraging AI for adaptive learning pathways, automated feedback, intelligent tutoring, and predictive analytics, educators can optimize instruction, streamline assessments, and improve student outcomes.

For new college professors, understanding how to effectively incorporate AI-driven tools into their teaching is essential for creating dynamic, inclusive, and student-centered learning environments. This section explores the role of AI in education, key AI tools for personalized learning and feedback, implementation strategies, and ethical considerations.

The Role of AI in Higher Education

AI technologies enable data-driven, responsive teaching methods that go beyond traditional approaches. AI enhances learning by:

Personalizing instruction based on student strengths, weaknesses, and learning styles.
Providing real-time feedback, helping students improve their work before final submission.
Automating administrative tasks, allowing instructors to focus on deeper student engagement.
Identifying at-risk students through predictive analytics, enabling early intervention.

By incorporating machine learning algorithms, predictive analytics, and natural language processing, AI tools augment, rather than replace, the educator's role, offering students more meaningful, customized, and accessible learning experiences.

AI Tools for Personalized Learning

AI-driven personalized learning adapts content, pacing, and feedback based on individual student progress. These tools help close knowledge gaps, reinforce comprehension, and optimize study time.

1. Adaptive Learning Platforms

Adaptive learning tools use AI algorithms to tailor coursework to each student's learning pace, strengths, and areas needing improvement.

- **Example Platforms**:
    - **Knewton Alta**: Customizes coursework based on student responses.
    - **Smart Sparrow**: Provides adaptive course modules with AI-powered assessments.
    - **Socratic by Google**: Uses AI-driven explanations and step-by-step solutions for problem-solving.

Best Practices for Implementation:

- Use adaptive quizzes and diagnostics to assess prior knowledge before instruction.
- Incorporate real-time adjustments that modify lesson plans based on student performance.
- Ensure that students understand how to engage with adaptive learning tools effectively.

2. AI-Powered Intelligent Tutoring Systems (ITS)

AI tutors provide personalized, interactive learning support, simulating human tutoring by identifying conceptual gaps and offering targeted explanations.

- **Example Platforms**:
    - IBM Watson Tutor: Provides AI-based student mentoring.

- Carnegie Learning's MATHia: Offers personalized tutoring in mathematics.
- Duolingo: Uses AI to customize language-learning experiences.

Best Practices for Implementation:

- Use AI tutors for supplementary instruction, ensuring students still engage with faculty for complex discussions.
- Combine AI tutoring with peer learning and instructor guidance to reinforce concepts.

3. AI-Enhanced Study Assistants and Chatbots

AI chatbots provide instant, 24/7 academic support, answering student queries, guiding research, and offering study recommendations.

- **Example Platforms**:
  - **ChatGPT**: Assists students in brainstorming, research, and writing refinement.
  - **Elicit**: AI-powered research assistant that synthesizes academic papers.
  - **Quizlet AI Tutor**: Generates adaptive quizzes and flashcards.

Best Practices for Implementation:

- Encourage individuals to use AI chatbots for clarification and exploratory learning rather than direct answers to assignments.
- Embed chatbot assistance into LMS platforms to provide seamless access to AI support.

AI Tools for Automated and Personalized Feedback

Providing timely and detailed feedback is one of the most critical aspects of effective teaching, yet it can be time-consuming for instructors. AI tools help streamline feedback by offering instant, data-driven, and personalized recommendations.

1. AI-Based Writing Evaluation and Feedback Tools

AI-driven writing assistants analyze grammar, structure, clarity, and argumentation, providing instant formative feedback.

- **Example Platforms**:
  - Grammarly: AI-powered writing refinement tool.
  - Turnitin Feedback Studio: Combines plagiarism detection with AI-assisted writing feedback.
  - ProWritingAid: Analyzes writing style, readability, and structure.

Best Practices for Implementation:

- Encourage students to review AI-generated feedback before submission, promoting self-editing.
- Use AI writing tools as a first-level review, with faculty providing deeper conceptual feedback.

2. AI-Powered Automated Grading Systems

AI can assist with grading objective and subjective assessments, reducing instructor workload while maintaining grading consistency.

- **Example Platforms**:
    - **Gradescope**: Uses AI to grade assignments, coding projects, and handwritten work.
    - **Peergrade**: AI-assisted peer review platform for structured feedback.

Best Practices for Implementation:

- Use AI grading for low-stakes assessments to free time for instructor-led feedback on critical assignments.
- Ensure human oversight in AI grading to avoid errors in subjective evaluation.

3. AI-Driven Voice and Video Feedback

AI can transcribe, analyze, and provide insights on student presentations, speeches, or video submissions.

- **Example Platforms**:
    - PitchVantage: AI-based speech analysis for presentations.
    - GoReact: Allows AI-enhanced video feedback for student performances.

Best Practices for Implementation:

- Provide blended AI and instructor feedback to maintain a personal connection with students.
- Encourage students to use AI-driven voice analysis to refine public speaking and communication skills.

Implementing AI in Teaching: Best Practices

1. Align AI Tools with Learning Objectives

- AI should enhance—not replace—faculty instruction.
- Select AI tools, aligning with course goals and student learning needs.

2. Maintain a Human-AI Balance

- AI tools should support faculty expertise and student autonomy, rather than making educational experiences overly mechanized.
- Foster interactive discussions alongside AI-driven insights.

3. Promote Ethical AI Use and Digital Literacy

- Educate students about responsible AI use, emphasizing academic integrity and critical evaluation of AI-generated responses.
- Address concerns about data privacy, bias, and AI reliability.

4. Encourage AI-Enhanced Reflection and Self-Regulated Learning

- Have students reflect on AI-generated feedback before making revisions.
- Use AI-driven learning dashboards to help students track their own progress.

Challenges and Ethical Considerations in AI-Powered Learning

While AI offers immense potential, critical challenges and ethical considerations must be addressed:

Bias in AI Algorithms: AI tools may reflect biases from training data, leading to skewed feedback or evaluation.
Data Privacy & Security: Ensure AI tools comply with FERPA and GDPR regulations to protect student data.
Over-Reliance on AI: Students may develop dependency on AI tools rather than honing independent problem-solving skills.

Professors should encourage mindful AI usage, integrating AI as a supplementary learning tool rather than a replacement for academic rigor and personal engagement.

Conclusion: AI as a Catalyst for Personalized and Effective Teaching

The integration of AI tools in higher education signifies a paradigm shift in the teaching and learning environment, offering unparalleled opportunities for personalized learning, automated feedback, and enhanced student engagement. When implemented strategically, AI can:

Empower learners to own their journey through adaptive and interactive tools.
Provide timely, data-driven feedback that enhances academic growth.
Support faculty in administrative and instructional tasks, freeing up time for deeper pedagogical interactions.

By embracing AI as an evolution of rather than a replacement for teaching, new college professors can cultivate dynamic, personalized, and student-centered learning environments, preparing students for a future where AI and human intelligence coexist in education and beyond.

Best Practices for Hybrid and Online Instruction: Creating Effective Digital Learning Environments

As technology continues to reshape higher education, hybrid and online instruction have become essential modes of teaching, offering flexibility, accessibility, and scalability. Whether delivering fully online courses or blending in-person and digital experiences through hybrid instruction, college professors must strategically design courses, foster engagement, and leverage technology to ensure meaningful learning outcomes.

Hybrid and online learning environments require more than simply transferring traditional lectures to a virtual format; they demand intentional course design, robust student support systems, and interactive digital strategies to create engaging and effective learning experiences. This section explores best practices for structuring online and hybrid courses, enhancing student engagement, utilizing technology effectively, and enabling equitable access for all learners.

Understanding Hybrid and Online Instruction

1. Online Learning: Fully Digital Course Delivery

Online instruction occurs entirely in a virtual environment, either synchronously (real-time sessions) or asynchronously (on-demand learning materials).

Synchronous Online Learning:

- Students and instructors engage in real-time virtual interactions via Zoom, Microsoft Teams, or Google Meet.
- Encourages immediate feedback and discussion but requires scheduling considerations across time zones.

Asynchronous Online Learning:

- Course materials (e.g., video lectures, discussion boards, assignments) are accessible anytime.
- Offers greater flexibility but requires strong self-regulation skills from students.

2. Hybrid Learning: A Blend of Instruction Approaches

Hybrid (or blended) learning combines face-to-face classroom experiences with online components, allowing for greater flexibility while maintaining personal interaction.

Flipped Classroom Model:

- Students review materials online before attending class, using in-person time for discussions, problem-solving, and applied learning.

Rotational Model:

- Students alternate between in-person and online sessions, ensuring consistent interaction in both environments.

By thoughtfully integrating online and in-person components, hybrid learning maximizes the advantages of both modalities, providing interaction, flexibility, and engagement.

Best Practices for Designing Hybrid and Online Courses

1. Establish Clear Course Structure and Expectations

Online and hybrid learners thrive in courses that are well-organized, transparent, and easy to navigate.

Use a Learning Management System (LMS) Effectively

- Organize content into modules or weekly sections within platforms like Canvas, Blackboard, or Moodle.
- Ensure a logical flow of materials, assessments, and activities.
- Clearly outline due dates, participation expectations, and grading policies.

Provide a Comprehensive Course Orientation

- Offer an introductory module with a course overview, syllabus breakdown, and LMS tutorial.
- Record a welcome video introducing yourself, the course, and best practices for success.

Communicate Expectations Clearly

- Establish email, discussion board, and office hour protocols for contacting the instructor.
- Set response time expectations for emails and feedback (e.g., "I will respond to inquiries within 24–48 hours").

2. Foster Engagement and Interaction in Online Spaces

One of the critical challenges of online instruction is preventing student isolation and disengagement.

Use Interactive Discussion Boards

- Replace traditional "post once, reply twice" prompts with debate-style discussions, case study analyses, and student-led questions.
- Utilize multimedia responses, allowing students to record video/audio replies instead of text-based posts.

Incorporate Active Learning Strategies

- Integrate collaborative tools such as Padlet, Google Docs, and Miro for brainstorming and group work.
- Use live polling (Mentimeter, Poll Everywhere) to check comprehension during synchronous sessions.

Leverage Small Group Interactions

- In synchronous sessions, use breakout rooms (Zoom, Microsoft Teams) for peer discussions and problem-solving.
- Assign team projects where students collaborate asynchronously using shared workspaces.

Encourage Instructor Presence

- Post weekly video announcements summarizing key takeaways and upcoming assignments.
- Engage in discussion boards with thoughtful feedback and guiding questions.
- Hold virtual office hours to provide direct student support.

3. Optimize Multimedia and Technology for Online Learning

Effective hybrid and online courses require intentional use of technology and multimedia to enhance, rather than overwhelm, students.

Use High-Quality Video and Audio

- Keep lecture videos concise (5–15 minutes) to maintain attention.
- Use professional microphones and clear visuals for recorded lectures.
- Ensure all videos have captions and transcripts for accessibility.

Gamify Learning with Interactive Elements

- Incorporate game-based learning platforms (Kahoot, Quizlet, and Badgr) to boost engagement.
- Use AI-based adaptive learning tools (Knewton, Duolingo) to personalize learning paths.

Balance Asynchronous and Synchronous Components

- Provide multiple ways for students to engage, such as recorded lectures for asynchronous review.
- Use low-bandwidth alternatives (PDF readings, discussion-based assignments) for students with limited internet access.

4. Design Effective Assessments for Online and Hybrid Learning

Traditional exams may not be ideal for remote learning environments, requiring innovative approaches to assessment.

Emphasize Authentic Assessments

- Replace high-stakes exams with case studies, research projects, and portfolio submissions.
- Use peer review to enhance learning through student-driven feedback.

Utilize AI-Driven and Automated Grading Tools

- AI-powered tools like Gradescope and Turnitin assist in evaluating assignments efficiently.
- Use auto-graded quizzes for formative assessments while reserving manual grading for deeper evaluations.

Encourage Self-Reflection and Metacognition

- Require students to submit learning journals, reflections, or self-assessments alongside assignments.
- Use scaffolded assignments (draft-submission cycles) to provide iterative feedback.

5. Support Student Success in Virtual Learning Environments

Hybrid and online students require guidance, motivation, and accessibility support to succeed.

Monitor Student Engagement Using LMS Analytics

- Track assignment submissions, discussion participation, and video watch time to identify at-risk students.
- Reach out via personalized messages if students show signs of disengagement.

Provide Technical Support and Resources

- Offer tutorials on using the LMS, submitting assignments, and troubleshooting technical issues.
- Direct students to institutional IT support and digital literacy workshops.

Be Flexible and Understanding

- Recognize challenges such as time zone differences, internet limitations, and personal circumstances.
- Offer alternative submission options for students facing technical barriers.

The Future of Hybrid and Online Instruction: Emerging Trends

As hybrid and online learning evolve, emerging technologies and pedagogical innovations are shaping the future of digital education:

Artificial Intelligence (AI) in Personalized Learning

- AI-powered chatbots and tutors can provide real-time academic support [140].

- AI-driven analytics predict student learning patterns to offer personalized study recommendations [141].

Virtual Reality (VR) and Augmented Reality (AR) for Immersive Learning

- Platforms like Labster and Google Expeditions enable virtual lab simulations and 3D explorations.
- AR-enhanced textbooks provide interactive, multi-sensory learning experiences.

Blockchain and Micro-Credentials

- Digital credentials, blockchain-based transcripts, and micro-certifications are gaining traction.
- Students can earn and display digital badges for competency-based achievements.

Conclusion: Creating Engaging and Effective Hybrid and Online Courses

Hybrid and online instruction offer powerful opportunities to expand learning beyond traditional classrooms, but effective implementation requires intentionality, innovation, and student-centered design.

By structuring courses clearly, fostering engagement, integrating technology effectively, and prioritizing student support, professors can create high-impact digital learning experiences that enhance accessibility, engagement, and academic success.

Ultimately, the goal is not just to deliver content online but to create a dynamic, interactive, and personalized learning environment that empowers students to succeed in a digital-first educational landscape.

Digital Accessibility and Universal Design for Learning (UDL): Creating Inclusive Learning Environments

As higher education embraces technology-driven instruction, digital accessibility and Universal Design for Learning (UDL) have become essential pillars of inclusive teaching. Ensuring digital content is accessible to all students—including those with disabilities—goes beyond legal compliance; it is about fostering an equitable learning environment where all learners, regardless of ability, can engage with course materials meaningfully.

For new college professors, integrating accessibility and UDL principles into course design enhances student engagement, retention, and overall learning outcomes. This section explores the importance of digital accessibility, the core principles of UDL, best practices for creating accessible course materials, and the role of technology in promoting inclusive learning.

Understanding Digital Accessibility in Higher Education

1. What Is Digital Accessibility?

Digital accessibility ensures that all individuals, including those with disabilities, can access and engage with online learning materials, tools, and resources. This includes individuals with:

- **Visual impairments** (blindness, low vision, color blindness).
- **Hearing impairments** (deafness, hard of hearing).
- **Motor impairments** (difficulty using a keyboard/mouse, limited mobility).
- **Cognitive and learning disabilities** (dyslexia, ADHD, autism spectrum disorders).

2. The Legal and Ethical Imperative

Institutions must comply with federal and international accessibility standards, including:
Americans with Disabilities Act (ADA) – Requires equal access to educational resources.
Section 508 of the Rehabilitation Act – Mandates digital accessibility for federally funded institutions.
Web Content Accessibility Guidelines (WCAG 2.1) – Provides global best practices for accessible digital content.

Beyond compliance, accessibility fosters student success and retention, ensuring that all learners can fully participate in academic life.

Universal Design for Learning (UDL): A Framework for Inclusive Teaching

1. What Is Universal Design for Learning (UDL)?

UDL is an instructional framework that proactively designs learning experiences to accommodate diverse student needs from the design phase, rather than retrofitting accessibility after barriers arise. It focuses on enabling multiple means of representation, engagement, and expression to support a wide range of learning abilities, preferences, and backgrounds.

2. The Three Core Principles of UDL

Principle 1: Multiple Means of Representation (The "What" of Learning)

- Students perceive and process information differently—some learn better through text, others through visuals, and others through auditory content.
- Provide multiple formats for instructional materials:
    - Text-based: Lecture transcripts, readable PDFs.
    - Visual-based: Infographics, concept maps, charts.
    - Audio-based: Recorded lectures, podcasts, screen readers.
    - Video-based: Captioned videos, ASL interpretations.

Principle 2: Multiple Means of Engagement (The "Why" of Learning)

- Students engage with learning in different ways—some thrive on collaborative discussions, while others prefer independent study.
- Strategies to enhance engagement:
    - Use interactive discussions and peer collaboration.
    - Incorporate gamification and scenario-based learning.
    - Provide self-paced learning options to accommodate different processing speeds.
    - Connect course material to real-world applications and student interests.

Principle 3: Multiple Means of Action and Expression (The "How" of Learning)

- Individuals demonstrate knowledge in diverse ways—not all excel in timed exams or essay writing.
- Offer flexibility in assessments, such as:
    - Written essays or recorded video reflections.
    - Multiple-choice quizzes or project-based assessments.
    - Presentations or interactive simulations.

By applying these UDL principles, instructors reduce barriers to learning, ensuring that all students can access and demonstrate their knowledge effectively.

Best Practices for Digital Accessibility and UDL Implementation

1. Designing Accessible Course Materials

Use Readable and Well-Structured Documents

- Headings and subheadings (H1, H2, H3) improve navigation for screen readers.
- Ensure sufficient contrast between text and background for visibility.
- Use sans-serif fonts (Arial, Verdana) for readability.

Ensure Accessible PDFs and Word Documents

- Avoid scanned PDFs—use OCR-enabled, searchable text.
- Enable alt text descriptions for images and graphs.

Make Presentations and Videos Accessible

- Provide captions and transcripts for video content.
- Use audio descriptions for visually complex media.
- Avoid excessive animations that can distract students with cognitive disabilities.

Provide Flexible Navigation in LMS

- Use consistent layouts in Blackboard, Canvas, or Moodle.
- Enable keyboard navigation for students with motor impairments.
- Label links clearly (e.g., "Download Syllabus [PDF]" instead of "Click Here").

2. Leveraging Technology for Inclusive Learning

AI-Powered Accessibility Tools

- Microsoft Immersive Reader: Converts text to speech, simplifies complex text.
- Grammarly & ProWritingAid: Assist students with dyslexia and language processing disorders.
- Kurzweil 3000 & Read&Write: Assistive technology for reading comprehension and note-taking.

Accessible Video and Audio Content

- Otter.ai & Rev.com: Auto-generate captions and transcripts.
- Panopto & YouTube Studio: Offer built-in captioning tools.

Speech-to-Text and Screen Readers

- Voice Typing (Google Docs) helps students with mobility impairments.
- NVDA, JAWS, and Apple VoiceOver provide screen reading for visually impaired learners.

Alternative Assessment Platforms

- Flipgrid: Allows students to submit video responses instead of written assignments.
- Canva & Piktochart: Enables visual learners to create infographics instead of essays.

Building an Inclusive Teaching Mindset

1. Normalize Accessibility Conversations

- Include a syllabus statement on accessibility resources.
- Offer anonymous feedback forms for students to request accommodations.

2. Adopt a Growth Mindset Toward Digital Accessibility

- Regularly audit course materials for accessibility.
- Seek institutional support and professional development on inclusive teaching practices.

3. Be Proactive, Not Reactive

- Design accessible courses from the start, rather than modifying them upon request.
- Apply UDL principles to all aspects of teaching, from lectures to assessments.

The Future of Digital Accessibility and UDL

As educational technology evolves, AI, machine learning, and immersive tools like VR/AR are shaping the future of accessibility in education.

AI-Driven Personalization

- AI-powered adaptive platforms alter content difficulty based on individual student needs [142].

VR/AR for Inclusive Learning

- Virtual simulations provide sensory-friendly learning environments for neurodivergent students [143].

Blockchain and Digital Credentials

- Micro-credentials allow students to showcase diverse skill sets beyond traditional grading models.

By embracing technology, innovation, and inclusive design, faculty can ensure that every student, regardless of ability, has equitable access to higher education.

Technology Integration Beyond Tools

Faculty in higher education often focus on learning specific instructional technologies—such as learning management systems, polling apps, or collaboration platforms—without adopting a strategic framework for technology use. While proficiency with tools is necessary, it is not sufficient. Effective technology integration requires thoughtful alignment with pedagogy, careful evaluation of new tools, leadership in adoption, and an eye toward equity, privacy, and sustainability. Without this broader perspective, technology risks becoming a distraction or an administrative burden rather than a catalyst for meaningful learning. Moving beyond tools toward intentional integration ensures that technology amplifies teaching effectiveness and enhances student learning.

Evaluating Emerging Educational Technologies

Because new technologies are constantly entering the educational marketplace, faculty must learn to evaluate strategically rather than reactively. Not every tool adds value, and chasing every innovation can fragment instruction. A structured evaluation process allows faculty to determine whether a tool is truly worth adopting.

- **Pedagogical Fit**
  The first and most important criterion is whether the technology supports core learning objectives. Tools should enhance teaching practices already known to be effective (e.g.,

active learning, formative assessment, collaborative problem-solving). Faculty should ask: *Does this tool allow students to achieve outcomes more effectively or efficiently than without it?* If the answer is no, the tool may be more of a novelty than a necessity.

- **Evidence of Effectiveness**
  Adoption should be guided by research, not marketing claims. Faculty can look for:
    - Peer-reviewed studies examining student learning outcomes.
    - Case reports from similar institutions or disciplines.
    - Pilot data collected within their own department or class.
      Technologies with little or no evidence of effectiveness should be approached cautiously.

- **Ease of Use**
  Even powerful tools can fail if they are too complex. Faculty must weigh the learning curve against the anticipated benefits. Considerations include:
    - Intuitive interface for both instructors and students.
    - Availability of training resources.
    - Reliability across devices and operating systems.
      If a tool requires significant setup or frequent troubleshooting, adoption may undermine the learning experience.

- **Institutional Support**
  Technologies supported by campus IT services or teaching and learning centers are more sustainable than ad hoc solutions. Supported tools benefit from:
    - Technical help desks for troubleshooting.
    - Integration with existing systems (e.g., LMS single sign-on).
    - Compliance with institutional privacy and accessibility policies.
      Unsupported tools, while tempting, may create long-term challenges if institutional approval is withdrawn.

- **Scalability**
  Faculty should consider whether the tool works in a variety of contexts:
    - Can it scale from small seminars to large lectures?
    - Is it adaptable for hybrid and fully online courses?
    - Does it support both synchronous and asynchronous use cases?
      Scalable tools maximize institutional investment and allow students to carry skills across courses.

Key Takeaway

Evaluating educational technology requires a framework of alignment, evidence, usability, support, and scalability. Faculty should adopt tools only when they demonstrably enhance pedagogy, are supported institutionally, and can serve a wide range of learners effectively. This approach ensures that technology strengthens teaching and learning rather than adding complexity without value.

Leading Technology Adoption Within Departments

Faculty leaders often serve as catalysts for innovation, guiding departments through decisions about which technologies to adopt and how to implement them into teaching. This leadership role requires more than technical expertise—it involves diplomacy, evidence-based advocacy, and the ability to navigate resistance. Technology adoption at the departmental level succeeds when it is collaborative, data-driven, and strategically managed, ensuring that decisions enhance pedagogy rather than simply adding new tools.

Building Consensus

Technology adoption decisions should not be imposed unilaterally. Faculty leaders must cultivate dialogue and shared ownership.

- Transparent Presentations: Introduce the proposed tool by outlining both its strengths and limitations. Avoid overselling, which can create skepticism if results fall short.
- Faculty Input: Encourage colleagues to voice concerns, questions, and alternative ideas. This inclusive process builds trust and buy-in.
- Shared Goals: Frame the technology in terms of department-wide teaching and learning priorities (e.g., improving student engagement, streamlining assessment, or supporting accreditation requirements).

Pilot Programs

Small-scale trials allow departments to test tools in controlled conditions before full implementation.

- Pilot Design: Select a limited number of courses or faculty volunteers to experiment with the technology.
- Data Collection: Gather both quantitative data (student outcomes, usage metrics) and qualitative data (student and faculty feedback).
- Iterative Refinement: Use pilot results to adjust implementation plans, identify training needs, or decide whether the technology is worth scaling.
- Risk Mitigation: Pilots reduce the cost of large-scale failures and provide real evidence for or against adoption.

Evidence-Based Advocacy

Faculty leaders must ground their recommendations in data rather than enthusiasm alone.

- Student Feedback: Collect surveys and testimonials showing how the tool affected learning, engagement, or accessibility.
- Performance Data: Compare student outcomes before and after implementation to demonstrate impact.
- Peer Examples: Share case studies from other institutions or disciplines to illustrate proven benefits.
- Cost-Benefit Analysis: Present financial and workload implications alongside pedagogical gains, providing a holistic picture for decision-making.

Change Management

Resistance to new technologies is natural, especially when faculty worry about increased workload, disruption, or loss of control. Effective leaders approach change management with empathy and support.

- Professional Development: Offer workshops, tutorials, and ongoing training to build confidence.
- Peer Mentoring: Pair early adopters with hesitant colleagues to provide informal support and encouragement.
- Clear Communication: Explain not just *how* the tool works but *why* it matters for student learning and departmental goals.
- Gradual Implementation: Allow flexibility by phasing in adoption rather than mandating immediate, universal use.
By recognizing concerns and providing support, leaders transform resistance into engagement.

Key Takeaway

Leading technology adoption within departments requires consensus-building, pilot testing, evidence-based advocacy, and thoughtful change management. Faculty leaders who combine transparency with strategic planning ensure new technologies are implemented in ways that are sustainable, pedagogically sound, and broadly supported by colleagues.

Training Colleagues on New Pedagogical Technologies

The successful integration of educational technology within a department or institution depends on more than individual adoption—it requires collective capacity-building. Faculty who have developed expertise in new tools can play a pivotal role in training their colleagues, lowering barriers to entry, and fostering a culture of shared experimentation. Effective training should be practical, accessible, and sustained, emphasizing pedagogy as much as technical skill.

Workshops and Demonstrations

Hands-on learning environments are the most effective way for faculty to explore new technologies.

- Low-Stakes Exploration: Workshops should allow colleagues to test tools without the pressure of immediate classroom implementation.
- Modeling Pedagogy: Demonstrations should not only explain *how* a tool works but also illustrate *why* it supports student learning. For example, a polling app demo can be paired with a live active learning exercise.
- Variety of Formats: Offer both in-person and online sessions to accommodate faculty schedules. Short "micro-workshops" (30–45 minutes) can increase participation compared to lengthy trainings.
- Follow-Up Support: Provide office hours or open labs where faculty can seek help while piloting the technology in their own courses.

Mentorship Models

Peer mentoring creates sustainable networks of support that extend beyond formal workshops.

- Early Adopter Mentors: Faculty who have successfully integrated a tool can mentor colleagues through the initial stages of adoption.
- Shadowing Opportunities: Colleagues can observe mentors using the technology in live teaching environments, seeing both benefits and troubleshooting in real time.
- Reciprocal Learning: Mentorship should be a two-way exchange, where experienced users gain new insights from the questions and perspectives of novice adopters.
- Departmental Pairing: Assign mentors within disciplines to contextualize training to subject-specific needs.

Resource Development

Faculty trainers can reduce barriers to adoption by creating reusable materials.

- Step-by-Step Guides: Written instructions with screenshots help colleagues follow along independently.
- Video Tutorials: Short recordings provide visual demonstrations that colleagues can revisit as needed.
- Template Course Shells: Pre-built LMS modules demonstrate best practices and give faculty a ready-made starting point.
- FAQs and Troubleshooting Sheets: Anticipating common questions saves time and reduces frustration for new users.

Peer Sharing Forums

Sustained adoption requires spaces where faculty can share both successes and failures.

- Regular Conversations: Host monthly or semesterly forums where colleagues discuss their experiences with technologies in different courses.
- Showcase Events: Highlight innovative uses of technology in teaching through teaching fairs or faculty panels.
- Failure as Learning: Normalize discussion of what did *not* work, reframing unsuccessful experiments as opportunities for collective learning.
- Online Communities: Use discussion boards, chat platforms, or faculty newsletters to maintain momentum between formal meetings.

Key Takeaway

Training colleagues on new pedagogical technologies is most effective when it is hands-on, supported by mentorship, reinforced with reusable resources, and sustained through peer sharing. By building collective capacity, faculty not only expand technological proficiency but also cultivate a culture of innovation and collaboration where experimentation is encouraged and supported.

Balancing Innovation with Proven Practices

Innovation in educational technology drives progress, but uncritical adoption can harm instructional quality and student outcomes. New tools often generate excitement, yet not every innovation delivers on its promise, and some may even distract from core learning objectives. Faculty must approach technology adoption with a mindset that balances pedagogical innovation with evidence-based practices that have already proven effective. This balance ensures students benefit from both cutting-edge experimentation and the stability of time-tested strategies.

Blend Old and New

Rather than discarding established practices when adopting new technologies, faculty should view technology as an enhancement to proven methods.

- Active Learning Strategies: For example, a traditional think–pair–share exercise can be amplified by a polling app that collects responses in real time, providing both engagement and data insights.
- Lecture Support: Instead of replacing lectures entirely, instructors might supplement them with video modules or interactive quizzes that reinforce key concepts.
- Group Work: Collaborative projects can maintain established teamwork practices while leveraging digital collaboration platforms (e.g., shared documents, project management apps) to extend learning beyond the classroom.
The most effective innovations extend or deepen existing pedagogy rather than displacing it.

Evaluate Outcomes Regularly

Innovation without assessment risks implementing technology that does not actually improve learning. Faculty should build continuous evaluation into their adoption process.

- Student Performance Data: Compare student grades, completion rates, or skill demonstrations before and after technology adoption.
- Student Feedback: Collect surveys and focus group input on usability, engagement, and learning impact.
- Faculty Reflection: Instructors should critically assess whether the tool improved efficiency, engagement, or instructional clarity—or whether it added unnecessary complexity.
- Iterative Adjustment: If outcomes do not align with expectations, faculty should adapt the technology use, supplement it with other strategies, or discontinue it altogether.

Avoid Technology for Its Own Sake

New technologies often create pressure to adopt simply because they are popular or trendy. Faculty must resist this tendency by asking fundamental questions:

- Does it enhance pedagogy? If the tool does not directly serve a course objective or support a teaching method, it should not be adopted.
- Is it sustainable? Tools that require steep learning curves or frequent updates may not provide long-term value.
- Is it equitable? Adoption must not exclude students with limited access to devices, bandwidth, or digital skills.
Innovation should never come at the cost of accessibility, student success, or instructional coherence.

Key Takeaway

Balancing innovation with proven practices means integrating new tools thoughtfully, evaluating their impact rigorously, and resisting adoption for novelty alone. When faculty pair technology with established pedagogical strategies, monitor outcomes, and remain focused on learning objectives, innovation becomes a driver of progress rather than a source of distraction.

Managing Technology Equity Issues Among Students

While technology can enhance learning, it can also widen gaps between students if access and support are uneven. Not all learners have the same devices, reliable internet, or digital literacy skills. Faculty must therefore adopt equity-centered approaches to ensure that technology integration does not exclude or disadvantage vulnerable students. By anticipating barriers and designing with inclusivity in mind, instructors can create a more level playing field that maximizes the benefits of digital tools for everyone.

Access Audits

Understanding student access to technology is the first step in addressing equity.

- Surveys at Course Start: Ask students whether they have reliable access to laptops, mobile devices, internet connections, and quiet study spaces.
- Anonymous Responses: Students may hesitate to disclose challenges directly; anonymous surveys help ensure honest input.
- Use Data to Adapt: If many students lack stable Wi-Fi, faculty may reduce reliance on synchronous video sessions and emphasize asynchronous options instead.

Device-Agnostic Materials

Students rely on a variety of devices, with some completing coursework primarily on smartphones. Faculty should design content that works across platforms.

- Mobile Compatibility: Ensure that LMS pages, readings, and assignments display correctly on phones and tablets.
- Flexible File Formats: Use PDFs, HTML text, and responsive designs rather than requiring specialized software that only runs on high-end devices.

- Avoiding "One-Device Assumptions": Do not assume all students have laptops with webcams or the ability to install large applications.

Low-Bandwidth Alternatives

High-speed internet is not universally available, and heavy reliance on video can create barriers. Faculty can provide lower-bandwidth alternatives without compromising rigor.

- Lecture Alternatives: Offer slide decks with detailed notes, audio-only recordings, or transcripts alongside video lectures.
- Downloadable Content: Provide readings, assignments, and resources that students can download and use offline.
- Flexible Engagement: Where possible, allow students to demonstrate learning through text-based or asynchronous participation rather than requiring live streaming.

Campus Resources

Institutions often provide technology support that students may not know about. Faculty can help by:

- Promoting Loan Programs: Informing students about laptop, tablet, or Wi-Fi hotspot loan programs available through libraries or IT offices.
- Computer Labs and Study Spaces: Directing students to on-campus facilities with reliable hardware and internet.
- Community Resources: Sharing information about public libraries, community centers, or nonprofit organizations that provide access to devices or internet.

Inclusive Design

Equity is not only about access to devices but also about ensuring that digital activities are usable by all learners. Faculty can apply Universal Design for Learning (UDL) principles:

- Multiple Means of Representation: Offer content in text, audio, and visual formats.
- Multiple Means of Engagement: Provide varied ways for students to interact with material (e.g., discussion boards, small group collaborations, individual reflections).
- Multiple Means of Expression: Allow flexibility in how students demonstrate learning (e.g., essays, recorded presentations, infographics).
Inclusive design ensures students with disabilities, language differences, or varying learning needs can fully participate.

Key Takeaway

Equitable technology use requires proactive planning, device-agnostic design, bandwidth-conscious materials, promotion of institutional resources, and inclusive pedagogy. When faculty adopt these practices, technology becomes a bridge rather than a barrier, ensuring that all students can engage fully with digital learning environments.

Data Privacy and Security in Educational Technology

Educational technologies provide powerful tools for teaching and learning, but also introduce significant risks related to student data privacy and cybersecurity. Many platforms collect personal information such as names, email addresses, grades, behavioral analytics, and even biometric identifiers. Faculty must act as responsible stewards of this data, ensuring compliance with legal standards, institutional policies, and ethical obligations. Protecting student privacy is not optional—it is a core responsibility that sustains trust between faculty, institutions, and learners.

Following FERPA and Institutional Policies

The Family Educational Rights and Privacy Act (FERPA) in the United States—and similar laws globally—sets strict limits on how student information can be collected, shared, and stored.

- FERPA Compliance: Faculty must ensure that tools used in courses meet FERPA requirements, particularly when storing or transmitting grades, attendance, or participation data.
- Institutional Oversight: Most universities have approved lists of educational technologies that have undergone legal and IT review. Faculty should prioritize these tools and consult IT services before adopting new platforms.
- International Students: When teaching students abroad, faculty should also consider local regulations such as GDPR (General Data Protection Regulation) in Europe, which carries additional restrictions on data use.

Avoiding Unauthorized Platforms

The appeal of "free" or widely available tools can be strong, but unauthorized platforms may compromise privacy.

- Unvetted Tools: Apps that track user behavior, sell data to third parties, or lack secure hosting should not be required for coursework.
- Consent Issues: Even when optional, students may feel pressured to use tools that expose their data. Faculty should provide secure alternatives.
- Institution-Approved Alternatives: When possible, select tools already licensed and supported by the institution, as these have undergone security vetting.

Transparency with Students

Students deserve to understand how their data is collected and used. Faculty should communicate clearly:

- What Data Is Collected: Specify whether the tool collects names, logins, participation records, location data, or usage analytics.
- Why It Is Collected: Explain how the data supports learning outcomes (e.g., analytics for engagement, tracking progress).

- Who Has Access: Clarify whether only the instructor, institutional staff, or third-party vendors can view or use the data.
- Options for Students: Provide alternatives when students have legitimate concerns about privacy, such as pseudonym use in public forums.

Secure Practices

Faculty themselves must adopt strong cybersecurity habits when handling student data.

- Passwords and Authentication: Use strong, unique passwords for educational platforms and enable multifactor authentication whenever possible.
- Restricted Access: Limit access to student records to only those with legitimate instructional responsibilities.
- Data Storage: Store sensitive student information only in institution-approved systems. Avoid using personal devices, unsecured cloud storage, or email attachments for grade or identity-related information.
- Regular Updates: Keep software, browsers, and operating systems updated to reduce vulnerability to cyberattacks.

Key Takeaway

Educational technology brings both opportunities and responsibilities. Faculty must safeguard student data by ensuring compliance with FERPA and institutional policies, avoiding unauthorized platforms, maintaining transparency with students, and practicing secure data management. When privacy and security are prioritized, faculty not only protect students but also build trust in the responsible use of technology in higher education.

Long-Term Technology Planning for Courses

The most effective use of educational technology is not reactive but strategically planned over time. Semester-to-semester decisions, made without a broader vision, often lead to inconsistency for students, wasted resources, and faculty frustration. Sustainable integration requires a long-term approach that anticipates change, manages costs, and aligns with institutional priorities. Faculty who plan strategically ensure that technology supports continuity, stability, and growth in their courses.

Develop Technology Roadmaps

Technology roadmaps provide a structured plan for adoption over multiple semesters.

- Continuity for Students: When students encounter consistent platforms and tools across courses, they spend less time learning technology and more time engaging with content.
- Faculty Efficiency: Long-term planning reduces the need to rebuild course materials every term. Templates, modules, and resources can be reused and refined.

- Strategic Sequencing: Faculty can plan when and how to introduce more advanced tools as students progress through a program, building digital literacy alongside disciplinary skills.
- Communication with Colleagues: Roadmaps also allow coordination across courses, preventing redundancy and ensuring students experience a balanced variety of tools.

Plan for Obsolescence

Technology changes rapidly, and tools that are cutting-edge today may be obsolete tomorrow. Faculty should plan for transitions in advance.

- Identify Vulnerable Tools: Watch for signs of limited vendor support, declining adoption rates, or lack of updates.
- Backup Strategies: Have alternatives ready so transitions are smooth rather than disruptive. For example, if a polling app is discontinued, know which LMS-native or institution-supported tool can replace it.
- Student Continuity: Avoid mid-semester tool changes unless absolutely necessary. Transitions should ideally occur between terms with clear communication to students.

Evaluate Costs

Cost considerations extend beyond subscription fees. Long-term planning requires careful budgeting of both financial and time investments.

- Direct Costs: Subscriptions, licenses, or pay-per-use fees must be factored into course budgets.
- Hidden Costs: Consider training time, setup workload, and student expenses for devices or materials.
- Return on Investment (ROI): Evaluate whether the pedagogical benefits justify the costs compared to free or institutionally provided alternatives.
- Equity Considerations: Avoid requiring tools that impose undue financial burden on students, particularly when free or low-cost options exist.

Institutional Alignment

Individual faculty choices should not exist in isolation from broader institutional strategies.

- Departmental Integration: Align tool use with departmental goals, ensuring consistency across courses and reducing redundancy.
- Institutional Support: Prioritize tools that IT services or teaching centers can support with training, troubleshooting, and compliance oversight.
- Accreditation and Assessment: Consider whether technologies support institutional reporting requirements or program-level learning outcomes.
- Collaborative Planning: Faculty should engage in conversations with colleagues and administrators to ensure their long-term technology plans contribute to, rather than conflict with, institutional initiatives.

Key Takeaway

Long-term technology planning ensures that integration is sustainable, cost-effective, and institutionally aligned. By developing technology roadmaps, anticipating obsolescence, evaluating costs, and coordinating with institutional strategies, faculty create continuity for students and efficiency for themselves. Combined with equity, privacy, and pedagogy-focused adoption, strategic planning positions technology as a durable force multiplier for learning rather than a disruptive trend.

Conclusion: The Responsibility of Inclusive Digital Teaching

Creating accessible and inclusive digital learning environments is not just about compliance—it is about equity, student success, and fostering a culture of belonging.

By integrating digital accessibility and UDL principles, educators can:
 Reduce barriers to learning and accommodate diverse student needs.
 Promote engagement and participation for all students.
 Enhance the effectiveness of technology-driven teaching.

By prioritizing accessibility from course design to assessment, instructors can empower students with the tools, flexibility, and support they need to succeed—ensuring that higher education remains a space of inclusion, innovation, and limitless learning opportunities.

The Future of Teaching with Technology

The integration of technology in teaching is no longer optional—it is a fundamental component of modern higher education. When used effectively, digital tools can enrich learning experiences, improve student outcomes, and create more flexible and inclusive educational environments. However, technology should always serve as a means to enhance teaching rather than replace sound pedagogical practices.

By embracing LMS platforms, interactive content, AI-driven personalization, and best practices for hybrid and online instruction, faculty can create dynamic and engaging courses that meet the needs of diverse learners. Additionally, prioritizing digital accessibility ensures all individuals have equal opportunities to succeed.

As educational technology continues to evolve, faculty must remain adaptable, continuously exploring new tools and refining their approaches to instruction. By thoughtfully integrating technology into their teaching, educators can foster innovation, enhance student engagement, and prepare indivdiuals for the digital demands of the future.

Chapter 8: Research, Scholarship, and Teaching Integration

The role of a professor extends beyond the classroom, encompassing research, scholarship, and service to the academic community. In higher education, professors are expected to contribute research to their respective industries while also delivering high-quality instruction. The integration of research and teaching is essential for cultivating intellectual curiosity, encouraging student engagement, and advancing knowledge within a discipline.

This chapter explores the balance between teaching, research, and institutional service, highlighting how faculty can integrate their scholarship into the classroom to enhance student learning. It also examines strategies for fostering

Figure 8.1. Integrating Disciplines [219].

student involvement in research, guiding them through scholarly inquiry, and mentoring them in academic writing and presentation. Additionally, the chapter addresses best practices for faculty research productivity, navigating peer-reviewed publication processes, and aligning research efforts with institutional goals.

By effectively combining teaching and research, faculty can cultivate an enriching learning environment not only imparting knowledge but also cultivating critical thinking, problem-solving skills, and a passion for discovery in students.

Balancing Teaching, Research, and Service: Navigating the Multifaceted Role of a College Professor

One of the defining characteristics of an academic career is the need to balance multiple professional responsibilities, namely teaching, research, and service. Unlike many professions that focus on a singular domain of expertise, faculty members must excel in the classroom, contribute to scholarly advancements, and engage in institutional and community service—all while maintaining a sustainable workload and career trajectory.

For new college professors, learning to harmonize these responsibilities is essential for professional success, personal fulfillment, and long-term career advancement. Effective time management, strategic planning, and intentional integration of these roles can transform potential overload into synergy, creating a productive and fulfilling academic career.

This section explores the three pillars of faculty work, the challenges associated with balancing them, and practical strategies for successfully navigating academic life.

The Three Core Responsibilities of Faculty Work

1. Teaching: The Foundation of Academic Life

Teaching is often the most visible and immediate responsibility of a faculty member, directly shaping student learning, engagement, and institutional reputation. Effective teaching demands more than industry expertise—it requires curriculum development, innovative pedagogy, student mentoring, and continuous improvement.

Key Components of Teaching Excellence:

- Designing engaging, student-centered courses with clear learning objectives.
- Employing innovative teaching strategies such as flipped classrooms, active learning, and technology integration.
- Assessing student learning through formative and summative evaluations.
- Providing meaningful feedback and mentorship to support student success.
- Continuously refining teaching approaches through self-assessment and professional development.

Common Challenges:

- Balancing large course loads with research and service obligations.
- Managing diverse student needs and expectations.
- Keeping up with pedagogical advancements and instructional technologies.

Strategies for Effective Teaching Management:

- Develop a well-structured syllabus that includes clear expectations and deadlines.
- Use Learning Management Systems (LMS) to automate grading, distribute materials, and streamline communication.
- Implement efficient grading techniques, such as rubrics and peer assessments, to manage workload.
- Dedicate consistent office hours and consider group advising sessions to maximize student support.

2. Research: Advancing Knowledge and Professional Growth

Research serves as the intellectual engine of academia, expanding knowledge, influencing policy, and driving innovation. Faculty members, especially those at research-intensive institutions, are expected to produce scholarly publications, secure funding, and contribute to disciplinary advancements.

Key Components of Research Productivity:

- Developing a focused research agenda aligned with expertise and institutional priorities.
- Writing and publishing peer-reviewed works, including journal books, articles, or conference papers.
- Securing grants and funding from governmental and private organizations.
- Engaging in collaborative research with colleagues, graduate students, and external partners.
- Presenting findings at academic conferences and public forums.

Common Challenges:

- Finding time for research amid teaching and service obligations.
- Securing funding and institutional support for research projects.
- Managing multiple research projects while maintaining quality and impact.

Strategies for Research Productivity:

- Establish a dedicated research schedule, blocking time for writing and data analysis.
- Collaborate with colleagues or students to share research responsibilities and resources.
- Apply for internal and external funding opportunities to support projects.
- Utilize technology tools for literature reviews, citation management (Zotero, EndNote), and writing efficiency (Scrivener, Overleaf).
- Align research with teaching and service by integrating research projects into coursework or community initiatives.

3. Service: Contributing to the Academic and Broader Community

Service is an integral, though often underappreciated, aspect of faculty work. It involves contributions to departmental, institutional, professional, and public service activities that support the functioning and mission of academia.

Key Areas of Faculty Service:

- Institutional Service: Participating in faculty governance, curriculum committees, and accreditation efforts.
- Professional Service: Reviewing journal articles, organizing conferences, serving on editorial boards.

- Community Engagement: Collaborating with local organizations, offering public lectures, or engaging in outreach programs.

Common Challenges:

- Overcommitting to service roles at the expense of research and teaching.
- Navigating institutional expectations without clear guidelines for service load.
- Balancing internal (university) and external (professional) service commitments.

Strategies for Effective Service Management:

- Prioritize service roles that align with personal and professional interests.
- Limit committee involvement to meaningful and impactful contributions.
- Learn to say no tactfully to excessive service requests.
- Seek mentorship on service expectations, particularly for tenure and promotion.

Achieving Balance: Strategies for Sustainable Academic Success

Balancing teaching, research, and service requires intentional planning, strategic decision-making, and ongoing self-reflection. Below are best practices for harmonizing these responsibilities effectively.

1. Time Management and Prioritization

- Use calendar blocking to allocate time for teaching prep, grading, research writing, and meetings.
- Set weekly and semester-long goals for research progress, course development, and service commitments.
- Follow the 80/20 Rule (Pareto Principle)—focus on the most impactful activities that yield the greatest results.

2. Leveraging Integration Across Roles

- Align research with teaching by designing courses that incorporate student-led research projects.
- Use service roles (e.g., faculty committees, journal reviewing) to network and advance research interests.
- Publish scholarship of teaching and learning (SoTL) studies to integrate pedagogy and research.

3. Setting Boundaries and Avoiding Burnout

- Recognize when to say no—not every request is equally important.
- Seek collaborative teaching and research models to share workload.

- Maintain a healthy work-life balance, ensuring time for personal commitments, development and well-being.

4. Seeking Mentorship and Institutional Support

Engage with senior faculty mentors for guidance on balancing responsibilities.
Utilize faculty development programs, writing retreats, and research grants for professional growth.
Collaborate with interdisciplinary teams to share research and service responsibilities.

Conclusion: Crafting a Sustainable and Fulfilling Academic Career

Balancing teaching, research, and service is an ongoing challenge, yet intentional planning, strategic alignment, and self-awareness can transform these responsibilities into a cohesive and fulfilling academic career.

By adopting efficient time management strategies, integrating responsibilities, and setting clear priorities, faculty members can excel in all three areas while maintaining well-being and professional satisfaction.

Ultimately, the goal is not to simply divide time evenly between teaching, research, and service but to create synergy between these roles, ensuring that each area enriches the others—leading to greater impact, career advancement, and a meaningful contribution to academia.

Incorporating Research into Teaching: Bridging Scholarship and Pedagogy for Enhanced Learning

The integration of research into teaching represents a hallmark of higher education, where faculty members are not only knowledge disseminators but also active scholars contributing to the advancement of their fields. This dynamic interplay between research and instruction transforms the classroom into an environment of intellectual discovery, critical inquiry, and evidence-based learning.

For new college professors, incorporating research into teaching elevates student engagement, fosters a culture of inquiry, and enhances the relevance of course content. By embedding current scholarship, research methodologies, and discipline-specific discoveries into teaching practices, faculty can inspire students to think critically, conduct independent research, and contribute meaningfully to their fields.

This section explores the pedagogical benefits of integrating research into teaching, effective strategies for doing so, and practical examples of how faculty can infuse their research expertise into coursework to create a dynamic, inquiry-driven learning experience.

The Importance of Integrating Research into Teaching

1. Enhancing Student Learning Through Inquiry and Discovery

Integrating research into teaching shifts the classroom dynamic from passive knowledge transfer to active exploration, fostering:

Critical thinking and analytical skills—Students learn to evaluate evidence, analyze data, and construct well-reasoned arguments.

Engagement with real-world applications—Research-based learning connects theoretical concepts to practical, discipline-specific issues.

Stronger problem-solving abilities—Students are exposed to methodologies that encourage investigative learning and experimental approaches.

2. Strengthening the Link Between Theory and Practice

By weaving current research findings and methodologies into coursework, faculty members demonstrate how knowledge is constructed, tested, and refined over time. This approach:

Reinforces the evolving nature of knowledge and helps students understand that disciplines are dynamic rather than static.

Encourages students to explore unanswered questions and contribute to the knowledge economy.

Helps students recognize research as an essential component of professional and academic growth.

3. Promoting Student Involvement in Research

Introducing research into teaching creates pathways for students to engage in independent and collaborative scholarly work. Benefits include:

Increased participation in undergraduate and graduate research projects.

Development of academic writing, data analysis, and presentation skills.

Enhanced preparation for graduate school and research-intensive careers.

By making research a visible and integral part of teaching, faculty can nurture the next generation of scholars, scientists, and thought leaders.

Strategies for Incorporating Research into Teaching

Effectively integrating research into teaching requires intentional course design, innovative pedagogy, and active engagement. The following strategies illustrate various ways in which faculty can seamlessly merge scholarship with instruction.

1. Infusing Course Content with Current Research

One of the simplest yet most impactful ways to integrate research is by incorporating recent studies, landmark research papers, and emerging debates into course readings and discussions.

Assign primary research articles instead of relying solely on textbooks.

Analyze case studies and current events using recent scholarly work.

Encourage students to critically evaluate research methods—What are the strengths and limitations of a particular study?

Use your own research findings as real-world examples, demonstrating the investigative process.

Example: In a psychology course, instead of solely teaching established theories, assign recent peer-reviewed studies on cognitive biases and discuss their implications in contemporary settings.

2. Engaging Students in Research-Based Assignments

Students develop deeper understanding when they apply research methodologies in hands-on projects. Faculty can create assignments that mirror scholarly investigation, such as:

Literature Reviews: Students synthesize existing research, identifying gaps and areas for further study.
Research Proposals: Students design a hypothetical study, including research questions, methodologies, and expected findings.
Data Analysis Projects: Students work with existing datasets or conduct small-scale experiments.
Case Studies and Policy Evaluations: Students apply research to solve real-world problems in their discipline.
Peer Reviews of Research Articles: Students critique research papers using academic journal review criteria.

Example: In a business strategy course, students conduct a market analysis using primary and secondary research data, then present recommendations based on empirical findings.

3. Incorporating Research-Based Pedagogies (Inquiry-Based Learning and Problem-Based Learning)

Inquiry-Based Learning (IBL) and Problem-Based Learning (PBL) encourage students to investigate complex problems, generate hypotheses, and explore solutions through research.

Inquiry-Based Learning (IBL)

- Students propose their own research questions and seek answers through structured investigation.
- Encourages autonomy, critical thinking, and evidence-based reasoning.

Problem-Based Learning (PBL)

- Students tackle practical real-world challenges using research-based solutions.
- Develops collaborative skills and interdisciplinary thinking.

Example: In an environmental science course, students analyze climate change impact reports, collect field data, and propose local sustainability initiatives based on research findings.

4. Integrating Students into Faculty-Led Research

Beyond the classroom, faculty can actively involve students in ongoing research projects, helping them gain firsthand experience in academic inquiry.

Offer research assistantships for students to engage in data collection, analysis, and manuscript preparation.

Encourage student co-authorship on publications and conference presentations.

Mentor students through independent research projects, honors theses, and capstone experiences.

Facilitate undergraduate research symposia where students present findings to academic audiences.

Example: A professor in public health integrates students into their epidemiological research, allowing them to analyze survey data, identify health trends, and contribute to scholarly publications.

Overcoming Challenges in Research-Integrated Teaching

While integrating research into teaching offers numerous benefits, faculty may encounter challenges such as time constraints, student preparedness, and institutional support limitations. The following strategies can help mitigate these barriers:

Time Management:

- Incorporate small-scale research activities rather than large, semester-long projects.
- Utilize collaborative research groups to distribute workload efficiently.

Supporting Students with Varied Research Backgrounds:

- Provide scaffolding for research assignments, including tutorials on research design, literature searches, and academic writing.
- Encourage peer mentoring where advanced students assist those new to research.

Institutional Support:

- Advocate for course-based undergraduate research experiences (CUREs), which integrate research systematically into the curriculum.
- Leverage institutional grants and research funding to support student involvement in faculty-led projects.

By anticipating these challenges and implementing strategic solutions, faculty can successfully cultivate a research-rich learning environment.

Conclusion: Transforming Students into Scholars

Incorporating research into teaching enriches student learning, strengthens the link between scholarship and pedagogy, and prepares students for future academic and professional pursuits.

By infusing course content with contemporary research, designing inquiry-driven assignments, engaging students in research methodologies, and mentoring them in faculty-led projects, professors bridge the gap between knowledge creation and knowledge dissemination.

Ultimately, a research-integrated approach transforms students from passive learners into active scholars, empowering them to think critically, generate new insights, and contribute meaningfully to their fields—a hallmark of higher education's enduring impact.

Encouraging Student Research and Collaboration: Fostering Inquiry and Academic Engagement

Encouraging student research and collaboration is central to integrative teaching and scholarship, enabling students to transition from passive recipients of knowledge to active contributors in their academic disciplines. When faculty members engage students in research, they cultivate intellectual curiosity, critical thinking, and methodological rigor, preparing them for advanced academic study, professional careers, and lifelong learning.

For new college professors, fostering student research requires intentional course design, structured mentorship, and collaborative opportunities that allow students to explore ideas, work with peers, and contribute to scholarly discourse. This section explores the importance of student research, effective strategies for fostering research engagement, and methods for encouraging collaboration in academic inquiry.

The Importance of Encouraging Student Research

Integrating research opportunities into undergraduate and graduate education enhances student learning by:

Developing Analytical and Problem-Solving Skills

- Assisting in research teaches students how to formulate inquiries, evaluate evidence, and synthesize findings.
- Encourages intellectual independence and critical reasoning.

Bridging Theory and Application

- Research allows students to connect theoretical knowledge with practical challenges.
- Helps students see their coursework as part of a larger scholarly conversation rather than isolated assignments.

Enhancing Career and Graduate School Preparedness

- Students gain valuable experience in academic writing, data analysis, and project management.
- Builds a strong foundation for graduate studies and professional fields requiring research competency.

Fostering Engagement and Academic Ownership

- Students who engage in research develop a deeper interest in their field and a sense of contribution to knowledge creation.

- Encourages self-motivation, intellectual curiosity, and scholarly identity formation.

By embedding research-based learning into the curriculum, faculty enable students to own their intellectual growth, preparing them for success in academia and beyond.

Strategies for Encouraging Student Research

1. Integrating Research into Coursework

Rather than limiting research opportunities to independent studies or capstone projects, faculty can incorporate research-based assignments and inquiry-driven learning into standard courses.

Incorporate Literature Reviews and Research Proposals

- Have students review existing scholarship, identify gaps, and propose new research directions.
- Encourage the use of academic databases and citation management tools (Zotero, EndNote, Mendeley).

Use Case-Based and Problem-Based Learning

- Provide learners with real-world problems and ask them to propose research-driven solutions.
- Example: In an environmental science course, students analyze pollution data and propose evidence-based policy recommendations.

Implement Course-Based Undergraduate Research Experiences (CUREs)

- CUREs allow students to engage in authentic, discipline-specific research within the structure of a course.
- Example: A biology professor designs a semester-long lab project where students collect and analyze original microbiological samples rather than replicating established experiments.

2. Creating Structured Research Mentorship Opportunities

Faculty mentorship holds a pivotal role in guiding students through the research process, helping them develop methodological skills and scholarly confidence.

Offer Research Assistantships

- Invite students to participate in ongoing faculty research projects.
- Provide gradual exposure to the research process, from data collection to publication.

Facilitate Independent Study Research Projects

- Allow students to pursue self-directed research under faculty guidance.
- Help them refine research questions, develop methodologies, and analyze findings.

Encourage Research Dissemination

- Mentor students on writing for academic journals, presenting at conferences, and applying for research grants.
- Example: A political science professor helps students submit policy analysis papers to undergraduate research journals.

By providing structured mentorship and research opportunities, faculty cultivate student confidence, scholarly identity, and professional research skills.

Encouraging Collaboration in Student Research

Collaboration is an essential component of academic inquiry, mirroring the team-based nature of research in most professional and academic fields. Faculty can encourage student collaboration through peer research teams, interdisciplinary partnerships, and faculty-student co-authorship.

1. Facilitating Collaborative Research Teams

Pair students with complementary skills (e.g., a strong writer with a strong data analyst).
Assign group research projects where students design experiments, conduct analyses, and co-author papers.
Encourage peer review sessions where students critique and improve each other's research.

Example: A professor in business administration assigns teams to analyze corporate financial reports, requiring students to synthesize data and produce a collaborative research paper.

2. Encouraging Interdisciplinary Research Collaboration

Encouraging students to work across disciplines broadens their perspectives and fosters innovative problem-solving approaches.

Develop cross-disciplinary research opportunities where students from different majors combine expertise to tackle complex problems.
Partner with other departments to offer joint research projects.
Example: A computer science and linguistics collaboration where students develop AI models for language processing.

3. Promoting Faculty-Student Research Collaboration

Engaging in co-authored research with students provides them with valuable experience in scholarly publishing and professional networking.

Co-Author Papers with Students

- Guide students in developing research for publication.
- Offer structured writing and revision support to prepare papers for submission.

Encourage Conference Presentations

- Support students in submitting research presentations to academic conferences.
- Example: A faculty member in psychology mentors students in preparing poster presentations for the APA conference.

Facilitate Research Showcases

- Organize campus-wide research symposia where students present their findings to faculty, peers, and external audiences.
- Provide guidance on effective research communication techniques.

By fostering collaborative research experiences, faculty prepare students for professional research environments while enhancing the visibility of student scholarship.

Overcoming Challenges in Encouraging Student Research

While student research has immense benefits, faculty may encounter challenges related to time constraints, student preparedness, and institutional resources. The following strategies help address these barriers:

Managing Faculty Workload

- Establish scalable research projects that integrate into existing coursework.
- Use structured mentorship models (group mentoring, peer research teams) to distribute workload.

Supporting Students with Limited Research Experience

- Provide step-by-step research guides and training in academic databases, methodology, and citation practices.
- Encourage peer mentoring where experienced students support new researchers.

Securing Institutional and External Funding

- Apply for grants and institutional research fellowships to support student-led research initiatives.
- Advocate for institutional recognition of undergraduate and graduate research programs.

By anticipating and addressing challenges, faculty can create sustainable models for student research engagement.

Conclusion: Cultivating a Research-Rich Academic Culture

Encouraging student research and collaboration transforms students into active contributors to knowledge creation, equipping them with the necessary skills, confidence, and practical experience necessary for academic and professional success.

By integrating research-based assignments, fostering structured mentorship, and creating opportunities for interdisciplinary and faculty-student collaboration, professors instill a culture of inquiry and intellectual curiosity in their students.

Ultimately, faculty who actively engage students in research not only cultivate student learning and career readiness but also contribute to a thriving academic community where scholarship is a shared endeavor—one that extends beyond the classroom and into the world of discovery, innovation, and lifelong inquiry.

Writing for Academic Publication and Professional Development: Establishing a Scholarly Identity

Writing for academic publication is a cornerstone of scholarly engagement, shaping both intellectual contributions to a field and professional development within academia. For new college professors, mastering the art of academic writing is essential—not only for securing tenure and promotion but also for establishing credibility, fostering interdisciplinary dialogue, and influencing the evolution of knowledge in their respective fields.

Beyond publication, engaging in professional development through scholarly writing enables faculty to refine research expertise, expand professional networks, and enhance teaching effectiveness. By consistently contributing to academic discourse, professors strengthen their scholarly identity and position themselves as thought leaders.

This section explores the role of academic publishing in faculty development, best practices for writing and submission, navigating the peer review process, and integrating scholarly writing into a sustainable professional trajectory.

The Role of Academic Publishing in Professional Development

1. Advancing Knowledge and Scholarly Contribution

Academic publishing is more than a professional requirement—it is an intellectual responsibility that enables scholars to:
 Generate new insights through empirical research, theoretical frameworks, and applied scholarship.
 Engage with disciplinary conversations, contributing to ongoing academic and societal debates.
 Influence policy, practice, and pedagogy, shaping the future of a given field.

2. Enhancing Career Advancement and Institutional Recognition

Most academic institutions emphasize publication records as part of tenure and promotion criteria.
 Faculty who publish consistently demonstrate a commitment to research excellence.
 Publications increase institutional reputation and can attract research funding.
 Active scholars gain opportunities for keynote speaking, consulting, and leadership roles in academic associations.

3. Strengthening Teaching Through Research Integration

Publishing enhances teaching by keeping faculty engaged with contemporary debates.
Faculty who publish can infuse courses with cutting-edge research, exposing students to real-world applications.
Engaging in scholarly writing fosters a research-based teaching approach, reinforcing inquiry-driven pedagogy.

By recognizing publishing as an integral aspect of both intellectual and professional growth, faculty can develop a sustainable, impactful scholarly career.

Best Practices for Writing and Publishing Academic Work

Writing for academic publication requires structured planning, clarity, and engagement with scholarly communities. The following strategies enhance writing productivity and publication success.

1. Establishing a Sustainable Writing Routine

Set dedicated writing time: Treat writing as an ongoing scholarly practice, not a last-minute task.
Break writing into manageable segments: Use the Pomodoro technique (focused writing sprints) to maintain productivity.
Create a research pipeline: Develop a systematic workflow for drafting, revising, and submitting manuscripts.

Example: A faculty member commits to writing three hours per week and submits one article per semester.

2. Selecting the Right Publication Venues

Identifying appropriate journals and publishers is key to maximizing impact. Consider:
Journal Scope and Audience: Does the journal align with your research field and intended readership?
Reputation and Impact Factor: Prioritize well-regarded, peer-reviewed journals that align with institutional expectations.
Acceptance Rates and Review Timelines: Consider submission timelines to strategically balance multiple writing projects.

Example: A historian researching postcolonial literature submits to a top-tier journal in cultural studies, ensuring alignment with scholarly discourse.

3. Structuring an Effective Academic Paper

Title and Abstract: Ensure clarity, conciseness, and alignment with the journal's audience.
Introduction: Establish a compelling research question, significance, and theoretical framework.
Literature Review: Situate the work within existing scholarship, highlighting gaps and contributions.
Methodology and Data Analysis: Provide transparent research design and justification of methods.
Findings and Discussion: Connect results to broader academic and practical implications.

Conclusion and Future Research: Suggest new avenues for inquiry and interdisciplinary engagement.

Example: A social sciences professor uses a clear, structured outline before drafting, ensuring logical coherence and alignment with submission guidelines.

4. Navigating the Peer Review and Revision Process

The peer review process is often rigorous and time-consuming. Faculty should:
Approach revisions constructively: Engage with reviewer comments as opportunities for refinement.
Prioritize clarity and defensibility: Address reviewer concerns thoughtfully and with evidence.
Resubmit strategically: If rejected, consider revising and submitting to another journal with an appropriate scope.

Example: A faculty member receives constructive feedback and revises the manuscript thoroughly, improving clarity and methodological transparency before resubmitting.

Expanding Professional Development Through Scholarly Writing

1. Writing Beyond Academic Journals: Engaging Broader Audiences

While journal articles are essential, faculty can enhance their scholarly impact through diverse writing formats:
Book Chapters and Edited Volumes: Contribute to collaborative scholarly collections.
Op-Eds and Public Scholarship: Publish research insights in mainstream media, blogs, and policy briefs.
Grant Proposals and White Papers: Translate academic research into applied solutions and institutional funding opportunities.

Example: A political science professor publishes peer-reviewed research in an academic journal and later adapts findings into a policy report for government agencies.

2. Leveraging Writing for Academic Networking and Collaboration

Present research at conferences: Transform conference papers into publishable journal articles.
Collaborate with interdisciplinary scholars: Co-author research to enhance publication impact and diversify perspectives.
Join editorial boards and peer review committees: Contribute to academic publishing processes while refining one's own scholarly writing.

Example: A faculty member collaborates with an international research team, producing a co-authored publication that broadens research exposure.

3. Integrating Writing into Mentorship and Student Research

Incorporate students into research projects: Co-author papers with undergraduates and graduate students.
Create writing groups: Establish faculty and student writing workshops for peer feedback.

Encourage student-led publications: Support students in submitting to undergraduate research journals and conference proceedings.

Example: A professor in psychology mentors students in qualitative research methods, leading to a co-authored journal article on mental health interventions.

Overcoming Challenges in Academic Publishing

1. Managing Rejection and Revision Stress

View rejection as part of the scholarly process—resilience and revision lead to success. Seek mentorship from senior faculty for insightful feedback on manuscript development.

Example: A faculty member tracks all manuscript submissions and sets revision deadlines for resubmissions, maintaining momentum.

2. Balancing Writing with Teaching and Service

Use sabbaticals, research leave, and writing retreats to prioritize long-term projects. Establish writing accountability groups with colleagues for structured progress.

Example: A professor schedules weekly writing sessions with a faculty research cohort, enhancing productivity.

Conclusion: Building a Sustainable and Impactful Writing Career

Writing for academic publication is a transformative process that enhances scholarly contributions, career advancement, and intellectual engagement. By developing structured writing habits, selecting appropriate publication venues, engaging in interdisciplinary collaboration, and mentoring students in research, faculty members establish a lasting academic legacy.

Ultimately, academic writing should be seen not as an isolated requirement but as an ongoing conversation with the scholarly community—one that shapes disciplines, informs teaching, and drives innovation in research. By cultivating a strategic, reflective, and collaborative approach to publishing, faculty can amplify their impact, expand professional opportunities, and contribute significantly to the advancement of knowledge.

Mentorship and Guiding Students Through Academic Research: Cultivating the Next Generation of Scholars

Mentorship is a cornerstone of academic success, shaping the professional and intellectual growth of students as they navigate the complexities of scholarly research. Effective mentorship goes beyond supervision; it involves guidance, collaboration, and empowerment, fostering a culture of critical inquiry, academic integrity, and independent thought.

For new college professors, learning to mentor students through the research process is an essential competency that enhances student learning, strengthens faculty-student engagement, and contributes to the broader academic community. Through structured mentorship, faculty can help students develop research skills, navigate academic challenges, and build confidence as emerging scholars.

This section explores the role of faculty as research mentors, best practices for guiding students through academic inquiry, and strategies for cultivating an inclusive and supportive research environment.

The Role of Mentorship in Academic Research

1. Mentorship as an Intellectual and Professional Partnership

Mentorship in research is not a one-directional transmission of knowledge but a collaborative, iterative process that cultivates:
Critical thinking and analytical reasoning—Students learn to evaluate evidence, formulate questions, and construct arguments.
Independence and intellectual ownership—Mentors provide scaffolding that allows students to take initiative in research design and execution.
Professional development—Students gain experience in academic writing, conference presentations, and research ethics.
Long-term academic engagement—Strong mentorship relationships extend beyond graduation, often leading to collaborative projects, graduate studies, and professional opportunities.

2. Enhancing Student Success Through Research Mentorship

Effective mentorship significantly impacts student retention, academic motivation, and career preparedness. Students who engage in faculty-mentored research experience:
Greater persistence in academic programs, particularly in STEM and research-intensive disciplines.
Higher rates of graduate school admission due to early exposure to scholarly inquiry.
Increased self-efficacy and confidence in conducting independent research and contributing to academic discourse.

By actively mentoring students in research, faculty empower students to become knowledge producers rather than passive consumers, fostering a culture of innovation, curiosity, and lifelong learning.

Best Practices for Mentoring Students in Research

1. Establishing a Structured Research Mentorship Model

Define Clear Expectations from the Start

- Outline roles, responsibilities, and research goals in an initial meeting.
- Provide students with timelines, benchmarks, and a structured roadmap for research progression.

Assess Student Readiness and Adapt Mentorship Approaches

- Identify students' prior experience with research methodologies.

- Offer tailored guidance for different levels—introductory research experiences, advanced independent studies, or thesis projects.

Encourage an Inquiry-Based Mindset

- Model curiosity by posing open-ended research questions.
- Teach students how to critically engage with literature and synthesize existing knowledge.

Example: A faculty mentor guides a student in formulating a research hypothesis by asking, *"What gap in the literature does your research address?"* instead of simply assigning a topic.

2. Guiding Students Through the Research Process

Students often struggle with navigating the complexity of academic research. Faculty can demystify the process by breaking it into clear, manageable steps.

Step 1: Developing Research Questions and Hypotheses

- Help students refine broad ideas into focused, researchable questions.
- Teach concept mapping techniques to explore relationships between key variables.

Step 2: Conducting a Literature Review

- Introduce students to academic databases (JSTOR, Google Scholar, PubMed, ProQuest).
- Teach students how to assess source credibility and identify research gaps.
- Use citation management tools like Zotero, EndNote, or Mendeley for organizing references.

Step 3: Designing a Research Methodology

- Guide students in selecting appropriate qualitative, quantitative, or mixed-methods approaches.
- Emphasize ethical research practices, including IRB protocols and informed consent.
- Discuss common challenges in data collection and analysis.

Step 4: Analyzing Data and Synthesizing Findings

- Provide hands-on training in statistical software (SPSS, R, NVivo) or qualitative coding techniques.
- Encourage students to interpret results critically rather than merely reporting them.

Step 5: Writing and Presenting Research

- Help students structure academic papers using IMRAD format (Introduction, Methods, Results, and Discussion).

- Provide feedback on clarity, argumentation, and coherence in writing.
- Encourage participation in student research symposia, undergraduate research journals, and conference presentations.

Example: A mentor working with a first-time research student might assign low-stakes writing exercises before expecting a full literature review.

3. Fostering Collaborative Research and Peer Mentorship

Encourage Research Teams

- Pair students with complementary skill sets (e.g., a strong writer with a skilled data analyst).
- Facilitate peer-led discussions and feedback workshops.

Incorporate Students into Faculty Research

- Offer research assistantships where students contribute to ongoing faculty projects.
- Provide opportunities for student co-authorship and grant-funded research collaborations.

Develop Research Communities

- Establish student-faculty research labs or reading groups.
- Connect students with graduate students and postdocs for interdisciplinary mentorship.

Example: A faculty mentor assigns senior research students as peer guides for first-year undergraduates, fostering a culture of collaborative learning.

4. Encouraging Student Autonomy and Scholarly Confidence

Cultivate a Growth Mindset in Research

- Normalize failure as a growth mindset and part of the research process.
- Encourage students to view setbacks as learning opportunities rather than barriers.

Guide Students in Publishing and Presenting Research

- Help students submit manuscripts to undergraduate journals and conference proceedings.
- Teach strategies for effective academic communication and poster presentations.

Recognize and Celebrate Achievements

- Nominate students for research awards and fellowships.
- Showcase student research through campus-wide symposiums and faculty research spotlights.

Example: A mentor encourages a student to present their findings at a regional conference, boosting their confidence in academic discourse.

Overcoming Challenges in Research Mentorship

1. Managing Time Constraints as a Faculty Mentor

Establish realistic mentorship loads—balance mentoring responsibilities with teaching and research commitments.
Use group mentorship models where students work collaboratively, reducing one-on-one time demands.

2. Supporting Students with Limited Research Experience

Provide step-by-step research training, rather than assuming prior knowledge.
Develop online research modules or workshops to teach foundational skills.

3. Addressing Equity and Inclusion in Research Mentorship

Offer opportunities to students from underrepresented backgrounds, ensuring diversity in research engagement.
Be mindful of implicit biases in student selection for research projects.

Example: A faculty mentor creates an inclusive research group by actively recruiting first-generation college students for research opportunities.

Research-Practice Integration Models

The integration of research, scholarship, and teaching is one of the hallmarks of higher education, distinguishing universities from other forms of postsecondary instruction. Yet this approach is not a one-size-fits-all endeavor. It varies across disciplines, student levels, and career stages, requiring faculty to balance advancing knowledge with preparing students for professional, scholarly, and civic life. Sustainable and impactful integration depends on understanding disciplinary traditions, aligning expectations with student readiness, and adopting practices that respect ethical and legal standards.

Discipline-Specific Research-Teaching Integration Strategies

Each academic discipline carries its own traditions of inquiry, methods of knowledge production, and expectations for student involvement. Faculty must align research-teaching integration with these disciplinary cultures to ensure both academic rigor and meaningful student engagement.

- **STEM Disciplines**
  In science, technology, engineering, and mathematics, research is often empirical and data-driven, making integration highly hands-on.
    - Laboratory Work: Students may engage in bench science, computational modeling, or engineering design projects that directly contribute to faculty research agendas.

- o Data Collection and Analysis: Undergraduates may gather environmental samples, run simulations, or analyze datasets, while graduate students design experiments or develop new methodologies.
- o Collaborative Teams: Research labs provide hierarchical mentorship models where undergraduates assist graduate students, who in turn are supervised by faculty.

  This approach prepares students for research careers while producing tangible outputs that advance faculty scholarship.
- Social Sciences

  Research integration in the social sciences often emphasizes applied, field-based, or policy-oriented projects.
  - o Fieldwork: Students may conduct interviews, ethnographies, or community observations that contribute to larger research initiatives.
  - o Survey and Data Analysis: Courses may incorporate the design and administration of surveys, followed by student-led statistical or qualitative analysis.
  - o Case Studies: Students apply theoretical frameworks to analyze contemporary issues such as inequality, political participation, or organizational behavior.

    This integration highlights the connection between theory and real-world social dynamics, reinforcing transferable skills in critical analysis and problem-solving.
- **Humanities**

  In humanities disciplines, integration often centers on interpretation, creativity, and archival discovery.
  - o Archival Research: Students may examine primary sources such as manuscripts, historical records, or oral histories.
  - o Textual and Cultural Analysis: Courses can include projects where students critically interpret literature, art, or media in ways that align with faculty research.
  - o Digital Humanities: Increasingly, humanities integration involves digital projects, such as building online archives, mapping cultural histories, or creating annotated digital editions of texts.

    This approach underscores intellectual inquiry and critical reflection, emphasizing how research contributes to cultural understanding.
- **Professional Fields (Business, Education, Health Sciences, etc.)**

  Professional programs typically prioritize applied research that connects directly to practice.
  - o Business: Students may consult with local organizations, conduct market analyses, or evaluate entrepreneurial models.
  - o Education: Teacher candidates often conduct classroom-based research projects, such as action research on instructional methods.
  - o Health Sciences: Nursing, public health, and allied health programs may emphasize program evaluations, patient outcome studies, or community health interventions.
  - o Community-Based Participatory Research (CBPR): Students collaborate with practitioners and stakeholders to co-create knowledge that addresses pressing societal needs.

    These approaches emphasize problem-solving, evidence-based practice, and professional identity development.

Key Takeaway

Discipline-specific approaches to research-teaching integration ensure that students engage in authentic scholarly practices relevant to their fields. By tailoring strategies to disciplinary norms—whether through labs, fieldwork, archives, or applied projects—faculty provide students with opportunities to practice the methods, values, and reasoning processes of their professions. At the same time, faculty advance their own research agendas, creating a mutually reinforcing cycle of scholarship and teaching.

Undergraduate vs. Graduate Research Mentorship Models

Research mentorship is not uniform—it varies significantly by degree level, reflecting differences in student preparation, disciplinary expectations, and developmental needs. Faculty must carefully calibrate mentorship approaches to ensure that undergraduates gain exposure to research without being overwhelmed, while graduate students are supported as they transition toward scholarly independence. Well-structured mentorship prepares students for the next stage of their academic or professional careers while sustaining the quality of faculty research.

Mentorship for Undergraduates

Undergraduate research experiences are often a student's first encounter with scholarly inquiry, so the emphasis should be on fundamentals and skill-building rather than original, high-level contributions.

- Introducing Research Fundamentals: Faculty should guide students through the basics of question formulation, literature review, methodological awareness, and ethical considerations.
- Small-Scale or Course-Embedded Projects: Undergraduate research is most effective when embedded into existing coursework (e.g., course-based undergraduate research experiences, or CUREs). These experiences allow students to practice research skills in a structured environment.
- Faculty-Aligned Research Tasks: Students may contribute to faculty projects through manageable roles such as coding qualitative data, running statistical analyses, or assisting in archival work.
- Skill Development: Beyond research content, undergraduates should gain confidence in time management, teamwork, and academic communication.
  The goal is not to produce professional-level scholarship but to build readiness for advanced study and cultivate curiosity.

Mentorship for Graduate Students

Graduate-level mentorship is more intensive, requiring faculty to prepare students for independence as scholars or practitioners.

- Project Design and Execution: Graduate students are expected to design their own research projects, often with faculty guidance on framing questions, selecting methods, and identifying feasible scopes.
- Advanced Methods: Faculty mentor students through sophisticated techniques, whether in statistical modeling, lab experimentation, or theoretical argumentation.
- Professional Development: Mentorship extends to publishing articles, presenting at conferences, and navigating peer review.
- Doctoral-Level Guidance: At the doctoral stage, faculty mentorship includes dissertation supervision, shaping theoretical contributions, and facilitating professional networks (e.g., introducing students to editors, research collaborators, and potential employers). Here the goal is not just knowledge acquisition but contribution—students are expected to generate new knowledge and establish themselves as independent thinkers.

Hybrid Mentorship Models

Some structures serve as bridges between undergraduate and graduate models, offering students increasing independence while still providing support.

- Capstone Projects: Often required in professional fields, capstones allow students to synthesize learning into applied projects, such as business plans, curriculum designs, or engineering prototypes.
- Honors Theses: Advanced undergraduates can pursue more independent research under close faculty supervision, often producing work of near-graduate-level rigor.
- Research Labs: Faculty-led labs often mix undergraduates and graduate students, creating tiered mentorship structures where advanced students help guide less experienced peers. This not only lightens faculty workload but also strengthens the mentorship culture.

Calibrating Expectations

The central challenge for faculty is matching expectations to student readiness:

- Setting the bar too low may limit student growth and engagement.
- Setting it too high risks overwhelming students and compromising research quality. Faculty should communicate expectations clearly, scaffold learning opportunities, and progressively increase autonomy as students advance.

Key Takeaway

Research mentorship must be tailored to student level: undergraduates need structured exposure and skill-building, graduates require preparation for independence, and hybrid models provide transition pathways. By calibrating expectations, faculty create developmental trajectories that both enhance student growth and sustain scholarly excellence.

Managing Research Supervision Workload

Faculty face constant pressure to balance the three pillars of higher education—teaching, scholarship, and service—with research supervision adding another layer of responsibility. While mentoring students in research is rewarding, it can quickly become overwhelming without careful workload management. Effective supervision requires clear boundaries, structured delegation, curricular integration, and realistic limits. By approaching supervision strategically, faculty can sustain both the quality of their scholarship and the developmental value for students.

Setting Boundaries

Boundaries establish structure and prevent mentorship from consuming disproportionate time and energy.

- Role Clarity: At the beginning of a project, faculty should define student responsibilities (e.g., data entry, literature review, independent analysis) and what tasks remain under faculty oversight.
- Meeting Frequency: Faculty should agree on how often students will meet for updates—weekly for graduate projects, biweekly or monthly for undergraduate roles.
- Communication Protocols: Establish preferred communication channels (e.g., email vs. LMS vs. shared drives) and response time expectations to avoid constant interruptions.
- Deliverable Milestones: Setting checkpoints ensures students stay on track and reduces last-minute crises that add to faculty workload.

Using Tiered Mentorship

Tiered mentorship leverages the expertise of more advanced students to support less experienced ones, creating a mentorship ecosystem.

- Graduate Student Leadership: Graduate students can mentor undergraduates in labs, fieldwork, or data analysis, easing the faculty burden while gaining leadership experience themselves.
- Peer Mentorship: Advanced undergraduates can supervise introductory-level research assistants, guiding them through basic tasks such as data entry or library research.
- Faculty Oversight: Faculty remain accountable for the overall quality and ethics of the project, but tiered systems allow them to focus on higher-level supervision.

Embedding Research in Courses

Course-based undergraduate research experiences (CUREs) align faculty research with teaching, reducing duplication of effort.

- Integrated Projects: Faculty design assignments that contribute to their own research agenda (e.g., class-wide data collection or archival transcription).
- Scalable Participation: Instead of supervising each student individually, faculty guide groups through structured projects during normal class hours.

- Skill Building for Students: Students gain authentic research experience while faculty advance their scholarship.
This model transforms supervision from an added obligation into a mutually beneficial teaching practice.

Recognizing Limits

Faculty must acknowledge that they cannot supervise every interested student without compromising quality.

- Selective Recruitment: Admit students to projects based on interest, preparation, and available capacity.
- Project Prioritization: Focus supervision on projects with the highest alignment to research goals or program outcomes.
- Quality over Quantity: One well-mentored student producing publishable work is often more impactful than many students contributing superficially.
- Protecting Well-Being: Faculty must safeguard their own research productivity and personal balance by resisting overcommitment.

Key Takeaway

Managing research supervision workload is about intentional structure and realistic capacity. By setting boundaries, using tiered mentorship, embedding research into courses, and recognizing limits, faculty create sustainable models of supervision. This ensures that both students and faculty benefit from research integration without sacrificing productivity, quality, or well-being.

Intellectual Property Considerations in Student Research

Collaborative research between faculty and students enriches learning while advancing scholarship, but it also raises complex questions about ownership of ideas, data, and products. Unlike traditional coursework, research often produces outputs with long-term value—datasets, publications, patents, or creative works—that must be governed by clear intellectual property (IP) policies. Misunderstandings can erode trust, damage mentoring relationships, and even lead to legal disputes. Faculty must therefore establish transparent agreements, follow institutional policies, and respect student rights from the outset of collaboration.

Clear Agreements

Written agreements protect both faculty and students by setting expectations before work begins.

- Scope of Work: Define what contributions students are expected to make (e.g., data collection, analysis, writing, or design).
- Ownership of Outputs: Clarify whether outputs belong to the faculty, student, institution, or are jointly owned. For example, student-generated software may remain theirs, while datasets created within a faculty lab may belong to the institution.

- Future Use: Outline how student-generated materials can be used after the project ends, including whether faculty may continue to develop the work if the student graduates.
- Publication Plans: Discuss authorship roles and contributions early, reducing the risk of conflict later.

Institutional Policies

Universities typically have formal guidelines governing IP, especially for research involving funding or commercialization potential.

- Grant-Funded Research: Funding agencies often stipulate that data and results belong to the institution, not individual faculty or students.
- Patentable Inventions: In STEM fields, discoveries made in labs may be subject to institutional ownership under technology transfer policies. Faculty must inform students of these policies when their work may contribute to patents.
- Creative Works: In the humanities and arts, student-created works such as essays, performances, or designs often remain the intellectual property of the student, unless contractual agreements state otherwise.
- Compliance: Faculty should consult with legal, technology transfer, or research offices to ensure compliance and to avoid unintended violations.

Student Rights

Respect for student contributions is essential to maintaining ethical mentoring relationships.

- Credit and Recognition: Students must be acknowledged for their intellectual and practical contributions, whether through authorship on publications, acknowledgment sections, or conference presentations.
- Ownership of Original Work: Theses, dissertations, and creative projects typically belong to students. Faculty should not use student work without explicit permission.
- Consent for Use: If faculty plan to use student-generated materials (e.g., class projects, essays, or datasets) in their own scholarship, they must obtain written consent.
- Protection from Exploitation: Students should not be pressured to surrender rights unnecessarily or excluded from credit for substantial contributions.

Transparency

Open communication is the most effective way to prevent disputes.

- Early Conversations: Discuss IP issues at the beginning of the project, not after valuable outputs have been created.
- Ongoing Updates: Revisit agreements as projects evolve, especially if outputs exceed the original scope.
- Documentation: Keep written records of contributions, agreements, and revisions to protect both parties.

- Ethical Culture: By modeling transparency, faculty teach students how to navigate IP issues professionally, preparing them for future collaborations.

Key Takeaway

Intellectual property in student research must be managed with clarity, institutional awareness, respect for student rights, and transparent communication. Faculty who establish agreements early, follow institutional policies, and recognize student contributions build trust while protecting the integrity of collaborative scholarship. This proactive approach ensures that research outcomes benefit both students and faculty without compromising fairness or ethics.

Publication Ethics When Working with Students

When faculty collaborate with students on research that leads to publications, they carry a dual responsibility: advancing scholarship while mentoring students in the professional and ethical practices of academic publishing. Because students often lack experience navigating authorship norms, peer review, and editorial processes, faculty must serve as both guides and gatekeepers. Failure to uphold ethical standards risks not only exploitation of students but also reputational harm to faculty and institutions. Clear communication, fairness in authorship, and attention to disciplinary standards are essential.

Authorship Credit

Authorship must reflect genuine intellectual or practical contributions.

- Criteria for Inclusion: Students should be listed as co-authors if they contribute significantly to research design, data analysis, interpretation, or manuscript preparation. Merely performing routine tasks under direction may not qualify for authorship but may warrant acknowledgment.
- Order of Authorship: Faculty should discuss the meaning of author order within the discipline—whether first authorship indicates the most substantial contribution (as in STEM) or if alphabetical order is customary (as in some humanities and social sciences).
- Written Agreements: Establishing authorship expectations early prevents conflict later, especially in multi-student collaborations.
Recognizing student contributions fairly models professional ethics and fosters trust in the mentoring relationship.

Avoiding Exploitation

Faculty must protect students from exploitation, both intentional and unintentional.

- Acknowledgment vs. Authorship: Students should never be denied authorship when their contributions meet disciplinary standards.
- Timely Publication: Faculty should not delay or suppress student publications to protect their own research agendas. For example, a student's thesis should not be withheld from submission while faculty prepare their own manuscript.

- Respect for Intellectual Independence: Faculty must avoid appropriating student ideas, arguments, or data without acknowledgment.
  Protecting students from exploitation ensures that collaboration remains mutually beneficial and ethically sound.

Mentorship in Publishing

Beyond including students in authorship, faculty have a duty to teach them how the publishing process works.

- Understanding Peer Review: Faculty should explain review procedures, including blind review, editorial decisions, and revision cycles.
- Guidance on Revisions: Students should be coached in how to respond to reviewer feedback constructively and professionally.
- Ethical Writing Practices: Faculty should model proper citation, paraphrasing, and avoidance of plagiarism.
- Encouraging Independence: Mentorship should prepare students to publish on their own, building confidence and competence for future scholarship.

Discipline-Specific Norms

Authorship conventions vary widely across disciplines, and students must be educated on these differences.

- STEM Fields: Authorship is often hierarchical, with first authorship denoting the largest contribution, senior authorship (last author) signaling the lab leader, and middle authors representing collaborators.
- Social Sciences: Practices may mirror STEM but often emphasize collaborative authorship and clear contribution statements.
- Humanities: Sole authorship is more common, but co-authorship can occur in digital humanities, edited volumes, or collaborative interpretation.
- Professional Fields: Applied disciplines such as business or education may include practitioner co-authors, requiring additional explanation of authorship norms.
  Faculty should clarify these expectations early so students understand how credit is determined in their field.

Key Takeaway

Publication ethics when working with students require fair credit, protection from exploitation, intentional mentorship, and transparency about disciplinary norms. Faculty must ensure that student contributions are acknowledged appropriately while also teaching the skills needed for independent scholarly publishing. Ethical collaboration not only safeguards students but also strengthens academic integrity and contributes to the development of future scholars.

Grant Writing That Includes Teaching Components

Research grants are often seen as vehicles to advance scholarship, but they can also serve as powerful tools for strengthening teaching and student engagement. Funding agencies increasingly expect faculty to demonstrate how their work benefits education and society, and integrating teaching components into proposals provides both credibility and resources. By explicitly connecting research activities with instructional initiatives, faculty can secure support for student development, course innovation, and broader community partnerships while enhancing the competitiveness of their proposals.

Broader Impacts Statements

Many funding agencies—such as the National Science Foundation (NSF)—require applicants to address how their projects contribute to society beyond academic research. Education-focused activities are highly valued in these sections.

- Student Engagement: Involving undergraduates and graduates in data collection, analysis, or dissemination highlights how the grant supports workforce preparation.
- Curriculum Development: Demonstrating how research findings will be integrated into courses strengthens the proposal's educational impact.
- Outreach Activities: Workshops, public lectures, or K–12 engagement programs linked to the research can also satisfy broader impact requirements.
Clear articulation of these educational outcomes positions the grant as advancing both scholarship and teaching.

Undergraduate Research Assistants

Equitable access to research experiences is often limited by students' financial circumstances. Grants can address this by funding stipends for undergraduate research assistants.

- Financial Access: Paid research positions allow students from underrepresented or economically disadvantaged backgrounds to participate fully without sacrificing income from other jobs.
- Skill Development: Stipends create structured roles where students gain transferable skills in research methods, teamwork, and communication.
- Retention and Success: Evidence shows that funded undergraduate research contributes to higher retention rates, graduate school enrollment, and professional readiness [144]. Budgeting for these roles ensures that teaching and mentorship are built into the grant's design.

Course Development Funds

Research grants can include funding to design or redesign courses that integrate research findings or methods.

- Research-Based Courses: Faculty can develop classes where students directly contribute to funded projects, such as analyzing data or piloting methodologies.
- Training Modules: Grants may support the creation of instructional materials or workshops that prepare students to use new tools or techniques developed during the research.
- Scalable Impact: By embedding grant-supported content into courses, faculty extend the reach of the funding from a small research team to hundreds of students over time. This approach ensures that research outputs enrich teaching beyond the duration of the grant.

Community Integration

Some grants encourage projects that involve community partnerships, blending research with service-learning or applied learning opportunities.

- Service-Learning Projects: Faculty can design community-based initiatives where students apply research methods to real-world challenges, such as public health interventions or local sustainability efforts.
- Applied Research Partnerships: Collaborations with nonprofits, government agencies, or industry can provide students with authentic experiences while fulfilling grant objectives.
- Mutual Benefits: Community integration enhances student learning, strengthens the proposal's societal impact, and demonstrates the university's commitment to civic engagement.

Key Takeaway

Integrating teaching into grant proposals makes them stronger, more competitive, and more impactful. By highlighting broader educational impacts, funding undergraduate research assistants, supporting course development, and incorporating community engagement, faculty can secure resources that advance both their research and their teaching missions. This dual focus not only benefits students and communities but also positions faculty as leaders who bridge the gap between scholarship and education.

Measuring Impact of Research-Integrated Teaching

Research-integrated teaching requires significant investment of time, resources, and institutional support. To sustain and improve these efforts, faculty must demonstrate measurable impact at multiple levels—student, faculty, and institution. Without clear evidence of effectiveness, integration risks being undervalued or underfunded. Rigorous assessment not only justifies the effort but also provides insights for refining practices and strengthening outcomes.

Student Outcomes

The most direct measure of impact lies in student achievement and opportunities that result from research engagement.

- Scholarly Outputs: Track student-authored or co-authored publications, poster sessions, and conference presentations. These outputs show how students move from consumers to producers of knowledge.
- Graduate and Professional School Admissions: Research experience is often a differentiator in applications to advanced degree programs [145]. Monitoring admission success highlights long-term benefits of integration.
- Employment Placement: Employers value applied research skills such as data analysis, problem-solving, and project management. Alumni surveys can capture how research experience contributes to career readiness [146].
- Retention and Completion: Research participation is linked to higher rates of persistence and graduation, especially among underrepresented students [147].

Learning Gains

Beyond external achievements, faculty should measure how students develop academically through research engagement.

- Critical Thinking and Problem-Solving: Pre- and post-course assessments or rubric-based evaluations of student work can capture growth in higher-order thinking.
- Research Literacy: Assessments can measure improvements in literature review skills, methodological understanding, and data interpretation.
- Self-Efficacy and Confidence: Surveys can track how research participation improves students' belief in their ability to contribute to scholarly or professional communities.
- Reflective Artifacts: Journals, portfolios, and essays provide qualitative evidence of student learning and meaning-making.

Faculty Outcomes

Faculty also benefit from integrating research and teaching, and these outcomes must be documented to demonstrate sustainability.

- Publications and Presentations: Co-authored works with students expand faculty scholarship while showcasing mentorship impact.
- Grant Success: Demonstrating student engagement strengthens broader impacts sections in grant proposals, leading to higher funding competitiveness.
- Teaching Evaluations: Courses that integrate research often enhance student engagement, which may be reflected in stronger course evaluations [148].
- Professional Recognition: Faculty may earn awards or leadership opportunities based on innovative integration models.

Institutional Impact

At the macro level, research-teaching integration contributes to institutional goals and reputation.

- Accreditation Metrics: Many accrediting bodies emphasize student research engagement as evidence of high-quality education [149].

- Retention and Recruitment: Prospective students are increasingly drawn to institutions that advertise undergraduate and graduate research opportunities [150].
- Reputation and Branding: Institutions that highlight faculty-student research collaborations strengthen their profile as places where scholarship and teaching intersect meaningfully.
- Community Engagement: Applied research partnerships with local or global organizations enhance institutional visibility and impact.

Assessment Practices

To ensure comprehensive evaluation, faculty and institutions should adopt structured assessment practices:

- Longitudinal Tracking: Follow cohorts of students to measure long-term outcomes such as graduate study or career success.
- Mixed-Methods Evaluation: Combine quantitative measures (grades, publications, surveys) with qualitative ones (interviews, reflections, case studies).
- Benchmarking: Compare outcomes with peer institutions to contextualize success.
- Feedback Loops: Use assessment results to refine program design, ensuring continuous improvement.

Key Takeaway

Measuring the impact of research-integrated teaching requires attention to student outcomes, learning gains, faculty productivity, and institutional contributions. By collecting and reporting robust evidence, faculty and institutions ensure that integration efforts are recognized, resourced, and continuously improved. This accountability reinforces the value of research-practice integration as a model where students not only learn about scholarship but actively participate in creating it, preparing them for advanced study, professional practice, and civic leadership.

Conclusion: Transforming Students into Independent Scholars

Effective research mentorship is more than guidance—it is a transformational process that empowers students to become independent thinkers, skilled researchers, and confident contributors to academic knowledge.

By providing structured support, fostering inquiry-based learning, and cultivating an inclusive research culture, faculty mentors enable students with the necessary skills for academic success, graduate study, and professional careers.

Ultimately, a well-mentored student does not merely complete a research project—they develop the intellectual curiosity, analytical acumen, and scholarly confidence to engage in lifelong inquiry and innovation, ensuring that the pursuit of knowledge extends beyond the academic environments and into the broader academic and professional world.

Advancing Knowledge Through Research-Integrated Teaching

Integrating research and teaching is not just beneficial—it is a cornerstone of higher education. Faculty members who engage in scholarship enrich their classrooms by incorporating current research findings, fostering analytical thinking, and mentoring students in academic inquiry. When students are exposed to faculty research, they gain valuable insights into the evolving nature of knowledge and are better prepared for careers that require critical thinking, innovation, and evidence-based decision-making.

By balancing teaching responsibilities with research productivity, faculty contribute to both their professional development and the academic reputation of their institutions. Encouraging student collaboration in research projects, guiding them in scholarly writing, and mentoring them through the research process fosters a culture of inquiry that benefits the entire academic community.

Ultimately, the successful integration of research, scholarship, and teaching empowers faculty to not only advance their fields but also inspire the next generation of scholars and professionals. By maintaining this synergy, educators create lasting impacts that extend beyond the classroom, shaping future researchers, leaders, and innovators.

Chapter 9: Student Inclusivity in Higher Education

Higher education institutions are increasingly diverse, with students from diverse backgrounds, cultures, and abilities. Professors play a critical role in fostering inclusivity by cultivating learning experiences where all individuals feel valued, respected, and supported in their academic journey. Inclusive teaching goes beyond accessibility; it involves actively addressing barriers to learning, integrating diverse perspectives, and ensuring all individuals—regardless of socioeconomic background, disability status, or cultural identity—have equal opportunities to succeed.

Figure 9.1. Inclusive Student Learning [219].

This chapter explores the essential principles of student inclusivity in higher education. It examines strategies for understanding diverse student backgrounds, designing culturally responsive course materials, addressing bias in grading and teaching, and supporting students with disabilities and learning differences. Additionally, this chapter provides practical methods for building an inclusive and supportive learning environment, ensuring that all students can thrive academically and professionally.

By adopting inclusive teaching practices, faculty contribute to a more equitable and engaging learning experience that benefits not only marginalized groups but all students, fostering a richer, more dynamic academic community.

Understanding Diverse Student Backgrounds: Cultivating Inclusive and Equitable Learning Environments

Higher education is becoming increasingly diverse, with students representing a wide range of cultural backgrounds, socioeconomic statuses, learning abilities, gender identities, life experiences, and educational pathways. For college professors, understanding these diverse backgrounds is critical to fostering an inclusive, equitable, and supportive learning environment—one in which all students, regardless of their identity or circumstances, feel valued and empowered to succeed.

Effective teaching is not just about delivering content; it is about recognizing the complex and varied experiences students bring to the classroom and designing courses that honor those experiences while promoting academic success for all learners. By understanding student diversity, professors can create responsive, student-centered learning environments that encourage engagement, reduce barriers, and promote equity in higher education.

This section explores the dimensions of student diversity, the impact of background on learning experiences, and strategies for creating an inclusive classroom, embracing and supports all students.

Dimensions of Student Diversity in Higher Education

Understanding student diversity requires acknowledging multiple intersecting factors that shape students' educational experiences. These include:

1. Cultural and Linguistic Diversity

International Students and Multilingual Learners

- Students from different cultural backgrounds may have varied academic expectations, communication styles, and levels of English proficiency.
- Some students may struggle with academic writing norms, class participation expectations, or group work dynamics due to cultural differences.

First-Generation College Students

- These students may lack family guidance on navigating higher education but bring resilience and unique perspectives.
- They often benefit from mentorship and structured academic support systems.

Religious and Ethnic Diversity

- Different religious practices may affect scheduling, dietary needs, and participation in class activities.
- Some students may face bias, microaggressions, or exclusionary behaviors that impact their academic experience.

Example: A professor implementing culturally responsive teaching may integrate global perspectives into course readings, recognizing diverse intellectual traditions rather than focusing solely on Western frameworks.

2. Socioeconomic Background and Access to Resources

Financial Barriers to Learning

- Students from low-income backgrounds may struggle with tuition, housing, and access to technology.
- The digital divide impacts individuals' ability to participate in online coursework, requiring professors to consider low-bandwidth alternatives for assignments and lectures.

Working and Caregiving Students

- Many students juggle full-time jobs, caregiving responsibilities, or financial stressors, impacting their availability for office hours, study sessions, and extracurricular involvement.
- Professors can offer flexible deadlines, asynchronous learning opportunities, and virtual office hours to accommodate these students.

Example: An instructor adopting an inclusive course design might provide textbook-free options by integrating open educational resources (OERs) to reduce financial burdens.

3. Neurodiversity and Learning Differences

Students with Disabilities (Visible and Invisible)

- Students may have physical, sensory, learning, or psychological disabilities that require accommodations, such as:
    - Extended time for exams.
    - Captioned videos and screen reader-friendly materials.
    - Alternative assignment formats.

Neurodiverse Students (e.g., ADHD, Autism Spectrum, Dyslexia)

- These students may thrive in structured, visually organized learning environments with clear expectations, predictable routines, and multimodal content delivery.

Example: A professor designing an accessible course syllabus uses plain language, provides structured weekly outlines, and offers multiple formats (audio, video, text) for content consumption to support neurodiverse learners.

4. Gender Identity, Sexual Orientation, and Inclusive Pedagogy

LGBTQ+ Students and Campus Climate

- Creating an inclusive environment involves using correct pronouns, incorporating diverse perspectives in curricula, and ensuring classroom discussions are respectful and affirming.
- Some students may feel unsafe disclosing their identity or may face discrimination in educational spaces.

Example: A faculty member normalizes pronoun-sharing by offering students the option to share their preferred name and pronouns in introductions and updating class rosters to reflect chosen names.

5. Non-Traditional, Returning, and Military-Affiliated Students

Adult Learners and Career-Changers

- These individuals face different issues than traditional college-aged students, such as balancing coursework with family and full-time work responsibilities.
- Professors can design courses with asynchronous content, flexible deadlines, and competency-based assessments to accommodate them.

Veteran and Military-Affiliated Students

- Some students transitioning from military service to academia may require structured guidance on academic expectations, time management, and civilian professional pathways.
- Providing clear instructions, direct feedback, and goal-oriented assessments can support their success.

Example: A faculty member uses case-based learning approaches that allow adult learners and veterans to apply their real-world experiences to academic concepts, making learning more relevant.

Creating an Inclusive Classroom for Diverse Students

1. Implementing Culturally Responsive Teaching

Acknowledge and integrate diverse perspectives into curricula rather than centering only dominant cultural narratives.
Encourage student voice by allowing students to bring in personal experiences, cultural knowledge, and interdisciplinary insights.

Example: In a literature class, a professor diversifies the reading list to include authors from various racial, cultural, and gender backgrounds, allowing students to engage with texts that reflect their identities.

2. Designing Equitable Course Policies

Offer flexibility in assignment formats to accommodate various learning preferences and life circumstances.
Implement inclusive grading practices, such as growth-based assessments that focus on student progress rather than rigid performance metrics.

Example: Instead of relying solely on high-stakes exams, an instructor allows students to demonstrate knowledge through research projects, creative assignments, or oral presentations.

3. Promoting an Inclusive Classroom Culture

Use inclusive language and address microaggressions proactively.
Encourage participation in multiple ways (verbal discussion, online discussion boards, written reflections).
Foster a sense of belonging by actively interacting with students, learning their names, and valuing their contributions.

Example: A professor uses small-group discussions and anonymous polling to ensure that students who are hesitant to speak in class still have ways to engage meaningfully.

4. Providing Academic and Institutional Support Resources

Direct students to tutoring centers, disability services, and financial aid resources when needed. Encourage mentorship programs that connect first-generation students or underrepresented groups with faculty mentors.

Example: A faculty member partners with the campus writing center to provide extra writing support for students unfamiliar with academic writing conventions.

Conclusion: Fostering a Culture of Equity and Inclusion

Understanding diverse student backgrounds is not just an academic exercise—it is a commitment to fostering an inclusive, equitable, and student-centered learning experience. By acknowledging the intersectional nature of student identities, designing accessible and culturally responsive courses, and promoting equitable classroom policies, faculty can ensure all students feel valued, supported, and empowered to succeed.

A truly inclusive higher education system does more than accommodate diversity—it celebrates it as a strength that enriches academic inquiry, fosters deeper learning, and prepares students to engage meaningfully in an increasingly complex and interconnected world.

Creating Culturally Responsive Teaching Materials: Enhancing Equity, Engagement, and Representation in Higher Education

In an increasingly diverse and globalized world, higher education must reflect the same complexity of cultural identities, histories, and societal perspectives. Traditional curricula have often been shaped by dominant cultural narratives, unintentionally marginalizing perspectives from underrepresented communities. Culturally responsive teaching (CRT) aims to remedy these gaps by intentionally designing teaching materials that affirm students' cultural backgrounds, promote diverse ways of knowing, and create more inclusive learning environments [151].

For new college professors, the development of culturally responsive teaching materials is not simply an academic exercise—it is a pedagogical responsibility that enhances student engagement, equity, and the relevance of higher education. This section explores the principles of culturally responsive teaching, strategies for developing inclusive course materials, and best practices for integrating diverse perspectives into the curriculum.

The Principles of Culturally Responsive Teaching

Culturally responsive teaching is an approach, recognizing, respecting, and incorporating individuals' cultural experiences into the learning environment. It is guided by the following principles:

1. Asset-Based Perspective on Diversity

Recognizing Diversity as an Academic Strength

- Instead of viewing cultural differences as challenges to overcome, culturally responsive teaching values diversity as an asset that enriches learning.
- Students bring unique experiences, linguistic skills, and worldviews that contribute to a more dynamic and enriched classroom discussion.

Example: A business professor acknowledges different global economic perspectives by incorporating case studies from non-Western economies, showing how business models vary based on cultural and historical contexts.

2. Decentering Dominant Narratives

Challenging Eurocentrism and Expanding Canonical Texts

- Many academic disciplines have been historically centered on Western, white, and male perspectives, often neglecting the contributions of Black, Indigenous, Latinx, Asian, and other historically marginalized scholars.
- Culturally responsive teaching broadens the curriculum to include multiple perspectives, epistemologies, and histories.

Example: A literature professor includes Chinua Achebe, Gloria Anzaldúa, and James Baldwin alongside Shakespeare and Hemingway, fostering a more representative literary canon.

3. Promoting Cultural Relevance in Course Materials

Relating Course Content to Students' Lives and Communities

- Students engage more deeply when they see themselves reflected in course content.
- Professors can integrate contemporary social issues, diverse case studies, and real-world applications, resonating with students' lived realities.

Example: A sociology professor discussing urban development includes examples from gentrification in diverse cities like Detroit, São Paulo, and Lagos, rather than solely focusing on Western urbanization models.

4. Incorporating Multilingual and Multimodal Learning Approaches

Valuing Linguistic Diversity

- Many students speak multiple languages or dialects, and their linguistic skills should be viewed as strengths rather than deficiencies.
- Professors can encourage students to explore research in different languages or analyze texts from multilingual perspectives.

Using Visuals, Media, and Interactive Tools

- Some students learn better through visuals, storytelling, or oral traditions, which are integral to many non-Western learning traditions.

- Professors can incorporate videos, infographics, podcasts, and oral histories to diversify learning methods.

Example: A professor in public health includes Indigenous health practices, traditional healing systems, and multilingual patient communication strategies to show how health equity depends on culturally aware healthcare approaches.

Strategies for Developing Culturally Responsive Teaching Materials

1. Expanding Reading Lists and Course Content

Diversify Assigned Readings

- Include scholars from different racial, gender, and cultural backgrounds.
- Ensure that theoretical frameworks reflect global and intersectional perspectives.

Example: In a history course on World War II, a professor includes readings on the contributions of Navajo Code Talkers, African American soldiers, and women in resistance movements, rather than focusing solely on European and U.S. military strategies.

Be Mindful of Language and Representation

- Avoid texts that reinforce stereotypes or deficit-based narratives.
- Encourage critical thinking by having students analyze biases within historical texts.

Example: In a psychology class, students examine the historical exclusion of marginalized groups in psychological research and discuss how this has impacted modern understandings of mental health.

2. Using Diverse Case Studies and Real-World Examples

Contextualizing Learning Through Global and Local Lenses

- Case studies should reflect varied geographic, economic, and cultural realities.
- Professors can use student-led projects where learners explore issues in their own communities.

Example: In an environmental science class, students compare water conservation policies in urban centers like Cape Town, Mexico City, and Los Angeles, illustrating how climate change impacts different communities uniquely.

Incorporating Cross-Cultural Problem-Solving Approaches

- Encourage students to analyze how different cultures approach ethics, law, medicine, business, or education.
- Use group discussions, debates, or role-playing activities that challenge students to engage with perspectives different from their own.

Example: In a law class, a professor compares Indigenous restorative justice practices with Western legal frameworks, allowing students to critique and appreciate alternative justice models.

3. Designing Inclusive Assessments and Assignments

Offering Multiple Ways for Students to Demonstrate Learning

- Traditional exams may not accommodate all learning styles or cultural backgrounds.
- Professors can use oral presentations, video projects, community-based research, or digital storytelling as assessment options.

Example: Instead of requiring a standard research paper, an anthropology professor allows students to create ethnographic documentaries that explore cultural traditions in their communities.

Providing Culturally Responsive Feedback

- Avoid grading approaches that assume a singular, "correct" way of expressing knowledge.
- Recognize the validity of different argumentation styles, linguistic patterns, and rhetorical traditions.

Example: A faculty member encourages multilingual students to incorporate bilingual sources in their research papers and values their ability to navigate multiple linguistic and cultural frameworks.

4. Creating an Inclusive Classroom Environment

Encourage Student Voice and Agency

- Give students opportunities to share cultural experiences and perspectives in discussions.
- Allow students to bring personal and community knowledge into academic discourse.

Example: A professor in a global health course invites students to share healthcare challenges faced by their own communities, encouraging an exchange of knowledge across cultural backgrounds.

Build Cultural Awareness Through Collaborative Learning

- Pair students from diverse backgrounds in group projects to encourage cross-cultural dialogue and teamwork.
- Foster interdisciplinary projects that allow students to draw from different cultural and academic traditions.

Example: A professor in international relations assigns mixed-nationality teams to analyze global conflicts from multiple perspectives, requiring them to integrate historical, economic, and cultural analysis.

Conclusion: Cultivating an Inclusive and Culturally Responsive Learning Experience

Creating culturally responsive teaching materials is not simply about adding diversity to the syllabus—it is about fundamentally transforming the learning experience to be more inclusive, reflective, and empowering for all students.

By broadening curricula, integrating multiple perspectives, designing inclusive assessments, and fostering culturally aware discussions, faculty can ensure that higher education reflects the diverse realities of students while preparing them for success in an interconnected world.

Ultimately, culturally responsive teaching fosters equity, engagement, and deeper learning, ensuring that all students see themselves as valued individuals in the global academic and professional landscape.

Addressing Bias in Teaching and Grading: Ensuring Fairness, Equity, and Student Success

Bias—whether conscious or unconscious—is an unavoidable aspect of human cognition. In higher education, bias can subtly shape teaching practices, classroom interactions, assessment methods, and grading in ways that perpetuate inequities and disadvantage certain student groups. While many educators strive to be objective, unexamined biases can affect who is called on in class, how student contributions are perceived, and how academic performance is evaluated.

For new college professors, acknowledging and addressing bias in teaching and grading is essential for fostering an inclusive, equitable, and just learning environment. By adopting evidence-based strategies, self-reflection, and transparent assessment practices, faculty can mitigate bias, ensure fairness in evaluations, and promote student success across diverse backgrounds.

This section explores the various types of bias that can affect teaching and grading, their impact on students, and best practices for ensuring objectivity and equity in higher education.

Understanding Bias in Teaching and Grading

Bias in academia does not always stem from intentional discrimination; more often, it is unconscious and shaped by societal norms, stereotypes, and institutional structures. Addressing bias requires faculty to actively recognize and counteract it in their interactions, pedagogy, and assessment strategies.

1. Types of Bias in Teaching

Confirmation Bias

- Faculty may unconsciously reinforce pre-existing beliefs about student ability based on past performance, demographics, or initial impressions.

- Example: Assuming that students from elite high schools will perform better than first-generation college students.

Implicit Bias

- Unconscious associations can affect who is called on in discussions, how student behavior is interpreted, and whose opinions are valued.
- Example: Expecting women in STEM courses to struggle more than male students or assuming that students from certain ethnic groups excel in specific subjects.

Cultural Bias

- Teaching methods that favor Western, Eurocentric, or dominant cultural norms can alienate students from diverse linguistic and cultural backgrounds.
- Example: Assigning only English-language sources without recognizing non-Western contributions to a field.

Affinity Bias

- Faculty may connect more easily with students who share similar backgrounds, interests, or cultural experiences, leading to unintended favoritism.
- Example: Engaging in more informal mentorship or offering more detailed feedback to students with similar socioeconomic or educational backgrounds.

Halo/Horns Effect

- A student's early impression (positive or negative) can influence future assessments, even when performance varies.
- Example: A student who impresses in the first-class discussion may receive more lenient grading later, while a student who struggles early may face harsher evaluation despite improvement.

Gender and Racial Bias in Student Perceptions

- Studies show that faculty may perceive and evaluate students differently based on gender, race, and perceived linguistic ability [152].
- Example: Women and students of color are often described in subjective terms like "hardworking" rather than "brilliant" in recommendation letters, affecting opportunities for graduate school or research.

Addressing Bias in Teaching Practices

1. Cultivating Awareness Through Self-Reflection and Training

Engage in Bias Awareness Training

- Participate in implicit bias workshops and self-assessments (e.g., Harvard's Implicit Association Test) to uncover unconscious biases [153].

Solicit Student Feedback

- Use anonymous surveys to gauge whether students perceive disparities in classroom interactions, participation opportunities, or grading practices.

Engage in Peer Observations

- Invite colleagues to observe classes and provide feedback on potential biases in student engagement.

Example: A faculty member notices they call on male students more frequently in STEM courses and implements randomized participation tracking to ensure balance.

2. Promoting Equitable Classroom Participation

Use Structured Discussion Techniques

- Implement strategies such as round-robin participation, think-pair-share, or digital polling to ensure that all voices are included.

Normalize Diverse Communication Styles

- Recognize that students from different cultural backgrounds may engage differently—some may feel uncomfortable with direct debate-style discussions but excel in written analysis or small-group discussions.

Example: A faculty member encourages students to submit discussion questions before class so that students who may be hesitant to speak verbally can still engage in meaningful ways.

Addressing Bias in Grading and Assessment

1. Ensuring Objectivity and Fairness in Grading

Use Rubrics to Standardize Evaluations

- Develop clear, specific, and transparent grading rubrics to minimize subjectivity.
- Ensure rubrics align with learning objectives and provide detailed criteria for assessment.

Blind Grading Where Possible

- When feasible, grade assignments without names to reduce unconscious biases based on student identity, previous performance, or participation levels.

Calibrate Grading with Colleagues

- Conduct grading norming sessions with colleagues to compare how assignments are evaluated and ensure consistency.

Example: In an essay-based course, the professor grades assignments anonymously, following a structured rubric to ensure impartial assessment.

2. Reducing Cultural and Linguistic Bias in Assessment

Recognize and Validate Different Forms of Academic Writing

- Be mindful that linguistic bias can disadvantage multilingual students whose writing may not conform to Western academic norms but still demonstrate deep analytical thinking.
- Offer revision opportunities and writing support instead of penalizing non-standard English grammar.

Offer Multiple Assessment Methods

- Provide varied assessment formats (e.g., oral presentations, multimedia projects, written essays) to cultivate diverse learning styles and cultural backgrounds.

Example: A history professor allows students to submit final projects in different formats—a traditional research paper, a digital documentary, or a visual exhibit.

3. Mitigating Bias in Course Policies and Expectations

Avoid Assumptions About Student Resources and Background Knowledge

- Recognize students have different levels of access to technology, research materials, and prior academic preparation.
- Offer accessible materials, low-cost textbook alternatives, and flexible learning options.

Be Flexible in Attendance and Participation Policies

- Some students may face barriers to attendance due to financial strain, caregiving responsibilities, or disability-related issues.
- Implement alternative participation methods (e.g., online discussion boards, recorded lectures).

Example: A professor does not penalize occasional absences but instead provides alternative assignments to ensure students can keep up without academic penalty.

Fostering an Ongoing Commitment to Equity in Teaching

Seek Continuous Professional Development

- Engage in equity-centered teaching workshops, antiracist pedagogy training, and cross-cultural competency seminars.

Regularly Revise Course Content and Policies

- Ensure that syllabi, assigned readings, and examples reflect diverse perspectives and avoid reinforcing stereotypes.

Be Transparent About Assessment Criteria

- Provide students with clear grading explanations and offer opportunities for constructive feedback and revision.

Example: A professor shares anonymized exemplary assignments to clarify grading expectations and model strong academic work.

Conclusion: Creating a More Equitable and Inclusive Academic Experience

Addressing bias in teaching and grading is a continuous process that requires self-awareness, intentional practice, and structural change. By recognizing the hidden biases that shape classroom interactions and assessment methods, faculty can create fairer, more inclusive learning experiences, empowering all students to succeed.

By implementing objective grading practices, equitable classroom participation strategies, and ongoing self-reflection, faculty can ensure that their teaching does not unintentionally reinforce inequities but instead fosters academic growth, confidence, and belonging for all students.

Supporting Students with Disabilities and Learning Differences: Building Inclusive and Accessible Higher Education

Higher education institutions increasingly recognize the importance of accessibility and inclusivity in ensuring that students with disabilities and learning differences can thrive academically. Students with disabilities—whether physical, sensory, cognitive, neurological, psychological, or chronic health-related—face unique challenges that require thoughtful accommodation, proactive support, and a commitment to equitable learning opportunities.

For new college professors, creating an inclusive classroom means going beyond compliance with legal requirements and actively fostering an environment in which all students, regardless of ability, can engage fully, demonstrate their knowledge, and succeed on their own terms. This section explores the diverse needs of individuals with disabilities, common barriers to learning, legal and ethical considerations, and best practices for providing accommodations and inclusive teaching strategies.

Understanding Disabilities and Learning Differences in Higher Education

Students with disabilities are a diverse and heterogeneous group, with varied experiences and needs. Some disabilities are visible, while others—such as learning disabilities, mental health conditions, ADHD, or chronic illnesses—are invisible and may go unrecognized without student disclosure.

1. Types of Disabilities and Learning Differences

Physical Disabilities

- May include mobility impairments, multiple sclerosis, chronic pain, arthritis, spinal cord injuries, or cerebral palsy.

- Students may require wheelchair-accessible seating, modified classroom layouts, voice recognition software, or ergonomic tools.

Sensory Disabilities

- Includes visual impairments (blindness, low vision) and hearing impairments (deafness, hard of hearing).
- Accommodations may include Braille materials, screen readers, captioned videos, or ASL interpreters.

Neurodiversity and Learning Disabilities

- Students may have dyslexia, dysgraphia, dyscalculia, auditory processing disorder, or ADHD.
- Support strategies include extra time on exams, note-taking assistance, structured learning environments, and multimodal instruction.

Autism Spectrum and Cognitive Disabilities

- May impact social interaction, sensory processing, and executive functioning.
- Students may benefit from clear expectations, reduced sensory distractions, structured routines, and alternative communication options.

Mental Health and Psychological Disabilities

- Includes anxiety, depression, PTSD, bipolar disorder, or schizophrenia.
- Flexible attendance policies, quiet exam environments, and access to mental health resources can provide crucial support.

Chronic Illnesses and Medical Conditions

- Conditions such as epilepsy, diabetes, Crohn's disease, or long-term effects of medical treatments may require adjustments in deadlines, class participation, or physical accommodations.

By understanding the spectrum of disabilities and learning differences, faculty can adopt inclusive teaching practices that reduce barriers and enhance student engagement.

Legal and Ethical Considerations in Disability Support

1. Institutional and Legal Frameworks for Disability Inclusion

Faculty members must comply with legal protections that ensure equitable access for students with disabilities, including:

Americans with Disabilities Act (ADA) & Section 504 of the Rehabilitation Act [154]

- Requires reasonable accommodations for students with disabilities.

- Mandates that institutions remove barriers to access and provide equal opportunity in academic programs.

The Individuals with Disabilities Education Act (IDEA)

- Although IDEA applies primarily to K-12, many students transition to college with Individualized Education Programs (IEPs) or 504 Plans.
- Faculty should coordinate with disability services offices to ensure continued support.

Confidentiality and Student Rights

- Disability status is protected under FERPA (Family Educational Rights and Privacy Act) [155].
- Professors should not inquire about disabilities directly but should encourage students to seek support through institutional disability services.

Example: A professor includes a disability accommodation statement in the syllabus, directing students to campus support resources and reassuring them that accommodations are welcome.

Best Practices for Supporting Students with Disabilities and Learning Differences

1. Creating an Accessible Classroom Environment

Ensure Physical and Digital Accessibility

- Arrange classrooms with wheelchair-accessible seating and clear pathways.
- Use accessible digital platforms (Canvas, Blackboard, Moodle) with screen-reader compatibility.

Use Clear and Consistent Communication

- Provide structured syllabi with clear deadlines and expectations.
- Use plain language, visual aids, and organizational tools to support students with processing difficulties.

Example: A professor uploads lecture notes and slides in advance, allowing students with cognitive processing challenges to review material at their own pace.

2. Implementing Universal Design for Learning (UDL) Principles

Multiple Means of Representation (How Information is Delivered)

- Provide text, audio, video, and interactive formats for course content.
- Ensure materials are colorblind-friendly and screen-reader compatible.

Multiple Means of Engagement (How Students Interact with Content)

- Incorporate low-distraction learning environments for students with sensory sensitivities.

- Offer structured discussion formats (written forums, small groups, one-on-one interactions) for students who struggle with large-group participation.

Multiple Means of Expression (How Students Demonstrate Learning)

- Allow students to submit projects in different formats (written, oral, multimedia) to accommodate varied learning needs.
- Provide alternative testing arrangements, extended time, or alternative formats when necessary [156].

Example: A history professor allows students to present final research projects as written papers, digital story maps, or recorded oral presentations.

3. Providing Accommodations Without Stigmatization

Offer Accommodations Proactively

- Instead of waiting for students to disclose disabilities, create an inclusive course design from the start.

Maintain Student Privacy and Dignity

- Do not single out students needing accommodations. Use neutral language and confidential processes.

Example: A professor privately emails students about available support services rather than asking them publicly in class.

4. Adapting Assessment and Grading Practices

Use Flexible and Accessible Assessments

- Offer low-stakes assessments and varied grading criteria to accommodate students with test anxiety or executive function challenges.

Example: Instead of a single high-stakes exam, a professor designs a series of short quizzes, open-book reflections, and take-home essays.

Provide Constructive and Inclusive Feedback

- Be mindful that neurodiverse students or those with dyslexia may struggle with traditional grading feedback.
- Use audio or video feedback tools to offer more nuanced, supportive critique.

Example: A faculty member records verbal feedback on assignments, allowing students to engage with the critique in a more accessible format.

5. Connecting Students to Institutional and Community Resources

Direct Students to Campus Disability Services

- Encourage students to seek formal accommodations through disability support offices.

Partner with Campus Support Networks

- Work with academic tutoring centers, writing labs, mental health services, and disability specialists.

Example: A professor collaborates with the writing center to provide one-on-one tutoring for students with dyslexia.

Conclusion: Creating a Culture of Accessibility and Inclusion

Supporting students with disabilities and learning differences is not just about compliance—it is about creating a higher education system that values equity, accessibility, and diverse ways of learning.

By incorporating universal design principles, flexible assessment methods, accessible teaching materials, and proactive accommodations, faculty can remove barriers, empower students, and ensure that all learners—regardless of ability—have the opportunity to succeed.

Ultimately, an inclusive classroom benefits everyone—not just students with disabilities—but all learners who thrive in environments that prioritize adaptability, accessibility, and academic success.

Building an Inclusive and Supportive Learning Environment: Cultivating Equity, Engagement, and Belonging in Higher Education

A truly inclusive and supportive learning experience is one in which all students, regardless of background, identity, or ability, feel valued, respected, and empowered to succeed. In higher education, where classrooms bring together individuals from diverse cultural, socioeconomic, and academic backgrounds, fostering inclusivity is both a pedagogical responsibility and an ethical imperative.

For new college professors, building an inclusive classroom requires intentionality, adaptability, and a commitment to equity. It involves rethinking traditional teaching approaches, eliminating systemic barriers, and fostering a culture of mutual respect and engagement. This section explores the key elements of an inclusive learning environment, the benefits of fostering inclusivity, and actionable strategies for creating a supportive classroom culture.

The Importance of Inclusive and Supportive Learning Environments

An inclusive classroom goes beyond diversity awareness—it actively ensures that every student can fully participate and succeed. Professors who cultivate an inclusive environment help students:

Feel a Sense of Belonging and Representation

- Students engage more when they see themselves reflected in course materials, discussions, and classroom interactions.

- Inclusion fosters a sense of academic identity and motivation.

Overcome Barriers to Learning

- Many students face hidden challenges, including disabilities, financial hardship, language barriers, and cultural adaptation struggles.
- A supportive environment ensures that these barriers do not hinder academic success.

Develop Critical Thinking Through Diverse Perspectives

- When classrooms welcome a range of viewpoints, backgrounds, and lived experiences, students gain a richer, more nuanced understanding of course material.

Achieve Higher Retention and Academic Success

- Research indicates learners who feel included and supported in the classroom are more likely to persist in their studies and perform well academically [157].

By designing courses and classroom interactions with inclusivity at the forefront, faculty contribute to a more just, equitable, and intellectually engaging academic experience.

Key Elements of an Inclusive and Supportive Learning Environment

1. Equity-Centered Course Design

Universal Design for Learning (UDL)

- Use multiple ways to present information, allowing students to engage with content in ways that match their learning styles.
- Example: Provide lecture recordings, transcripts, infographics, and interactive discussions instead of relying solely on text-based readings.

Flexible Assessments and Grading Practices

- Not all students perform best on traditional exams or essays.
- Example: Allow students to demonstrate learning through written papers, video presentations, group projects, or hands-on work.

Transparent Course Expectations

- Clearly define grading rubrics, deadlines, and participation requirements to eliminate confusion.
- Example: A professor provides a detailed syllabus with a structured weekly breakdown so that students can plan ahead.

2. Creating a Classroom Culture of Respect and Belonging

Establish Ground Rules for Inclusive Discussions

- Set guidelines for respectful dialogue, ensuring that all students feel safe expressing their thoughts.
- Example: A professor encourages students to use "I" statements in discussions to promote constructive debate rather than personal attacks.

Address Implicit Bias and Microaggressions

- Recognize and correct unintentional biases in classroom interactions.
- Example: If a student's ideas are dismissed in discussion, the professor actively re-centers the conversation to acknowledge and validate their contribution.

Learn and Use Students' Preferred Names and Pronouns

- Addressing students correctly fosters a sense of recognition and respect.
- Example: On the first day, the professor invites students to share their preferred names and pronouns, making it standard practice in class.

Encourage Peer Support and Collaboration

- Promote group activities and peer mentoring to foster community.
- Example: A professor pairs international students with domestic students in projects to enhance cross-cultural learning.

3. Representation and Inclusive Curriculum Development

Diversify Course Content

- Ensure that course materials reflect multiple perspectives, cultures, and contributions.
- Example: A history professor includes Black, Indigenous, Latinx, and Asian voices in discussions of historical movements.

Use Case Studies and Examples Relevant to All Students

- Avoid centering examples on only Western, male, or dominant cultural perspectives.
- Example: A business professor incorporates case studies from global markets rather than only U.S.-centric models.

Recognize Different Ways of Knowing

- Value oral traditions, storytelling, and experiential knowledge alongside traditional academic sources.
- Example: In a science class, a professor acknowledges Indigenous environmental knowledge alongside Western ecological theories.

4. Supporting Students with Varied Needs

Make Course Materials Accessible

- Ensure content is compatible with screen readers, captioned for hearing-impaired students, and formatted for visual clarity.
- Example: A professor provides alternative text for all images in PowerPoint presentations for students using screen readers.

Offer Flexible Participation Options

- Not all students feel comfortable speaking in class—offer alternative ways to contribute.
- Example: Allow students to participate in online discussion boards, small group chats, or reflective journals.

Be Mindful of Mental Health and Well-Being

- Acknowledge the pressures of academic life and provide resources for students struggling with mental health.
- Example: A professor includes a statement in the syllabus directing students to campus mental health services.

5. Encouraging Faculty-Student Mentorship and Support

Hold Regular Office Hours in Accessible Formats

- Provide both in-person and virtual options for students with time constraints.
- Example: A professor holds "drop-in Zoom office hours" in the evening for working students.

Foster Inclusive Research and Internship Opportunities

- Encourage students from historically underrepresented backgrounds to pursue research, internships, and leadership roles.
- Example: A faculty mentor actively recruits first-generation college students for research assistant positions.

Recognize and Address Power Dynamics

- Cultivate an experience where students feel comfortable to ask for help without fear of judgment.
- Example: A professor frames feedback as a conversation rather than a critique, reinforcing a growth mindset.

Overcoming Common Challenges to Inclusion

Recognizing and Addressing Implicit Bias

- Faculty must reflect on personal biases and actively work to unlearn discriminatory assumptions.
- Solution: Engage in implicit bias training and inclusive pedagogy workshops.

Balancing Academic Rigor with Flexibility

- Inclusivity does not mean lowering expectations—it means providing equitable access to success.
- Solution: Maintain high academic standards while offering multiple pathways for students to demonstrate mastery.

Managing Resistance to Inclusion Initiatives

- Some faculty and students may resist changes to traditional teaching methods.
- Solution: Frame inclusivity as an evidence-based approach that benefits all students, improving learning outcomes, retention, and engagement.

Global and Cultural Competency Development

In today's interconnected world, higher education institutions are no longer local or national enterprises—they are global. Classrooms frequently include students from a wide array of countries, cultural traditions, and linguistic backgrounds. This diversity offers rich opportunities for broadening perspectives and fostering global awareness, but it also presents challenges for faculty who may not be fully prepared to address the varied needs of international and multicultural student groups. Developing global and cultural competency is therefore not optional; it is a professional responsibility for educators committed to inclusivity and to preparing graduates for work and citizenship in a multicultural world.

Cultural competency requires more than awareness of diversity. Faculty must employ intentional strategies that foster equity, belonging, and global engagement. This involves adapting pedagogy, redesigning curricula, and strengthening institutional systems that support international and multilingual students, while also encouraging domestic students to broaden their worldviews.

Teaching International Students Effectively

International students bring unique strengths and perspectives, but they also face distinct challenges in adapting to new academic environments. Faculty who adopt intentional practices can ease these transitions and help students succeed.

- **Clarifying Expectations**
  Academic practices vary widely around the world. For example, expectations around classroom participation, group work, and the definition of plagiarism differ significantly by culture. Faculty should:
    - Provide explicit guidelines on participation norms and grading rubrics.

- o Offer detailed explanations of citation and referencing practices, especially where academic integrity expectations differ from those in students' home countries.
  - o Use orientation sessions or short tutorials to explain the academic culture of their institution.
- **Using Multiple Teaching Modalities**
  International students may come from systems that emphasize rote memorization or lecture-based instruction. To bridge these differences:
  - o Combine lectures with visuals, diagrams, or multimedia to reinforce comprehension.
  - o Incorporate interactive components such as discussion, group projects, or problem-based learning.
  - o Provide hands-on activities where students can apply theories in practical contexts, reinforcing understanding through experience.
- **Creating Welcoming Environments**
  International students often experience social isolation or are relegated to token roles in group settings. Faculty can counter this by:
  - o Pairing international students with domestic peers in group projects to promote cross-cultural exchange.
  - o Encouraging peer mentorship programs that connect students across cultural backgrounds.
  - o Modeling inclusivity by affirming diverse perspectives during discussions and ensuring all voices are heard.
- **Providing Early Feedback**
  Transitioning into a new academic culture can be overwhelming, particularly when grades are tied to high-stakes assessments. Faculty can ease adjustment by:
  - o Assigning small, low-stakes tasks early in the semester to help students gauge expectations.
  - o Offering constructive, formative feedback that emphasizes growth and improvement rather than just evaluation.
  - o Scheduling one-on-one check-ins to discuss progress and address challenges before they escalate.

Key Takeaway

Teaching international students effectively requires a combination of clarity, pedagogical flexibility, inclusive practices, and formative support. Faculty who adopt these strategies not only help international students succeed but also enrich the classroom environment for all learners by fostering intercultural exchange and deeper global understanding.

Incorporating Global Perspectives into Curriculum

Global competency cannot be developed if students are only exposed to a narrow set of cultural frameworks or scholarly traditions. A curriculum that reflects diverse voices and contexts prepares students to think critically about global interdependence, appreciate cultural variation, and apply knowledge in ways that are relevant beyond their immediate environment. Faculty play a crucial role in broadening perspectives by intentionally designing courses that move beyond Western or local-centric views and highlight the interconnectedness of global challenges and opportunities.

Diversify Readings

Course materials should represent a wide range of cultural and intellectual traditions.

- **Non-Western Scholarship**: Include works by authors from Africa, Asia, Latin America, and the Middle East, not just as supplemental readings but as central voices in the curriculum.
- **Local and Indigenous Knowledge**: Recognize knowledge systems often marginalized in academic discourse, such as indigenous ecological practices or community-based problem-solving approaches.
- **Multilingual Sources**: When possible, expose students to translated works, reinforcing that valuable scholarship is not limited to English-language publications.
By diversifying readings, faculty validate multiple perspectives and encourage students to critically examine whose voices are included in knowledge production.

Global Case Studies

Analyzing issues across cultural and geographic contexts helps students see the global relevance of their discipline.

- **Comparative Lens**: For example, climate change can be studied through its impact on coastal communities in Southeast Asia, agricultural regions in Sub-Saharan Africa, and urban centers in North America.
- **Field-Specific Relevance**: In business courses, students might compare consumer behavior in emerging economies with that in industrialized markets. In health sciences, they could examine how cultural beliefs shape approaches to wellness and treatment.
- **Contextual Awareness**: Global case studies emphasize that solutions effective in one region may fail in another due to cultural, political, or economic differences.

Comparative Assignments

Assignments that require students to analyze problems through multiple cultural frameworks deepen critical thinking.

- **Healthcare Systems**: Compare universal healthcare models in Europe with privatized systems in the United States or community-based models in rural Asia.
- **Governance and Policy**: Contrast democratic practices in different regions, or examine how cultural values shape policy priorities.
- **Business Ethics**: Explore how cultural norms affect concepts such as bribery, corporate responsibility, and sustainability.
These assignments help students develop cultural agility—the ability to adapt knowledge and practices across contexts.

Collaborative International Projects

Technology now makes it possible to integrate cross-border collaboration into coursework, even without physical travel.

- **Virtual Exchange Programs**: Partner courses across institutions globally, where students work together through online platforms to address shared research questions or case studies.
- **Joint Capstone Projects**: Create opportunities for students to co-author reports or presentations with peers from partner universities abroad.
- **Cross-Cultural Dialogue**: Facilitate structured discussions where students reflect on differences in perspectives, communication styles, and problem-solving approaches. Such projects foster intercultural communication skills and mirror the global teamwork common in professional fields.

Key Takeaway

Incorporating global perspectives into curriculum means going beyond tokenism and embedding diverse voices, comparative analysis, and international collaboration into the fabric of academic learning. By diversifying readings, analyzing global case studies, designing comparative assignments, and fostering cross-border collaboration, faculty equip students with the intellectual agility and cultural awareness needed to succeed in a globalized world.

Managing Cultural Differences in Learning Styles

Students' approaches to learning are shaped not only by individual preferences but also by the cultural and educational systems in which they were raised. In some traditions, students are taught to show respect through silence and deference to authority, while in others, challenging ideas and debating with professors is encouraged as a sign of engagement. These cultural differences can create misunderstandings in diverse classrooms if faculty interpret behaviors through only one lens—for example, mistaking quietness for disengagement or assertiveness for disrespect. Effective teaching in multicultural contexts requires awareness, flexibility, and validation of multiple ways of learning.

Recognize Variability

Faculty must avoid essentializing or stereotyping students by cultural group. Not every student from a particular background will conform to assumed norms.

- **Contextual Awareness**: Recognize that patterns may exist but remain open to variation within groups.
- **Observation and Dialogue**: Pay attention to how individual students prefer to engage and ask them about their learning needs directly when appropriate.
- **Interpret with Care**: A quiet student may be processing ideas deeply rather than disengaged; an outspoken student may simply reflect a cultural emphasis on verbal participation.

Blend Pedagogies

A mix of instructional approaches ensures that diverse learning preferences are respected.

- **Lecture-Based Instruction**: Retain structured content delivery for students accustomed to teacher-centered learning environments.
- **Active Learning Strategies**: Integrate problem-based learning, peer collaboration, or experiential exercises for students who thrive on engagement and discussion.
- **Variety in Assessment**: Balance exams and essays with presentations, portfolios, and group projects, giving students multiple ways to demonstrate learning.
Blended pedagogies create inclusive classrooms where no single cultural learning style dominates.

Facilitate Participation

Participation norms vary across cultures, and faculty can use strategies to ensure all voices are included.

- **Structured Turn-Taking**: Roundtable formats or calling on students systematically reduces dominance by a few voices.
- **Small-Group Discussions**: Some students feel more comfortable contributing in smaller groups before sharing with the larger class.
- **Anonymous Polling and Digital Tools**: Platforms like clickers or online discussion boards allow hesitant students to contribute without the social pressure of speaking publicly.
- **Wait Time**: Allowing longer pauses after asking questions accommodates students who need more time to formulate responses, especially in a second language.

Normalize Multiple Approaches

Faculty should explicitly acknowledge that there is more than one valid way to learn and participate.

- **Validation**: Reinforce that both reflective and outspoken learners contribute meaningfully to the academic environment.
- **Explicit Framing**: Explain to students that the classroom will include a range of pedagogical strategies, and all are valuable.
- **Cultural Self-Awareness**: Faculty should reflect on their own cultural biases in teaching, recognizing that what feels "normal" in their classroom may not be universal.

Key Takeaway

Managing cultural differences in learning styles means recognizing variability, blending pedagogies, facilitating participation, and normalizing diverse approaches. By intentionally designing inclusive classrooms, faculty not only support international and multicultural students but also model for all learners the adaptability and respect needed in global professional and civic contexts.

Cross-Cultural Communication Strategies

In classrooms with students from diverse cultural and linguistic backgrounds, communication is not simply about transmitting information, it is about building mutual understanding across differences. What seems clear to one student may be confusing, intimidating, or even disrespectful to another due to variations in language proficiency, cultural norms, and communication styles. Faculty must therefore model communication practices that both bridge divides and teach students how to engage respectfully in global and multicultural contexts.

Plain Language

Academic jargon, idioms, and culturally specific references can create barriers for individuals whose first language is not English or individuals who come from different educational systems.

- **Clarity First**: Use direct, simple language when giving instructions or explaining key concepts. Avoid slang, metaphors, or cultural references that may not translate.
- **Supplementary Materials**: Provide written instructions alongside verbal explanations, and reinforce concepts with visuals or diagrams.
- **Consistent Terminology**: Use the same terms for core concepts throughout the course to reduce confusion.
  Plain language helps all students—not just non-native speakers—by making expectations and content more transparent.

Active Listening

Listening across cultural boundaries requires more than hearing words; it requires effort to understand intent and meaning.

- **Paraphrasing Contributions**: Restate student comments to confirm understanding and validate their ideas.
- **Clarifying Questions**: Ask follow-up questions rather than making assumptions about meaning, especially when language barriers exist.
- **Encouraging Voices**: Show appreciation for contributions, even when phrased imperfectly, to build confidence and encourage participation.
  Active listening signals respect and models inclusive communication practices for students.

Nonverbal Awareness

Nonverbal cues—gestures, facial expressions, eye contact, and silence—carry different meanings across cultures. Misinterpretation can easily lead to tension or alienation.

- **Eye Contact**: While some cultures see direct eye contact as respect, others interpret it as confrontational or inappropriate.
- **Gestures**: Hand signals or body language may be benign in one culture but offensive in another.
- **Silence**: In some traditions, silence reflects deep thought or respect, while in others it suggests confusion or disengagement.
Faculty should avoid overinterpreting nonverbal behavior and instead create space for students to explain their communication preferences.

Conflict Mediation

Multicultural classrooms may experience miscommunication or disagreement stemming from cultural differences in how opinions are expressed. Faculty can guide students toward respectful engagement by:

- **Establishing Ground Rules**: At the start of the course, outline norms for respectful dialogue, including listening without interruption and critiquing ideas rather than individuals.
- **Modeling Respectful Disagreement**: Demonstrate how to challenge ideas constructively without dismissing or demeaning others.
- **Intervening Quickly**: If a discussion escalates, faculty should step in early to redirect conversation and prevent misunderstandings from hardening into conflict.
- **Teaching Communication Tools**: Introduce strategies such as "I statements" or cultural dialogue frameworks to help students express themselves while respecting differences.

Key Takeaway

Cross-cultural communication in higher education requires intentional clarity, respectful listening, cultural sensitivity to nonverbal cues, and structured conflict mediation. Faculty who model these practices not only foster inclusive classroom environments but also prepare students with essential skills for navigating multicultural workplaces and societies.

Understanding Visa and Immigration Impacts on Student Experience

For international students, academic success is deeply intertwined with immigration status. Visa regulations affect where they can work, how many credits they must take, whether they can participate in internships, and even their ability to remain in the country. These policies create layers of stress and uncertainty that domestic students typically do not face. Faculty who understand the impact of immigration rules on student life can better support international students, not by acting as legal advisors, but by demonstrating awareness, flexibility, and empathy.

Be Informed

Faculty should have a working knowledge of how visa restrictions influence international students' academic and professional options.

- **Work Eligibility**: Most student visas restrict employment, limiting students to on-campus jobs or requiring special authorization (e.g., CPT or OPT in the U.S.) for internships or professional placements. Faculty must avoid assuming students can accept unpaid or off-campus work without considering visa rules.
- **Course Load Requirements**: Many visa types require students to maintain full-time enrollment. Dropping below the minimum credit requirement can jeopardize immigration status, even for legitimate academic or personal reasons.
- **Program Changes**: Switching majors, extending time to degree, or taking online courses may require immigration approval. Faculty should guide students to appropriate advisors when such changes are considered.

Flexibility in Scheduling

Immigration-related issues often disrupt academic schedules in ways beyond students' control.

- **Visa Delays**: Students may arrive late at the start of the semester due to consular processing backlogs. Faculty can accommodate by providing early access to course materials online.
- **Travel Restrictions**: International crises or political changes can prevent students from leaving or re-entering the host country. Faculty should allow remote participation when possible.
- **Mandatory Appointments**: Immigration office visits, biometric screenings, or court dates may conflict with class or exam schedules. Faculty should provide flexibility in rescheduling deadlines or assessments.

Referral to Resources

Faculty are not immigration experts, but they can connect students to the right support systems.

- **Campus Immigration Services**: Most institutions have international student offices that provide advising on visas, work authorization, and compliance.
- **Legal Support**: Universities may offer access to immigration attorneys or legal aid clinics for more complex cases.
- **Emergency Aid**: Financial assistance programs may be available for students who face unexpected costs due to visa restrictions or travel interruptions.
  Knowing where to refer students ensures they receive accurate information without faculty overstepping professional boundaries.

Empathy in Advising

Perhaps the most important role faculty can play is acknowledging the emotional and psychological toll of navigating immigration systems.

- **Recognizing Stress**: Visa uncertainty can create chronic anxiety about the future, affecting academic performance.

- **Showing Understanding**: Simple gestures—such as acknowledging the difficulty of balancing legal compliance with academic rigor—can help students feel supported.
- **Avoiding Assumptions**: Faculty should not assume all international students face the same circumstances; immigration rules vary by country of origin, visa category, and personal situation.
- **Encouraging Communication**: Creating an open, supportive environment allows students to share challenges without fear of penalty or judgment.

Key Takeaway

International students' academic experiences are inseparable from the visa and immigration systems that govern their presence in the host country. Faculty cannot solve immigration issues, but by being informed, flexible, resource-aware, and empathetic, they can reduce unnecessary barriers and provide meaningful support. Such practices not only promote student success but also signal institutional commitment to creating a welcoming global learning environment.

Religious Accommodation in Academic Settings

Religion shapes the daily lives, schedules, and identities of many students, yet it is often overlooked in academic planning. Inclusive teaching requires not only awareness of students' faith practices but also proactive steps to ensure that religious obligations do not conflict with academic participation or success. When faculty respect students' religious commitments, they create learning environments that affirm diversity and demonstrate fairness.

Scheduling Awareness

Religious holidays and observances may fall outside widely recognized public calendars, making it essential for faculty to plan inclusively.

- **Avoiding Conflicts**: Do not schedule major exams, project deadlines, or mandatory events on significant religious holidays (e.g., Yom Kippur, Eid al-Fitr, Diwali).
- **Academic Calendars**: Some institutions publish interfaith calendars; faculty should review these when designing syllabi.
- **Advance Communication**: Invite students early in the term to inform faculty about potential conflicts so adjustments can be made respectfully.

Flexible Attendance

Many faith traditions require regular rituals, prayers, or community gatherings that may conflict with class times.

- **Excused Absences**: Allow students to miss class for religious observances without penalty.
- **Alternative Assignments**: Provide make-up opportunities or alternative assessments so students are not disadvantaged.

- **Respect for Routine Practices**: Recognize daily or weekly observances (e.g., Friday prayers, Sabbath restrictions) and accommodate where possible, particularly with scheduling group work or evening events.

Dietary Considerations

Academic events often include food, and neglecting dietary restrictions can unintentionally exclude students.

- **Religious Diets**: Be mindful of halal, kosher, vegetarian, or fasting practices tied to faith traditions.
- **Inclusive Event Planning**: When food is served at academic functions, provide labeled options that accommodate religious dietary needs.
- **Sensitivity During Fasting**: Recognize that students observing fasts (e.g., during Ramadan) may need scheduling flexibility for exams, presentations, or physically demanding activities.

Respectful Dialogue

Religion can be a sensitive and personal subject, but academic contexts sometimes require its discussion. Faculty must model respectful engagement.

- **Creating Safe Spaces**: Encourage dialogue that allows students to share perspectives without fear of ridicule or marginalization.
- **Focusing on Ideas, Not Individuals**: When religion is part of the curriculum (e.g., in history, philosophy, or social sciences), frame discussions around beliefs and practices rather than personalizing debates.
- **Managing Conflict**: Intervene if discussions become disrespectful, reinforcing that academic spaces require civility even when disagreements are strong.
- **Encouraging Critical Thinking**: Support exploration of religious ideas while maintaining sensitivity to students' lived identities.

Key Takeaway

Religious accommodation is a cornerstone of inclusive education. By practicing scheduling awareness, offering flexible attendance, respecting dietary restrictions, and fostering respectful dialogue, faculty ensure that students of all faiths can fully participate in academic life. These practices not only comply with equity standards but also affirm the dignity and belonging of every student.

Language Support Strategies for Non-Native English Speakers

Language is one of the most immediate barriers that non-native English-speaking students encounter in higher education. Even when these students possess strong academic preparation, linguistic challenges can affect their ability to fully participate in class discussions, understand complex instructions, or demonstrate their knowledge in writing. Faculty play a critical role in creating inclusive environments where students' ideas are valued independently of language proficiency and where communication support is built into instruction.

Simplifying Materials

Course materials should be designed with clarity and accessibility in mind.

- **Concise Instructions**: Provide step-by-step directions for assignments and assessments, using straightforward language.
- **Avoiding Idioms**: Expressions like "hit the ground running" or "think outside the box" can confuse non-native speakers. Replace them with literal, unambiguous wording.
- **Consistency in Terminology**: Use the same terms throughout a course to reduce confusion, particularly with technical or discipline-specific vocabulary.
- **Written + Verbal Instructions**: Reinforce oral explanations with written summaries so students can process material at their own pace.

Supplemental Resources

Faculty should connect students with resources that strengthen their language skills.

- **Writing Centers**: Direct students to campus services where they can receive individualized feedback on essays, lab reports, and presentations.
- **ESL Support Services**: Encourage use of English language courses, tutoring, or conversation groups that build academic language proficiency.
- **Online Tools**: Recommend grammar checkers, translation aids, or vocabulary-building apps while clarifying their appropriate academic use.
- **Faculty Office Hours**: Provide additional support by clarifying assignment expectations or reviewing drafts with students one-on-one.

Multimodal Teaching

Reinforcing content through multiple modes of delivery increases comprehension and retention.

- **Visual Aids**: Use diagrams, charts, infographics, and slide decks to anchor complex ideas.
- **Recorded Lectures**: Allow students to replay material at their own pace, supporting comprehension.
- **Demonstrations and Examples**: Pair abstract explanations with concrete illustrations, making material more accessible.
- **Interactive Tools**: Online quizzes or visual annotation software can provide immediate reinforcement of key concepts.

Peer Support

Peer collaboration offers non-native speakers opportunities to practice academic English in supportive, low-pressure contexts.

- **Mixed-Language Groups**: Pair international students with domestic peers to foster reciprocal learning—language support for one, global perspective-building for the other.
- **Peer Review**: Structured peer feedback sessions help students improve clarity in writing while strengthening collaborative skills.
- **Mentorship Programs**: Encourage participation in formal or informal peer mentorship networks, particularly those that connect new international students with experienced ones.

Assessment Flexibility

Faculty should design assessments that recognize the difference between language accuracy and conceptual understanding.

- **Content First**: Evaluate the quality of ideas, analysis, and evidence independently from minor grammar or syntax errors, especially in early drafts or formative assignments.
- **Multiple Assessment Formats**: Use oral presentations, visual projects, or group work to allow students to demonstrate knowledge beyond written English.
- **Formative Opportunities**: Provide practice assessments where students can receive feedback on both content and language without high stakes attached.
  This flexibility ensures that students are evaluated fairly for what they know, not penalized disproportionately for how they express it.

Key Takeaway

Supporting non-native English speakers requires clarity in materials, access to supplemental resources, multimodal teaching strategies, peer support systems, and fair assessment practices. By embedding language support into pedagogy, faculty create inclusive environments where all students can demonstrate their knowledge and thrive. This commitment to language inclusion strengthens overall global and cultural competency, equipping graduates with the skills to communicate and collaborate across linguistic and cultural boundaries.

Conclusion: Fostering an Equitable and Engaging Learning Community

Building an inclusive and supportive learning environment is not a one-time initiative—it is an ongoing commitment that requires self-reflection, adaptability, and a dedication to student success.

By designing equitable courses, diversifying curriculum content, fostering respectful classroom dialogue, and providing necessary accommodations, faculty can remove barriers and create spaces where all students can thrive.

Ultimately, an inclusive classroom benefits not only marginalized students but all learners, fostering critical thinking, cultural competence, and academic excellence in higher education.

Advancing Inclusion in Higher Education

Inclusivity in higher education is not just a policy requirement—it is a commitment to fostering an environment where all students can learn, grow, and contribute meaningfully. Professors have the power to shape classroom experiences in ways that empower students, encourage diverse perspectives, and dismantle barriers to success.

By implementing culturally responsive teaching, addressing biases in grading and instruction, and supporting students with diverse needs, faculty members create a more accessible and equitable academic landscape. These efforts do more than improve student outcomes; they cultivate a culture of respect, critical thinking, and collaboration that prepares students for success in an increasingly diverse world.

Ultimately, the goal of inclusive teaching is not simply to accommodate differences but to celebrate them—ensuring that every student has the opportunity to excel and make meaningful contributions to their field of study. By embracing inclusivity as a core value, faculty strengthen both their institutions and the broader educational community, fostering a future of higher education that is truly equitable and transformative.

Chapter 10: Communication and Professionalism

Effective communication and professionalism are fundamental to success in higher education. Professors serve as educators, mentors, and institutional representatives, requiring them to navigate complex interactions with students, colleagues, and administrators. Beyond subject matter expertise, faculty must develop strong communication skills to foster an engaging learning environment, uphold academic integrity, and maintain professional relationships within their institutions.

This chapter explores key principles of professional communication, including clarity, respect, and responsiveness in student interactions, collaboration with colleagues, and

Figure 10.1. Professional Communication [219].

engagement in institutional governance. It also addresses best practices for managing workload, setting professional boundaries, and maintaining ethical standards in academic environments. By mastering these skills, faculty can create a positive learning atmosphere, contribute to institutional effectiveness, and establish themselves as respected members of the academic community.

Professional Communication with Students and Colleagues: Fostering Clarity, Respect, and Academic Integrity

Effective professional communication is a cornerstone of academic success, shaping relationships between faculty, students, and colleagues while cultivating a culture of respect, transparency, and collaboration. In higher education, faculty members engage in a wide range of communication—whether providing feedback to students, corresponding with colleagues, navigating institutional policies, or presenting scholarly work. The ability to communicate clearly, professionally, and ethically is critical for building trust, managing conflicts, and ensuring a productive academic environment [158].

For new college professors, developing a professional communication style requires nuance, adaptability, and an awareness of institutional norms. This section explores the principles of professional communication, best practices for engaging with students and faculty, and strategies for handling challenges in academic interactions.

The Foundations of Professional Communication in Higher Education

Effective communication in academia is built on **three core principles**:

Clarity and Precision

- Communication should be concise, structured, and free from ambiguity.
- Professors should articulate expectations, feedback, and institutional policies clearly to prevent misunderstandings.

Respect and Civility

- Academic communication must be professional, respectful, and mindful of tone—whether verbal, written, or digital.
- This includes active listening, acknowledging differing viewpoints, and managing conflicts diplomatically.

Ethical and Confidential Conduct

- Faculty must uphold confidentiality in student interactions, comply with FERPA (Family Educational Rights and Privacy Act), and handle academic matters with discretion and fairness.

By prioritizing these principles, faculty members set the tone for productive and professional relationships with students and colleagues alike.

Professional Communication with Students

Students rely on faculty communication for guidance, academic feedback, and mentorship. Professors serve as academic role models, and their communication style significantly influences student engagement, motivation, and academic success [159].

1. Setting Clear Communication Expectations

Define Communication Policies in the Syllabus

- Include expectations regarding email response times, office hours, discussion board etiquette, and preferred communication methods.
- Example: *"I respond to emails within 24 hours on weekdays and within 48 hours on weekends. Please include your course title in the subject line."*

Offer Multiple Avenues for Communication

- Students have different communication preferences; offer in-person office hours, virtual meetings, and asynchronous discussion forums.
- Example: A professor holds "drop-in" Zoom hours for remote students who cannot attend in-person meetings.

2. Email and Written Correspondence with Students

Email is the primary mode of communication in higher education, but poorly structured emails can lead to misunderstandings, delays, or unprofessional exchanges [160].

Best Practices for Professional Emails to Students

- Use a formal yet approachable tone (e.g., "Dear [Student's Name]," rather than "Hey" or an unstructured greeting).
- Clearly state the purpose of the email in the subject line.
- Provide context and actionable next steps to ensure clarity.
- Example:

✉ **Subject:** Follow-Up on Your Research Proposal Feedback

Dear [Student Name],

I appreciate your thoughtful engagement with the research proposal assignment. I've attached my comments for your review. Please let me know if you have any questions or would like to discuss revisions during office hours.

Best,
Professor [Last Name]

Managing Student Email Etiquette

- Many students lack experience with professional communication. Faculty can model proper email etiquette by maintaining consistency in their own responses.
- Example: If a student writes an informal email, reply professionally while gently modeling formal communication:

✉ **Student Email:** "Hey Prof, I need an extension for my paper. Let me know. Thanks."

✉ **Professor Response:**

Dear [Student Name],

Thank you for reaching out. If you require an extension, please submit a formal request via the extension policy outlined in the syllabus. Let me know if you'd like to discuss this further.

Best,
Professor [Last Name]

By responding professionally yet empathetically, faculty reinforce communication norms without discouraging students from reaching out.

3. Providing Constructive Feedback

Feedback is one of the most critical forms of professor-student communication, directly influencing academic development and motivation [161].

Best Practices for Feedback Communication

- Be clear and actionable—avoid vague comments like *"Needs improvement,"* provide clear guidance on how to improve.

- Use a balanced approach—highlight strengths before addressing weaknesses (the "feedback sandwich" method).

- Example: *"Your argument is well-structured, but your evidence could be more developed. Consider expanding on [specific point] by incorporating more primary sources."*

Handling Difficult Conversations

- Some discussions—such as academic integrity violations, failing grades, or behavioral concerns—require sensitivity and professionalism.

- Best approach: Address concerns privately, remain factual, and focus on solutions.

- Example: Instead of saying, *"Your work is below expectations,"* say, *"Your recent assignments suggest some challenges. Let's discuss strategies to support your progress."*

By fostering a feedback-rich environment, faculty can enhance learning while maintaining professionalism and approachability.

Professional Communication with Colleagues

Interpersonal communication among faculty, administrators, and staff shapes academic collaboration, institutional culture, and professional reputation [162]. Professors must navigate departmental meetings, collaborative projects, and faculty governance with diplomacy and professionalism [163].

1. Faculty and Departmental Communication

Practice Active Listening in Meetings

- Engage thoughtfully in discussions, avoid interrupting, and acknowledge others' contributions.

- Example: "That's a great point, and I'd like to build on that by adding…"

Use Constructive Language in Disagreements

- Higher education involves debating ideas, but disagreements should be framed collegially and solution-focused.

- Example: Instead of *"That proposal doesn't make sense,"* say, *"I see the rationale, but I have concerns about implementation. Can we explore alternative approaches?"*

Respect Institutional Hierarchies and Protocols

- Address administrators, senior faculty, and staff respectfully, following formal protocols where necessary.

- Example: When corresponding with department chairs, use formal salutations and professional tone, even in casual exchanges.

2. Collaborative Research and Interdisciplinary Work

Maintain Professional Boundaries in Joint Research

- Clearly define roles, authorship agreements, and expectations upfront to prevent conflicts.

Respond Promptly in Academic Correspondence

- Faculty collaboration often requires timely responses for project efficiency.

Example: When working on a co-authored publication, a professor ensures all email exchanges remain courteous and document progress.

3. Managing Difficult Conversations with Colleagues

Address Conflicts Privately and Respectfully

- If disagreements arise, handle them in one-on-one conversations rather than public meetings.

Use Mediation Strategies When Necessary

- If conflicts escalate, seek mediation through department leadership or faculty committees.

Example: If a faculty member feels excluded from a project, instead of expressing frustration publicly, they request a private discussion with colleagues to clarify expectations.

Conclusion: Cultivating a Culture of Professional Communication

Professional communication in academia is more than etiquette—it is foundational to building trust, fostering collaboration, and creating an environment where both students and faculty can thrive. By maintaining clarity, respect, and ethical responsibility, professors set the standard for an academically enriching and professionally rewarding experience.

By mastering effective communication with students and colleagues, faculty ensure that their professional interactions support academic integrity, inclusivity, and institutional success—hallmarks of excellence in higher education.

Setting Boundaries and Managing Workload Effectively: Strategies for Sustainable Academic Success

The role of a college professor is multifaceted, requiring a delicate balance between teaching, research, service, and administrative responsibilities. Without intentional boundary-setting and workload management, faculty members risk burnout, reduced productivity, and diminished job satisfaction [162].

For new college professors, developing strategies to protect time, establish professional boundaries, and prioritize tasks effectively is essential for maintaining well-being, sustaining career growth, and ensuring high-quality engagement with students and colleagues. This section explores the importance of setting boundaries, practical workload management techniques, and strategies for fostering a balanced, fulfilling academic career.

The Importance of Setting Boundaries in Academia

Academic environments often **blur work and personal life**, as professors juggle [162]:
Teaching responsibilities (lectures, grading, curriculum development).
Research and publishing (manuscript preparation, grant writing, conference presentations).
Service commitments (committee work, faculty meetings, mentorship).
Administrative duties (advising, accreditation tasks, program coordination).

Without clear boundaries, professors may find themselves overcommitted, overworked, and struggling to maintain a sustainable workflow [162].

1. Common Challenges Without Boundaries

- Excessive work hours and constant availability—responding to emails late at night or working through weekends.
- Unclear expectations from students and colleagues—feeling obligated to take on additional tasks.
- Neglecting personal well-being—sacrificing sleep, exercise, and leisure due to workload overload.
- Decreased effectiveness and burnout—leading to reduced teaching quality, stalled research progress, and mental fatigue.

By setting intentional, well-communicated boundaries, professors can protect their time, energy, and professional effectiveness while maintaining a fulfilling career trajectory.

Strategies for Setting Boundaries in Academia

1. Establishing Clear Communication Boundaries

Professors often feel pressure to be constantly available to students and colleagues, but defining communication expectations early can prevent misunderstandings.

Define Response Time Expectations for Emails

- Include in your syllabus: *"I respond to emails within 24 hours on weekdays and within 48 hours on weekends. Please allow adequate time for responses."*
- Use email scheduling tools to delay responses and avoid setting expectations for immediate replies.

Limit After-Hours Availability

- Set "email-free" hours or use an auto-response indicating when you will be available.

- Example: "Thank you for your email. I check messages during office hours and will respond accordingly."

Encourage Student Independence

- Direct students to office hours, FAQs, and course resources before seeking immediate faculty intervention.
- Example: Instead of answering individual grading queries via email, use a dedicated discussion board for general questions.

2. Managing Teaching and Grading Workload Effectively

Teaching is time-intensive, but structured planning can prevent grading overload and last-minute course preparation.

Use Rubrics for Transparent Grading

- A detailed grading rubric ensures consistency, reduces subjectivity, and minimizes time spent justifying grades.
- Example: Pre-set feedback comments (e.g., "Your argument is well-structured, but your evidence needs more depth. See rubric criteria for analysis.").

Batch Similar Tasks

- Grade assignments in dedicated blocks of time rather than intermittently throughout the day.
- Example: "Tuesdays for grading essays, Wednesdays for discussion board replies."

Leverage Technology for Efficiency

- Use auto-graded quizzes, plagiarism checkers, and LMS grading tools (Canvas SpeedGrader, Turnitin) to streamline grading.

Implement "No-Grading Days"

- Set boundaries by designating days off from grading to prevent cognitive fatigue.
- Example: "I do not grade on Sundays—this is my designated rest day."

3. Prioritizing Research and Scholarship

Many new professors struggle to balance teaching obligations with research productivity, yet publishing is essential for career advancement [163].

Block Out Research Time in Your Schedule

- Treat research time as non-negotiable, just like a class meeting.
- Example: "Fridays from 9 AM–12 PM are reserved for writing—no meetings scheduled."

Use the "Write First" Strategy

- Prioritize research early in the day before email and administrative work consume time.
- Example: "I commit to writing for 60 minutes each morning before checking my inbox."

Break Research into Manageable Tasks

- Instead of waiting for large uninterrupted blocks of time, use short, focused writing sprints.
- Example: "Today's goal: Draft one paragraph of the methodology section."

Collaborate Strategically

- Engage in co-authorship and interdisciplinary projects to share the workload and diversify research output.

4. Setting Boundaries on Service and Administrative Responsibilities

Professors are often asked to serve on multiple committees, mentor students, and take on institutional projects, but overcommitting to service can derail research and teaching goals [164].

Learn to Say No Politely and Strategically

- Not all requests align with your professional goals—declining excessive commitments is essential for career sustainability.
- Example: *"Thank you for thinking of me for this committee. Unfortunately, I am currently at full capacity with my research commitments."*

Prioritize High-Impact Service Roles

- Choose service opportunities that align with your expertise and professional growth, rather than accepting every request out of obligation.
- Example: A faculty member declines a time-intensive committee role but agrees to mentor one graduate student per semester.

Delegate When Possible

- Share committee responsibilities, research tasks, and mentorship duties with colleagues and teaching assistants.
- Example: "Instead of serving as the primary event coordinator, I can assist by reviewing proposals for speakers."

5. Maintaining Work-Life Balance and Well-Being

Set Physical and Digital Boundaries

- Have a dedicated workspace for professional tasks and designate "off" hours for personal time.

- Example: No work emails after 7 PM—professors need downtime too.

Prioritize Self-Care

- Just as students need breaks, faculty must schedule mental health and well-being activities.
- Example: "Every Friday evening is reserved for personal time—no work commitments."

Engage in Professional Development Without Overcommitting

- Attend conferences, workshops, and networking events strategically to prevent professional overload.
- Example: "I will attend two key conferences per year rather than saying yes to every opportunity."

Overcoming Challenges in Boundary-Setting and Workload Management

Managing External Pressures

- Some faculty struggle with saying no due to fear of disappointing colleagues or missing career opportunities.
- Solution: Frame boundary-setting as a way to enhance effectiveness—prioritizing key tasks leads to higher-quality contributions.

Addressing Student Pushback

- Some students may expect immediate responses or extended availability.
- Solution: Reinforce expectations consistently, directing them to office hours and course resources.

Balancing Adaptability with Firm Boundaries

- Professors should be flexible for emergencies but avoid compromising all personal time.
- Solution: Evaluate each request based on long-term workload impact.

Conclusion: Creating a Sustainable and Fulfilling Academic Career

Setting boundaries and managing workload effectively is not about doing less—it's about doing the right things well. By establishing clear communication guidelines, prioritizing key responsibilities, and protecting personal well-being, faculty members can enhance productivity, maintain job satisfaction, and sustain a long, rewarding career in academia.

Ultimately, the ability to balance professional responsibilities with personal well-being defines academic excellence, leadership, and longevity in higher education.

Handling Student Concerns and Complaints Professionally: Fostering Transparency, Fairness, and Resolution

In higher education, student concerns and complaints are inevitable. Whether the issue involves grading disputes, course policies, academic integrity, or interpersonal challenges, how a professor responds can significantly impact student trust, engagement, and institutional reputation. Addressing concerns with professionalism, empathy, and structured resolution strategies ensures that students feel heard while upholding academic integrity and institutional policies.

For new college professors, mastering the art of handling student complaints professionally requires a balance of fairness, diplomacy, and adherence to institutional guidelines. This section explores common types of student concerns, best practices for managing complaints effectively, and strategies for maintaining professionalism while resolving conflicts constructively.

The Importance of Professionalism in Handling Student Concerns

Handling student concerns professionally serves multiple purposes:

Preserving Student-Instructor Trust

- Students are more likely to respect course policies and faculty authority when they feel that their concerns are handled fairly and transparently.

Maintaining Institutional Standards

- Universities and colleges have formal policies governing academic disputes, grade appeals, and student grievances. Professors must ensure their responses align with institutional guidelines [165].

Reducing Conflict and Escalation

- A proactive and respectful approach can prevent minor concerns from escalating into formal complaints or legal disputes.

Fostering a Positive Learning Environment

- When students feel comfortable expressing concerns, it enhances communication and engagement, leading to a more supportive classroom culture.

By treating complaints as opportunities for constructive dialogue, faculty can demonstrate professionalism while upholding academic rigor and fairness.

Common Student Concerns and Complaints

Professors should be prepared to handle a range of student concerns, including:

1. Grading Disputes and Grade Appeals

Students may challenge low grades, misunderstand rubric expectations, or feel they were graded unfairly. Some students request grade changes due to personal circumstances rather than academic performance.

Example: A student contests a B+ on a final paper, claiming it should be an A based on effort rather than rubric criteria.

2. Course Policy Complaints

Students may disagree with attendance policies, late work penalties, participation requirements, or exam structures.
Some concerns stem from miscommunication or misinterpretation of syllabus guidelines.

Example: A student argues that the late submission policy is unfair after missing a deadline due to personal reasons.

3. Perceived Unfair Treatment or Bias

Students may feel singled out, misjudged, or treated unfairly due to race, gender, disability, or personal beliefs. Concerns may arise about implicit bias, favoritism, or cultural insensitivity in grading or classroom interactions.

Example: A student claims that their contributions in class discussions are dismissed while others receive more engagement.

4. Classroom Conflicts and Interpersonal Issues

Disputes may arise between students over group projects, participation dynamics, or classroom behavior. Some students may feel uncomfortable due to microaggressions, harassment, or disruptive behavior from peers.

Example: A student reports that a group project partner refused to contribute, leading to an unfair workload distribution.

5. Academic Integrity and Misconduct Allegations

Students may challenge plagiarism accusations, cheating penalties, or violations of institutional policies. Some concerns arise due to unclear expectations about citation practices, collaboration policies, or AI use in assignments.

Example: A student denies plagiarizing a paper after a Turnitin report flags high similarity.

Best Practices for Handling Student Complaints Professionally

Handling complaints effectively requires a structured approach that balances fairness, empathy, and adherence to academic standards.

1. Create a Transparent and Open Communication Environment

Set Clear Expectations Early

- A well-structured syllabus with detailed policies on grading, late submissions, participation, and academic integrity prevents confusion.

- Example: "All grade appeals must be submitted in writing within five days of receiving feedback, with specific references to rubric criteria."

Encourage Students to Raise Concerns Promptly

- Waiting too long to address issues leads to resentment and escalated conflicts.
- Example: A professor regularly reminds students to discuss grading concerns early rather than at the end of the semester.

Foster a Culture of Respectful Discourse

- Model open, professional, and calm communication so students feel comfortable approaching concerns without fear of retaliation.

2. Actively Listen and Respond with Empathy

Give the Student Your Full Attention

- When a student expresses a concern, avoid dismissing their feelings or interrupting.
- Use active listening techniques: "I understand that you're frustrated. Let's go through your concern step by step."

Validate the Concern Without Immediately Agreeing

- Acknowledge emotions while remaining neutral and objective.
- Example: "I see why this feels unfair to you. Let's review the grading rubric together to clarify expectations."

Remain Calm and Professional in Difficult Situations

- Some students may express frustration emotionally or aggressively. Professors must de-escalate rather than react defensively.
- Example: If a student raises their voice, remain composed: "I hear that you're upset. Let's take a step back and go through this calmly."

3. Follow Institutional Policies and Document All Interactions

Adhere to University Grievance Procedures

- Know your institution's grade appeal process, student conduct guidelines, and mediation protocols.
- If necessary, refer students to academic advisors, ombuds offices, or department chairs for further resolution.

Keep Written Records of Complaints and Resolutions

- Document student emails, meeting summaries, and grade appeal discussions in case issues escalate.

- Example: After a grading dispute, a professor sends a summary email of the discussion and agreed resolution.

Use a Professional, Fact-Based Approach

- Base responses on syllabus policies, grading rubrics, and institutional guidelines, not personal opinions.
- Example: "Your final grade reflects the rubric criteria outlined in the syllabus. Let's go over the areas where deductions occurred."

4. Offer Solutions While Maintaining Academic Integrity

Identify Reasonable Accommodations Without Compromising Standards

- If a complaint is valid, offer a fair and consistent solution.
- Example: If an error is found in grading, correct it without hesitation while explaining the reasoning behind the decision.

Encourage Growth and Learning from the Situation

- Frame the resolution as a learning opportunity instead of a punishment or concession.
- Example: "I appreciate your effort in discussing this. Let's focus on strategies to improve in future assignments."

If the Complaint Is Unfounded, Provide a Professional Explanation

- Some students may seek grade changes or policy exceptions without merit.
- Example: "I understand your request for extra credit, but to ensure fairness across the class, I adhere to the grading policy stated in the syllabus."

Dealing with Escalated or Persistent Complaints

Involve Academic Support Services

- If an issue persists, direct students to department chairs, academic advisors, or student support offices.

Maintain Boundaries and Professionalism

- If a student becomes hostile or refuses to accept a decision, remain firm but respectful.
- Example: "I understand your frustration, but my decision is final based on the grading criteria outlined in the syllabus."

Seek Mediation for Complex Cases

- If a dispute escalates, seek formal mediation or institutional intervention rather than handling it alone.

Conclusion: Turning Complaints into Constructive Dialogue

Handling student complaints professionally is not about conceding to every request but about engaging in fair, respectful, and structured communication. By implementing clear policies, active listening, and institutional procedures, professors can turn student concerns into opportunities for learning, clarity, and academic growth.

Ultimately, a well-managed approach to student complaints fosters trust, professionalism, and a culture of mutual respect in higher education.

Writing Effective Recommendation Letters: Crafting Thoughtful and Impactful Endorsements

A well-written recommendation letter can serve as a powerful endorsement of a student's abilities, character, and potential [166]. Whether for graduate school applications, scholarships, internships, or job opportunities, faculty members are often asked to provide letters that help shape a student's future.

For new college professors, learning to write clear, persuasive, and ethically responsible recommendation letters is an essential professional skill. A strong letter can open doors for students, showcase their strengths, and provide credibility to their applications, while a poorly written or vague letter may fail to convey the student's true qualifications [167].

This section explores best practices for writing compelling recommendation letters, structuring effective endorsements, and maintaining professional and ethical considerations.

The Purpose and Impact of Recommendation Letters

Advocating for Student Success

- A well-crafted recommendation letter serves as a bridge between a student's achievements and their future opportunities, providing insight beyond transcripts and resumes.

Providing Credibility to an Applicant's Strengths

- Universities, employers, and selection committees rely on faculty recommendations to assess intellectual abilities, work ethic, leadership potential, and character.

Building Faculty-Student Professional Relationships

- Writing strong recommendations demonstrates **investment in students' futures**, reinforcing faculty mentorship and student trust.

Example: A former student applying to law school requests a recommendation highlighting their research, analytical skills, and leadership in class discussions. A well-written letter provides concrete evidence supporting these attributes.

Best Practices for Writing Effective Recommendation Letters

1. Determine Whether You Can Write a Strong Letter

Before agreeing to write a letter, consider:

Do You Know the Student Well Enough?

- If you have limited interaction with the student, your letter may lack depth and credibility.
- If unsure, ask: *"Can you provide me with details about your goals and experiences?"*

Are You Comfortable Endorsing This Student?

- If a student performed poorly in your class or lacked engagement, a lukewarm or negative letter can harm their application.
- It is ethically responsible to decline writing a letter if you cannot provide a genuine and positive endorsement.

Example: If a struggling student requests a recommendation, politely decline:
"I appreciate your request, but I believe another professor who knows your work more closely would provide a stronger recommendation."

2. Gather Essential Information Before Writing

To craft a **detailed and specific** letter, request:

-The student's resume or CV (to understand their academic background and experiences).
-The purpose of the letter (graduate school, job, fellowship, etc.).
-Details about the program, job, or scholarship (to tailor the recommendation accordingly).
-Key skills or qualities the student wants highlighted (e.g., research skills, leadership, collaboration).
-Relevant coursework or projects the student completed under your supervision.

Example: A student applying to a data science master's program requests emphasis on coding proficiency and analytical reasoning—the letter should highlight coursework, assignments, and projects demonstrating these skills.

3. Structuring an Effective Recommendation Letter

A well-organized letter typically follows this structure:

A. Introduction: Establish Your Relationship with the Student

-State your position, title, and department.
-Mention how long you have known the student and in what capacity (e.g., professor, research advisor).
-Provide a brief preview of the student's qualifications.

- **Example Introduction:**

"It is with great enthusiasm that I recommend [Student's Name] for [Program/Position]. As a professor in [Department], I had the pleasure of teaching [Student] in [Course], where they consistently demonstrated intellectual curiosity, analytical rigor, and exceptional problem-solving skills."

B. Body Paragraphs: Highlight Specific Strengths with Evidence

Discuss academic performance, skills, and work ethic with specific examples.
Mention leadership qualities, research contributions, or class participation.
Connect the student's abilities to the opportunity they are applying for.

- **Example Body Paragraph:**

"In my [Advanced Economics] course, [Student Name] ranked in the top 5% of the class, demonstrating an exceptional ability to apply theoretical concepts to real-world case studies. Their final research project on [Topic] was one of the most insightful I have seen, showcasing a sophisticated understanding of market trends and economic modeling. Beyond coursework, [Student] served as a peer mentor, helping classmates grasp complex quantitative methods—a testament to their leadership and communication skills."

C. Conclusion: Reinforce Endorsement and Provide a Strong Closing

Reiterate enthusiasm and confidence in the student's potential.
Offer to provide further details if needed.
End with a formal, professional closing.

- **Example Conclusion:**

"Based on [Student Name]'s intellectual abilities, analytical skills, and leadership qualities, I have no doubt they will excel in [Program/Job]. I wholeheartedly recommend them without reservation. Please feel free to contact me at [Email] should you require additional insights."

4. Avoiding Common Mistakes in Recommendation Letters

- **Vague or Generic Praise**

    - Avoid overused phrases like *"a great student"* or *"very hardworking"*—instead, provide specific anecdotes.

- **Overly Long or Rambling Letters**

    - Keep letters concise (typically 1–1.5 pages) while maintaining depth.

- **Failure to Tailor the Letter**

    - A generic letter (e.g., using the same letter for multiple students) may weaken the student's application.

- **Unbalanced Criticism or Faint Praise**

- If a letter contains only neutral or slightly positive remarks, selection committees may interpret this in a negative fashion.

- **Excessive Personal Information**
  - Avoid discussing unrelated personal details that could violate student privacy or introduce bias.

Example of Weak vs. Strong Praise:

- *"[Student] was a decent student in my class and did well overall."*
- *"[Student] consistently produced insightful, well-researched work and demonstrated strong critical thinking in class discussions."*

5. Ethical and Professional Considerations

Maintain Confidentiality and Honesty

- Never exaggerate or fabricate details—letters should be honest yet supportive.
- If you cannot provide a strong recommendation, decline the request professionally.

Adhere to Institutional Guidelines

- Some institutions have specific policies for letters of recommendation (e.g., requiring submission through official portals) [168].

Submit the Letter on Time

- Respect deadlines to ensure students' applications remain competitive.

Retain a Professional Tone

- Avoid overly casual language, humor, or informal anecdotes that may seem unprofessional.

Conclusion: Writing Impactful and Professional Recommendations

Writing an effective recommendation letter is both an academic responsibility and a professional skill that can shape students' academic and career trajectories. By structuring letters thoughtfully, providing clear examples, and maintaining professionalism, faculty members enhance students' opportunities while upholding ethical standards.

Ultimately, a strong, well-crafted recommendation serves as a powerful testament to a student's potential, reinforcing the essential role of faculty mentorship in higher education.

Ethics in Higher Education and Avoiding Conflicts of Interest: Upholding Integrity, Fairness, and Professionalism

Ethical conduct is the foundation of academic integrity, institutional credibility, and faculty professionalism in higher education. Professors are entrusted with the intellectual and professional development of students, the advancement of research, and the fair administration of academic policies. With this responsibility comes the necessity to navigate ethical dilemmas, uphold institutional values, and avoid conflicts of interest that could compromise the integrity of teaching, research, or service.

For new college professors, understanding the ethical dimensions of higher education and implementing strategies to prevent conflicts of interest is crucial to maintaining fairness, objectivity, and credibility in academic roles. This section explores core ethical principles in academia, types of conflicts of interest, and best practices for ensuring ethical decision-making in teaching, research, and professional interactions.

The Foundations of Ethical Conduct in Higher Education

Ethical principles in higher education serve as guiding values that shape professional conduct, academic policies, and institutional governance. The core tenets include:

Integrity – Professors must demonstrate honesty, transparency, and consistency in their teaching, research, and administrative duties.

Fairness and Equity – Faculty should ensure that all students and colleagues are treated equitably, free from discrimination, favoritism, or bias.

Accountability – Professors are responsible for upholding institutional policies, reporting ethical violations, and maintaining academic standards.

Respect for Intellectual Freedom – Faculty must foster an environment where diverse ideas are encouraged, debated, and examined with academic rigor.

Confidentiality and Student Privacy – Professors must protect student records, research data, and confidential institutional information in compliance with FERPA (Family Educational Rights and Privacy Act) and other ethical guidelines [169].

By adhering to these principles, faculty not only safeguard their professional integrity but also contribute to a culture of trust, respect, and ethical academic engagement.

Recognizing and Avoiding Conflicts of Interest in Academia

A conflict of interest occurs when a faculty member's personal, financial, or professional interests interfere with their academic responsibilities. Such conflicts can compromise objectivity, fairness, and institutional credibility if not properly managed.

1. Types of Conflicts of Interest in Higher Education

A. Conflicts in Teaching and Student Relationships

Favoritism and Preferential Treatment

- Professors must ensure that grading, mentorship, and classroom interactions remain fair and unbiased.

- **Example:** Offering special privileges (extra credit, extensions, or mentorship opportunities) to a student based on personal connections rather than merit.

Romantic or Inappropriate Relationships with Students

- Many institutions prohibit faculty-student romantic relationships due to the power imbalance [170].
- Such relationships create ethical dilemmas, perceptions of favoritism, and conflicts with institutional policies.

Financial Transactions with Students

- Faculty should not engage in business dealings (e.g., selling books, tutoring services, or consulting) with students they directly oversee, as it creates a conflict between financial interest and professional responsibility.

Example: A professor requires students to purchase their self-published book, profiting directly from their own class—raising ethical concerns.

B. Conflicts in Research and Scholarship

Bias in Research Funding and Publications

- Faculty must disclose any financial ties, sponsorships, or external pressures that could influence research outcomes.
- **Example:** A professor receives corporate funding for research on a product but fails to disclose this potential conflict in published work.

Authorship and Credit Disputes

- Professors should ensure that students, research assistants, and colleagues receive proper credit for their contributions.
- **Example:** Taking sole authorship for research largely conducted by graduate students without proper acknowledgment.

Using Institutional Resources for Personal Gain

- Faculty should not exploit university labs, funding, or student labor for personal consulting work or private research projects.

C. Conflicts in Service, Hiring, and Institutional Governance

Nepotism and Hiring Bias

- Faculty must avoid hiring or promoting family members, close friends, or individuals with whom they have a personal relationship without transparent oversight.
- Example: A professor sits on a hiring committee and advocates for a close relative without disclosing their connection.

Undue Influence in Committee Decisions

- Professors must ensure that institutional decisions (e.g., curriculum development, tenure reviews) are made based on academic merit rather than personal relationships or financial interests.

Example: A faculty member reviews a colleague's tenure application but has a prior personal dispute with them, potentially leading to biased evaluation.

By recognizing these conflicts, faculty can take proactive steps to ensure their professional conduct remains professional, transparent, ethical and aligned with institutional values.

Strategies for Avoiding and Managing Conflicts of Interest

1. Maintain Transparency and Disclosure

Report Potential Conflicts Proactively

- If there is a perceived or actual conflict of interest, disclose it to department chairs, research boards, or ethics committees.
- Example: A professor discloses financial ties before accepting research funding from a corporate sponsor.

Use Institutional Guidelines for Ethical Decision-Making

- Familiarize yourself with institutional conflict-of-interest policies, research integrity protocols, and faculty codes of conduct.

2. Establish Clear Boundaries in Student-Faculty Relationships

Avoid Personal Relationships that Compromise Professionalism

- Maintain academic distance and fairness in all student interactions.
- **Example:** If a former student applies for a job in your department, recuse yourself from hiring decisions.

Apply the Same Standards to All Students

- Ensure grading, mentorship, and recommendation letters are based on merit and academic performance, not personal relationships.

3. Ensure Ethical Research Practices

Maintain Objectivity in Research

- Disclose funding sources, affiliations, and any potential biases in research publications.
- Example: *A professor includes a statement of disclosure when publishing a study funded by an organization that may have a vested interest in the results.*

Give Proper Credit to Collaborators

- Clearly define authorship expectations before research begins.

Follow Institutional Ethics Review Board (IRB) Guidelines

- Obtain proper approval for human-subject research and ensure ethical treatment of participants.

4. Uphold Institutional Integrity in Service and Administration

Recuse Yourself from Decisions Where Personal Bias May Exist

- If a hiring, tenure, or policy decision involves a close friend or adversary, recuse yourself to avoid ethical conflicts.

Adhere to Institutional Financial Ethics

- Avoid misusing university funds for personal or external projects.

Example: A faculty member declines participation in a committee reviewing a grant application submitted by their spouse.

Handling Ethical Dilemmas and Reporting Violations

Seek Guidance from Ethics Committees or Department Leadership

- When faced with a complex ethical decision, consult with institutional ethics committees or senior faculty.

Report Ethical Violations Through Proper Channels

- If a colleague engages in unethical behavior, follow institutional procedures for reporting misconduct, ensuring confidentiality and professionalism.

Example: A professor notices favoritism in tenure decisions and reports concerns to the academic integrity office.

Conclusion: Fostering a Culture of Ethics and Integrity in Academia

Ethical behavior in higher education is not just about following rules—it is about cultivating trust, fairness, and professional responsibility. By recognizing potential conflicts of interest, maintaining transparency, and adhering to ethical standards in teaching, research, and service, faculty members ensure that their work remains credible, objective, and aligned with the mission of higher education.

Ultimately, ethical decision-making strengthens academic institutions, fosters student success, and upholds the integrity of scholarly contributions, ensuring that higher education remains a pillar of knowledge, equity, and professionalism.

Fostering a Culture of Professionalism in Academia

Professionalism and effective communication are essential for fostering a productive and respectful academic environment. Faculty members who demonstrate clear, thoughtful, and ethical communication contribute to student success, strengthen collegial relationships, and uphold the integrity of their institutions.

By setting boundaries, managing workload efficiently, and adhering to ethical standards, professors can navigate the challenges of higher education while maintaining a healthy work-life balance. Additionally, engaging in professional development and institutional collaboration ensures continued growth and effectiveness as educators and scholars.

Ultimately, professionalism in academia is not just about personal conduct—it shapes the culture of higher education, influencing student experiences, institutional reputation, and the broader academic community. By prioritizing clear communication, ethical decision-making, and respectful engagement, faculty members uphold the highest standards of teaching, mentorship, and scholarship.

Chapter 11: Teaching Evaluations and Continuous Improvement

Effective teaching is an evolving process, requiring reflection, adaptation, and a commitment to professional growth. Teaching evaluations—whether through student feedback, peer reviews, or institutional assessments—serve as essential tools for assessing instructional effectiveness, refining pedagogical approaches, and ensuring student success. However, evaluations should not be viewed merely as a judgment of faculty performance; rather, they should be leveraged as opportunities for continuous improvement and professional development.

Figure 11.1. Teaching Improvement [219].

This chapter explores the purpose, structure, and best practices for interpreting student evaluations and faculty reviews. It examines the importance of self-assessment and reflective teaching, helping faculty use feedback constructively rather than reactively. Additionally, the chapter addresses common challenges such as bias in student evaluations, handling critical feedback, and developing strategies for implementing meaningful improvements in teaching.

By understanding and embracing the role of evaluations, faculty members can cultivate a culture of continuous learning and excellence, enhancing both their effectiveness as educators and the overall student experience.

Understanding Student Evaluations and Faculty Reviews: Leveraging Feedback for Teaching Excellence

Teaching evaluations and faculty reviews serve as essential tools in assessing instructional effectiveness, guiding professional development, and informing institutional decisions on tenure, promotion, and teaching improvement. These evaluations—whether student-generated course feedback, peer assessments, or administrative reviews—provide valuable insights into faculty performance, instructional quality, and areas for growth.

For new college professors, navigating student evaluations and faculty reviews requires a balanced approach—acknowledging their importance while understanding their limitations and potential biases. By analyzing feedback critically and using it for continuous improvement, faculty can refine their teaching methods, enhance student engagement, and contribute to a culture of excellence in higher education.

This section explores the purpose, structure, and interpretation of student evaluations and faculty reviews, addressing common challenges, biases, and best practices for integrating feedback into professional growth.

The Purpose and Importance of Teaching Evaluations and Faculty Reviews

Effective teaching is an iterative process that requires reflection, adaptation, and responsiveness to student needs. Evaluations and reviews help assess faculty effectiveness, ensure accountability, and support faculty development in the following ways:

Enhancing Teaching Quality

- Feedback from students and peers helps identify instructional strengths and opportunities for improvement, enabling faculty to refine their approach [171].

Promoting Institutional Accountability and Accreditation

- Teaching evaluations contribute to institutional assessment and accreditation processes, ensuring courses meet educational standards [171].

Supporting Tenure, Promotion, and Career Advancement

- Faculty reviews often play a critical role in tenure and promotion decisions, providing evidence of teaching effectiveness and student engagement [171].

Fostering an Environment of Continuous Improvement

- Engaging with feedback demonstrates a commitment to student success, pedagogical innovation, and self-reflection.

By understanding how to interpret and apply evaluation results, faculty can transform assessments into meaningful professional development tools rather than viewing them solely as judgmental metrics.

Understanding Student Evaluations

Student evaluations provide consistent teaching assessment, offering direct insights into student perceptions of course effectiveness, engagement, and faculty performance.

1. Components of Student Evaluations

Most institutions use standardized student evaluation forms, which may include:

Quantitative Ratings

- Likert-scale questions on teaching clarity, engagement, fairness, responsiveness, course difficulty, and overall satisfaction.

Qualitative Feedback

- Open-ended comments that provide specific insights into student experiences, course strengths, and suggested improvements.

Course and Learning Outcome Assessments

- Questions evaluating how well course objectives were met and whether the structure facilitated learning.

Instructor Effectiveness and Approachability

- Feedback on faculty communication, availability, grading fairness, and instructional delivery methods.

2. Common Challenges and Limitations of Student Evaluations

While student evaluations provide valuable feedback, they also present potential challenges and biases that faculty should recognize:

- Bias Based on Identity and Demographics

- Research shows that women, faculty of color, and non-native English speakers often receive lower evaluations due to implicit biases [172].
- **Solution:** Faculty should contextualize ratings within broader institutional trends and advocate for bias-awareness training in evaluation processes.

- Focus on Popularity Over Learning Outcomes

- Students may rate professors highly for being entertaining rather than pedagogically effective.
- **Solution:** Institutions should incorporate multiple measures of teaching effectiveness beyond student opinions, such as peer reviews or course design assessments.

- Disproportionate Weight on Grading Difficulty

- Students may evaluate instructors lower if they find the course challenging or receive lower grades.
- **Solution:** Professors can explain grading criteria clearly and emphasize that rigor and fairness are essential components of learning.

- Vague or Unconstructive Feedback

- Comments like *"This class was boring"* or *"Too much reading"* lack actionable insights.
- **Solution:** Professors can encourage students to provide specific feedback on course structure, instructional methods, and assignments.

Interpreting and Responding to Student Evaluations

Faculty should approach evaluation results with a growth mindset, identifying both strengths to maintain and areas for refinement.

1. Looking for Patterns Rather Than Individual Comments

Focus on recurring themes across multiple student responses rather than fixating on outliers.
Example: If multiple students note unclear assignment expectations, adjustments to instructions or rubrics may be necessary.

2. Comparing Across Semesters

Track feedback over time to identify consistent trends or improvements in response to past changes.

3. Separating Emotional Reactions from Constructive Criticism

Negative comments can be discouraging, but faculty should view them as opportunities for improvement rather than personal attacks.
Example: Instead of reacting defensively to *"The professor is too strict,"* reflect on whether grading policies are transparent and consistently applied.

Understanding Faculty Reviews and Peer Evaluations

In addition to student evaluations, peer reviews and faculty assessments provide a broader perspective on teaching effectiveness. These reviews typically include:

Classroom Observations

- Senior faculty or department chairs observe teaching sessions, evaluating pedagogical techniques, engagement strategies, and instructional clarity.

Teaching Portfolios

- Faculty submit syllabi, course materials, assessments, and reflections to demonstrate teaching effectiveness.

Self-Reflection Reports

- Some institutions require professors to analyze their evaluations, identify areas for growth, and outline improvements.

Service and Research Contributions

- Faculty reviews may also assess contributions to curriculum development, mentorship, and institutional service.

Best Practices for Constructive Faculty Reviews

Approach Peer Feedback with an Open Mind

- Recognize that peer observations are meant to enhance teaching, not critique personal style.

- Engage in post-review discussions to clarify suggestions and implement changes.

Use Faculty Reviews as Evidence of Growth

- Document teaching innovations, adjustments based on feedback, and student learning improvements.

Advocate for Holistic Teaching Evaluations

- Encourage institutions to assess multiple dimensions of faculty effectiveness, including peer reviews, student evaluations, curriculum development, and research contributions.

Seek Mentorship and Professional Development

- Engage with teaching workshops, faculty support communities, and pedagogical training to refine teaching practices.

Using Evaluations for Continuous Improvement

Teaching evaluations and faculty reviews should not be viewed as static judgments but rather as dynamic tools for growth. Faculty can leverage feedback to:

Refine Course Design and Teaching Methods

- Example: If students struggle with course pacing, consider modifying assignment schedules or incorporating more active learning techniques.

Enhance Student Engagement Strategies

- Example: If evaluations indicate low class participation, integrate group discussions, case studies, or flipped learning models.

Develop Stronger Communication and Clarity

- Example: If students report unclear grading policies, improve transparency by revising rubrics and offering grading workshops.

Strengthen Faculty Development and Teaching Effectiveness

- Participate in faculty mentoring programs, instructional design workshops, and assessment training to improve pedagogy.

Conclusion: Cultivating a Culture of Constructive Feedback and Growth

Student evaluations and faculty reviews, when approached with a growth mindset and a commitment to professional development, serve as invaluable resources for enhancing teaching effectiveness, fostering student success, and contributing to a high-quality academic environment.

By interpreting feedback thoughtfully, addressing concerns constructively, and continuously refining teaching practices, professors demonstrate a commitment to excellence and lifelong learning.

Ultimately, the goal of evaluations is not perfection but progress—using reflective teaching practices to create engaging, impactful, and inclusive educational experiences for students.

Self-Assessment and Reflective Teaching Practices: Cultivating a Growth-Oriented Approach to Teaching Excellence

Teaching is an evolving, iterative process that requires faculty to constantly evaluate their effectiveness, adapt to diverse student needs, and refine their instructional methods. While external evaluations—such as student feedback and faculty reviews—play an important role in assessing teaching effectiveness, self-assessment and reflective teaching practices allow professors to engage in ongoing, personal, and meaningful professional development.

For new college professors, developing a habit of self-reflection is essential for continuous improvement, ensuring that teaching methods remain engaging, inclusive, and aligned with student learning outcomes. By systematically assessing their own teaching, professors can enhance course design, improve classroom interactions, and cultivate a mindset of lifelong learning.

This section explores the importance of self-assessment in higher education, practical strategies for reflective teaching, and ways to integrate self-reflection into daily academic practices.

The Importance of Self-Assessment in Higher Education

Self-assessment in teaching involves critical examination of one's instructional practices, student engagement strategies, and course effectiveness. Professors who engage in self-assessment benefit in the following ways:

Identifying Strengths and Areas for Improvement

- Professors can assess which teaching strategies are effective and which need refinement.

Enhancing Student Learning Outcomes

- Reflection allows faculty to adjust course delivery, assessment methods, and engagement strategies to better support students.

Encouraging Adaptability and Innovation

- Self-assessment fosters a culture of experimentation, leading to new teaching methodologies, technology integration, and pedagogical innovations [173].

Building Confidence and Professional Growth

- Regular self-reflection empowers faculty to become proactive in their development, reducing uncertainty and increasing teaching effectiveness over time [173].

Strengthening Student-Faculty Relationships

- A reflective professor is more likely to be empathetic, responsive, and engaged, creating a positive and inclusive learning environment [173].

By incorporating structured self-assessment and reflective teaching practices, faculty can develop a sustainable, growth-oriented approach to teaching improvement [173].

Key Strategies for Self-Assessment in Teaching

1. Engaging in Structured Self-Reflection

Self-reflection should be intentional, structured, and actionable. Professors can ask themselves critical questions after each class session or semester, such as:

Course Effectiveness:

- *Did students grasp the key concepts as intended?*
- *Were the learning outcomes successfully met?*

Student Engagement:

- *Were students actively engaged in discussions, projects, or activities?*
- *Did I create an inclusive and welcoming learning environment?*

Instructional Methods:

- *Did my teaching style accommodate diverse learning preferences?*
- *Were there alternative approaches I could have used?*

Assessment and Feedback:

- *Did my grading and feedback methods support student growth?*
- *Were my expectations clear and fair?*

Personal Reflection:

- *What went well in this course, and why?*
- *What challenges did I face, and how can I address them next time?*

Example: After a challenging class discussion where students seemed disengaged, a professor reflects on possible reasons—was the topic too abstract? Were students hesitant to speak? Could small-group discussions have encouraged participation? Based on this reflection, the professor adjusts their approach for the next session.

2. Collecting and Analyzing Teaching Artifacts

Teaching Portfolios:

- Maintain a portfolio with syllabi, lesson plans, student work samples, and self-reflections to track progress over time.
- Example: A professor compares syllabi from past semesters to assess how course content has evolved and whether past modifications improved student learning.

Recorded Lectures for Self-Review:

- Reviewing recorded lectures helps faculty evaluate clarity, pacing, and student engagement.
- Example: A professor notices they spend more time lecturing than facilitating discussion and decides to incorporate active learning strategies.

Student Performance Data:

- Analyzing exam results, participation trends, and assignment performance can reveal patterns in student learning outcomes.
- Example: If many students struggle with a particular concept, the professor adjusts how they introduce or reinforce that material.

3. Seeking Student Input Beyond Course Evaluations

Mid-Semester Feedback Surveys

- Instead of relying solely on end-of-semester evaluations, professors can use mid-term feedback surveys to adjust teaching in real-time.
- Example: A survey reveals students find lectures too fast-paced, prompting the professor to slow down and integrate more discussion breaks.

One-on-One Student Conversations

- Engaging in informal discussions with students provides direct insights into their learning experiences and challenges.

Exit Tickets or Reflection Assignments

- At the end of class, students can submit one key takeaway and one area they found confusing, helping faculty adjust accordingly.
- Example: After a math lesson, students submit index cards noting which concepts were clear and which need further explanation.

4. Engaging in Peer Observation and Faculty Learning Communities

Invite Colleagues for Classroom Observations

- A trusted colleague can provide constructive feedback on teaching methods, student engagement, and course pacing.
- Example: A fellow professor observes a lecture and suggests using case studies to make abstract concepts more relatable.

Join Faculty Learning Communities (FLCs)

- Participate in collaborative discussions, workshops, and interdisciplinary teaching groups to exchange ideas and best practices.
- Example: A faculty member joins a teaching and learning seminar focused on integrating active learning techniques.

Engage in Cross-Disciplinary Dialogue

- Exposure to teaching methods from different disciplines can spark new approaches to instruction and assessment.

5. Setting Professional Development Goals and Action Plans

Establish Specific, Measurable, Achievable, Relevant, and Time-Bound (SMART) Goals

- Rather than broad goals like *"improve student engagement,"* set specific objectives:
    - *"Incorporate three active learning strategies into lectures this semester."*
    - *"Reduce reliance on lectures by integrating more problem-based learning."*

Document Changes and Measure Impact

- Keep track of teaching adjustments and evaluate their effects on student performance and engagement.
- Example: A professor implements more collaborative projects and measures whether student participation improves over two semesters.

Seek Mentorship and Continuous Training

- Attend teaching development workshops, online courses, or conferences to stay informed about emerging pedagogical practices.

Overcoming Common Challenges in Reflective Teaching

- Time Constraints

- Solution: Dedicate small increments of time (e.g., 10 minutes after each class) for quick self-reflections.

- Fear of Negative Feedback

- Solution: View feedback as a tool for growth rather than criticism—even seasoned educators evolve.

- Resistance to Change

- Solution: Implement small, gradual improvements rather than overhauling teaching methods all at once.

- Bias in Self-Assessment

- Solution: Combine self-reflection with peer feedback and student insights for a well-rounded perspective.

Conclusion: Cultivating a Mindset of Continuous Growth in Teaching

Self-assessment and reflective teaching practices empower faculty to become intentional, adaptable, and student-centered educators. By analyzing instructional effectiveness, seeking feedback, and implementing iterative improvements, professors foster a culture of innovation and academic excellence [174].

Ultimately, the best educators are not those who teach flawlessly, but those who reflect, evolve, and continuously strive to improve their teaching for the benefit of their students [174].

Peer Observations and Collaborative Teaching Improvement: Enhancing Instruction through Collegial Feedback and Shared Learning

Teaching in higher education is not a solitary endeavor; rather, it thrives on collegial exchange, continuous refinement, and shared pedagogical innovation. One of the most effective strategies for professional development in teaching is peer observation and collaborative teaching improvement [175], which allow faculty members to engage in constructive feedback, interdisciplinary dialogue, and evidence-based teaching enhancement.

For new college professors, participating in peer observations and collaborative teaching initiatives offers an opportunity to gain new perspectives, refine instructional strategies, and contribute to a culture of collective growth. When conducted thoughtfully and with a focus on developmental feedback, peer observations foster a non-evaluative, growth-oriented approach to improving teaching effectiveness.

This section explores the principles of peer observation, best practices for conducting productive teaching reviews, and strategies for engaging in collaborative teaching improvement efforts within an academic community.

The Value of Peer Observation in Higher Education

Unlike student evaluations, which provide insights based on student perceptions, peer observations offer an expert lens on teaching methodologies, classroom dynamics, and curriculum alignment. Peer observation is beneficial for:

Providing Constructive, Faculty-Led Feedback

- Peers can evaluate instructional clarity, engagement strategies, and pedagogical techniques from an instructor's perspective.

Encouraging Reflective Teaching Practices

- Observing colleagues allows faculty to critically examine their own approaches by contrasting them with different styles and strategies.

Fostering a Culture of Collegiality and Professional Growth

- Peer review strengthens mentorship, interdisciplinary exchange, and shared responsibility for student success.

Enhancing Course Design and Pedagogical Innovation

- Faculty can exchange ideas, best practices, and novel instructional techniques to improve student learning outcomes.

Providing Formative, Non-Evaluative Feedback

- Unlike formal performance reviews, peer observations emphasize growth, experimentation, and improvement over judgment.

By integrating peer observations into professional development, faculty create a collaborative environment where teaching quality is continuously refined through mutual learning and constructive dialogue [177].

Best Practices for Conducting Peer Observations

1. Establishing Clear Goals and Expectations

To ensure a productive and structured observation process, both the observer and the observed faculty member should [178]:

Define the Purpose of the Observation

- Is the focus on student engagement, assessment strategies, course structure, or instructional clarity?

Set Expectations for Feedback

- Determine whether feedback will be written, verbal, structured, or informal.
- Example: *"I'd like feedback on how I facilitate discussions and encourage diverse student participation."*

Emphasize Growth Rather Than Evaluation

- Observations should be framed as collaborative learning experiences rather than performance assessments.

Establish Confidentiality and Trust

- Feedback should be shared only between participants and used for personal growth, not for administrative evaluation.

2. Structuring the Peer Observation Process

A well-organized peer observation cycle consists of three key phases:

A. Pre-Observation Meeting

- Discuss the focus areas (e.g., lecture delivery, student interaction, assessment methods).

- Review course objectives and teaching materials to provide context.
- Set guidelines for feedback format (written notes, structured rubric, open discussion).

Example: A faculty member asks a colleague to observe how they integrate active learning techniques in a flipped classroom setting.

B. Classroom Observation

- Take objective, detailed notes on teaching strategies, student reactions, and engagement levels.
- **Focus on specific teaching elements**, such as:
    - Pacing and clarity of explanations
    - Use of technology or multimedia
    - Effectiveness of discussion facilitation
    - Student participation and response dynamics
- **Minimize disruption**—observers should blend into the background rather than interfere with class flow.

Example: A peer observer notes that students engage more in small-group discussions than in full-class discussions, suggesting ways to improve large-group interactions.

C. Post-Observation Reflection and Feedback

- Schedule a debriefing session soon after the observation to discuss insights.
- Frame feedback constructively, emphasizing both strengths and opportunities for improvement.
- Encourage self-reflection by asking the observed faculty member what they felt worked well and what they would change.

Example: Instead of saying, *"Your lecture was too fast-paced,"* frame feedback constructively:

- - *"Your lecture covered a lot of valuable content, but students might benefit from periodic pauses for discussion or reflection."*

Collaborative Teaching Improvement Strategies

1. Reciprocal Peer Observations

Faculty can engage in mutual observations where both parties observe and exchange feedback. This creates a two-way learning experience, benefiting both instructors.

Example: A history professor observes a physics class to gain insights into visual demonstrations and real-world applications in lectures.

2. Team-Teaching and Cross-Disciplinary Collaboration

Professors from different disciplines can co-teach or guest lecture in each other's courses, exposing students to interdisciplinary perspectives.
Faculty can jointly design assignments or case studies that blend different fields.

Example: A psychology professor partners with an education professor to co-teach a seminar on cognitive learning theories in the classroom.

3. Faculty Learning Communities (FLCs)

Faculty can form small groups dedicated to discussing and improving teaching strategies.
These communities serve as safe spaces for sharing challenges, best practices, and classroom innovations.

Example: An FLC on active learning meets monthly to discuss new research, conduct peer observations, and refine classroom engagement techniques.

4. Video Recording and Self-Observation

In addition to peer feedback, faculty can record their own lectures and review them critically. This allows instructors to assess clarity, pacing, and engagement strategies firsthand.

Example: A professor records a lecture and notices they rely heavily on one-way communication, prompting them to incorporate more student interaction.

5. Institutional Support for Collaborative Teaching

Universities can formalize peer observation programs by offering:

- Teaching workshops and training sessions on best practices.
- Mentorship programs pairing new faculty with experienced educators.
- Grant funding for collaborative curriculum development.

Example: A university's teaching and learning center sponsors a faculty mentorship program, encouraging experienced professors to mentor new faculty through structured observations and feedback sessions.

Overcoming Challenges in Peer Observation and Collaboration

- Fear of Judgment

- Solution: Frame observations as non-evaluative and developmental rather than as critiques.

- Scheduling Conflicts

- Solution: Plan observations in advance and integrate them into faculty development schedules.

- **Resistance to Feedback**
    - Solution: Encourage faculty to approach feedback with a growth mindset, recognizing its value in professional development.

- **Inconsistencies in Peer Review Quality**
    - Solution: Use structured observation rubrics to maintain fairness and clarity in feedback.

Conclusion: Building a Collaborative Culture of Teaching Excellence

Peer observations and collaborative teaching improvement initiatives cultivate a culture of shared learning, innovation, and faculty development. By engaging in structured peer feedback, interdisciplinary collaboration, and reflective teaching discussions, faculty can enhance their pedagogical approaches, enrich student learning experiences, and foster a community of continuous improvement.

Ultimately, the most effective educators are those who remain open to feedback, seek diverse perspectives, and actively engage in professional development, ensuring that higher education remains dynamic, responsive, and student-centered.

Using Data Analytics for Course Improvement: Leveraging Evidence-Based Insights to Enhance Teaching and Learning

In today's data-driven academic environment, faculty have access to an unprecedented amount of information about student performance, engagement, and learning patterns. By effectively utilizing data analytics, professors can move beyond subjective impressions and anecdotal feedback, using quantifiable insights to refine instructional methods, optimize course design, and improve student outcomes.

For new college professors, developing data-informed teaching strategies allows for continuous improvement based on measurable evidence rather than intuition alone. Whether through learning management system (LMS) analytics, student assessment trends, engagement metrics, or predictive modeling, data analytics serves as a powerful tool for enhancing curriculum design, identifying at-risk students, and personalizing learning experiences.

This section explores the importance of data analytics in course improvement, key metrics to track, tools for gathering and interpreting data, and strategies for applying insights to refine teaching effectiveness.

The Role of Data Analytics in Teaching and Learning

Enhancing Decision-Making with Evidence-Based Insights

- Faculty can use quantitative and qualitative data to make informed adjustments to instructional methods, assessment design, and student engagement strategies.

Identifying Patterns and Trends in Student Learning

- Data analytics helps detect student performance trends, pinpoint common misconceptions, and assess the effectiveness of course materials.

Improving Student Engagement and Retention

- Professors can monitor participation rates, detect disengagement early, and intervene with targeted support strategies.

Personalizing Learning Experiences

- Adaptive learning systems can individualize coursework and resources based on individual student progress and learning needs.

Optimizing Course Design and Assessment Strategies

- By analyzing assignment outcomes, quiz scores, and discussion board activity, faculty can refine grading rubrics, content delivery, and assessment methods.

By embracing data-driven teaching improvement, faculty move from reactive problem-solving to proactive course optimization, ensuring that their instruction remains dynamic, responsive, and student-centered.

Key Data Points and Metrics for Course Improvement

1. Student Performance Analytics

Tracking student success through **grades, assessment results, and completion rates** helps faculty determine:

Which topics students struggle with most
How well assessments align with learning objectives
The effectiveness of different instructional strategies

Example: A professor analyzes exam performance data and discovers that students consistently perform poorly on one particular concept, prompting a revision of the teaching approach for that topic.

2. Student Engagement Metrics

Tracking attendance, discussion participation, assignment submissions, and LMS activity reveals how engaged students are with the course.

Indicators of engagement:

- Frequency of login activity on the LMS
- Discussion board interactions and peer responses
- Completion rates of non-mandatory learning resources

Example: A professor notices that students who watch recorded lectures more frequently tend to perform better on exams, suggesting that reinforcing asynchronous content could be beneficial.

3. Assessment and Learning Outcomes Analysis

By examining assessment data, faculty can determine:

Whether test questions fairly assess intended learning outcomes
Which question types (multiple-choice, essay, application-based) yield better comprehension
Whether students improve over time or struggle with cumulative knowledge retention

Example: A professor compares quiz performance before and after introducing active learning exercises to determine if student comprehension has improved.

4. Predictive Analytics for Student Success

Early identification of at-risk students

- Data analytics tools can flag students with low engagement, missing assignments, or poor performance trends, allowing faculty to intervene early.

Example: If LMS data shows that a subset of students has not logged in for two weeks, the professor can send personalized outreach emails encouraging them to reconnect with the course.

Data Analytics Tools for Faculty

Modern teaching platforms provide faculty with built-in analytics dashboards to track student activity, assess performance, and analyze trends. Key tools include:

Learning Management Systems (LMS) Analytics

- Platforms like Canvas, Blackboard, Moodle, and D2L provide dashboards with:
    - Student login frequency and engagement tracking
    - Assignment completion and submission timestamps
    - Quiz and assessment performance trends

Survey and Feedback Tools

- Google Forms, Qualtrics, and SurveyMonkey allow faculty to collect student feedback on course effectiveness and instructional methods.

Student Information Systems (SIS) and Institutional Data Dashboards

- Universities often provide institution-wide analytics dashboards that integrate student performance trends across multiple courses.

AI and Adaptive Learning Platforms

- EdTech tools like Coursera, Knewton, and Smart Sparrow use AI-driven data to customize learning pathways based on student needs.

Example: A professor uses Canvas analytics to track which students fail to open course materials regularly and sends proactive reminders to encourage engagement.

Applying Data Insights for Course Improvement

1. Refining Course Content and Delivery Methods

If LMS data shows students skipping certain readings or lectures, instructors can adjust materials to be more engaging or interactive.

If exam results indicate widespread difficulty with a specific concept, faculty can incorporate alternative explanations, case studies, or peer teaching sessions.

Example: A professor integrates short video lectures instead of long readings after noticing that text-heavy materials receive low engagement rates.

2. Enhancing Student Support and Retention Strategies

Use data to tailor student interventions:

- If a student consistently misses assignments, schedule a one-on-one meeting to discuss challenges.
- If a class wide engagement drop is detected, **adjust teaching methods mid-semester.**

Example: A professor notices a drop in discussion board participation mid-semester and introduces weekly prompts with extra credit incentives to re-engage students.

3. Improving Assessment Design

Analyze quiz and exam performance trends to ensure that assessments:

- Accurately measure learning outcomes
- Are neither too difficult nor too easy
- Align with instructional materials and in-class discussions

Example: After reviewing test analytics, a professor sees that students struggle with application-based exam questions but excel in recall-based questions. To address this gap, the professor incorporates more real-world case studies into lectures.

4. Iterative Course Design Based on Data Trends

Faculty can compare data across semesters to track improvements and refine course structures. Using longitudinal data, professors can determine whether curricular changes lead to better learning outcomes over time.

Example: A faculty member notices that class averages increased by 10% after incorporating active learning sessions, confirming the effectiveness of the new strategy.

Overcoming Challenges in Using Data Analytics for Teaching Improvement

- **Data Overload**

- Solution: Focus on key performance indicators (KPIs) most relevant to student learning and engagement.

- **Interpreting Data Without Context**

    - Solution: Combine quantitative data with qualitative insights from student feedback and peer observations.

- **Avoiding a One-Size-Fits-All Approach**

    - Solution: Recognize individual student learning differences and adjust strategies accordingly.

- **Privacy and Ethical Concerns**

    - Solution: Ensure that data collection complies with institutional policies and student privacy regulations (FERPA, GDPR, etc.).

Conclusion: Data-Driven Teaching for Continuous Improvement

Using data analytics for course improvement empowers faculty with actionable insights that enhance teaching effectiveness, optimize student engagement, and personalize learning experiences. By tracking performance trends, refining course materials, and leveraging predictive analytics, professors can make informed decisions that drive student success.

Ultimately, data analytics transforms teaching from intuition-based decision-making to evidence-based practice, ensuring that higher education remains adaptive, responsive, and student-centered in an evolving academic landscape.

Staying Current with Educational Trends and Pedagogical Research: Advancing Teaching Excellence through Lifelong Learning

Higher education is a dynamic and ever-evolving field, shaped by advancements in technology, shifts in student demographics, new learning methodologies, and emerging research in cognitive science and pedagogy. To remain effective educators, college professors must continuously update their teaching strategies, integrate evidence-based practices, and adapt to new trends in higher education.

For new college professors, staying informed about educational trends and pedagogical research is essential for maintaining relevance, engagement, and instructional effectiveness. The integration of modern teaching innovations, inclusive learning strategies, and data-driven assessment methods ensures that students receive an education that aligns with contemporary academic and professional demands.

This section explores the importance of staying current in pedagogy, strategies for engaging with ongoing research, and best practices for incorporating emerging trends into teaching practice.

The Importance of Staying Current with Pedagogical Research

Enhancing Teaching Effectiveness

- New research provides insights into how students learn best, what instructional strategies are most effective, and how faculty can optimize course delivery.

Improving Student Engagement and Learning Outcomes

- By incorporating innovative teaching methods and evidence-based learning techniques, faculty can create more dynamic and interactive classrooms.

Adapting to Changes in Student Needs and Expectations

- Today's students have diverse backgrounds, learning preferences, and technological fluency—requiring faculty to continuously adjust and refine their approach.

Aligning with Institutional and Accreditation Standards

- Universities frequently update their curriculum frameworks, assessment strategies, and accreditation requirements—faculty must remain informed to maintain program integrity.

Fostering Lifelong Professional Growth

- Engaging with ongoing research and educational discourse ensures professors remain intellectually engaged, adaptable, and effective throughout their careers.

By embracing a mindset of continuous learning, professors position themselves as leaders in higher education, committed to innovation and student success.

Key Sources for Staying Informed on Educational Trends

Professors can stay updated on cutting-edge pedagogical research and trends by engaging with the following:

1. Academic Journals and Research Publications

Leading journals publish peer-reviewed research on instructional strategies, student cognition, and curriculum development.

Recommended Journals:

- *The Journal of Higher Education*
- *Innovative Higher Education*
- *Teaching in Higher Education*
- *Journal of Educational Psychology*
- *Active Learning in Higher Education*

Example: A professor reads a study in *The Journal of Higher Education* on active learning strategies and incorporates collaborative problem-solving techniques into their lecture format.

2. Conferences and Professional Development Workshops

Conferences provide opportunities to learn from experts, engage in discussions, and explore new teaching technologies.

Top Higher Education Conferences:

- *American Association of Colleges and Universities (AAC&U) Conference*
- *Educause (Technology and Higher Ed)*
- *Lilly Conference on Teaching and Learning*
- *Society for Teaching and Learning in Higher Education (STLHE) Conference*

Example: A faculty member attends an Educause session on AI in education, prompting them to explore AI-driven adaptive learning tools for their online courses.

3. Faculty Learning Communities (FLCs) and Interdisciplinary Collaboration

Participating in teaching circles, faculty development workshops, or cross-disciplinary discussions allows faculty to exchange ideas and learn from colleagues.

Example: A professor in the humanities collaborates with a STEM faculty member to explore project-based learning techniques that engage students in real-world problem-solving.

Engagement Strategies:

- Join university-sponsored faculty development groups.
- Attend departmental teaching and pedagogy meetings.
- Collaborate on cross-disciplinary research on student learning.

4. Online Courses, Webinars, and MOOCs on Pedagogy

Platforms like Coursera, EdX, and LinkedIn Learning offer certifications in higher education teaching, instructional design, and digital learning.

Example: A faculty member takes a Harvard EdX course on "Rethinking Teaching in the Digital Age", learning to incorporate gamification into their assessments.

Top Online Courses for Professors:

- *"Evidence-Based Teaching" (FutureLearn)*
- *"Learning How to Learn" (Coursera)*
- *"Teaching with Technology" (Harvard EdX)*

5. Higher Education Blogs, Podcasts, and Newsletters

Engaging with short-form content from experts provides quick, digestible insights into new teaching methodologies and challenges in higher education.

Recommended Blogs and Podcasts:

- *The Chronicle of Higher Education* (blog & newsletter)
- *Teaching in Higher Ed Podcast*
- *The EdSurge Higher Ed Podcast*
- *Faculty Focus Blog*

Example: A professor listens to the *Teaching in Higher Ed Podcast* episode on "Addressing Student Motivation," inspiring them to revise their syllabus to emphasize intrinsic learning incentives.

6. Institutional Teaching and Learning Centers (TLCs)

Many universities have dedicated Teaching and Learning Centers (TLCs) that offer:

- Workshops on instructional innovation
- Mentorship programs for new faculty
- Support for curriculum redesign and digital learning

Example: A professor consults their university's Teaching and Learning Center to redesign their assessments for inclusivity, integrating universal design principles.

Emerging Trends in Higher Education Pedagogy

Active and Experiential Learning

- Flipped classrooms, project-based learning, and case-study approaches are reshaping traditional lectures.

Technology-Enhanced Learning

- AI-driven assessments, virtual reality (VR) learning, and adaptive learning platforms are enhancing digital instruction.

Equity, Diversity, and Inclusion (EDI) in Teaching

- Faculty are incorporating culturally responsive teaching methods and universal design for learning (UDL) to support diverse student populations.

Competency-Based and Personalized Learning

- Institutions are shifting toward mastery-based education, modular learning, and flexible course pathways.

Data-Driven Teaching Strategies

- Learning analytics help professors assess student engagement, predict at-risk students, and refine assessment methods.

Example: A professor adopts learning analytics tools to track which students engage most with online course materials, allowing for targeted support interventions.

Strategies for Integrating New Research into Teaching Practices

Experiment with One New Teaching Technique Per Semester

- Start small—implement a new discussion format, assessment method, or technology tool.

Seek Student Feedback on New Strategies

- Ask students if new methods enhance their learning experience and make adjustments accordingly.

Collaborate with Colleagues on Pedagogical Innovations

- Partner with faculty to test active learning techniques, redesign courses, or conduct research on student engagement.

Document Changes in a Teaching Portfolio

- Keep track of teaching evolution and research-based adjustments for tenure and promotion portfolios.

Faculty Peer Review and Collaborative Improvement

Effective teaching in higher education requires continuous reflection, feedback, and refinement. Student evaluations, while useful for gauging satisfaction and perceptions, provide only a limited perspective. They often reflect factors unrelated to pedagogy—such as course difficulty, grading policies, or instructor demographics—making them insufficient as the sole measure of teaching effectiveness. Faculty peer review and collaborative improvement offer a richer, more developmental framework for growth. Unlike one-time or informal observations, comprehensive systems emphasize ongoing dialogue, accountability, and shared innovation. When embedded into academic culture, structured peer review and collaborative models foster teaching excellence that is both sustainable and collegial.

Structured Peer Review Protocols Beyond Observation

Traditional peer review often stops at the classroom visit, but true developmental feedback requires a multi-stage, systematic process that engages faculty before, during, and after observation.

- **Pre-Observation Planning**
  The process begins with intentional preparation.
    - Faculty should meet in advance to review the course syllabus, assignments, and stated learning outcomes.
    - The observed faculty member can share specific areas where feedback is desired (e.g., student engagement, clarity of explanations, or assessment design).

- o Setting goals beforehand ensures that the review is not a generic evaluation but a targeted opportunity for professional growth.
- **Observation Frameworks**
  Observations should follow structured criteria rather than rely solely on subjective impressions.
  - o Standardized rubrics can include categories such as clarity of learning objectives, use of inclusive teaching practices, evidence of active learning, and alignment between activities and outcomes.
  - o Reviewers should also note how the instructor responds to student questions, integrates technology, or manages classroom dynamics.
  - o Using shared frameworks increases fairness and consistency across departments while ensuring that feedback is pedagogically meaningful.
- **Post-Observation Dialogue**
  Feedback should be dialogical rather than one-directional.
  - o After the observation, reviewers and instructors should meet for a reflective conversation.
  - o The observed faculty member can begin by sharing their perspective—what went well, what challenges they experienced, and where they seek improvement.
  - o Reviewers can then provide constructive feedback, highlighting strengths while offering specific strategies for growth.
  - o This reflective dialogue positions peer review as collaborative problem-solving rather than evaluative judgment.
- **Documentation and Follow-Up**
  A record of the peer review ensures accountability and supports professional development.
  - o Summaries may include key feedback, action steps, and resources for further improvement.
  - o Faculty can use these documents to demonstrate teaching development in annual reviews, promotion dossiers, or teaching portfolios.
  - o Importantly, follow-up observations or check-ins should be scheduled to track progress and reinforce that improvement is an ongoing process.

Key Takeaway

Structured peer review protocols transform classroom visits from isolated events into developmental systems. By including pre-observation planning, rubric-based evaluations, reflective dialogue, and documentation, faculty ensure that reviews are consistent, constructive, and growth-focused. When scaled across departments, these systems embed teaching improvement into academic culture, positioning pedagogy as a shared professional responsibility rather than an individual pursuit.

Cross-Disciplinary Teaching Consultation Models

While faculty expertise often develops within the boundaries of specific disciplines, teaching challenges are not always discipline-specific. Issues such as motivating students, designing assessments, or integrating technology cut across fields. By engaging in cross-disciplinary consultation, faculty gain access to new pedagogical strategies, broaden their perspectives, and reduce the risk of teaching in isolation. These consultations help create a culture where teaching is understood not just as a private activity but as a shared professional craft.

Cross-Unit Pairings

Pairing faculty from different departments fosters one-on-one exchange of strategies that might not emerge within disciplinary silos.

- **Example in Practice**: A business professor could work with a humanities colleague to strengthen writing assignments by incorporating rhetorical analysis or scaffolding techniques common in writing-intensive courses. Conversely, a humanities professor could learn from STEM colleagues how to integrate visualizations, simulations, or data-driven problem sets.
- **Mutual Benefit**: Cross-unit pairings are not about one faculty member acting as the "expert" but about reciprocal learning, where each shares strengths shaped by disciplinary norms.
- **Application**: These pairings can be formalized by teaching and learning centers or developed informally through collegial networking.

Interdisciplinary Panels

When multiple perspectives are brought together, course design and teaching strategies benefit from holistic feedback.

- **Panel Structure**: A group of faculty from different fields reviews a syllabus, assignment sequence, or assessment framework.
- **Comprehensive Lens**: A STEM faculty member might focus on clarity of instructions and data use, while a social scientist emphasizes student engagement strategies, and a humanities scholar highlights critical thinking and reflection.
- **Institutional Support**: Teaching centers can organize panels as part of workshops or curriculum review initiatives, ensuring that feedback is constructive and grounded in pedagogical evidence.

Shared Pedagogical Practices

Cross-disciplinary dialogue also facilitates the transfer of effective teaching methods that have been tested in different contexts.

- **Active Learning**: Techniques like think–pair–share, peer instruction, and case-based discussion are common in some fields but underutilized in others.
- **Problem-Based Learning (PBL)**: Widely used in medical and engineering education, PBL can also enhance humanities or social science classrooms by framing debates or case analyses as problems to be solved collaboratively.
- **Digital and Technological Tools**: STEM fields may pioneer the use of data visualization tools or coding platforms, while humanities faculty may lead in digital storytelling and

multimodal assignments.

By sharing strategies, faculty avoid reinventing the wheel and discover adaptable practices that enhance teaching across contexts.

Broader Impacts

Cross-disciplinary consultations break down the silos that often define academic culture.

- **Perspective Expansion**: Faculty gain insight into how students encounter learning in other disciplines, helping them better understand the diverse educational journeys of their students.
- **Curricular Coherence**: When faculty align teaching strategies across departments, students experience smoother transitions between courses and programs.
- **Innovation Culture**: Exposure to diverse practices encourages experimentation, helping faculty remain adaptable in rapidly changing educational landscapes.

Key Takeaway

Cross-disciplinary consultation enriches teaching by bringing fresh perspectives, encouraging reciprocal learning, and spreading effective strategies across fields. Through cross-unit pairings, interdisciplinary panels, and shared pedagogical practices, faculty broaden their teaching repertoire while contributing to a culture of collaboration and innovation. This approach helps dismantle disciplinary insularity and positions teaching as a collective, institution-wide pursuit of excellence.

Faculty Learning Communities and Teaching Circles

While workshops and one-time consultations provide valuable insights, sustainable teaching improvement requires ongoing collaboration and dialogue. Faculty learning communities (FLCs) and teaching circles provide structured yet collegial spaces where educators can reflect on practice, share strategies, and support one another's professional growth. These groups foster not only skill development but also a sense of community, reducing the isolation faculty may feel in their teaching roles.

Learning Communities

Faculty Learning Communities (FLCs) are typically formal, long-term groups that meet consistently over a semester or academic year.

- **Thematic Focus**: Each FLC usually centers on a specific theme, such as inclusive pedagogy, digital teaching, writing across the curriculum, or assessment reform.
- **Structured Activities**: Meetings may include reading scholarly literature, piloting new teaching methods, or engaging in collaborative action research.
- **Institutional Support**: Many institutions provide funding, release time, or professional development credit for participation, ensuring that FLCs are recognized as meaningful faculty work.

- **Outcomes**: FLCs often produce tangible results, such as redesigned courses, published scholarship of teaching and learning (SoTL), or campus-wide teaching initiatives.

Teaching Circles

Teaching circles are smaller, more informal groups that prioritize peer conversation and immediate problem-solving.

- **Regular Meetings**: Faculty meet periodically—sometimes over coffee or lunch—to discuss classroom challenges, share resources, and exchange ideas.
- **Peer-to-Peer Support**: Teaching circles thrive on collegial trust, allowing faculty to be candid about difficulties and seek constructive advice.
- **Flexible Agendas**: Unlike FLCs, teaching circles may not have a set theme or deliverable; instead, they evolve based on participants' needs.
- **Accessibility**: Because they are low-cost and informal, teaching circles are an easy entry point for faculty who are new to collaborative professional development.

Accountability and Support

Both FLCs and teaching circles succeed because they combine professional accountability with collegial encouragement.

- **Safe Experimentation**: Faculty can test new teaching strategies knowing they will receive supportive feedback rather than punitive evaluation.
- **Constructive Feedback**: Peers provide suggestions grounded in shared experience, helping colleagues refine their practices in real time.
- **Motivation Through Community**: Group membership reinforces the idea that improving teaching is not a solitary pursuit but a shared commitment.
- **Long-Term Growth**: The consistent, relational nature of these groups promotes lasting changes in teaching practice, rather than short-term adjustments.

Key Takeaway

Faculty learning communities and teaching circles provide sustained, collegial environments where faculty can reflect, experiment, and grow. While FLCs offer structured, theme-based engagement and often yield institutional outcomes, teaching circles create informal peer networks for sharing strategies and troubleshooting challenges. Together, they normalize continuous teaching improvement as a collective professional responsibility, shifting the culture of higher education toward collaboration and excellence.

Collaborative Curriculum Development Processes

Curriculum design is often imagined as the work of individual faculty members building their own courses. While individual creativity is important, curriculum is most effective when designed through collaborative processes that ensure coherence across courses, programs, and even departments. Collaboration helps align expectations, avoids redundancy, and ensures students progress through a well-structured learning pathway rather than experiencing a series of disconnected courses.

Course Alignment Workshops

Faculty teaching multiple sections of the same course can greatly enhance student learning by aligning content and expectations.

- **Shared Learning Outcomes**: Instructors agree on a common set of learning objectives so all students—regardless of section—develop the same essential skills and knowledge.
- **Consistent Assessments**: Faculty collaborate to design shared exams, assignments, or rubrics, ensuring fairness across sections.
- **Flexibility Within Structure**: While core outcomes and assessments remain consistent, instructors retain freedom to use different pedagogical approaches.
- **Institutional Benefit**: Alignment also supports accreditation processes by demonstrating consistency in student achievement.

Program-Level Collaboration

Departments can strengthen curricula by ensuring that courses work together to scaffold learning progressively across a student's academic journey.

- **Skill Development Pathways**: Introductory courses might focus on foundational skills (e.g., critical reading, basic statistics), while advanced courses build toward independent research or applied practice.
- **Avoiding Redundancy**: Collaboration reduces the risk that students repeatedly encounter the same content without progression.
- **Capstone Integration**: Designing backward from capstone projects or senior theses ensures that earlier courses provide the preparation students need.
- **Regular Review**: Department-wide curriculum mapping exercises allow faculty to identify gaps, overlaps, and areas needing reinforcement.

Cross-Departmental Initiatives

Interdisciplinary programs require collaboration to balance disciplinary contributions and integrate diverse perspectives.

- **Joint Planning Committees**: Faculty from multiple departments meet to design course sequences that weave together disciplinary strengths.
- **Shared Ownership**: Interdisciplinary courses or minors work best when participating departments share responsibility for learning outcomes, rather than treating them as add-ons.
- **Student Perspective**: Cross-departmental collaboration ensures students experience interdisciplinary programs as coherent and purposeful rather than fragmented.

- **Innovation Opportunities**: Collaborative design often sparks new course ideas, such as pairing computer science with the humanities in digital humanities programs, or business with environmental science in sustainability curricula.

Broader Benefits of Collaboration

Collaborative curriculum development strengthens higher education in ways that extend beyond course design.

- **Faculty Development**: Collaboration exposes faculty to new pedagogical strategies and disciplinary perspectives.
- **Institutional Efficiency**: Shared resources reduce duplication of effort, saving time and improving quality.
- **Student Success**: Most importantly, students benefit from curricula that are intentional, integrated, and clearly scaffolded, leading to better retention, progression, and preparation for professional or academic futures.

Key Takeaway

Curriculum design is strongest when it is collective rather than isolated. Through course alignment workshops, program-level collaboration, and cross-departmental initiatives, faculty create curricula that are coherent, efficient, and meaningful. This collaborative approach reduces redundancy, strengthens scaffolding, and ensures that students experience higher education as a connected learning journey rather than a series of disconnected courses.

Peer Mentorship Programs for Teaching Improvement

Formal mentorship programs are among the most effective ways to strengthen teaching capacity within higher education. By pairing experienced educators with newer faculty—or those seeking to refresh their practice—institutions create structured opportunities for knowledge transfer, skill development, and cultural integration. Unlike one-time workshops, peer mentorship fosters relationships that extend over semesters or years, providing ongoing support as faculty refine their teaching. Importantly, mentorship is not a one-way exchange; both mentors and mentees grow through reflective dialogue, experimentation, and shared accountability [178].

Mentor Roles

Mentors serve as guides, coaches, and role models for teaching practice.

- **Course Design Support**: Mentors help mentees align learning outcomes with assessments, design inclusive syllabi, and select appropriate teaching strategies.
- **Classroom Management**: Experienced faculty can share strategies for facilitating discussion, managing large classes, and addressing disruptive behaviors constructively.
- **Assessment Practices**: Mentors provide feedback on grading rubrics, exam design, and methods for offering formative feedback that supports student learning.

- **Institutional Navigation**: Beyond pedagogy, mentors help mentees understand local teaching policies, evaluation criteria, and available campus resources.

Reciprocal Growth

While mentorship is often framed as a benefit to newer faculty, senior faculty also gain by participating.

- **Reflective Practice**: Explaining and modeling teaching choices prompts mentors to reflect on their own methods and assumptions.
- **Exposure to Innovation**: Mentees may bring fresh ideas, new technologies, or different disciplinary approaches that enrich the mentor's practice.
- **Leadership Development**: Serving as a mentor builds leadership skills and positions faculty for roles in administration or faculty development.
- **Renewed Purpose**: Many mentors find renewed motivation and pride in seeing colleagues succeed and in contributing to a culture of teaching excellence.

Structured Programs

Effective mentorship requires more than informal pairings—it benefits from clear structures and institutional support.

- **Formal Matching**: Teaching and learning centers or academic departments can pair faculty based on complementary needs and expertise.
- **Clear Expectations**: Programs should outline goals, meeting frequency, confidentiality agreements, and expected outcomes.
- **Timelines**: Semester- or year-long commitments ensure sustained engagement and give mentees enough time to apply and refine new strategies.
- **Recognition of Mentors**: Institutions should value mentorship by providing service credit, professional development funds, or public acknowledgment in annual reviews.

Broader Impact on Institutional Culture

Peer mentorship strengthens higher education by positioning teaching as a collective craft rather than an isolated responsibility.

- **Community Building**: Mentorship creates connections across rank, discipline, and background, reinforcing collegiality.
- **Consistency in Quality**: As teaching practices are shared, departments benefit from greater alignment in expectations and standards.
- **Retention and Success**: Newer faculty often feel more supported and integrated into the institution, reducing attrition and improving morale.
- **Teaching Innovation**: Mentorship fosters a culture of experimentation where faculty feel safe trying new methods, knowing they have guidance and feedback.

Key Takeaway

Peer mentorship programs elevate teaching by combining guidance, reflection, and institutional support. With clear roles, structured programs, and recognition for contributions, mentorship ensures that teaching excellence is not left to chance but cultivated intentionally. In doing so, institutions strengthen their culture of collaboration, positioning teaching as a shared professional responsibility passed between colleagues and across generations of faculty.

Group Problem-Solving for Teaching Challenges

Faculty across disciplines often encounter recurring challenges: disengaged students, uneven participation, classroom management in large sections, or integrating new technologies effectively. While these issues can feel isolating when faced alone, many colleagues are wrestling with similar concerns. Group problem-solving transforms these challenges into opportunities for collective learning. By pooling expertise, testing solutions, and sharing results, faculty accelerate innovation and create a culture where teaching is approached as a collaborative craft rather than a solitary struggle.

Case-Based Discussions

One of the simplest and most effective formats for group problem-solving is case-based dialogue.

- **Structured Sharing**: A faculty member presents a specific classroom challenge—such as low engagement in online discussions or high rates of plagiarism—and outlines the context.
- **Collective Brainstorming**: Peers offer strategies, share similar experiences, and suggest alternative perspectives.
- **Applied Takeaways**: The group distills key ideas into actionable steps that the presenting faculty can test in their classroom.
This approach is low-cost, highly adaptable, and helps normalize open discussion of teaching struggles.

Action Research Teams

For deeper exploration, faculty can form action research teams that systematically study teaching challenges.

- **Pilot Solutions**: Teams design and implement experimental strategies, such as using gamification to boost participation or restructuring group projects to enhance accountability.
- **Data Collection**: Faculty track outcomes through student surveys, grade analysis, or observation.
- **Iterative Refinement**: Teams adjust approaches based on findings, creating a cycle of continuous improvement.
- **Dissemination**: Results can be shared at faculty meetings, teaching workshops, or conferences, contributing to institutional knowledge and potentially the scholarship of teaching and learning (SoTL).

This model elevates problem-solving into a scholarly endeavor, linking practice with evidence-based improvement.

Workshops and Retreats

Dedicated, structured time allows for more in-depth exploration of shared challenges.

- **Workshops**: Short, focused sessions (1–3 hours) provide space for collaborative exploration of specific issues like assessment redesign, inclusive pedagogy, or integrating AI tools.
- **Retreats**: Multi-day or off-campus retreats encourage deeper reflection and team building, allowing faculty to step back from daily pressures and think holistically about teaching.
- **Collaborative Outputs**: These sessions often generate shared resources such as sample assignments, rubrics, or teaching guides that benefit the wider faculty community. Workshops and retreats create momentum by embedding problem-solving into institutional rhythms of professional development.

Benefits of Collaborative Problem-Solving

- **Reduces Isolation**: Faculty recognize that teaching challenges are common and solvable through shared wisdom.
- **Accelerates Adoption**: When solutions are tested collectively, successful practices spread more quickly across departments.
- **Encourages Experimentation**: Collaborative groups create a low-risk environment for innovation, where failure is framed as learning.
- **Builds Institutional Memory**: Documenting and sharing solutions ensures continuity, especially as faculty turnover occurs.

Key Takeaway

Group problem-solving empowers faculty to turn shared teaching challenges into collective opportunities for growth. Through case-based discussions, action research teams, and dedicated workshops or retreats, institutions cultivate a culture of collaboration, experimentation, and evidence-based improvement. Integrated within peer review and collaborative systems, this approach ensures that teaching is not only continuously refined but also owned collectively, strengthening both faculty development and student learning.

Conclusion: A Commitment to Lifelong Learning in Higher Education

Staying current with educational trends and pedagogical research is an essential component of teaching excellence. By engaging with scholarly research, attending professional development events, experimenting with new teaching strategies, and leveraging technology, faculty can ensure that their courses remain engaging, effective, and aligned with the evolving needs of students.

Ultimately, the most impactful educators are those who remain lifelong learners themselves, continuously refining their pedagogy to create dynamic, inclusive, and evidence-based learning environments in higher education.

Fostering a Growth-Oriented Approach to Teaching

Teaching evaluations and faculty reviews should not be seen as static assessments but as dynamic tools for professional growth. When approached with a mindset of continuous improvement, these evaluations provide valuable insights that help faculty refine their teaching strategies, enhance student engagement, and align their instruction with institutional and pedagogical goals.

By engaging in self-assessment, actively seeking feedback, and implementing constructive changes, faculty can cultivate more effective learning environments, benefiting both students and educators. Furthermore, addressing evaluation biases and using multiple forms of assessment ensures a fairer, more comprehensive understanding of teaching effectiveness.

Ultimately, the goal of teaching evaluations is not perfection but progress. Faculty who embrace ongoing reflection and adaptation demonstrate a commitment to educational excellence, fostering a culture of innovation, inclusivity, and student-centered learning in higher education.

Chapter 12: Continuous Improvement

Higher education is constantly changing, evolving, and requiring faculty to engage in ongoing professional development and instructional refinement. Continuous improvement is essential for maintaining teaching effectiveness, staying informed of educational advancements, and ensuring that students receive the highest quality learning experiences. By adopting a mindset of lifelong learning, faculty members can refine their teaching methodologies, integrate innovative technologies, and respond to the changing needs of students and institutions.

Figure 12.1. Continuous Teaching Improvement. [219]

This chapter explores key aspects of continuous improvement, including tenure and promotion processes, building a strong teaching portfolio, documenting instructional effectiveness, and expanding leadership opportunities within academia. Additionally, it highlights the importance of professional networking and engagement in faculty development initiatives to stay at the forefront of pedagogical research and best practices.

By committing to continuous improvement, faculty members not only enhance their own careers but also contribute to the broader academic community, ensuring that higher education remains dynamic, inclusive, and impactful.

Understanding Traditional Tenure and Promotion Processes and Promotional Opportunities

In academia, tenure and promotion serve as foundational pillars that define faculty career progression, academic contributions, and long-term institutional commitment. While tenure systems vary across institutions, they traditionally function as mechanisms to recognize faculty excellence in teaching, research, and service, ensuring both job security and academic freedom. Promotion processes, whether within a tenure-track system or in alternative faculty career paths, are designed to reward professional growth, scholarly contributions, and leadership within the institution.

At Walsh College, promotional opportunities follow a distinct framework aligned with the institution's mission, faculty contributions, and strategic priorities. Understanding both traditional tenure models and Walsh's specific promotion structure enables faculty to navigate career advancement effectively while aligning their professional development with institutional goals.

This section explores the traditional tenure and promotion system, alternative faculty promotion models, and specific career advancement opportunities at Walsh College.

Traditional Tenure and Promotion Processes in Higher Education

In many universities, tenure and promotion function as a structured, multi-year process that assesses faculty across three primary dimensions:

Teaching Excellence – Effective pedagogy, curriculum development, student mentorship, and innovative instructional practices.
Scholarly Research and Publications – Contributions to academic knowledge through peer-reviewed publications, conference presentations, and research grants.
Service to the Institution and Community – Participation in faculty governance, committee leadership, mentorship, and community engagement.

These evaluations are conducted through peer review, administrative oversight, and faculty committees, culminating in a tenure decision that grants long-term academic appointment and career stability [179].

1. The Tenure Process: A Traditional Perspective

Tenure is typically a multi-stage process spanning five to seven years, consisting of:

Initial Appointment (Year 1-2): Faculty are hired into tenure-track positions, focusing on establishing teaching effectiveness, research contributions, and institutional service involvement [179].

Mid-Tenure Review (Year 3-4): Faculty undergo a formative review, assessing progress in teaching, research, and service, receiving feedback for improvement [179].

Tenure Application (Year 5-7): Faculty submit a comprehensive tenure dossier, including:

- Teaching evaluations and innovations
- Published research and scholarly contributions
- Evidence of institutional service and leadership [179]

Final Tenure Decision: Faculty committees and senior administrators review the tenure dossier, conduct peer evaluations, and vote on tenure status.

Post-Tenure Responsibilities: Once granted, tenure ensures job security, academic freedom, and increased leadership responsibilities within the institution [179].

2. Alternative Faculty Promotion Models

While traditional tenure-track systems remain prominent in research-intensive universities, many institutions—including Walsh College—adopt alternative faculty promotion structures tailored to their teaching-focused and industry-driven missions [179].

Non-Tenure-Track Faculty Career Paths

- Some institutions offer renewable contract positions that include structured promotion pathways without tenure commitments.

Teaching-Focused Promotions

- In institutions prioritizing professional education and applied learning, faculty promotions emphasize teaching effectiveness, industry experience, and instructional leadership rather than traditional research output.

Hybrid Models: Blending Teaching, Research, and Service

- Some faculty roles integrate applied scholarship, industry partnerships, and institutional service rather than requiring extensive peer-reviewed research.

Example: A business professor in a non-tenure-track role advances to a Senior Lecturer or Professor of Practice based on teaching excellence and professional contributions to the field.

Promotional Opportunities at Walsh College

Walsh College, as a career-focused institution emphasizing professional education in business and technology, structures faculty promotions around teaching excellence, curriculum leadership, industry collaboration, and institutional contributions rather than a traditional tenure model.

Faculty promotions at Walsh College are designed to:

Recognize Teaching Innovation and Excellence

- Faculty who demonstrate outstanding student engagement, curriculum development, and pedagogical advancements are considered for higher academic ranks.

Encourage Industry and Professional Engagement

- Given Walsh's strong ties to the business and technology sectors, faculty promotions may be influenced by industry impact, professional credentials, and applied research contributions.

Support Leadership in Institutional Initiatives

- Faculty who contribute to faculty governance, program development, accreditation efforts, and strategic institutional initiatives can advance within Walsh's promotional structure.

1. Faculty Ranks and Promotion Criteria at Walsh College

While specific titles and advancement paths may evolve, Walsh College faculty promotions generally follow a tiered structure, moving from:

Assistant Professor → Associate Professor → Full Professor

- Faculty progress through these ranks based on teaching excellence, curriculum contributions, and professional engagement.

Lecturer → Senior Lecturer → Distinguished Lecturer

- Non-tenure-track faculty may follow a pathway emphasizing instructional excellence and student mentorship.

Professor of Practice → Distinguished Professor of Practice

- Faculty with significant industry experience may advance based on professional expertise, thought leadership, and business impact.

2. Key Promotion Considerations at Walsh

Instructional Effectiveness as a Primary Criterion

- Unlike tenure-track universities that emphasize research, Walsh prioritizes teaching innovation, student mentorship, and curriculum leadership as key promotion criteria.

Industry Collaboration and Professional Contributions

- Faculty with strong industry ties, consulting work, or applied research experience are recognized for their contributions to bridging academia with real-world applications.

Institutional Service and Leadership

- Faculty engagement in faculty committees, curriculum development, accreditation efforts, and student success initiatives strengthens promotion applications.

Example: A faculty member who leads an initiative to integrate AI-driven analytics into business courses while actively engaging with local industry leaders may be considered for promotion based on teaching excellence and professional impact.

3. Preparing for Promotion at Walsh College

Faculty seeking promotion should proactively:

Document Teaching Effectiveness and Innovations

- Maintain teaching portfolios, student evaluations, curriculum redesigns, and instructional methodologies that demonstrate continuous improvement.

Engage in Institutional Service and Faculty Leadership

- Serve on faculty committees, participate in accreditation projects, or mentor junior faculty to strengthen institutional contributions.

Demonstrate Industry and Professional Contributions

- Engage in consulting, corporate partnerships, applied research, and industry training programs that align with Walsh's mission of business and technology education.

Develop a Strong Promotion Portfolio

- A promotion dossier should include:
    - Teaching evaluations and student success metrics
    - Curriculum development contributions
    - Professional and industry engagement activities
    - Institutional leadership roles and service contributions

Seek Mentorship and Guidance

- Engage with senior faculty, department chairs, and academic leadership to receive feedback on promotion readiness and areas for growth.

Example: A faculty member who redesigns a finance curriculum to integrate real-world simulations, mentors junior instructors, and collaborates with business leaders may build a compelling case for promotion.

Conclusion: Navigating Faculty Career Advancement at Walsh College

Understanding traditional tenure and promotion models provides a foundational framework, but advancing at Walsh College requires aligning faculty development with the institution's distinctive mission. By prioritizing teaching excellence, industry engagement, and institutional contributions, faculty can build meaningful academic careers that bridge theoretical knowledge with applied professional expertise.

Ultimately, faculty promotion at Walsh College is not about adhering to rigid tenure models but about fostering continuous growth, leadership, and impact within the evolving landscape of business and technology education.

Building a Strong Teaching Portfolio: Showcasing Excellence, Growth, and Impact in Higher Education

A teaching portfolio serves as a comprehensive, reflective, and evidence-based document that illustrates a professor's philosophy, effectiveness, and contributions to student learning. In higher education, a well-crafted portfolio is essential for faculty promotion, professional development, tenure considerations, and continuous improvement [180]. Beyond being an evaluative tool, a strong teaching portfolio also serves as a self-reflective artifact, enabling educators to assess their own pedagogical growth, adapt to evolving student needs, and refine instructional strategies.

For new college professors, developing a dynamic and compelling teaching portfolio is a key step toward career advancement, professional credibility, and enhanced instructional impact. This section explores the essential components of a teaching portfolio, strategies for presenting an authentic and data-driven narrative, and best practices for continuous refinement.

The Purpose and Value of a Teaching Portfolio

Demonstrating Teaching Effectiveness

- A well-organized portfolio showcases teaching innovations, student engagement strategies, and instructional success.

Documenting Professional Growth and Pedagogical Evolution

- The portfolio serves as a self-reflective record, illustrating adaptations, refinements, and new teaching methodologies over time.

Providing Evidence for Promotion and Career Advancement

- Many institutions require a teaching portfolio for tenure, promotion, or faculty evaluations to assess teaching impact, student learning outcomes, and curricular contributions [181].

Enhancing Self-Reflection and Continuous Improvement

- The process of compiling a portfolio encourages faculty to evaluate their strengths, identify areas for growth, and set professional development goals.

Showcasing Teaching Scholarship and Innovations

- A strong portfolio highlights curriculum design, integration of new technologies, interdisciplinary teaching, and contributions to faculty development.

By creating a portfolio that is intentional, structured, and evidence-based, faculty can craft a compelling narrative of their teaching excellence and professional growth.

Key Components of a Strong Teaching Portfolio

A teaching portfolio typically includes both qualitative reflections and quantitative evidence that illustrate a faculty member's approach to instruction, effectiveness in the classroom, and contributions to student learning.

1. Teaching Philosophy Statement

A concise, reflective statement (1-2 pages) that articulates:

- Core teaching values and beliefs
- Instructional methods and pedagogical approach
- How learning is facilitated in diverse student populations
- Commitment to continuous improvement and adaptability

Example: A faculty member writes about active learning strategies in business education, emphasizing real-world case studies, experiential learning, and technology integration.

2. Course Materials and Curriculum Development

Syllabi, Lesson Plans, and Course Descriptions

- Showcases how courses are structured, assessed, and aligned with learning objectives.

Innovative Teaching Materials

- Examples of lecture slides, digital resources, case studies, and problem-based learning exercises.

Curriculum Redesign Contributions

- Documentation of course innovations, program development, and interdisciplinary collaborations.

Example: A professor integrates AI-driven analytics into finance courses, refining assessments to reflect industry-relevant problem-solving.

3. Evidence of Student Learning and Engagement

Assessment Data and Learning Outcomes

- Summarizes student performance trends, assignment evaluations, and improvement metrics over time.

Examples of Student Work (With Permission)

- Showcases exceptional projects, research papers, or case studies that demonstrate deep engagement.

Student Engagement Strategies

- Describes how faculty foster interactive learning, classroom discussions, and real-world application of concepts.

Example: A professor tracks student participation in interactive simulations and problem-solving workshops, using feedback surveys to measure effectiveness.

4. Student Evaluations and Feedback

Summarized Student Evaluations (Quantitative and Qualitative)

- Documents trends in student satisfaction, course impact, and teaching effectiveness.
- **Example:** "Over the past three years, 92% of students reported that course concepts were effectively connected to industry applications." [182]

Mid-Semester Feedback and Adjustments

- Illustrates how faculty respond to student concerns and refine teaching strategies in real time.

Letters of Student Appreciation

- Optional section featuring emails or testimonials from students describing impactful learning experiences.

5. Peer Reviews and Teaching Observations

Faculty Peer Evaluations

- Summarizes observations from senior faculty, department chairs, or peer mentors.

Mentorship and Collaborative Teaching Initiatives

- Highlights engagement in faculty learning communities, interdisciplinary teaching, or co-teaching experiences.

Example: A professor includes peer review feedback from a faculty mentor who observed their lecture on case-based decision-making in strategic management.

6. Teaching Awards, Grants, and Professional Development

Recognition for Excellence in Teaching

- Includes teaching awards, institutional recognition, or student-nominated honors.

Grants for Pedagogical Research or Course Development

- Lists funding received for innovative teaching projects, instructional technology integration, or curriculum enhancements.

Professional Development Activities

- Participation in teaching workshops, higher education conferences, and industry certifications.

Example: A professor documents attendance at the AACSB Teaching & Learning Conference and subsequent implementation of new case-study approaches in business analytics courses.

7. Reflection and Future Teaching Goals

Self-Assessment of Teaching Growth

- A reflective narrative on lessons learned, challenges overcome, and areas for continued improvement.

Future Teaching Innovations and Pedagogical Goals

- Outlines planned teaching advancements, course enhancements, and new instructional strategies.

Example: A faculty member sets a goal to incorporate more experiential learning into online courses and tracks progress over two semesters.

Best Practices for Building and Maintaining a Strong Teaching Portfolio

Keep the Portfolio Dynamic and Continuously Updated

- Revisit and refine teaching materials, student feedback, and assessment data regularly.

Use a Digital or Web-Based Portfolio for Accessibility

- Consider hosting a teaching portfolio on a personal website, institutional repository, or professional e-portfolio platform.

Balance Reflection with Evidence

- Combine self-reflection with concrete data and artifacts to create a compelling teaching narrative.

Tailor the Portfolio for Specific Audiences

- Customize sections for promotion, tenure, grant applications, or institutional reviews.

Seek Feedback from Colleagues and Mentors

- Engage in peer review of teaching portfolios to refine clarity, structure, and presentation.

Overcoming Common Challenges in Teaching Portfolio Development

- Too Much or Too Little Information

- Solution: Focus on impact-driven content—highlight key accomplishments with supporting evidence rather than including every detail.

- Unclear Teaching Philosophy

- Solution: Articulate a concise, student-centered teaching statement grounded in pedagogical principles.

- Lack of Quantifiable Evidence

- Solution: Use assessment data, student learning outcomes, and engagement metrics to substantiate teaching effectiveness.

- Failure to Reflect on Growth and Future Goals

- Solution: Demonstrate evolution in teaching practices—how past experiences shape future instructional strategies.

Conclusion: Crafting a Compelling Teaching Portfolio for Academic Excellence

A strong teaching portfolio is more than just a record of past achievements—it is a living document that reflects an educator's philosophy, effectiveness, and commitment to student success. By integrating qualitative reflections with quantitative data, documenting student learning impact, and engaging in continuous pedagogical improvement, faculty can build a portfolio that not only supports promotion and professional advancement but also fosters ongoing self-reflection and instructional excellence.

Ultimately, a well-crafted teaching portfolio serves as both a personal roadmap for continuous growth and a professional testament to the transformative power of effective teaching in higher education.

Documenting Teaching Effectiveness: A Comprehensive Approach to Measuring and Showcasing Instructional Impact

Teaching effectiveness is a central pillar of faculty success, influencing student learning outcomes, institutional reputation, and professional advancement in higher education [183]. However, effective teaching is multifaceted and dynamic, encompassing not only course delivery and student engagement but also pedagogical innovation, assessment design, and contributions to curriculum development. Documenting teaching effectiveness is essential for faculty evaluations, tenure and promotion applications, accreditation reviews, and continuous instructional improvement.

For new college professors, developing a structured, evidence-based approach to measuring and documenting teaching effectiveness enables them to:
Reflect on and enhance their instructional methods
Provide concrete evidence of student success and engagement
Strengthen promotion and tenure applications
Demonstrate contributions to institutional goals and student development

This section explores key components of teaching effectiveness, data sources for documentation, and best practices for presenting evidence in a compelling and meaningful way.

Understanding Teaching Effectiveness in Higher Education

Teaching effectiveness extends beyond delivering lectures or grading assignments; it involves a comprehensive impact on student learning, curriculum innovation, and institutional service. Effective instructors:

Facilitate Active Learning

- Engage students through interactive discussions, problem-solving activities, and experiential learning experiences.

Cultivate Critical Thinking and Skill Development

- Encourage students to analyze, synthesize, and apply practical knowledge in real-world contexts.

Utilize Inclusive and Adaptive Teaching Strategies

- Design courses that accommodate diverse learning styles and accessibility needs.

Assess and Respond to Student Learning Needs

- Use formative and summative assessments to gauge progress and adapt instruction accordingly.

Engage in Pedagogical Innovation

- Incorporate new teaching technologies, flipped classrooms, and data-driven instructional strategies.

Contribute to Curriculum Development and Institutional Goals

- Collaborate on program improvements, accreditation efforts, and faculty mentoring.

Because teaching effectiveness is multidimensional, documentation must reflect both qualitative and quantitative evidence [184].

Sources of Evidence for Documenting Teaching Effectiveness

Faculty can document teaching effectiveness through three primary categories of evidence:

1. Direct Measures of Student Learning and Performance

Student Achievement Data

- Course completion rates, grade distributions, and student progression in subsequent courses.

Assessment Results and Learning Gains

- Comparison of pre- and post-course assessments to demonstrate knowledge acquisition.

Example: A faculty member tracks student performance on case-study analysis assignments over multiple semesters, demonstrating growth in critical thinking and applied problem-solving skills.

2. Student Feedback and Evaluations

Formal Student Course Evaluations

- Quantitative ratings and qualitative feedback on teaching clarity, engagement, and learning support.

Mid-Semester Feedback and Exit Surveys

- Customized surveys allowing students to provide specific feedback on instructional methods, course design, and content delivery.

Example: A professor includes data from end-of-semester evaluations showing consistent student satisfaction with instructional clarity and accessibility.

3. Peer and Administrative Evaluations

Faculty Peer Reviews

- Classroom observations conducted by colleagues or department chairs evaluating teaching style, student interaction, and content delivery.

Departmental or Institutional Teaching Awards

- Recognition of teaching excellence through faculty-nominated or student-selected awards.

Example: A faculty member documents a peer observation report highlighting innovative case-based teaching approaches in business analytics.

4. Teaching Artifacts and Instructional Contributions

Sample Course Materials and Syllabi

- Provides evidence of well-structured learning objectives, innovative teaching methods, and course alignment with institutional goals.

Innovative Teaching Strategies

- Documentation of blended learning techniques, flipped classrooms, gamification, or experiential learning initiatives.

Example: A professor includes a syllabus revision showing the integration of AI-driven analytics projects into a finance curriculum to enhance real-world application.

5. Evidence of Professional Development and Pedagogical Scholarship

Faculty Learning Communities and Professional Development Workshops

- Participation in teaching-focused seminars, learning communities, and pedagogical research initiatives.

Publications and Conference Presentations on Teaching Strategies

- Engagement in scholarship of teaching and learning (SoTL), demonstrating a commitment to research-based instructional improvement.

Example: A faculty member includes a published paper on best practices in active learning strategies and documentation of their presentation at a faculty workshop on curriculum innovation.

Best Practices for Presenting Teaching Effectiveness in a Compelling Manner

Effectively documenting teaching effectiveness requires a clear structure, relevant evidence, and a reflective narrative that illustrates professional growth.

1. Develop a Teaching Portfolio

Organize materials into a structured portfolio with:

- Teaching philosophy statement
- Sample syllabi and course materials
- Student evaluation summaries
- Peer review reports and observation feedback
- Assessment results and student learning data
- Professional development and scholarship contributions

Example: A faculty member maintains a digital teaching portfolio showcasing course redesign efforts, assessment improvements, and student feedback trends.

2. Use Quantitative and Qualitative Evidence Together

Combine numerical data with narrative insights to contextualize impact.
Example: Instead of just listing student evaluation scores, a professor analyzes trends over multiple semesters, identifying improvements and adjustments made in response to feedback.

3. Highlight Teaching Innovations and Adaptability

Demonstrate growth by documenting pedagogical experiments and refinements.
Example: A professor includes a before-and-after analysis of student performance following the introduction of flipped classroom techniques.

4. Showcase Institutional and Community Contributions

Demonstrate impact beyond the classroom by documenting participation in curriculum development, faculty mentoring, and service to the academic community.
Example: A faculty member includes evidence of leadership in an accreditation review process, detailing their role in assessing learning outcomes and refining program objectives.

Overcoming Challenges in Documenting Teaching Effectiveness

- **Challenge:** Difficulty Quantifying Teaching Impact
Solution: Use multiple forms of assessment and trend analysis to demonstrate long-term effectiveness.

- **Challenge:** Interpreting Mixed or Conflicting Student Evaluations
Solution: Provide a balanced reflection, acknowledging challenges and documenting efforts to address feedback.

- **Challenge:** Time Constraints in Data Collection
Solution: Maintain an ongoing teaching journal or digital repository to streamline documentation.

- **Challenge:** Resistance to Self-Assessment
 Solution: Engage in peer collaborations and faculty mentoring to gain objective insights into teaching growth.

Conclusion: Creating a Meaningful Record of Teaching Excellence

Documenting teaching effectiveness is not just an administrative task—it is a valuable tool for self-reflection, professional growth, and instructional innovation. By gathering a diverse range of evidence, integrating qualitative and quantitative insights, and demonstrating a commitment to continuous improvement, faculty can create a compelling, evidence-based record of their impact on student learning and academic success.

Ultimately, a well-documented teaching journey strengthens faculty credibility, informs professional development, and enhances the broader mission of excellence in higher education.

Leadership Opportunities Within Academia: Pathways for Faculty Growth and Institutional Impact

Leadership in academia extends far beyond administrative roles—it encompasses mentorship, curricular development, faculty governance, and institutional innovation. Faculty members at all career stages can engage in leadership, whether through departmental service, program development, research initiatives, or academic policy-making. Leadership in higher education is not about hierarchy but about influencing positive change, fostering collaboration, and advancing institutional excellence.

For new college professors, understanding leadership pathways, identifying areas of influence, and cultivating essential leadership skills can lead to professional growth, career advancement, and meaningful contributions to the academic community. Leadership is not reserved for deans and department chairs; it exists in committee work, faculty mentoring, curriculum innovation, student advocacy, and pedagogical research.

This section explores key leadership roles in academia, strategies for developing leadership skills, and the impact of faculty leadership on institutional success.

The Importance of Leadership in Higher Education

Shaping Institutional Policies and Academic Programs

- Faculty leaders contribute to curriculum reform, accreditation processes, and strategic planning initiatives.

Enhancing Student Learning and Success

- Leadership in mentoring, student advising, and academic support initiatives directly impacts student retention and achievement.

Fostering Faculty Development and Collegial Collaboration

- Academic leadership plays a key role in mentoring junior faculty, supporting interdisciplinary collaboration, and driving research initiatives.

Advocating for Institutional and Disciplinary Advancements

- Faculty leaders engage in higher education advocacy, accreditation processes, and professional organizations to influence broader academic trends.

Encouraging Diversity, Equity, and Inclusion (DEI) Initiatives

- Leadership in academia is essential for promoting inclusive teaching practices, equitable hiring policies, and student success initiatives.

By embracing leadership opportunities, faculty contribute not only to their own career progression but also to the broader mission of higher education as a transformative force.

Types of Leadership Roles Within Academia

Leadership opportunities in academia can be categorized into formal administrative roles, faculty governance positions, and informal leadership in research, teaching, and mentorship.

1. Formal Administrative Leadership Roles

Faculty who transition into administrative roles take on institutional responsibilities, strategic planning, and decision-making.

Department Chair/Program Director

- Oversees curriculum development, faculty hiring, course scheduling, and departmental governance.

Dean/Associate Dean

- Provides academic leadership at the college or school level, overseeing faculty, budgets, and institutional policies.

Provost/Vice President of Academic Affairs

- Directs institution-wide academic strategy, accreditation, and faculty development initiatives.

Example: A faculty member with a strong track record in curriculum innovation and student engagement may be appointed Department Chair, leading efforts to redesign programs and enhance faculty collaboration.

2. Faculty Governance and Committee Leadership

Many leadership opportunities exist within faculty-led governance structures, shaping academic policies and institutional priorities.

Faculty Senate Membership

- Engages in institutional decision-making, policy development, and faculty advocacy.

Curriculum Committee Leadership

- Oversees course approvals, program reviews, and learning outcome assessments.

Academic Conduct and Integrity Committees

- Ensures ethical standards, academic honesty policies, and student disciplinary procedures.

Promotion and Tenure Committees

- Evaluates faculty teaching effectiveness, research contributions, and service for career advancement decisions.

Example: A faculty member serving on the Faculty Senate helps develop new policies for hybrid learning, ensuring alignment with student needs and accreditation requirements.

3. Research and Scholarly Leadership

Leadership in research involves mentoring student researchers, securing grants, and directing interdisciplinary initiatives.

Principal Investigator (PI) on Research Grants

- Leads funded research projects, oversees research teams, and disseminates findings through publications and conferences.

Director of Research Centers or Institutes

- Establishes collaborative research initiatives, interdisciplinary partnerships, and institutional research priorities.

Editorial Board Membership and Peer Review Leadership

- Serves as an editor or peer reviewer for academic journals, shaping the discourse in a discipline.

Example: A professor leading a cybersecurity research initiative secures external funding, mentoring graduate students and faculty collaborators.

4. Leadership in Teaching and Curriculum Innovation

Faculty can lead in academic excellence by advancing pedagogical innovations, designing new programs, and mentoring educators.

Faculty Mentor or Teaching Coach

- Supports new faculty members and adjunct instructors in developing effective teaching strategies.

Director of Teaching and Learning Centers (TLCs)

- Leads faculty development workshops on active learning, assessment strategies, and technology integration.

Course Coordinator or Program Lead

- Oversees multi-section courses, ensures instructional consistency, and evaluates teaching effectiveness.

Example: A faculty member who develops a new competency-based assessment model for business students is invited to lead a faculty training workshop on innovative assessment techniques.

5. Student-Focused Leadership and Mentorship

Faculty who take leadership roles in student development contribute to mentorship, career readiness, and co-curricular learning opportunities.

Faculty Advisor for Student Organizations

- Provides guidance for student clubs, professional associations, and academic honor societies.

Director of Undergraduate/Graduate Research Initiatives

- Leads student research conferences, innovation labs, and mentoring programs.

Academic Advisor or Career Development Liaison

- Supports students in course selection, research opportunities, and professional pathways.

Example: A professor who advises a Data Science student club facilitates networking events, industry partnerships, and student research presentations.

Strategies for Developing Leadership Skills in Academia

1. Engage in Faculty Development Programs

Attend Leadership Training Workshops

- Many institutions offer faculty leadership academies focusing on academic administration, conflict resolution, and strategic planning.

Example: A faculty member participates in a Higher Education Leadership Institute, developing skills in budget management, accreditation, and faculty engagement.

2. Seek Mentorship and Networking Opportunities

Learn from Experienced Faculty Leaders

- Shadow a department chair, senior faculty mentor, or research director to understand academic leadership dynamics.

Example: A faculty member partners with an Associate Dean to gain insights into strategic curriculum planning.

3. Contribute to Institutional Initiatives

Take on Small Leadership Roles First

- Serve on committees, lead faculty learning communities, or coordinate academic events before pursuing formal administrative roles.

Example: A faculty member begins by chairing a curriculum revision subcommittee, later moving into a department chair role.

4. Pursue Cross-Disciplinary Collaboration

Lead Interdisciplinary Projects and Partnerships

- Engage in multi-departmental research, faculty workshops, and cross-disciplinary program development.

Example: A faculty member in cybersecurity collaborates with the business school to design a fintech security course, demonstrating cross-disciplinary leadership.

Conclusion: Cultivating Leadership for Institutional and Professional Growth

Leadership within academia is not limited to administrative roles—it is about influencing change, fostering collaboration, and advancing the educational mission. By embracing leadership in faculty governance, research, curriculum innovation, and student mentorship, faculty members enhance their professional impact while contributing to institutional success.

For new college professors, developing leadership skills through mentorship, faculty engagement, and institutional service can lead to career advancement, meaningful contributions, and greater influence in shaping higher education. Ultimately, academic leadership is about building a culture of excellence, mentorship, and lifelong learning—creating a legacy, extending into the broader academic community.

Networking and Professional Development for Faculty: Expanding Influence, Knowledge, and Career Growth

In academia, professional success is not solely determined by teaching effectiveness, research output, or administrative contributions—it is also shaped by meaningful professional connections and ongoing development. Faculty members who actively engage in networking and professional growth opportunities gain access to new research collaborations, funding opportunities, leadership roles, and pedagogical advancements.

For new college professors, establishing a strong professional network and engaging in continuous development are essential strategies for:
Enhancing teaching and research effectiveness
Building interdisciplinary collaborations and academic partnerships
Navigating career advancement opportunities

Staying informed about emerging trends in higher education
Gaining visibility in academic and industry circles

Networking and professional development are not passive processes—they require intentional engagement, strategic participation, and a commitment to lifelong learning. This section explores key networking strategies, faculty development opportunities, and best practices for maximizing professional impact.

The Value of Networking in Academia

Networking in academia serves multiple functions beyond simple career advancement [185]. It fosters:

Collaborative Research and Scholarship

- Expands opportunities for multi-institutional and interdisciplinary research collaborations [185]

Knowledge Exchange and Best Practices Sharing

- Allows faculty to learn from colleagues' teaching innovations, research methodologies, and assessment techniques [185].

Institutional Influence and Policy Advocacy

- Faculty with strong networks contribute to academic governance, policy development, and institutional decision-making [185].

Career Advancement and Mentorship

- Relationships with senior faculty and academic leaders open doors to tenure-track positions, grants, and administrative roles [185].

Access to External Funding and Grant Opportunities

- Strong networks provide insights into funding sources, industry partnerships, and collaborative grant proposals [185].

Industry and Community Engagement

- Faculty benefit from networking with industry professionals, policymakers, and community organizations to bridge academic and real-world applications [185].

By developing a broad, multidisciplinary network, faculty enhance both their professional trajectory and the overall academic community [185].

Key Networking Strategies for Faculty

Networking requires strategic engagement across academic, institutional, and industry landscapes.

1. Institutional and Departmental Networking

Engage in Faculty Learning Communities (FLCs)

- Join interdisciplinary discussion groups focused on pedagogical research, curriculum development, or leadership training.

Participate in Faculty Governance and Committees

- Contribute to curriculum development, faculty hiring, and accreditation processes to build internal institutional influence.

Seek Mentorship from Senior Faculty

- Develop relationships with experienced professors, department chairs, and administrators for guidance on career advancement and tenure expectations.

Example: A new faculty member attends faculty senate meetings and joins a curriculum review committee, gaining visibility and influence in institutional decision-making.

2. Conferences, Workshops, and Academic Associations

Attend and Present at Academic Conferences

- Engage with leading scholars, share research, and discover emerging trends in one's field.

Join Professional Associations

- Membership in disciplinary organizations (e.g., AACSB for business faculty, IEEE for technology educators, or MLA for humanities scholars) provides networking, grant opportunities, and access **to industry research**.

Participate in Leadership and Teaching Workshops

- Engage in pedagogical development sessions to refine teaching methods and integrate innovative instructional practices.

Example: A faculty member attends the Lilly Conference on Teaching & Learning, learning new techniques in active learning strategies while connecting with educators from diverse institutions.

3. Digital and Online Academic Networking

Utilize Professional Networking Platforms (LinkedIn, ResearchGate, Academia.edu)

- Share research publications, teaching innovations, and grant opportunities with global academic peers.

Engage in Online Faculty Forums and Webinars

- Platforms like Inside Higher Ed, The Chronicle of Higher Education, and Twitter/X academic threads provide real-time discussions on higher education policies and instructional trends.

Develop an Online Scholarly Presence

- Maintaining a personal academic website or blog showcases research projects, publications, and teaching philosophies to broaden professional visibility.

Example: A faculty member creates a digital portfolio showcasing research and teaching methodologies, leading to invites for guest lectures and panel discussions.

4. Cross-Disciplinary and Industry Networking

Engage in Interdisciplinary Research Collaborations

- Partner with faculty from other disciplines to explore emerging research areas and grant opportunities.

Collaborate with Industry Leaders and Community Organizations

- Strengthen applied learning initiatives, corporate partnerships, and real-world research applications.

Join Advisory Boards or Professional Panels

- Serving on corporate or nonprofit advisory boards positions faculty as thought leaders bridging academia and industry.

Example: A professor in cybersecurity partners with business faculty to develop a fintech security certification program, integrating industry expertise and academic rigor.

Faculty Professional Development Opportunities

1. Teaching and Pedagogical Development

Attend Workshops on Innovative Teaching Methods

- Explore flipped classrooms, AI-assisted instruction, and competency-based assessments.

Enroll in Faculty Development Programs

- Institutions often **offer formal training in instructional design, technology integration, and diversity, equity, and inclusion (DEI) initiatives**.

Example: A faculty member completes a certification in Universal Design for Learning (UDL) to enhance inclusive teaching strategies.

2. Research and Scholarly Growth

Seek Internal and External Research Grants

- Engage with university-sponsored research initiatives and external funding agencies.

Publish in Peer-Reviewed Journals and Present at Conferences

- Developing a strong publication record enhances tenure applications and professional reputation.

Example: A faculty member secures a National Science Foundation (NSF) grant for research on AI ethics in higher education, expanding their academic impact.

3. Leadership and Administrative Development

Participate in Academic Leadership Training

- Programs such as the American Council on Education (ACE) Fellows Program prepare faculty for department chair, dean, and provost positions.

Engage in Institutional Strategic Initiatives

- Leading accreditation efforts, faculty mentorship programs, or community engagement initiatives fosters institutional impact and career advancement.

Example: A faculty member leads a committee on hybrid learning policies, positioning themselves for a future role as an Associate Dean.

Best Practices for Maximizing Networking and Development Opportunities

Be Proactive and Intentional

- Schedule regular professional development activities and actively seek networking opportunities.

Follow Up and Maintain Relationships

- After conferences, connect with colleagues via email or LinkedIn, fostering long-term collaborations.

Diversify Networking Engagement

- Engage in both academic and industry connections to expand professional opportunities.

Set Professional Development Goals

- Establish annual goals for conference participation, leadership engagement, and research dissemination.

Example: A professor sets a goal to publish two articles per year, present at one conference, and mentor at least one junior faculty member.

Faculty Leadership and Institutional Change

Faculty leadership is central to sustaining continuous improvement in higher education. While administrators set institutional policies and allocate resources, it is faculty who define the academic experience through curriculum design, pedagogy, scholarship, and mentorship. Effective faculty leaders go beyond excellence in their own classrooms; they act as change agents, guiding colleagues, shaping institutional practices, and fostering a culture where teaching is valued alongside research and service. This requires skills in change management—building consensus, navigating institutional politics, addressing resistance, and ensuring that improvements are not short-lived but embedded in institutional culture.

Leading Curriculum Reform Initiatives

Curriculum reform represents one of the most visible and impactful avenues of faculty leadership. Because curricula define what students learn, how they progress, and how programs align with external standards, reform efforts demand faculty insight and leadership at every stage [186].

- **Needs Assessment**
  Successful curriculum reform begins with identifying where change is needed.
    - Faculty leaders analyze student outcomes data (e.g., graduation rates, retention rates, course pass rates) to identify performance gaps.
    - Program reviews, accreditation reports, and employer feedback highlight areas where curricula may no longer align with professional or societal needs.
    - Comparative benchmarking against peer institutions helps identify missing components or innovative practices worth adopting.

    This diagnostic stage ensures that reform is evidence-driven rather than reactive.
- **Inclusive Design**
  Faculty-led reform must engage a wide range of stakeholders to ensure legitimacy and relevance.
    - **Faculty Across Ranks**: Including adjuncts, early-career faculty, and senior professors ensures multiple perspectives.
    - **Students**: Focus groups and surveys provide insight into lived experiences, course sequencing challenges, and unmet learning needs.
    - **Employers and Alumni**: These stakeholders highlight skills and competencies graduates need to thrive in the workforce.
    - **Interdisciplinary Voices**: Involving faculty from multiple departments ensures curricula reflect the realities of complex, cross-disciplinary challenges.

    Inclusive design builds broad ownership, making adoption smoother and more credible.
- **Implementation Strategy**
  Reform requires careful planning to avoid disruption and ensure faculty adoption.
    - **Course Redesign**: Leaders coordinate updates to learning outcomes, assignments, and assessment tools.
    - **Sequencing Adjustments**: Prerequisites and course pathways are mapped to ensure logical skill development.
    - **Faculty Development**: Training sessions help instructors adopt new pedagogical strategies aligned with revised curricula.
    - **Communication Plans**: Clear timelines and regular updates reduce confusion and resistance.

    Effective implementation balances ambition with practicality, ensuring reform does not overwhelm faculty or students.

- **Sustainability**
  Reform is not a one-time achievement but an ongoing process of renewal.
    - **Review Cycles**: Curricula should be revisited on a set schedule (e.g., every five years) to remain aligned with disciplinary advances and workforce demands.
    - **Feedback Mechanisms**: Regular student and employer feedback should inform adjustments.
    - **Scalability**: Leaders should design reforms that can evolve, such as integrating new technologies, embedding experiential learning, or adapting to accreditation changes.
    - **Institutionalization**: Reforms must be codified in departmental policies and program requirements so they endure beyond individual faculty leaders.

Key Takeaway

Curriculum reform is where faculty leadership is most visible and consequential. Through evidence-based needs assessment, inclusive design, strategic implementation, and ongoing review, faculty leaders ensure that curricula are not static but responsive to disciplinary advances, workforce needs, and societal change. By guiding reform, faculty establish themselves as institutional stewards of academic quality and innovation, positioning teaching and learning as central to the mission of higher education.

Building Consensus Among Faculty Peers

In higher education, shared governance is the foundation of decision-making. Unlike corporate or hierarchical models where leaders can enforce top-down directives, academic institutions rely on faculty input and collective approval for meaningful, lasting change. Whether the initiative involves curriculum reform, assessment practices, or pedagogical innovation, no change can succeed—or endure—without broad faculty support. Building consensus is therefore a critical leadership skill that requires dialogue, transparency, and shared ownership [187].

Collaborative Dialogue

Consensus begins with genuine opportunities for colleagues to voice concerns, contribute ideas, and shape outcomes.

- **Open Forums**: Faculty leaders can organize town halls, departmental retreats, or small-group meetings where colleagues discuss proposed initiatives in an inclusive setting.
- **Active Listening**: Leaders must demonstrate they are not simply presenting pre-determined plans but are open to adjusting based on feedback.
- **Safe Environment**: Creating spaces where dissent is welcomed rather than punished builds trust and reduces underground resistance.
- **Iterative Process**: Dialogue should be ongoing, not one-time; faculty buy-in grows when they see their input integrated into subsequent drafts of proposals.

Transparency

Faculty respect leaders who are honest about goals, processes, and trade-offs.

- **Clear Rationale**: Leaders should explain not just what changes are proposed, but why—linking initiatives to student learning, accreditation requirements, or institutional mission.
- **Process Mapping**: Outlining the steps in decision-making (committee reviews, faculty votes, administrative approvals) makes the pathway visible and predictable.
- **Trade-Offs and Constraints**: Leaders build credibility when they acknowledge limitations (e.g., budget restrictions, accreditation mandates) rather than overselling benefits.
- **Documentation**: Providing written summaries of meetings, proposals, and feedback loops ensures transparency and prevents miscommunication.

Shared Ownership

Successful faculty leaders frame initiatives as collective projects rather than personal agendas.

- **Collaborative Language**: Use "we" and "our" when framing goals, signaling that reforms belong to the faculty body, not to an individual or administrative office.
- **Distributed Leadership**: Invite colleagues to co-chair committees, lead subprojects, or present progress reports. Involvement deepens investment.
- **Recognition of Contributions**: Acknowledging faculty who contribute ideas or lead components of reform fosters goodwill and encourages wider participation.
- **Flexibility in Design**: Allowing for departmental or disciplinary variation within broader reform frameworks prevents feelings of imposed uniformity.

Transforming Resistance into Engagement

Consensus-building is not simply about eliminating resistance but about harnessing it productively.

- Resistance often reveals valid concerns about workload, academic freedom, or unintended consequences. By addressing these concerns transparently, leaders improve the quality of reforms.
- When faculty see their ideas reflected in the final product, skepticism turns into ownership.
- Broad engagement ensures reforms are resilient, surviving leadership transitions and enduring beyond the influence of individual champions.

Key Takeaway

Building consensus among faculty peers requires more than persuading colleagues—it requires collaborative dialogue, transparent communication, and shared ownership. Faculty leaders who cultivate inclusive, open processes transform potential resistance into active engagement, ensuring that reforms are not only adopted but sustained as part of the institutional fabric.

Navigating Institutional Politics and Hierarchies

Faculty leadership does not occur in a vacuum. Every initiative unfolds within the complex political and hierarchical structures of higher education institutions. Understanding how decisions are made, who influences them, and how to align reform efforts with institutional priorities is essential for faculty leaders who want to effect change. Successful navigation of politics and hierarchies requires not manipulation but strategic awareness, relationship-building, and principled diplomacy—anchored always in the mission of advancing student learning.

Understanding Governance Systems

Change in higher education follows established pathways, and faculty leaders must understand these systems to avoid unnecessary delays or resistance [188].

- **Formal Structures**: Proposals often move through faculty senates, curriculum committees, department councils, provost offices, and finally boards of trustees. Leaders must know which body has the authority to approve which type of change.
- **Timing**: Governance calendars matter—curricular reforms may only be reviewed at certain times of the year, making strategic planning crucial.
- **Accreditation and Policy Constraints**: Some initiatives must also align with external accreditation requirements or state-level regulations.
- **Informal Influences**: Beyond formal processes, informal networks (e.g., influential senior faculty, respected committee chairs) can shape outcomes significantly.

Strategic Alliances

No faculty leader can drive reform alone. Building alliances within the institutional hierarchy amplifies influence.

- **Department Chairs and Program Directors**: They are often the first gatekeepers and can either champion or block initiatives. Early collaboration with them ensures smoother progress.
- **Deans and Associate Deans**: Faculty leaders should align reforms with college-level priorities to secure administrative support and resources.
- **Provosts and Vice Presidents**: High-level administrators respond to initiatives that clearly support the institution's strategic plan or enhance accreditation compliance.
- **Coalitions Across Departments**: Broad coalitions prevent reforms from being dismissed as "niche" or "departmental" concerns.

Diplomacy

Institutional change often involves negotiation, compromise, and balancing diverse interests.

- **Balancing Stakeholder Interests**: Leaders must weigh the concerns of faculty autonomy, administrative efficiency, student needs, and budgetary constraints.

- **Compromise Without Capitulation**: Effective leaders find middle ground where possible while keeping essential student-focused goals intact.
- **Communication Style**: Diplomatic leaders frame reforms in language that resonates with each audience—using learning outcomes for faculty peers, accreditation standards for administrators, and student success metrics for trustees.
- **Conflict Resolution**: Leaders should anticipate points of resistance and prepare respectful, evidence-based responses.

Credibility

Faculty leaders gain influence not through titles alone but through earned credibility.

- **Competence**: Demonstrating deep knowledge of teaching, scholarship, and governance builds respect.
- **Fairness**: Leaders who consider multiple viewpoints and avoid favoritism are more likely to gain trust.
- **Integrity**: Commitment to student learning and institutional mission, rather than personal advancement, establishes legitimacy.
- **Consistency**: Leaders who follow through on promises and communicate transparently maintain credibility even when initiatives face setbacks.

Key Takeaway

Navigating institutional politics and hierarchies is an essential skill for faculty leaders. By understanding governance systems, building strategic alliances, practicing diplomacy, and maintaining credibility, leaders can move initiatives through complex structures without losing focus on student learning and institutional mission. This strategic navigation ensures that reforms are not only proposed but successfully implemented and sustained.

Managing Resistance to Pedagogical Innovation

Introducing new teaching practices—whether active learning, flipped classrooms, technology integration, or competency-based assessments—can provoke strong resistance among faculty. This resistance is rarely irrational; it is often rooted in legitimate concerns about tradition, academic freedom, workload, or skepticism about effectiveness [189]. Faculty leaders must recognize that resistance is part of the change process and can even be productive if managed well. Effective leadership requires listening, evidence, incremental implementation, and robust support systems to transform skeptics into gradual adopters.

Listening First

Before proposing solutions, leaders must understand the roots of resistance.

- **Philosophical Concerns**: Some faculty resist innovations they perceive as fads or as threats to disciplinary traditions and academic freedom.

- **Practical Barriers**: Others worry about time demands, lack of training, or inadequate classroom infrastructure.
- **Cultural Context**: Resistance may also stem from negative past experiences with top-down mandates or poorly supported initiatives.
- **Respectful Engagement**: By inviting dissenting voices into early conversations, leaders show respect for concerns and can identify barriers that need to be addressed.

Pilot Programs

Small-scale, low-risk trials help reduce fear of the unknown and demonstrate feasibility.

- **Proof of Concept**: Pilots allow faculty to test innovations in one class or module before committing to wider implementation.
- **Data Collection**: Leaders can gather evidence of student outcomes, engagement, or satisfaction from pilot efforts.
- **Iterative Refinement**: Feedback from early adopters and students informs adjustments before broader rollout.
- **Modeling Success**: Showcasing positive pilot results provides credibility and encourages cautious colleagues to try new methods.

Evidence-Based Advocacy

Data is often more persuasive than abstract claims.

- **Student Outcomes**: Share quantitative improvements such as higher exam scores, improved retention, or reduced achievement gaps.
- **Qualitative Feedback**: Highlight student testimonials about increased engagement or confidence in learning.
- **Peer-Reviewed Research**: Cite studies from the scholarship of teaching and learning (SoTL) that validate the effectiveness of proposed practices.
- **Comparative Examples**: Show how similar institutions successfully implemented innovations, reducing perceptions of risk.
  Grounding advocacy in evidence shifts discussions from personal preference to measurable impact.

Support Structures

Even when faculty are open to change, inadequate support can derail innovation.

- **Professional Development**: Offer workshops, peer mentoring, and ongoing consultations to build confidence.
- **Workload Adjustments**: Recognize the additional time required to redesign courses or learn new tools, and provide course releases or stipends where possible.
- **Infrastructure**: Ensure that classrooms, labs, or online platforms can actually support the new methods.

- **Peer Networks**: Encourage teaching circles or faculty learning communities to provide collegial support during transitions.
Support structures make innovation feel like a shared institutional investment rather than an individual burden.

Key Takeaway

Managing resistance to pedagogical innovation requires patience, persistence, and empathy. By listening to concerns, piloting initiatives, using evidence-based advocacy, and providing strong support systems, faculty leaders can gradually transform resistance into cautious adoption. Over time, innovation becomes normalized, skepticism diminishes, and institutions develop a culture where experimentation and continuous improvement are expected rather than feared.

Advocating for Teaching Resources and Support

Strong pedagogy does not happen in a vacuum—it requires investment in people, tools, and infrastructure. Faculty leaders are uniquely positioned to identify needs, articulate their importance, and advocate for institutional and external support. Unlike administrators, who may view teaching primarily through a budgetary lens, faculty leaders connect resources directly to the lived realities of classroom instruction. Effective advocacy ensures that teaching excellence is recognized as a priority equal to research and service, and that resources are distributed fairly across the institution.

Identifying Needs

The first step in advocacy is clarifying what is required to support effective teaching.

- **Instructional Support**: This may include teaching assistants, graders, or instructional designers who reduce workload and improve quality.
- **Technology and Infrastructure**: Faculty leaders can articulate needs such as updated classroom technology, accessible learning management systems, or flexible spaces that support active learning.
- **Professional Development**: Resources may include funding for conferences, workshops, or faculty learning communities that enhance teaching practice.
- **Student Support Services**: Effective teaching is bolstered by tutoring centers, writing labs, and supplemental instruction programs that faculty can advocate to expand.
Clear articulation of needs ensures that advocacy is grounded in specific, actionable requests rather than vague appeals.

Making the Case

Effective advocacy requires translating teaching needs into terms that resonate with institutional priorities.

- **Student Success**: Frame requests in terms of improved retention, graduation rates, and equity in outcomes.

- **Accreditation Standards**: Highlight how resources address requirements for assessment, learning outcomes, or faculty qualifications.
- **Institutional Reputation**: Connect strong pedagogy to rankings, student recruitment, and alumni satisfaction, all of which affect long-term viability.
- **Cost-Benefit Framing**: Show how investments in teaching yield measurable returns, such as reduced attrition saving tuition revenue.
  By aligning teaching needs with institutional goals, faculty leaders strengthen their case for resource allocation.

Leveraging External Funding

Faculty leaders can expand resources by integrating teaching into external funding opportunities.

- **Grant Proposals**: Many research grants allow for "broader impacts" sections that include undergraduate or graduate teaching components.
- **Teaching Innovation Funds**: Leaders can pursue grants specifically designed for pedagogy, technology integration, or curriculum reform.
- **Industry Partnerships**: Collaborations with employers may generate funding for experiential learning, labs, or co-curricular programs.
- **Philanthropy**: Endowed chairs, faculty fellowships, and donor-supported teaching initiatives can provide long-term support.
  Leveraging external funding relieves institutional budgets while still securing resources for teaching.

Ensuring Equity

Resource allocation must be fair, transparent, and responsive to the full range of academic programs.

- **Departmental Balance**: High-demand programs often receive disproportionate attention; leaders must advocate for smaller departments to avoid neglect.
- **Faculty Rank**: Adjunct and early-career faculty often have fewer resources but carry significant teaching loads; equity requires addressing these gaps.
- **Student Demographics**: Resources should support programs serving underrepresented or high-need student populations, ensuring access and fairness.
- **Transparency**: Clear criteria for resource distribution reduce perceptions of favoritism and build institutional trust.
  Equity in advocacy ensures that resources strengthen the whole institution rather than concentrating benefits narrowly.

Key Takeaway

Advocating for teaching resources requires clear identification of needs, strategic framing, pursuit of external funding, and commitment to equity. Faculty leaders who master these skills secure the tools, support, and infrastructure necessary for effective instruction while ensuring that resources are distributed fairly. In doing so, they elevate teaching to its rightful place as a core institutional priority and a driver of student success.

Mentoring Junior Faculty in Teaching Excellence

Developing the next generation of faculty leaders requires more than hiring talented scholars—it requires intentional mentorship in teaching excellence. While new faculty often arrive well-prepared in research, many have had limited formal preparation in pedagogy [190]. Mentorship fills this gap by helping junior faculty acclimate to institutional culture, refine their teaching practices, and understand how teaching contributes to long-term career success. Strong mentorship ensures that teaching quality does not depend on trial and error but develops through guided support and reflection.

Orientation and Onboarding

The first months of a faculty member's appointment are critical to establishing effective teaching habits.

- **Institutional Culture**: Senior faculty can explain the institution's mission, student demographics, and distinctive pedagogical values (e.g., liberal arts focus, applied learning orientation).
- **Teaching Expectations**: Mentors help clarify workload norms, assessment standards, use of technology, and policies for academic integrity or accessibility.
- **Available Resources**: Junior faculty often underutilize teaching centers, library services, or instructional design teams. Mentors can guide them toward these supports early. Effective onboarding prevents common pitfalls and accelerates a new faculty member's confidence in the classroom.

Ongoing Support

Mentorship should not end after orientation; it must evolve into regular, constructive engagement.

- **Classroom Observation**: Mentors can attend classes not as evaluators but as coaches, offering targeted feedback on clarity, pacing, or engagement strategies.
- **Syllabus and Assignment Review**: Reviewing course materials together helps mentees align learning outcomes with activities and assessments.
- **Regular Check-Ins**: Scheduled meetings allow mentees to ask questions about grading policies, managing student concerns, or adjusting pedagogy mid-semester.
- **Resource Sharing**: Mentors can provide sample syllabi, assignments, and rubrics to model best practices.
  This ongoing support reduces isolation and creates a reliable feedback loop for teaching improvement.

Modeling Excellence

Mentors influence mentees not only through advice but also through demonstration of effective practice.

- **Transparency in Practice**: Inviting mentees to observe their classes allows mentors to model active learning, inclusive pedagogy, or innovative assessment strategies.
- **Reflective Dialogue**: After observations, mentors explain the rationale behind choices, showing that good teaching is intentional rather than accidental.
- **Encouraging Experimentation**: By modeling both successes and challenges, senior faculty normalize the idea that teaching improvement involves risk-taking and iteration. This modeling inspires junior faculty to develop their own authentic teaching style grounded in evidence-based practice.

Career Advancement

Teaching mentorship must also prepare junior faculty to integrate pedagogy into their professional trajectory.

- **Promotion and Tenure**: Mentors clarify how teaching excellence is documented and evaluated in review processes, such as through peer reviews, student evaluations, or teaching portfolios.
- **Professional Recognition**: Junior faculty should be encouraged to apply for teaching awards, fellowships, or pedagogical grants.
- **Scholarship of Teaching and Learning (SoTL)**: Mentors can introduce mentees to opportunities for publishing or presenting on innovative teaching practices.
- **Balanced Identity**: Mentorship helps junior faculty see teaching not as competing with research but as an integral part of academic identity and leadership.

Key Takeaway

Mentoring junior faculty in teaching excellence requires structured onboarding, sustained support, authentic modeling, and guidance for career advancement. Faculty leaders who invest in mentorship ensure that new colleagues not only survive the early years of teaching but thrive as innovative, reflective educators. This process builds institutional continuity, strengthens teaching culture, and develops future leaders who will carry forward a commitment to continuous improvement in higher education.

Contributing to Institutional Teaching Culture

Faculty leaders play a pivotal role in shaping the teaching culture of their institutions. While individual teaching excellence is important, sustainable improvement emerges only when teaching is valued collectively, supported systematically, and embedded in the institution's identity. Faculty leadership ensures that teaching is not treated as a private activity but as a shared professional practice aligned with institutional mission and societal responsibility. By advocating for recognition, fostering collaboration, articulating a long-term vision, and championing cultural shifts, faculty leaders create environments where continuous teaching improvement becomes the norm rather than the exception.

Recognition Systems

Elevating the status of teaching requires visible acknowledgment of its value.

- **Teaching Awards**: Faculty leaders can advocate for institutional awards that recognize innovation, inclusivity, mentorship, or excellence in pedagogy.
- **Promotion and Tenure Criteria**: Leaders can push for teaching effectiveness—documented through peer reviews, student outcomes, and teaching portfolios—to carry weight equal to research in advancement decisions.
- **Public Acknowledgment**: Highlighting teaching achievements in newsletters, convocation ceremonies, or faculty meetings signals institutional commitment.
- **Equity in Recognition**: Recognition should extend across faculty ranks, including adjuncts and lecturers who often carry heavy teaching loads.
Such systems legitimize teaching as a core scholarly activity and motivate faculty to continually refine their practice.

Community-Building

Culture thrives when faculty engage in shared spaces for reflection, experimentation, and collaboration.

- **Teaching Circles and Learning Communities**: Small groups provide forums for sharing strategies, discussing challenges, and building peer support networks.
- **Innovation Labs**: Dedicated centers or initiatives can bring faculty together to experiment with new pedagogical technologies or active learning approaches.
- **Collaborative Projects**: Joint curriculum design, co-teaching initiatives, and interdisciplinary workshops foster relationships that strengthen the teaching culture.
- **Inclusive Participation**: Faculty leaders should ensure that these communities are accessible to all ranks and disciplines, reinforcing a culture of openness and shared ownership.
Community-building shifts the perception of teaching from isolated effort to collective enterprise.

Long-Term Vision

Faculty leaders must link teaching to the broader mission of the institution and the evolving needs of students and society.

- **Mission Alignment**: Effective teaching strategies should reflect the institution's identity, whether focused on liberal arts, professional preparation, or research.
- **Student Demographics**: Leaders must account for the needs of diverse learners, including first-generation students, adult learners, and international populations.
- **Societal Needs**: Curricula and pedagogy should prepare students for global citizenship, ethical leadership, and workforce demands in rapidly changing industries.
- **Forward-Looking Planning**: Visionary leaders anticipate challenges such as technological disruption, demographic shifts, and new accreditation pressures,

embedding teaching into strategic institutional planning.
By articulating a long-term vision, faculty leaders position teaching as central to institutional resilience and relevance.

Cultural Shift

Sustained change requires shifting institutional values so that teaching excellence is expected, celebrated, and continuously improved.

- **Championing Teaching**: Faculty leaders set the tone by modeling excellence and advocating for teaching in decision-making forums.
- **Embedding Continuous Improvement**: Regular assessment, peer review, and faculty development ensure that teaching evolves in response to evidence and feedback.
- **Balancing Teaching and Research**: Leaders promote a culture where teaching is recognized as complementary to scholarship, not secondary to it.
- **Celebrating Diversity in Pedagogy**: Recognizing that there are multiple valid ways to teach fosters inclusivity and innovation.
When teaching is championed as central to academic life, institutions become learning organizations, adaptable to change and committed to student success.

Key Takeaway

Faculty leaders influence institutional teaching culture by advocating for recognition systems, building collaborative communities, articulating long-term visions, and driving cultural shifts. Their leadership ensures that teaching is valued as much as research, embedded in institutional identity, and continuously improved. By shaping culture, faculty leaders secure the foundation for lasting institutional change—adaptive, inclusive, and committed to preparing students for an evolving global landscape.

Conclusion: Lifelong Networking and Professional Growth in Academia

Networking and professional development are not one-time events but continuous processes that enhance faculty influence, career advancement, and institutional contributions. By strategically engaging in faculty communities, interdisciplinary collaborations, teaching workshops, and leadership initiatives, professors expand their impact beyond the classroom and into the broader academic landscape.

For new college professors, building a strong professional network and actively pursuing professional growth ensures long-term success in teaching, research, and leadership. Ultimately, faculty who invest in continuous learning and meaningful professional connections remain adaptable, innovative, and highly influential in shaping the future of higher education.

A Commitment to Lifelong Learning and Excellence

Continuous improvement in higher education is not just a professional responsibility—it is a fundamental pillar of effective teaching and academic leadership. Faculty members who actively engage in professional development, document their teaching effectiveness, and pursue leadership opportunities set themselves up for long-term career success while positively influencing their students and institutions.

By understanding the tenure and promotion process, refining teaching portfolios, and embracing faculty development initiatives, educators create a foundation for sustained excellence in teaching and research. Furthermore, professional networking and collaboration with colleagues foster innovation and keep faculty informed of emerging trends and best practices.

Ultimately, the most impactful educators are those who embrace lifelong learning, continually refining their approaches to teaching and scholarship. By prioritizing continuous improvement, faculty members not only enhance their own careers but also contribute to the advancement of higher education, shaping future generations of learners and scholars.

Chapter 13: Mentorship and Student Support Services

Faculty hold a crucial role in shaping student success beyond the classroom. Effective mentorship and student support services help guide students through academic challenges, career planning, and personal development. While institutional advising services assist with course scheduling and degree requirements, faculty mentorship provides discipline-specific guidance, intellectual support, and professional networking opportunities that shape students' educational and career trajectories.

Figure 13.1. Mentorship and Student Support [219].

This chapter explores the key functions of faculty in academic advising and mentorship, distinguishing between their roles as advisors—focused on course planning and academic progress—and mentors, who provide career guidance, research support, and personal development coaching. Additionally, it discusses strategies for building meaningful faculty-student relationships, best practices for mentorship, and ways faculty can connect students with critical institutional support services such as tutoring centers, counseling resources, and career development programs.

By understanding and embracing their dual role as both advisors and mentors, faculty members contribute to higher student retention, increased academic performance, and better career readiness for students [191].

The Role of Faculty in Academic Advising and Mentorship: Guiding Students Toward Academic and Professional Success

Faculty have a critical role in academic advising and mentorship, serving as educators, advisors, and professional role models who guide students through their academic journey, career preparation, and personal development. While students rely on institutional advising services for course scheduling and degree completion, faculty advisors provide discipline-specific guidance, intellectual mentorship, and industry insights that shape students' educational and professional trajectories.

For new college professors, understanding the responsibilities and best practices of academic advising and mentorship is essential for fostering student engagement, retention, and success. Effective faculty mentorship contributes to higher graduation rates, career readiness, and a stronger institutional culture of student support [192].

This section explores the core functions of faculty advising, mentorship best practices, and strategies for creating meaningful faculty-student relationships that promote academic and career success.

Understanding the Dual Role of Faculty as Advisors and Mentors

While academic advising and mentorship are closely related, they serve distinct yet interconnected functions:

Academic Advising – Focuses on helping students navigate their degree programs, course selections, and academic policies to ensure timely progress toward graduation.

Mentorship – Involves long-term guidance, professional development support, and fostering intellectual curiosity, often extending beyond coursework to career exploration, networking, and research involvement.

Example: A faculty member advising a student on their degree path might recommend specific courses based on career goals, while mentoring involves helping the student secure an internship, develop research skills, or explore graduate school options.

Effective faculty members balance both roles, supporting students academically, professionally, and personally throughout their educational journey.

1. Faculty Responsibilities in Academic Advising

Academic advising ensures that students:
-Understand degree requirements and academic policies
-Select courses that align with career and academic goals
-Receive guidance on internships, research opportunities, and study abroad programs
-Address academic challenges and improve study strategies

Best Practices for Faculty in Academic Advising

Develop a Personalized Approach

- Take time to understand each student's goals, interests, and challenges, rather than providing generic course recommendations.

Be Proactive and Accessible

- Encourage students to meet regularly, discuss academic progress, and seek help before issues arise.

Stay Informed About Institutional Policies

- Keep up-to-date on graduation requirements, transfer credit policies, financial aid considerations, and institutional resources to provide accurate guidance.

Collaborate with Student Services and Academic Support Offices

- Connect students with tutoring centers, mental health resources, career services, and learning disability accommodations when needed.

Example: A professor notices a student struggling with coursework in an advanced economics class and refers them to a peer tutoring program while also helping them develop study strategies.

2. Faculty as Mentors: Supporting Student Development Beyond the Classroom

Mentorship goes beyond academic planning to support students in their intellectual, professional, and personal growth. Faculty mentors:

-Help students set long-term educational and career goals
-Provide research guidance and skill development
-Offer networking opportunities and professional connections
-Encourage critical thinking, problem-solving, and lifelong learning
-Foster resilience, confidence, and self-advocacy in students

Best Practices for Faculty Mentorship

Foster Meaningful Relationships

- Build trust through regular, open, and supportive conversations about students' aspirations, challenges, and opportunities.

Encourage Professional Development and Research Engagement

- Support students in attending conferences, publishing research, securing internships, and developing professional skills.

Promote Inclusive and Culturally Responsive Mentorship

- Recognize and address diverse student backgrounds, learning styles, and personal challenges to ensure equitable support.

Act as a Connector to Industry and Professional Networks

- Introduce students to alumni, professional organizations, and industry leaders who can provide additional guidance and career opportunities.

Example: A faculty mentor helps a student prepare a research proposal for a national conference while also connecting them with a former student who now works in the same field.

3. Addressing Common Challenges in Faculty Advising and Mentorship

- Time Constraints
Solution: Set dedicated advising hours, utilize group mentoring, and create structured resources (FAQs, course planning templates) to maximize efficiency.

- Students Who Are Unsure of Their Academic Path
Solution: Encourage exploratory coursework, introduce students to career assessment tools, and connect them with professionals in different fields.

- Students Facing Academic or Personal Struggles
Solution: Be supportive but also refer students to counseling services, tutoring programs, and student affairs professionals when necessary.

- Balancing Guidance with Student Independence
Solution: Provide structured guidance while empowering students to make their own decisions and take responsibility for their academic journey.

- Mentorship Bias and Unequal Access
Solution: Ensure that mentoring relationships are inclusive, equitable, and supportive of all students, especially those from underrepresented backgrounds.

Example: A faculty member implements a structured mentorship program to ensure that all students—not just the most proactive ones—receive guidance and professional development opportunities.

4. Strengthening Faculty-Student Connections: Building a Culture of Academic Support

Host Faculty-Student Networking Events

- Organize informal coffee chats, research discussion groups, or career panels to engage students outside the classroom.

Create a Welcoming Advising Environment

- Maintain an open-door policy, use clear and encouraging communication, and actively listen to student concerns.

Encourage Peer Mentorship and Alumni Involvement

- Develop mentoring programs where upper-level students or alumni offer guidance to undergraduates.

Example: A professor organizes a quarterly networking event where alumni return to campus to share insights with current students about career pathways.

5. The Impact of Effective Faculty Advising and Mentorship on Student Success

Higher Student Retention and Graduation Rates

- Research reveals students with strong faculty mentorship are more likely to complete their degrees and pursue graduate education.

Stronger Career Readiness and Workforce Preparedness

- Faculty mentors help students develop skills, build confidence, and transition smoothly into professional roles [193].

Enhanced Institutional Engagement and Satisfaction

- Individualss who feel supported by faculty are more likely to stay engaged, participate in research, and become active alumni contributors.

Example: A student struggling with career uncertainty receives faculty mentorship, completes an industry internship, and secures a full-time job before graduation.

Conclusion: The Transformational Role of Faculty in Student Advising and Mentorship

Faculty advising and mentorship are more than administrative duties—they are essential to student success, academic growth, and career readiness. Professors who engage deeply in academic advising and mentorship foster an environment where students:

-Receive tailored academic guidance
-Gain confidence in their professional aspirations
-Develop critical skills and real-world connections
-Feel valued, supported, and empowered to succeed

By committing to intentional advising, personalized mentorship, and student-centered engagement, faculty create a lasting impact on students' lives, ensuring they graduate not only with knowledge but with the confidence and skills to excel in their careers and beyond.

Identifying Students at Risk and Offering Support: A Faculty Guide to Early Intervention and Student Success

Higher education is a transformative experience for students, but many face academic, personal, and socio-economic challenges that put them at risk of poor performance, disengagement, or withdrawal. Faculty members play a critical role in identifying at-risk students early, intervening with appropriate support, and connecting them with resources that promote academic persistence and personal well-being.

For new college professors, developing an awareness of early warning signs, implementing proactive intervention strategies, and fostering a supportive classroom environment are essential components of effective student mentorship and academic success initiatives. By recognizing and addressing risk factors early, faculty can help retain students, boost confidence, and contribute to a culture of student-centered learning and holistic support.

This section explores key indicators of at-risk students, intervention strategies, faculty roles in student support, and best practices for creating an inclusive academic environment that promotes retention and success.

1. Understanding Risk Factors: Who Are At-Risk Students?

At-risk students are those who face significant barriers to academic achievement and may struggle with engagement, coursework completion, or overall well-being. These challenges can stem from academic, financial, psychological, or social factors.

Common Risk Factors for Student Struggles

Academic Difficulties

- Low grades on early assignments and exams
- Difficulty understanding course material or keeping up with readings
- Poor attendance and lack of participation in discussions

Personal and Psychological Challenges

- Stress, anxiety, depression, or mental health struggles
- Lack of self-confidence in academic abilities
- Overwhelm from balancing work, family, and school responsibilities

Financial and Socio-Economic Barriers

- Difficulty affording tuition, textbooks, or basic necessities
- Working multiple jobs while attending classes
- Unstable housing or food insecurity

Lack of Institutional Belonging or Social Support

- Feeling disconnected from peers or faculty
- First-generation college student status
- Underrepresentation in academic disciplines or lack of mentorship

Technology and Accessibility Issues

- Limited access to reliable internet, laptops, or software tools
- Learning disabilities or physical disabilities requiring accommodations

Example: A student who struggles to submit assignments on time, frequently misses class, and avoids participating in discussions may be dealing with academic or personal stressors that require faculty intervention and support.

2. Early Identification: Recognizing Warning Signs of At-Risk Students

Faculty members are often the first point of contact when a student begins to struggle. Recognizing early warning signs allows for timely intervention before issues escalate into academic failure or withdrawal.

Indicators of At-Risk Students in a Classroom Setting

Attendance and Participation Decline

- Frequent absences without explanation
- Minimal engagement in discussions or group work

Missed or Incomplete Assignments

- Late submissions or lack of submissions for major coursework
- Decreasing assignment quality over time

Sudden Drop in Academic Performance

- Declining test scores after previously strong performance
- Inconsistent performance across different assignments

Signs of Distress or Mental Health Struggles

- Expressing feelings of being overwhelmed or discouraged
- Noticeable changes in behavior, mood, or demeanor

Lack of Connection or Engagement with Faculty and Peers

- Avoiding office hours or advising sessions
- Not responding to emails or feedback

Example: A student who starts the semester actively participating but gradually becomes silent, misses assignments, and stops attending class may be experiencing personal, mental health, or financial struggles that require faculty support.

3. Intervention Strategies: How Faculty Can Offer Support

Once a faculty member identifies an at-risk student, early intervention is key to helping them re-engage with their coursework and seek appropriate resources. Faculty do not need to act as counselors or case managers but should serve as trusted guides who connect students with institutional support systems.

Best Practices for Faculty in Supporting At-Risk Students

Proactive Communication and Outreach

- Reach out personally via email or in class to express concern.
- Avoid accusatory language; instead, ask open-ended, supportive questions:

- o *"I noticed you haven't been in class lately—how are things going?"*
- o *"Would you like to discuss any challenges you're facing? I'm happy to help."*

Encourage Office Hours and One-on-One Meetings

- Offer a low-pressure, private space for students to share their concerns.
- Listen empathetically and avoid judgment.

Refer to Campus Resources

- Direct students to academic tutoring, writing centers, financial aid offices, and counseling services.
- Provide links to mental health services, career development resources, and disability support offices.

Help Develop a Recovery Plan

- Break down coursework into manageable steps for overwhelmed students.
- Offer extra resources, study strategies, or peer mentoring.

Create a Classroom Culture of Support and Inclusion

- Establish a welcoming, objective environment where students feel safe seeking help.
- Use flexible teaching approaches, such as extended deadlines or alternative assessments, when appropriate.

Example: A professor notices a student falling behind on assignments and sends a personalized email offering a one-on-one meeting. During the meeting, the student shares that they struggle with balancing coursework and a full-time job. The professor connects the student with an academic advisor and offers suggestions for time management strategies.

4. Faculty Roles in a Student Support Network

Faculty play a collaborative role in a broader system of student support that includes:

Academic Advising and Faculty Mentorship

- Help students choose appropriate courses and explore career paths.

Collaboration with Student Affairs and Support Services

- Work with advisors, financial aid officers, and mental health counselors to ensure students receive holistic support.

Supporting First-Generation and Underrepresented Students

- Be intentional about mentorship and outreach to students who may lack family or institutional knowledge about navigating college life.

Example: A faculty member partners with the university's student support office to implement an early alert system, where faculty report students showing signs of disengagement so advisors can intervene proactively.

5. Preventive Measures: Fostering a Proactive Approach to Student Retention

Build Relationships Early in the Semester

- Learn student names, interests, and backgrounds.
- Establish a class culture where students feel seen and valued.

Normalize Asking for Help

- Regularly remind students that seeking support is a strength, not a weakness.
- Provide structured check-ins and mid-semester feedback.

Offer Flexible and Inclusive Teaching Strategies

- Use universal design for learning (UDL) principles to accommodate different learning needs.
- Provide alternative assessment methods for students facing challenges.

Example: A professor integrates a mid-term self-assessment survey, allowing students to reflect on their progress and share any challenges they need help overcoming.

Conclusion: Faculty as a Vital Link in Student Success

Identifying and supporting at-risk students is not just an institutional responsibility—it is an essential faculty role in fostering student success, retention, and well-being. Professors who practice early intervention, proactive communication, and structured support strategies help students overcome challenges and reach their full potential.

By integrating compassionate mentorship, academic guidance, and a strong support network, faculty contribute to a more inclusive, engaged, and resilient student body, ensuring that every student has the resources, encouragement, and strategies needed to thrive in higher education and beyond.

Navigating Campus Student Services: Maximizing Institutional Resources for Student Success

Institutions deliver a broad spectrum of student support services designed to enhance academic success, personal well-being, and career readiness. However, many students underutilize or remain unaware of these essential resources, leading to missed opportunities for academic improvement, mental health support, and professional development. Faculty members play a critical role in bridging this gap, serving as guides who connect students with appropriate campus services and empower them to seek the help they need.

For new college professors, understanding how to navigate and refer students to counseling, tutoring, and career services is a fundamental competency. Faculty who proactively integrate student support resources into their courses, advising, and mentorship efforts contribute to higher retention rates, increased student engagement, and overall institutional success [194].

This section explores key campus student services, best practices for faculty referrals, and strategies for fostering a culture where students actively engage with available support systems.

1. Understanding Key Campus Student Services

Institutions offer a variety of student support services to enhance academic performance, promote well-being, and prepare students for their careers. The three core categories of student services that faculty should be familiar with are:

-Counseling and Mental Health Services
-Academic Tutoring and Learning Support Centers
-Career Services and Professional Development Resources

A. Counseling and Mental Health Services

College life presents students with academic stress, social pressures, and personal challenges that can impact their mental well-being. Campus counseling centers provide:

-Confidential mental health counseling (individual and group sessions)
-Crisis intervention and referrals for severe psychological concerns
-Workshops on stress management, mindfulness, and resilience
-Support groups for students facing academic or personal difficulties

Faculty Role:

- Be attentive to signs of student distress, such as withdrawal from class discussions, changes in behavior, or excessive absences.

- Encourage students to seek counseling services if they exhibit signs of stress, anxiety, or depression.

- Normalize mental health discussions by including counseling resources in the syllabus and classroom announcements.

Example: A student expresses feelings of being overwhelmed during office hours. The professor responds supportively and provides information about on-campus counseling services, encouraging the student to seek help.

B. Academic Tutoring and Learning Support Centers

Academic support services help students strengthen subject comprehension, refine study skills, and improve performance in challenging courses. These services include:

-One-on-one tutoring and peer-assisted study sessions
-Workshops on exam preparation, time management, and study skills

-Writing centers that assist with research papers, essays, and reports
-Supplemental instruction programs for high-demand courses

Faculty Role:

- Identify students who may benefit from tutoring based on early academic struggles or declining performance.

- Provide tutoring center information in syllabi, emails, and learning management system (LMS) announcements.

- Reduce stigma around tutoring by emphasizing that strong students also seek academic support as part of high-achieving behaviors.

Example: A student struggling in a statistics course seeks help from the professor. Instead of solely reviewing concepts during office hours, the professor also directs the student to the campus tutoring center for additional support.

C. Career Services and Professional Development Resources

Beyond academic success, colleges strive to prepare students for life after graduation by providing career guidance, internship placements, and networking opportunities. Career services typically offer:

-Resume and cover letter workshops
-Mock interviews and career coaching sessions
-Internship and job placement assistance
-Networking events and employer recruitment fairs
-Graduate school application support

Faculty Role:

- Encourage learners to visit career services early in their academic journey, not just before graduation.

- Invite career counselors to speak in class about professional development and industry expectations.

- Connect students with alumni networks, professional organizations, and internship opportunities.

Example: A faculty mentor works with a student interested in marketing. The professor suggests meeting with a career advisor to refine their resume, then refers them to a former student now working at a top marketing firm for networking advice.

2. Best Practices for Faculty in Referring Students to Campus Services

Faculty should adopt a proactive and supportive approach when guiding students to use campus resources.

Normalize Campus Resource Utilization

- Include information about counseling, tutoring, and career services in course syllabi.
- Regularly remind students that seeking help is a proactive step toward success, not a sign of weakness.

Make Personalized, Encouraging Referrals

- When referring a student, explain the benefits of the service and, if possible, help them schedule an appointment.
- Avoid simply directing students to a website; instead, describe how the service has helped other students in similar situations.

Follow Up on Referrals

- After recommending a service, check in with the student later to see if they found it helpful.
- Encourage continued engagement with support services, reinforcing that improvement takes time and persistence.

Example: Instead of vaguely saying, *"You should check out the tutoring center,"* a professor might say:

- *- "Many students in this class have found the tutoring center really helpful, especially for writing assignments. Would you like me to connect you with someone there?"*

3. Creating a Culture of Support and Resource Engagement

To maximize the impact of student services, faculty should integrate support systems into classroom culture and advising practices.

Host Faculty-Student Resource Orientation Sessions

- Invite counselors, career advisors, and tutoring center staff to present in class.

Use Learning Management Systems (LMS) to Share Campus Resources

- Post links to student services, mental health hotlines, and career event announcements in the course portal.

Recognize Student Barriers to Seeking Help

- Some students may hesitate to use campus services due to stigma, lack of awareness, or scheduling conflicts.
- Faculty should proactively dispel misconceptions and emphasize that successful students actively seek support.

Example: A professor creates a "Student Success" section in the syllabus with clear information on tutoring, counseling, and career services, along with personal endorsements like:

- *"I highly encourage you to use the writing center for major assignments—many students who went there saw significant improvement in their grades."*

4. The Long-Term Impact of Connecting Students with Campus Support Services

When faculty actively engage students with campus resources, institutions see:

Higher Student Retention and Graduation Rates

- Students who access tutoring and counseling services are more likely to persist in their studies [195].

Improved Academic Performance

- Data shows that students who use tutoring services achieve higher grades and develop stronger study habits [195].

Enhanced Career Readiness and Employment Outcomes

- Early engagement with career services leads to better job placement rates, networking opportunities, and graduate school admissions [195].

Stronger Faculty-Student Relationships

- Faculty who integrate student services into their teaching build trust with students, increasing their likelihood of seeking help when needed.

Conclusion: Faculty as Key Navigators of Student Success

Faculty members play an essential role in helping students access the full range of academic, mental health, and career resources available on campus. By proactively identifying student needs, making personalized referrals, and fostering a supportive learning environment, professors empower students to take advantage of services that enhance their success both in and beyond the classroom.

Ultimately, a student's ability to navigate support systems is a skill that extends beyond college—preparing them for lifelong resilience, self-advocacy, and professional growth. Faculty who embrace this role not only contribute to student success but also strengthen the overall academic community by fostering a culture of engagement, support, and achievement.

Encouraging Professional Development and Career Readiness in Students: The Faculty's Role in Bridging Academia and the Workforce

The transition from higher education to professional life is a critical milestone for students, requiring more than just academic knowledge. Employers today seek graduates who possess technical expertise, problem-solving abilities, professional communication skills, and adaptability. Faculty play a crucial role in mentoring students beyond the classroom, equipping them with the skills, resources, and experiences necessary for career success and lifelong professional development.

For new college professors, fostering career readiness and professional development means integrating industry insights, career-oriented learning experiences, and networking opportunities into their teaching and mentorship. By doing so, faculty help students:

  Develop practical and transferable skills that enhance employability
  Gain exposure to industry trends, workplace expectations, and career pathways
  Build confidence in professional communication and job search strategies
  Strengthen critical thinking, leadership, and problem-solving skills
  Engage in internships, research projects, and professional networking

This section explores effective faculty strategies for integrating professional development into coursework, mentoring students on career readiness, and ensuring graduates are well-prepared for the evolving job market.

1. Understanding Career Readiness: What Do Employers Look For?

Employers today expect college graduates to enter the workforce with a blend of technical competencies, workplace skills, and professional experience. The National Association of Colleges and Employers (NACE) outlines key career readiness competencies, including:

 -Critical Thinking and Problem-Solving – Ability to analyze information, make decisions, and address workplace challenges.
 -Oral and Written Communication – Clear and effective communication with colleagues, clients, and stakeholders.
 -Teamwork and Collaboration – Capacity to work effectively in diverse teams.
 -Digital and Technological Fluency – Proficiency with industry-relevant tools, software, and digital communication platforms.
 -Leadership and Professionalism – Initiative, work ethic, and ability to take responsibility in professional settings.
 -Career Self-Management – Understanding how to navigate job searches, networking, and career advancement.

Example: A faculty member teaching business analytics incorporates case studies and real-world data analysis projects into coursework, helping students develop critical thinking and analytical skills relevant to industry needs.

2. Faculty Strategies for Integrating Career Readiness into Academia

A. Embedding Career-Focused Learning in the Classroom

Faculty can design coursework and assignments that mirror real-world workplace tasks, encouraging students to apply their academic knowledge in practical, career-oriented ways.

Incorporate Project-Based Learning and Case Studies

- Use real-world scenarios, problem-solving tasks, and data analysis exercises to teach students how to apply theoretical knowledge in workplace settings.

Develop Industry-Aligned Assignments

- Require students to create professional deliverables such as business reports, policy briefs, or software prototypes to simulate workplace tasks.

Encourage Group Work and Cross-Disciplinary Collaboration

- **Simulate team-based work environments where students collaborate on projects, present findings, and refine leadership skills.**

Example: An engineering professor assigns students a semester-long capstone project where they work in teams to develop a prototype for a real client, reinforcing problem-solving, teamwork, and communication skills.

B. Promoting Professional Communication and Workplace Etiquette

Students entering the workforce must communicate effectively, navigate professional settings, and develop networking skills. Faculty can help by:

Assigning Written and Verbal Communication Exercises

- Require students to draft professional emails, cover letters, project proposals, and presentations.
- Teach effective public speaking skills through classroom presentations and networking simulations.

Integrating Mock Interviews and Elevator Pitches

- Organize mock job interviews and pitch sessions where students practice introducing themselves professionally.

Example: A marketing professor assigns students to conduct mock client pitches, preparing them for future sales and branding roles.

C. Encouraging Student Engagement in Internships, Research, and Work-Based Learning

Experiential learning opportunities—such as internships, research projects, and apprenticeships—provide students with firsthand exposure to industry expectations and opportunities to apply their skills in real-world settings.

Help Students Identify Internship and Research Opportunities

- Regularly share internship postings, research assistantship openings, and industry fellowship programs.
- Provide guidance on applying for internships and maximizing experiential learning.

Encourage Students to Present Research and Publish Work

- Help students submit research papers to academic journals, present at conferences, and participate in student competitions.

Example: A faculty mentor helps a student secure an internship at a cybersecurity firm, then encourages them to document their experience in a portfolio for job applications.

3. Mentoring Students in Career Exploration and Professional Growth

A. Faculty as Career Mentors

Schedule Career Development Conversations

- Regularly discuss career interests, professional aspirations, and skill-building strategies during office hours or mentorship sessions.

Expose Students to Different Career Paths

- Introduce students to traditional, alternative, and emerging career opportunities within their field.
- Encourage exploration of graduate programs, entrepreneurship, and interdisciplinary careers.

Example: A professor mentoring an economics major discusses careers in data analysis, policy advising, and fintech, helping the student clarify their professional direction.

B. Connecting Students with Industry and Alumni Networks

Leverage Alumni and Industry Partnerships

- Invite guest speakers, alumni panels, and employer networking sessions to provide industry insights.

Encourage Professional Organization Memberships

- Recommend joining industry associations, attending conferences, and pursuing certifications.

Example: A professor connects a graduating senior with an alum working at a Fortune 500 company, leading to a mentorship and internship opportunity.

C. Supporting Students in Job Searches and Graduate School Applications

Review Resumes, Cover Letters, and Application Materials

- Offer workshops and one-on-one reviews to help students refine job application documents.

Prepare Students for Interviews and Workplace Expectations

- Conduct mock interviews with industry professionals to boost confidence.
- Discuss common workplace challenges and professional ethics.

Example: A professor assists a student in preparing for a graduate school application by providing a recommendation letter and feedback on their personal statement.

4. Creating a Campus Culture of Career Readiness

Faculty should collaborate with career services, alumni networks, and industry partners to create a campus-wide culture of career preparation.

Partner with Career Services Offices

- Encourage students to attend resume workshops, career fairs, and job search webinars.
- Collaborate with career advisors to design industry-aligned curricula.

Develop Professional Development Courses or Programs

- Create certificate programs, micro-credentialing opportunities, or career boot camps tailored to specific industries.

Example: A faculty committee works with the career services department to develop a career readiness certificate that students earn through workshops, internships, and networking events.

5. The Long-Term Impact of Faculty-Driven Career Readiness Initiatives

When faculty actively support student career development, institutions see:

Higher Employment and Graduate School Acceptance Rates

- Students who engage in faculty-led career initiatives secure competitive jobs and admission to top graduate programs [196].

Stronger Industry and Alumni Engagement

- Graduates who feel supported by faculty remain connected to their alma mater and contribute to mentoring and networking efforts.

Increased Student Confidence and Professional Growth

- Students who develop career readiness skills early experience smoother transitions into the workforce.

Conclusion: Faculty as Catalysts for Student Career Success

Encouraging professional development and career readiness is not just the responsibility of career services—it is an essential role of faculty in higher education. By integrating real-world applications into coursework, mentoring students on professional pathways, and fostering industry connections, professors ensure that students graduate with the skills, confidence, and networks needed to thrive in their careers.

Ultimately, faculty who embrace career mentoring shape not only students' academic journeys but also their long-term professional success, reinforcing the value of higher education as a bridge between knowledge and meaningful employment.

Supporting Students in Research, Internships, and Career Placements: A Faculty Guide to Professional and Academic Development

The journey from college to career is not solely dependent on coursework—it requires hands-on experiences, industry exposure, and professional connections. Faculty play a pivotal role in guiding students through research opportunities, internships, and career placements, ensuring they gain practical experience, develop essential skills, and transition smoothly into the workforce or graduate studies.

For new college professors, supporting students in these areas means acting as mentors, advisors, and professional connectors—helping them navigate opportunities, refine their career paths, and build a strong foundation for long-term success. Faculty who actively engage in student research, internship guidance, and career mentorship contribute to higher student retention, increased employment rates, and stronger institutional reputation.

This section explores effective faculty strategies for mentoring students in research, assisting them in securing internships, and guiding them toward successful career placements.

1. The Faculty Role in Supporting Student Research

Undergraduate and graduate research enhance students' analytical skills, critical thinking, and academic engagement, preparing them for graduate studies, industry research positions, or specialized careers. Faculty serve as research mentors, advisors, and collaborators, helping students develop:

Research Methodology and Inquiry Skills

- Guidance on data collection, experimental design, and literature review techniques.

Academic Writing and Scholarly Communication

- Support in writing research papers, grant proposals, and conference presentations.

Presentation and Publication Experience

- Opportunities to present findings at academic conferences or publish in peer-reviewed journals.

Example: A faculty mentor advises a student on a cybersecurity research project, helping them develop a research question, analyze real-world case studies, and present findings at a national conference.

A. Strategies for Faculty in Supporting Student Research

Identify and Recruit Promising Research Students

- Encourage students who demonstrate curiosity, analytical skills, or strong academic performance to engage in research.

Provide Structured Research Training

- Teach research ethics, data analysis techniques, and scholarly writing skills through hands-on mentorship.

Facilitate Student Participation in Academic Conferences

- Help students prepare abstracts, secure funding, and practice presentation skills.

Encourage Research Collaboration and Networking

- Connect students **with faculty research teams, interdisciplinary projects, and professional organizations.**

Example: A professor in environmental science leads a research lab where students collaborate on sustainability projects, later co-authoring papers with faculty mentors.

2. Faculty Support in Internship Guidance

Internships deliver real-world experience, industry exposure, and professional networking opportunities. Faculty members can help students secure internships, maximize learning outcomes, and translate internship experiences into career opportunities.

A. Helping Students Identify and Secure Internships

Encourage Early Exploration of Internship Opportunities

- Guide students in identifying internship programs relevant to their field of study.

Assist in Resume Building and Application Preparation

- Provide feedback on resumes, cover letters, and interview preparation.

Leverage Faculty and Alumni Networks for Internship Referrals

- Connect students with industry partners, alumni, and professional contacts.

Example: A business professor introduces a student to an alum working at a top consulting firm, leading to a competitive internship offer.

B. Ensuring Students Gain Value from Internships

Encourage Reflection and Skill Development During Internships

- Assign post-internship reflection papers or presentations to help students articulate their experiences.

Advocate for High-Quality, Paid Internship Opportunities

- Support students in securing internships that offer mentorship, meaningful projects, and career advancement opportunities.

Integrate Internship Experiences into Academic Learning

- Allow students to connect classroom knowledge with practical applications through discussions and assignments.

Example: A marketing professor requires students to create a professional portfolio showcasing projects from their internship experiences.

3. Faculty Role in Career Placement and Workforce Preparation

While career services provide job search assistance, faculty bring discipline-specific expertise, industry connections, and mentorship that help students transition into the workforce. Professors who actively support career placement ensure that students:

Understand Job Market Expectations

- Learn about industry trends, required skills, and career growth opportunities.

Develop Professional Networks

- Gain access to alumni mentors, industry events, and employer connections.

Refine Job Search and Interview Strategies

- Receive resume reviews, job application support, and mock interview practice.

Example: A computer science professor hosts a panel discussion with software engineers from major tech companies, giving students insights into industry hiring practices.

A. Faculty Strategies for Career Placement Support

Help Students Identify Career Pathways

- Discuss varied job roles, specialization options, and potential career trajectories within the field.

Encourage Students to Build a Professional Online Presence

- Guide students in creating LinkedIn profiles, personal websites, and digital portfolios.

Organize Employer and Alumni Networking Opportunities

- Invite guest speakers, alumni panels, and company recruiters to campus events.

Example: An accounting professor partners with local firms to host an annual "Meet the Firms" event, where students network with potential employers.

B. Supporting Students Interested in Graduate or Professional School

Assist with Graduate School Applications

- Help students select programs, write personal statements, and secure recommendation letters.

Encourage Research on Funding and Scholarships

- Guide students through fellowship applications and financial aid opportunities.

Example: A faculty mentor helps a political science student apply for a Fulbright scholarship, refining their research proposal and statement of purpose.

4. Creating a Culture of Research, Internship, and Career Readiness

Faculty can integrate professional development into classroom culture, ensuring that career preparedness is a central part of the academic experience.

Embed Career-Related Assignments in Coursework

- Require students to conduct industry research, interview professionals, or draft career plans.

Collaborate with Career Services for Faculty-Led Career Initiatives

- Work with career offices to organize industry speaker events and career readiness workshops.

Encourage Professional Certification and Skills Training

- Recommend micro-credentials, industry certifications, and professional development programs.

Example: A finance professor integrates Bloomberg Terminal certification into coursework, enhancing students' marketability in the finance sector.

5. The Long-Term Impact of Faculty Mentorship in Research, Internships, and Career Placement

Higher Student Retention and Graduation Rates

- Students engaged in research and internships are more likely to persist and graduate [197].

Stronger Career Readiness and Workforce Competitiveness

- Faculty-supported students enter the job market with real-world experience and professional confidence [198].

Enhanced Institutional Reputation and Alumni Engagement

- Successful graduates contribute to stronger employer partnerships and alumni mentoring programs [199].

Example: A student mentored through a research project, internship, and faculty-supported job application secures a competitive position at a top consulting firm, later returning as a guest speaker to mentor current students.

Conclusion: Faculty as Catalysts for Student Success in Research, Internships, and Careers

Faculty members are instrumental in preparing students for life beyond the classroom, guiding them through academic research, professional internships, and career placements. By actively mentoring students, facilitating experiential learning opportunities, and leveraging industry connections, professors help students transition seamlessly from education to professional success.

Ultimately, faculty-driven support in research, internships, and career placement strengthens student confidence, enhances employability, and fosters lifelong professional growth, ensuring that graduates are equipped to thrive in an evolving global workforce.

Faculty as a Vital Link in Student Success

Mentorship and student support are essential components of higher education, ensuring that students receive the guidance and resources needed to thrive academically and professionally. Faculty members who take an active role in advising and mentoring create an environment where students feel valued, supported, and empowered to achieve their goals.

By fostering strong faculty-student relationships, providing tailored academic guidance, and proactively connecting students with institutional resources, professors can significantly improve student retention, engagement, and career readiness. Additionally, recognizing and addressing student challenges—such as academic struggles, mental health concerns, and career uncertainties—helps create a more inclusive and supportive academic community.

Ultimately, the impact of faculty mentorship extends far beyond graduation, shaping students' lifelong learning habits, professional networks, and career trajectories. By embracing their role as advisors, mentors, and advocates, faculty members play a transformative role in shaping the future of higher education and the success of their students.

Chapter 14: Academic Conduct, Integrity, and Proper Attribution

Academic integrity is the keystone of higher education, ensuring that scholarly work is conducted with honesty, fairness, and accountability. It upholds the credibility of institutions, reinforces ethical research practices, and maintains the integrity of degrees and credentials. Faculty members play a crucial role in fostering a culture of academic honesty by modeling ethical scholarship, setting clear expectations for students, and addressing potential misconduct.

This chapter explores the principles of academic integrity, including plagiarism prevention, proper attribution of sources, and ethical use of artificial intelligence and emerging

Figure 14.1. Academic Integrity [219].

technologies. It also examines the institutional frameworks that support integrity, including academic policies, codes of conduct, and enforcement procedures. Additionally, faculty will learn strategies for designing assessments that promote integrity, handling academic misconduct cases fairly, and creating a classroom culture that prioritizes ethical learning.

By embedding these values into teaching and research, faculty members can cultivate a learning environment where students develop a deep respect for intellectual property, uphold ethical academic practices, and carry these principles into their professional careers.

Understanding Academic Integrity in Higher Education

Academic integrity serves as the foundation of higher education, reinforcing the credibility, fairness, and intellectual rigor that define scholarly work. It is not merely an ethical ideal but a fundamental expectation that shapes institutional culture, ensuring that learning and research are conducted with honesty, respect, and accountability. In this section, we explore the definition and significance of academic honesty, the critical role faculty play in fostering integrity, and the institutional frameworks that uphold these values through policies and codes of conduct.

Definition and Importance of Academic Honesty

Academic honesty refers to the ethical commitment of students, faculty, and researchers to produce and present work that is original, properly attributed, and free from deceitful practices. It encompasses principles such as truthfulness in research, fairness in assessments, and respect for intellectual property. At its core, academic honesty fosters an environment where knowledge is advanced through authentic inquiry rather than misrepresentation or plagiarism.

The importance of academic integrity extends beyond individual coursework or research projects—it is central to the legitimacy of academic degrees, scholarly publications, and institutional reputation. When students engage in dishonest behaviors such as plagiarism, unauthorized collaboration, or fabrication of data, they undermine not only their own learning but also the trust that academia relies upon. Moreover, breaches of academic integrity can have long-term consequences, from disciplinary actions at the institutional level to reputational damage that can affect professional careers.

By embedding integrity within academic processes, institutions cultivate ethical scholars and professionals who carry these values into their careers, reinforcing integrity in their respective industries and communities. Upholding academic honesty is not simply about compliance with rules—it is about nurturing a culture of responsibility, critical thinking, and respect for the intellectual contributions of others.

Role of Faculty in Upholding Academic Integrity

Faculty members serve as both educators and ethical stewards in higher education, playing a crucial role in shaping students' understanding and adherence to academic integrity. Their responsibilities in this regard extend across multiple dimensions:

1. **Setting Expectations** – Professors must clearly communicate academic integrity policies within their syllabi, outlining acceptable and unacceptable behaviors in assignments, exams, and collaborative work. Defining expectations for citation practices, group projects, and use of generative AI tools helps prevent misunderstandings that may lead to unintentional violations.

2. **Modeling Ethical Scholarship** – Faculty should exemplify integrity in their own research, writing, and professional conduct. By demonstrating proper citation practices, transparency in methodology, and ethical decision-making, they reinforce these values for students.

3. **Fostering a Culture of Honesty** – Creating an environment where students feel encouraged to ask questions about attribution, research ethics, and citation standards is essential. When faculty actively discuss ethical dilemmas and academic integrity in their courses, students are more likely to internalize these principles.

4. **Designing Assessments That Promote Integrity** – Thoughtfully designed assignments can discourage dishonest behavior. For example, open-ended essay prompts, application-based problems, and scaffolded research projects make it more difficult for students to engage in plagiarism or contract cheating. Leveraging technology, such as plagiarism detection software, can serve as a deterrent, but it should be complemented with educational efforts to teach students about proper attribution.

5. **Enforcing Policies Fairly and Consistently** – Faculty must ensure that academic integrity violations are addressed according to institutional policies, applying sanctions equitably while maintaining due process. Rather than solely focusing on punitive measures, faculty should use violations as teachable moments to educate students on ethical academic practices.

By embracing these roles, faculty help cultivate a learning environment where integrity is valued not just as a rule to be followed, but as an essential component of intellectual growth.

Institutional Policies and Codes of Conduct

Academic institutions establish policies and codes of conduct to provide a structured framework for maintaining academic integrity. These guidelines serve several critical functions: defining ethical expectations, detailing prohibited behaviors, outlining reporting procedures, and specifying consequences for violations. While specific policies vary by institution, they commonly address the following elements:

1. **Definitions of Academic Misconduct** – Institutions typically outline what constitutes plagiarism, cheating, fabrication, unauthorized collaboration, and other forms of academic dishonesty. Clarity in definitions ensures that students and faculty have a shared understanding of academic expectations.

2. **Responsibilities of Students and Faculty** – Policies delineate the roles of both students and instructors in upholding integrity. Students are expected to adhere to citation standards, complete work independently unless otherwise specified, and report observed violations. Faculty, in turn, must enforce policies impartially and provide guidance on proper academic practices.

3. **Reporting and Adjudication Processes** – Institutions provide procedures for reporting suspected violations, investigating claims, and determining outcomes. This process often includes a review board or academic integrity committee that ensures fairness and due process for all parties involved.

4. **Sanctions for Violations** – Consequences for academic misconduct can range from warnings and resubmission requirements to course failure or expulsion in severe cases. Institutions often emphasize an educational approach, offering workshops or remediation programs to help students understand proper attribution and ethical scholarship.

5. **Support Resources for Academic Integrity** – Many colleges and universities provide writing centers, research ethics workshops, and online citation tools to help students develop skills that prevent academic integrity violations. Faculty training programs on integrity-related topics further reinforce institutional commitment to ethical academic practices.

A well-implemented academic integrity policy does more than deter misconduct; it fosters a scholarly environment where ethical behavior is expected, supported, and recognized as fundamental to academic and professional success. Through faculty engagement and institutional commitment, the principles of honesty and integrity become embedded within the educational experience, shaping future generations of ethical scholars and professionals.

Plagiarism and Proper Attribution

Plagiarism is one of the most critical ethical concerns in higher education, affecting the credibility of scholarly work, the integrity of academic institutions, and the intellectual development of students. Proper attribution is not merely a technical requirement—it is an essential component of ethical scholarship that ensures recognition of original ideas and contributes to the collective body of knowledge [200]. Faculty members play a vital role in teaching students to understand plagiarism, guiding them in proper citation practices, and leveraging technology to uphold academic integrity.

What Constitutes Plagiarism? *(Intentional vs. Unintentional)*

Plagiarism occurs when someone presents another's work, ideas, or expressions as their own without proper acknowledgment. It can take many forms, ranging from verbatim copying to paraphrasing without attribution. Plagiarism is often categorized into two primary types: **intentional** and **unintentional** plagiarism [201].

1. **Intentional Plagiarism**

    - **Direct Copying:** Submitting an entire work or significant portions of a work that was not authored by the student, often without citation.
    - **Fabrication of Citations:** Making up sources or misattributing information to misleading references.
    - **Contract Cheating:** Paying someone else to write a paper or using unauthorized AI-generated content without acknowledgment.
    - **Self-Plagiarism:** Submitting previously written work for multiple assignments without proper disclosure or permission.

2. **Unintentional Plagiarism**

    - **Improper Paraphrasing:** Altering a few words from the original source but retaining the sentence structure without proper citation.
    - **Omitting Citations:** Forgetting to cite a source, even when the intent was not to claim ownership of the idea.
    - **Misuse of Quotation Marks:** Using another's words but failing to indicate direct quotations properly.
    - **Inaccurate or Incomplete Citations:** Providing incorrect details in a citation, making it difficult to verify the source.

While intentional plagiarism often results in severe academic consequences, unintentional plagiarism highlights gaps in students' understanding of research ethics. Faculty must recognize that many students plagiarize unintentionally due to a lack of familiarity with citation conventions, ineffective note-taking, or misunderstanding what constitutes common knowledge. Addressing both types through education rather than punitive measures can help students develop stronger research and writing habits.

Citation Styles: APA, MLA, Chicago, and When to Use Them

Academic writing relies on standardized citation styles to ensure clarity, consistency, and proper attribution of sources. Different disciplines follow different citation conventions, and it is essential for faculty to familiarize students with the appropriate style for their field of study [201].

1. **American Psychological Association (APA)**
   - **Used in:** Social sciences (e.g., psychology, sociology, business, education).
   - **Key Features:** Author-date in-text citations (Smith, 2023); reference list with detailed source information.
   - **Why It's Used:** Emphasizes the currency of research by prioritizing publication dates.

2. **Modern Language Association (MLA)**
   - **Used in:** Humanities (e.g., literature, philosophy, cultural studies).
   - **Key Features:** Author-page in-text citations (Smith 23); Works Cited page at the end.
   - **Why It's Used:** Prioritizes textual analysis and literary interpretation with a focus on authorial intent.

3. **Chicago/Turabian Style**
   - **Used in:** History, fine arts, and some business disciplines.
   - **Key Features:** Footnotes or endnotes for citations and a bibliography at the end.
   - **Why It's Used:** Offers flexibility in citing diverse sources and accommodates historical and archival references.

4. **Other Citation Styles**
   - **IEEE (Institute of Electrical and Electronics Engineers):** Used in engineering and computer science.
   - **AMA (American Medical Association):** Used in medical and health sciences.
   - **Bluebook:** Used in legal writing.

Faculty should emphasize not only how to format citations correctly but also why citation styles vary, demonstrating how different disciplines' structure knowledge and prioritize different aspects of scholarship.

Teaching Students How to Properly Cite Sources

Students often struggle with proper attribution because citation rules can feel overwhelming and tedious. However, teaching citation skills should go beyond mechanics—it should focus on fostering an appreciation for ethical academic writing. Effective strategies for teaching proper citation include:

1. **Contextualizing Citation in Academic Integrity**
    - Explain that citations serve as intellectual breadcrumbs, allowing readers to verify sources and trace the evolution of ideas.
    - Discuss ethical implications—how plagiarism undermines research credibility and why giving credit fosters scholarly dialogue.

2. **Using Interactive Exercises**
    - **Paraphrasing Workshops:** Provide students with original text excerpts and guide them through the process of paraphrasing with proper attribution.
    - **Citation Games:** Have students format sample citations incorrectly and correct each other's mistakes.
    - **Group Research Exercises:** Assign collaborative citation tasks where students analyze sources and cite them properly in different styles.

3. **Integrating Citation Tools into Assignments**
    - Encourage students to use reference management tools like Zotero, Mendeley, or EndNote to automate citation formatting.
    - Assign annotated bibliographies to help students develop citation skills before writing full-length papers.

By making citation instruction engaging and accessible, faculty can help students view proper attribution not as a chore, but as an essential academic skill that enhances their credibility and critical thinking.

Using Plagiarism Detection Tools *(Turnitin, Grammarly, AI Detection Tools)*

Technology has transformed the way academic integrity is monitored. Plagiarism detection tools provide faculty with additional resources to identify potential academic misconduct while also serving as learning aids for students [202]. However, these tools should be used as teaching instruments rather than punitive measures.

1. **Turnitin**

- o   Evaluate submissions against a vast database of publications.
- o   Generates similarity reports, highlighting potentially plagiarized content and improper citations.
- o   Faculty can use these reports to discuss proper citation techniques with students rather than simply penalizing them.

2. **Grammarly and AI-Based Writing Assistants**
   - o   Offers real-time feedback on grammar, writing style, and plagiarism detection.
   - o   Can help students refine paraphrasing and avoid accidental plagiarism.

3. **AI Detection Tools (GPTZero, Winston AI, Originality.ai)**
   - o   With the rise of generative AI, new detection tools analyze text to determine if it was AI-generated [203].
   - o   These tools help institutions address emerging challenges related to students using AI to complete assignments without proper attribution.
   - o   Faculty should establish clear guidelines for AI use in coursework, outlining when AI tools are permitted and how students must document AI-assisted research.

Conclusion

Plagiarism and proper attribution are foundational to academic integrity, and faculty play a crucial role in ensuring students understand both the ethical and technical aspects of citation. By distinguishing between intentional and unintentional plagiarism, teaching students how to navigate different citation styles, and leveraging plagiarism detection tools as educational aids, professors can cultivate a culture of academic honesty. Rather than treating plagiarism as a mere infraction to be penalized, institutions should focus on education, prevention, and skill-building, helping students become responsible scholars who value proper attribution as a fundamental part of their academic and professional success.

Ethical Use of AI and Emerging Technologies

The rapid advancement of artificial intelligence (AI) and emerging technologies is transforming higher education, influencing how students conduct research, generate content, and engage with learning materials. While AI-assisted tools such as ChatGPT, Grammarly, and research automation platforms offer tremendous benefits, they also present ethical challenges related to academic integrity, authorship, and proper attribution. Faculty must navigate this evolving landscape by defining clear ethical boundaries, establishing guidelines for students, and ensuring responsible AI integration in the learning environment.

AI-Generated Content: What's Ethical and What's Not?

AI-generated content spans a broad spectrum of applications, from writing assistance and automated summarization to data analysis and predictive modeling [204]. However, ethical concerns arise when AI-generated material is presented as original student work without proper disclosure or when AI tools are used in ways that circumvent academic rigor. The ethical use of AI can be categorized into permissible, conditional, and unethical practices:

1. **Permissible AI Use** *(When AI is used as a supplement, not a substitute for intellectual effort)*

    - **Grammar and Clarity Enhancement:** AI-based tools like Grammarly or Hemingway Editor can assist students in refining their writing but should not replace critical thinking.

    - **Research Assistance:** AI can help generate research summaries, suggest relevant literature, or structure outlines, provided that students verify sources and contribute their own analysis.

    - **Coding and Data Analysis Support:** AI can assist in debugging or optimizing code, but students should understand and modify outputs to reflect their knowledge.

2. **Conditional AI Use** *(When AI use is acceptable with transparency and proper attribution)*

    - **AI-Generated Drafts with Attribution:** If a student uses AI to generate portions of an essay, it must be disclosed with proper acknowledgment of AI's role in content creation.

    - **AI-Assisted Translations and Summaries:** Using AI to translate texts or summarize complex topics is permissible, but students must ensure accuracy and cite original sources.

    - **Idea Generation and Brainstorming:** AI can help generate discussion topics or refine thesis statements, but students should expand upon AI-generated ideas with independent thought.

3. **Unethical AI Use** *(When AI is used in ways that compromise academic integrity)*

    - **Submitting AI-Generated Work as Original:** Presenting AI-written essays, research papers, or assignments as one's own without disclosure constitutes academic dishonesty.

    - **Fabricated Citations or Data:** Some AI tools generate incorrect or fictitious citations—students must verify all sources to maintain research integrity.

    - **AI for Unauthorized Exam Assistance:** Using AI-powered tools to answer exam questions or complete assignments designed to assess individual understanding violates academic ethics.

- **Excessive Dependence on AI Without Intellectual Engagement:** When students rely entirely on AI for content creation without critical analysis or modification, they risk academic stagnation rather than skill development.

By establishing these ethical distinctions, faculty can guide students toward responsible AI use while preserving the integrity of academic work.

Guidelines for Students Using AI-Assisted Research Tools

As AI technologies become integrated into research and writing processes, students require structured guidance on using these tools responsibly. Institutions should implement AI usage policies that clearly define acceptable and unacceptable practices, ensuring that students develop ethical research habits [205]. The following guidelines provide a foundation for responsible AI-assisted learning:

1. **Transparency and Disclosure**
   - Students should explicitly acknowledge AI's role in their work. If an AI tool was used for writing, summarization, or translation, a footnote or appendix should disclose its usage.
   - Courses should incorporate standardized AI citation guidelines (e.g., APA's evolving stance on AI-generated text citation).

2. **Verification of AI-Generated Content**
   - AI-generated summaries, references, and factual claims should always be cross-checked with authoritative sources.
   - Students should be encouraged to apply critical thinking to AI outputs, questioning the validity and bias of the information presented.

3. **Enhancement, Not Replacement**
   - AI should serve as a learning aid rather than a shortcut. Students must demonstrate their own analytical and critical thinking skills in all AI-assisted submissions.
   - Assignments should require students to reflect on their research process, explaining how AI was used and how they verified its outputs.

4. **Avoiding Intellectual Overreliance**
   - Faculty should encourage students to balance AI usage with traditional research methods, such as engaging with primary texts, conducting peer discussions, and seeking faculty mentorship.
   - Overreliance on AI can diminish students' ability to synthesize information, form arguments, and develop independent research skills.

5. **Ethical Citation of AI-Generated Content**
    - If AI-generated content significantly contributes to a written work, it should be cited according to emerging citation standards.
    - Example citation for ChatGPT (APA format):
    OpenAI. (2023). ChatGPT (Version 4) [Large language model]. https://openai.com

Institutions should also offer workshops or digital literacy training on AI ethics to ensure that students fully grasp these principles.

Faculty Responsibilities in AI-Integrated Learning Environments

The increasing presence of AI in education demands that faculty proactively shape policies, foster digital literacy, and design assessments that reflect academic integrity. Faculty responsibilities in AI-integrated classrooms include:

1. **Establishing Clear AI Policies in Course Syllabi**
    - Clearly define the scope of AI usage permitted in coursework, including whether AI tools can be used for brainstorming, research, or writing assistance.
    - Provide students with examples of proper AI disclosure and citation practices.
    - Differentiate between assignments where AI assistance is acceptable (e.g., literature reviews) and those where it is strictly prohibited (e.g., personal reflection essays, closed-book exams).

2. **Redesigning Assessments to Promote Original Thought**
    - Shift from traditional recall-based assignments to application-based and critical analysis tasks that require deeper engagement.
    - Incorporate oral defenses, reflective writing, and iterative drafts to reduce reliance on AI-generated content.
    - Utilize active learning methods, such as debates, case studies, and collaborative projects, to assess independent reasoning rather than rote responses.

3. **Utilizing AI Detection Tools Ethically**
    - Tools such as Turnitin AI Detection, GPTZero, and Winston AI can help identify AI-generated submissions. However, these tools should be used responsibly to avoid false accusations.
    - Faculty should engage in discussions with students before taking disciplinary action, ensuring that AI usage is assessed contextually rather than punitively [206].

4. **Encouraging AI Literacy and Ethical AI Use**

- Faculty should educate students about the strengths and limitations of AI, helping them develop critical AI literacy [207].

- Assigning research projects that evaluate AI bias, misinformation, and ethical dilemmas can deepen students' understanding of AI's societal impact.

- Providing ethical case studies on AI misuse in academia and industry can reinforce responsible AI engagement.

5. **Staying Informed on AI Developments**

    - As AI technology evolves, faculty must continuously adapt their instructional approaches and update policies accordingly.

    - Engaging in faculty development programs, interdisciplinary discussions, and AI ethics training ensures that educators remain at the forefront of responsible AI integration.

Conclusion

AI and emerging technologies present both opportunities and challenges for academic integrity. Ethical AI use requires a balance between leveraging technological advancements and maintaining rigorous academic standards. By distinguishing ethical AI use from misconduct, guiding students in responsible AI-assisted research, and adapting teaching strategies for AI-integrated environments, faculty can help students develop both technical proficiency and academic integrity. As AI continues to evolve, it is the role of educators to ensure that these powerful tools enhance learning rather than erode the principles of scholarly honesty and intellectual responsibility.

Preventing Academic Dishonesty

1. **Encouraging Critical Engagement with Sources**

    - Assign tasks that require students to compare, contrast, and critique different scholarly perspectives rather than simply summarizing material.

    - Incorporate reflection questions asking students to explain how their sources influenced their thinking.

    - Use self-assessment rubrics, where students reflect on their research process, source credibility, and attribution methods.

2. **Leveraging Technology for Integrity and Skill-Building**

    - Introduce students to plagiarism detection tools like Turnitin, not just for punitive purposes but as a learning tool to refine citation and paraphrasing skills.

    - Provide access to AI-powered writing assistants (such as Grammarly or Hemingway Editor) while emphasizing that these tools should aid rather than replace critical thinking.

- Require students to submit a source-verification statement, explaining how they located and validated their references.

By integrating scaffolded writing strategies, faculty encourage authentic intellectual engagement, making it less likely that students will resort to dishonest shortcuts.

Addressing Unauthorized Collaboration and Contract Cheating

Two of the most challenging forms of academic dishonesty to detect and prevent are unauthorized collaboration (working with peers beyond allowed limits) and contract cheating (outsourcing work to third parties, such as essay mills or freelancers). Faculty must be proactive in both recognizing the risks and implementing strategies to mitigate them.

1. **Setting Clear Expectations for Collaboration**
    - Explicitly define what constitutes permissible vs. unauthorized collaboration in assignments. For example:
        - "Group discussion is encouraged, but all written responses must be independently formulated."
        - "Collaboration is allowed on problem-solving but not on final write-ups."
    - Utilize contract-style agreements in group projects where students outline individual contributions, reducing the likelihood of unbalanced participation or ghostwriting.

2. **Detecting and Preventing Contract Cheating**
    - Be alert to sudden changes in writing style, vocabulary, or complexity, which may indicate work completed by an external party.
    - Use plagiarism detection software to check for recycled papers from essay mills or public repositories.
    - Require students to submit reflection statements discussing their research and writing process, making outsourcing more difficult.
    - Incorporate oral follow-ups where students briefly discuss key elements of their work, reinforcing accountability.

3. **Cultivating a Culture of Academic Integrity**
    - Discuss the ethical implications of contract cheating, including how it devalues the student's education and future professional credibility.
    - Foster an environment where learners feel comfortable seeking help with research, time management, and writing struggles—reducing the pressure to cheat.

- Offer alternative assessment methods, such as project-based learning or authentic assessments, to shift the focus from high-stakes testing to ongoing learning.

By addressing unauthorized collaboration and contract cheating through a mix of clear expectations, proactive detection, and ethical discourse, faculty can create an academic culture that prioritizes genuine learning over dishonest shortcuts.

Conclusion

Preventing academic dishonesty requires a proactive, multi-layered approach that combines effective assignment design, structured writing processes, and clear policies on collaboration and contract cheating. By developing assessments that minimize opportunities for misconduct, guiding students through ethical research practices, and fostering an academic culture that values integrity, faculty can help ensure that students engage authentically with their learning. Ultimately, the goal is not just to prevent cheating but to cultivate an academic environment where intellectual honesty and original thought are intrinsic to the learning experience.

Handling Academic Misconduct Cases

Addressing academic misconduct is one of the most delicate responsibilities a professor must navigate. While upholding academic integrity is crucial, handling violations requires a balanced approach that integrates fairness, due process, and educational opportunities for students. Faculty must be able to identify signs of academic dishonesty, follow proper reporting and documentation procedures, understand institutional disciplinary policies, and communicate with students in a way that reinforces learning rather than simply punishing misconduct. The goal is not just to enforce rules but to cultivate a culture where students understand and uphold academic integrity as a core principle of scholarship.

Identifying Signs of Academic Dishonesty

Recognizing academic misconduct early is essential for maintaining a fair learning environment. While some cases of dishonesty are obvious, others require careful analysis. Faculty should be familiar with the common indicators of academic misconduct across different types of assessments.

1. **Signs of Plagiarism**
    - Sudden shifts in writing style, vocabulary, or complexity that do not match the student's previous work.
    - Disjointed sections of text that suggest copying and pasting from multiple sources.
    - Missing or incorrect citations, especially when sources are misattributed or nonexistent.
    - Overuse of AI-generated language patterns or non-contextual academic phrasing.

- Unusual formatting inconsistencies that suggest text was copied from another document.

2. **Signs of Cheating on Exams and Assignments**
    - Similar or identical responses from multiple students on exams or essays, especially in take-home or online assessments.
    - Illogical answers or formula application errors that suggest a student copied a response without understanding it.
    - Unusual timing of submissions, such as last-minute changes in work quality or students submitting assignments at the same exact timestamp.
    - Use of unauthorized materials, such as hidden notes, smart devices, or AI-generated answers during assessments.

3. **Signs of Unauthorized Collaboration and Contract Cheating**
    - Student work does not align with their previous academic performance.
    - Vague or generic explanations when asked to discuss their own work.
    - Highly polished assignments that lack the expected process work (e.g., no drafts, no edits, no engagement in feedback).
    - Work that closely resembles an external tutoring service, academic ghostwriting service, or an AI-generated report.

While these signs may indicate misconduct, they should not be treated as proof without investigation. Faculty must approach each case with neutrality, verifying concerns before making accusations.

Steps for Reporting and Documenting Incidents

Once academic dishonesty is suspected, faculty must follow structured procedures to ensure that cases are handled fairly and consistently. Proper documentation and adherence to institutional guidelines prevent misunderstandings and protect both faculty and students.

1. **Gather and Review Evidence**
    - Collect original student work, drafts, and prior submissions to identify inconsistencies.
    - Use plagiarism detection tools (e.g., Turnitin) but do not rely solely on software results—cross-check sources manually.
    - Compare the student's work with known AI-generated responses if AI misuse is suspected.

- Retain relevant exam logs, timestamp data, or discussion board history if cheating occurred in an online setting.

2. **Consult Institutional Policies**
    - Review the university's academic integrity policies, including definitions of misconduct, faculty responsibilities, and required procedures for reporting violations.
    - Determine if the case falls under low-level violations (e.g., improper citation due to lack of understanding) or serious violations (e.g., contract cheating or repeated offenses).

3. **Communicate with the Student (If Applicable)**
    - If institutional policy allows, schedule a confidential meeting with the student to discuss concerns.
    - Avoid accusations—instead, ask the student to explain their work.
    - If the student admits to misconduct, guide them toward remedial resources (e.g., writing center, citation workshops) if the institution offers an educational intervention option.

4. **Officially Report the Incident**
    - Complete the required academic misconduct report, detailing:
        - The nature of the violation (e.g., plagiarism, unauthorized collaboration).
        - Supporting evidence (e.g., side-by-side comparison of sources, similarity report).
        - Steps taken to verify the misconduct.
        - Any prior offenses (if applicable).
    - Submit the report to the appropriate academic integrity office or disciplinary committee.

5. **Maintain Confidentiality**
    - Avoid discussing the case with other students or faculty unless required by policy.
    - Protect student privacy while ensuring the issue is handled transparently within institutional frameworks.

Proper documentation and adherence to formal reporting procedures protect both faculty and students, ensuring fairness and due process.

Institutional Procedures for Disciplinary Actions

Each institution has a structured process for reviewing academic misconduct cases, typically involving:

1. **Initial Faculty Review**
   - Faculty may assign a penalty within their authority (e.g., grade reduction, rewrite opportunity) for minor first-time violations.
   - For severe cases, the misconduct must be escalated to an institutional review board or academic conduct office.

2. **Academic Integrity Hearing or Review Board**
   - A panel consisting of faculty members, administrators, and sometimes student representatives may assess the case.
   - The student is typically given an opportunity to respond to the allegations and present their side.

3. **Sanctions and Consequences** *(Determined by Institutional Policies)*
   - **Minor Violations:** Formal warning, required academic integrity workshops, opportunity to revise work.
   - **Moderate Violations:** Assignment failure, course failure, notation on academic record.
   - **Severe Violations:** Suspension, expulsion, permanent academic misconduct record.

4. **Appeals Process** *(if applicable)*
   - Most institutions offer an appeal process where students can contest the decision under specific conditions (e.g., procedural errors, new evidence).

Understanding these procedures ensures faculty follow due process and avoid personal bias in enforcement.

Communicating with Students About Misconduct in a Constructive Manner

Approaching academic misconduct with a constructive, educational mindset rather than solely punitive measures helps students understand their mistakes and prevent future violations. Effective communication strategies include:

1. **Use a Neutral, Non-Confrontational Tone**
   - Avoid accusatory language (e.g., "You cheated on this paper.") and instead use open-ended statements:
     - "I noticed some inconsistencies in your writing. Can you walk me through your research process?"

- "I'm concerned about some similarities between your paper and another source. Can we discuss your approach?"

2. **Frame the Conversation as a Learning Opportunity**
    o If the misconduct is unintentional, focus on skill development:
        - "I see that citation was a challenge here. Let's work on improving your source attribution."
    o For intentional violations, emphasize accountability while encouraging ethical academic habits:
        - "Integrity is important in academic work, and I want to help you understand how to navigate challenges ethically moving forward."

3. **Explain Institutional Policies Clearly**
    o Walk students through the academic misconduct process, ensuring they understand potential consequences and their rights in the review process.

4. **Encourage Remediation When Possible**
    o If policies allow, provide students with resources such as:
        - Writing center workshops on plagiarism.
        - Academic integrity training.
        - Opportunities to revise and resubmit work under faculty supervision.

By handling academic misconduct transparently and educationally, faculty can reinforce ethical scholarship while deterring future violations.

Conclusion

Effectively addressing academic misconduct requires a structured yet compassionate approach—faculty must be vigilant in identifying dishonest behaviors, follow proper reporting procedures, and engage students in meaningful discussions about integrity. While disciplinary actions serve as deterrents, the ultimate goal should be education over punishment, ensuring that students develop the skills and ethical reasoning necessary for long-term academic and professional success. By fostering a culture of integrity through proactive engagement, faculty can reduce incidents of misconduct and empower students to take ownership of their learning with honesty and accountability.

Cultivating a Culture of Integrity

Academic integrity is not merely a set of rules to be followed—it is a fundamental ethos that underpins scholarly work, intellectual honesty, and the credibility of higher education. Creating a culture of integrity requires a proactive, holistic approach that goes beyond enforcing policies to instilling ethical values in students. Faculty play a crucial role in shaping this culture by fostering ethical scholarship, setting clear expectations, supporting students in ethical decision-making, and serving as role models for integrity in research and teaching. When students internalize academic honesty as a core value rather than an obligation, they are more likely to engage in responsible scholarship throughout their academic and professional lives.

Promoting a Classroom Culture of Ethical Scholarship

A culture of integrity begins with intentional course design, inclusive discussions, and a supportive academic environment where students understand the importance of honest scholarship. Professors can embed ethical scholarship into their teaching practices through the following strategies:

1. **Integrate Integrity into Course Discussions**
    - Discuss why academic honesty matters, not just in terms of policy enforcement but as a foundational principle of scholarship.
    - Relate integrity to professional fields—engineers, doctors, and business leaders must adhere to ethical standards, just as students must in academia.
    - Use real-world examples of academic fraud, retracted research, and ethical dilemmas to illustrate the consequences of dishonesty.

2. **Encourage Open Dialogue About Integrity**
    - Create a judgment-free space where students feel comfortable asking about proper attribution, collaboration boundaries, and ethical dilemmas.
    - Encourage students to share challenges they face with citations, time management, and pressure to succeed—many instances of dishonesty stem from academic stress rather than malicious intent.
    - Address misconceptions about plagiarism and academic misconduct, ensuring students know the difference between unintentional mistakes and clear violations.

3. **Design Assessments That Reinforce Integrity**
    - Use process-based assignments where students submit outlines, annotated bibliographies, and drafts before the final paper to discourage last-minute dishonesty.
    - Incorporate reflective writing where students explain their research process, cite sources critically, and justify their methodological choices.
    - Provide alternative assessment methods (oral exams, case studies, peer-reviewed projects) that measure learning beyond standard essays and multiple-choice tests.

By embedding discussions of ethical scholarship into the classroom experience, faculty create an environment where integrity becomes an expectation rather than an afterthought.

Encouraging Academic Honesty Through Clear Expectations

An effective way to prevent academic dishonesty is to establish clear, explicit expectations regarding ethical conduct. Students often struggle with academic integrity not because they wish to cheat, but because they are uncertain about boundaries, citation expectations, or collaboration policies. Faculty can minimize ambiguity by providing well-defined guidelines.

1. **Clearly Articulate Academic Integrity Policies**
    - Include an academic honesty statement in the syllabus, outlining:
        - What constitutes plagiarism, unauthorized collaboration, and AI misuse.
        - Specific citation requirements (APA, MLA, Chicago) for coursework.
        - Institutional policies on academic misconduct, reporting procedures, and consequences.

2. **Clarify Permissible Use of AI and Online Tools**
    - As AI becomes more integrated into education, specify acceptable vs. unethical AI-assisted work.
    - Provide students with examples of proper AI attribution and emphasize that AI should supplement, not replace, critical thinking.

3. **Set Clear Collaboration Boundaries**
    - Clearly define what level of group work is permitted for assignments.
    - Differentiate between peer discussions, collaborative projects, and unauthorized help—students should understand when working with others crosses ethical lines.

4. **Use Rubrics to Reinforce Ethical Scholarship**
    - Provide detailed grading rubrics that assess originality, citation quality, and critical engagement with sources.
    - Include a self-assessment checklist in assignments, asking students to confirm they have adhered to integrity guidelines.

By establishing transparency around expectations, faculty eliminate ambiguity and empower students to make ethical academic choices.

Supporting Students in Ethical Decision-Making

Academic integrity is not just about following rules—it is about developing ethical reasoning skills that help students make sound decisions even when faced with challenges. Many instances of misconduct stem from academic pressure, fear of failure, or lack of time management, rather than deliberate dishonesty. Faculty can support students in making ethical choices through proactive interventions.

1. **Teach Ethical Decision-Making Frameworks**
   - Introduce students to ethical reasoning models, such as:
     - **The Consequentialist Approach** – Examining the impact of dishonest actions on themselves, peers, and the institution.
     - **The Rights-Based Approach** – Emphasizing fairness, respect for intellectual property, and scholarly honesty.
     - **The Virtue Ethics Approach** – Encouraging students to act in ways that align with their personal and professional integrity.

2. **Address Time Management and Academic Stress**
   - Provide resources for time management, study strategies, and dealing with academic pressure.
   - Normalize discussions about academic struggles—students who feel supported are less likely to resort to dishonesty.
   - Encourage students to seek help before deadlines, offering revision opportunities and office hours to reduce panic-driven plagiarism.

3. **Offer Alternative Resolutions for Minor Violations**
   - Instead of immediately penalizing unintentional plagiarism, consider remediation strategies such as:
     - Requiring students to attend an academic integrity workshop.
     - Allowing rewrites with guided feedback on citation and paraphrasing.

By equipping students with ethical reasoning tools and academic support, faculty reduce the likelihood of misconduct and foster independent, responsible scholars.

Faculty as Role Models for Integrity in Research and Teaching

Students look to faculty as examples of academic integrity and ethical leadership. Professors who model honesty, fairness, and scholarly responsibility create an environment where students are more likely to uphold similar values. Faculty should demonstrate integrity in research, teaching, grading, and professional conduct.

1. **Model Proper Citation and Attribution in Teaching**
   - Consistently cite sources in lectures, slides, and handouts, emphasizing that even educators must follow attribution standards.
   - When discussing AI-generated content or external materials, acknowledge their sources transparently.

2. **Adhere to Fair and Transparent Grading Practices**

- Grade work consistently and objectively, avoiding favoritism or leniency for certain students.
- Provide clear feedback on assignments, explaining why points were deducted rather than making vague comments.
- Be willing to admit errors in grading or assessment if mistakes occur—demonstrating humility reinforces integrity.

3. **Engage in Ethical Research Practices**
    - Uphold research ethics by avoiding data manipulation, properly crediting co-authors, and following institutional research protocols.
    - Discuss real-world cases of research misconduct (e.g., data falsification, predatory publishing) to emphasize the long-term consequences of dishonesty in academia.

4. **Encourage a Growth Mindset Around Integrity**
    - Avoid framing academic dishonesty as a "gotcha" moment—instead, reinforce that ethical scholarship is a skill students can develop over time.
    - Praise students for original thinking, strong citation habits, and ethical research practices rather than just penalizing misconduct.

By embodying integrity in their teaching, research, and interactions, faculty create a learning environment where academic honesty becomes the norm rather than the exception.

Conclusion

Creating a culture of integrity requires deliberate effort from faculty, institutions, and students. By fostering ethical scholarship, setting clear expectations, equipping students with decision-making tools, and modeling integrity in research and teaching, professors lay the groundwork for an academic environment where honesty and responsibility flourish. Academic integrity is not about punishment—it is about developing ethical, independent thinkers who value scholarship, respect intellectual contributions, and carry these principles into their professional lives. Through education, transparency, and mentorship, faculty can instill academic integrity as a guiding principle rather than just a rule to follow.

Upholding Ethical Scholarship and Integrity

Academic integrity is more than just a set of rules—it is a fundamental principle that defines the credibility of education, research, and scholarly contributions. Faculty members serve as both role models and enforcers of these ethical standards, ensuring that students understand the importance of honesty, proper attribution, and responsible scholarship.

By proactively addressing academic misconduct, implementing fair policies, and promoting ethical research practices, institutions create an environment where integrity is valued and upheld. Faculty who engage students in discussions about academic ethics, design assessments that minimize opportunities for dishonesty, and fairly adjudicate cases of misconduct contribute to a culture of trust and respect within academia.

Ultimately, fostering academic integrity goes beyond preventing violations—it prepares students to become responsible scholars, ethical professionals, and lifelong learners. Through faculty commitment to these principles, institutions can sustain a strong academic culture that benefits students, researchers, and the broader educational community.

Chapter 15: Faculty Well-Being and Psychological Resilience

The Unique Psychological Landscape of Higher Education

Higher education professionals operate in an environment that combines intellectual intensity with organizational complexity. Faculty roles are not limited to teaching; they extend to research, service, advising, and administrative responsibilities. Each domain carries distinct expectations, metrics of success, and accountability structures. The simultaneous demand to excel in all areas creates a cumulative psychological burden that is qualitatively different from other professions [207].

Figure 15.1. Academic Integrity [219].

The teaching dimension requires constant preparation, curriculum updates, and adaptation to diverse student populations. Instructors must balance the delivery of disciplinary expertise with student-centered pedagogy, technology integration, and increasingly diverse learner needs. The requirement to demonstrate both subject mastery and innovative instructional methods heightens the sense of professional pressure.

The research dimension is equally demanding. Faculty are expected to maintain a steady record of scholarly output, secure external funding, and contribute to the intellectual reputation of their institution. This research productivity is often tied directly to promotion, tenure, or contract renewal, creating a high-stakes environment where lapses in output may have significant career consequences.

The service and governance dimension includes committee work, student advising, mentoring junior colleagues, and institutional planning. While these contributions are essential to the functioning of the academic community, they are often undervalued in formal evaluation systems. The resulting imbalance—high effort with limited recognition—creates a persistent source of frustration.

The administrative dimension has grown steadily in complexity. Faculty must comply with accreditation standards, reporting requirements, and policy changes related to higher education funding, assessment, and compliance. These obligations require extensive documentation and often compete directly with time allocated for research and teaching.

The culture of academia reinforces these pressures by normalizing overwork. Long hours, blurred boundaries between professional and personal life, and expectations of constant availability are often perceived as implicit requirements for success. Many faculty carry work home, grading papers or writing research articles during evenings and weekends, which reduces opportunities for rest and recovery.

Adding to this landscape are external and systemic pressures: shifting institutional policies, performance-based funding models, rapidly evolving technologies, and heightened scrutiny from the public and policymakers. The pace of change in higher education means faculty must continually adapt their teaching methods, research strategies, and service commitments. These layers of responsibility expand the scope of stress well beyond the core work of teaching and scholarship.

Key Insight: The psychological demands of academia are not limited to workload volume. They arise from the intersection of multiple high-stakes roles, the undervaluation of service labor, the normalization of overwork, and the expectation of continuous adaptation in an evolving educational environment.

Chronic Stressors in Academic Life

Several persistent stressors define the academic profession, creating sustained pressures that shape faculty well-being and performance over the course of a career. Unlike temporary challenges, these stressors are embedded in the structure of higher education and therefore require deliberate recognition and management.

Job Market Pressures

The academic labor market is intensely competitive, with far more qualified candidates than available tenure-track positions. Early-career scholars face years of temporary contracts, adjunct roles, or postdoctoral appointments before securing stable employment. Even after obtaining a position, the pressure does not subside. Concerns about tenure, promotion, contract renewal, or departmental restructuring create ongoing uncertainty. In some cases, entire programs are eliminated due to budget cuts or shifting institutional priorities, leaving faculty vulnerable to job loss despite strong performance. This continual state of precarity erodes psychological safety and contributes to chronic anxiety.

Funding Uncertainties

For research-active faculty, the ability to secure and maintain external funding is essential for sustaining laboratories, hiring graduate assistants, and advancing scholarly agendas. Grant competitions are rigorous, with success rates often in the single digits [208]. The constant cycle of proposal writing, peer review, rejection, and resubmission consumes vast amounts of time and emotional energy. Even established scholars face pressures to continually generate funding streams in order to maintain institutional support. For faculty in fields with limited funding opportunities, the challenge is compounded, forcing them to balance research ambitions with financial constraints.

Publication Demands

The maxim "publish or perish" continues to define faculty evaluation, particularly in research-focused institutions. Publication is often the primary criterion for tenure and promotion decisions, creating a relentless pressure to produce high-quality scholarship at a rapid pace. This demand requires balancing multiple, often conflicting, responsibilities: teaching, service, administrative duties, and personal life. The peer review process adds another layer of strain, as rejection and revision cycles are frequent and can extend timelines for years [209]. Faculty who are unable to sustain consistent publication records may experience diminished professional identity and stalled career advancement.

Workload Imbalances

Beyond research and teaching, faculty carry extensive responsibilities in advising, mentoring, committee service, and accreditation reporting. These tasks are essential to institutional function and student success but are often undervalued in formal recognition systems. The result is a mismatch between effort and reward, with faculty devoting substantial time to "invisible labor" that does not directly advance their careers. Service expectations can be disproportionately distributed, with women and faculty of color often shouldering heavier advising and mentoring responsibilities due to student demand for relatable role models [210]. Over time, these imbalances create frustration, fatigue, and inequity across the faculty body.

Key Insight: Chronic stressors in academia are structural, not incidental. Job insecurity, funding competition, relentless publication demands, and undervalued service work create a cycle of sustained pressure that requires intentional institutional and individual strategies to mitigate.

Variation Across Institution Types

While these stressors are present across higher education, their intensity and form vary by institutional mission:

- **Research Universities (R1 and R2)**
    - Funding and publication dominate faculty stress profiles. The expectation to secure external grants and publish in high-impact journals is paramount.
    - Service obligations may be lighter compared to teaching-intensive institutions, but administrative reporting related to grants and compliance is significant.
    - Faculty in these environments often experience pressure to maintain international visibility while mentoring graduate students and managing research teams.
- **Community Colleges**
    - Teaching loads are the primary source of stress, with faculty often teaching five or more courses per semester [211].
    - Research is typically not required, but heavy advising and student support responsibilities create intense demands on time and emotional energy.
    - Limited resources for professional development and fewer opportunities for tenure-track advancement can heighten job insecurity.
- **Liberal Arts Colleges**
    - Faculty are expected to balance teaching excellence with scholarly productivity, though the weight given to each varies by institution.
    - Small class sizes and close student-faculty relationships can increase mentoring and advising loads, which, while rewarding, may also lead to burnout.

- o Research expectations may not focus on external funding, but faculty are still under pressure to publish regularly, often without the infrastructure of large research universities.
- **Regional Public and Teaching-Oriented Universities**
  - o Faculty face a hybrid stress profile: teaching-heavy loads, moderate research expectations, and substantial service requirements.
  - o Accreditation reporting, program reviews, and community partnerships add additional layers of responsibility.
  - o Stress often emerges from role conflict—being expected to perform at research-university levels while meeting teaching and service demands more typical of community colleges.

Key Insight: Although the structural stressors of academia—job insecurity, funding competition, publication pressure, and undervalued service—are universal, their expression differs across institutional contexts. Tailored strategies are required to address the unique balance of pressures within each type of institution.

Seasonal Patterns of Academic Stress

Faculty stress does not remain constant throughout the year; it follows cyclical rhythms tied closely to the academic calendar. These recurring patterns create predictable peaks of workload and psychological strain that can accumulate over time if not actively managed.

Semester Cycles
Each term brings a unique set of stress points. At the beginning of the semester, faculty must finalize syllabi, update course materials, and prepare lectures or online modules. New student cohorts require orientation, advising, and early interventions to support success. By mid-semester, grading responsibilities escalate, student performance issues emerge, and faculty are called upon to provide feedback that balances encouragement with accountability. The end of the semester is typically the most intense, combining final grading, exam administration, and submission of grades with simultaneous administrative demands such as assessment reports, course evaluations, and faculty activity summaries. This recurring cycle leaves little time for recovery, as preparation for the next term begins almost immediately.

Conference Seasons
Academic conferences, often scheduled in late fall and spring, are vital for professional development, networking, and scholarly visibility. However, they add significant pressure. Preparing conference papers, presentations, and travel logistics requires time carved out from teaching and research obligations. For faculty presenting high-stakes work—such as preliminary dissertation findings, grant-funded projects, or book proposals—the performance expectations can be daunting. Travel itself introduces additional stressors, from financial costs and jet lag to disruptions in personal and family routines. While conferences can provide rejuvenation through intellectual exchange, they also intensify faculty workload before and after the event.

Job Market Timing
The academic job market follows a relatively fixed seasonal rhythm, with application deadlines

clustered in the fall and interviews or campus visits concentrated in the winter and spring. This cycle affects both job-seekers and faculty serving on search committees. Early-career scholars face the stress of assembling application materials, tailoring cover letters, and navigating rejection cycles, all while maintaining existing teaching or research duties. Senior faculty experience parallel stress as they evaluate hundreds of applications, conduct interviews, and coordinate candidate visits. The dual burden of mentoring job-seekers and participating in searches further amplifies workload intensity during these seasons.

Accreditation and Reporting Cycles

Beyond semester and hiring rhythms, faculty also encounter periodic institutional demands tied to accreditation, program review, and assessment cycles. These tasks often occur on multi-year schedules, yet they bring concentrated bursts of work when deadlines arrive. Accreditation reviews require extensive documentation of curriculum design, student outcomes, faculty qualifications, and resource allocations. Even when administrative staff provide support, faculty bear the responsibility for preparing evidence of learning effectiveness, revising curricula, and demonstrating compliance with external standards. Because these cycles often overlap with end-of-semester duties, they compound stress at already high-pressure times of the year.

Key Insight: The cyclical nature of academic stress means that faculty are rarely free from high-pressure demands. Instead, stress intensifies in predictable patterns linked to teaching, research dissemination, hiring processes, and accountability measures. Recognizing these cycles allows institutions and individuals to plan proactively, distributing workload more evenly and building in recovery periods where possible.

Recognizing Early Warning Signs of Burnout and Compassion Fatigue

Understanding the indicators of psychological strain is critical for early intervention. Burnout and compassion fatigue rarely emerge suddenly; they develop gradually as unresolved stress accumulates over time. By identifying early warning signs, faculty and institutions can implement timely strategies to prevent long-term impairment.

Emotional Indicators

Persistent irritability, cynicism, or emotional withdrawal from colleagues and students often signal the onset of burnout. Faculty may notice a loss of enthusiasm for teaching, research, or service, finding little joy in activities that once felt meaningful. Emotional detachment can also manifest as impatience with students, reduced empathy during advising, or avoidance of collaborative work. Over time, this emotional numbing creates distance from both professional responsibilities and supportive social networks, which worsens isolation.

Cognitive Indicators

Burnout and compassion fatigue also impair mental functioning. Faculty may experience difficulty concentrating, indecisiveness, or reduced problem-solving capacity. Tasks that once felt manageable—designing a syllabus, drafting a manuscript, or evaluating student work—can feel overwhelming. Creativity and intellectual curiosity, central to academic identity, may diminish. A faculty member who once thrived on exploring new research directions may instead default to rote tasks, signaling cognitive fatigue.

Physical Indicators

Chronic stress often manifests somatically. Common warning signs include persistent fatigue, disrupted sleep patterns, frequent headaches, or gastrointestinal problems. Faculty may notice a decline in immune function, leading to recurrent illness during peak stress periods, such as midterms or finals. Because academia often normalizes exhaustion, these physical signals are easily dismissed as part of the job rather than acknowledged as indicators of unsustainable strain.

Behavioral Indicators

Behavioral changes frequently accompany burnout and compassion fatigue. Faculty may increasingly rely on avoidance strategies such as procrastination, excessive delegation, or withdrawal from departmental service. Professional communities that once provided support may be neglected, leading to decreased engagement in conferences, faculty meetings, or collaborative projects. Some may adopt unhealthy coping mechanisms, such as overconsumption of caffeine, alcohol, or reliance on late-night work patterns that further disrupt recovery.

Burnout vs. Compassion Fatigue

- Burnout develops when prolonged stress depletes emotional and physical resources, leaving faculty feeling exhausted, disengaged, and ineffective. It is most strongly tied to workload, organizational culture, and mismatched expectations.
- Compassion fatigue, by contrast, often stems from sustained exposure to the struggles of students or colleagues. Faculty engaged in mentoring, counseling, or working with vulnerable populations may find themselves emotionally drained by repeated exposure to hardship. While burnout is more structural, compassion fatigue is more relational. Both conditions overlap, diminishing teaching effectiveness, research productivity, and overall job satisfaction if left unaddressed.

Key Takeaways

- Burnout and compassion fatigue are gradual, cumulative responses to unresolved stress in academia.
- Early warning signs appear in emotional, cognitive, physical, and behavioral domains.
- Burnout is largely tied to workload and institutional structures, while compassion fatigue emerges from emotional investment in others.
- Early recognition and proactive intervention are essential to preserve faculty well-being, professional effectiveness, and long-term career satisfaction.

Imposter Syndrome in Academic Contexts

Despite their advanced expertise and demonstrated accomplishments, many faculty members struggle with a persistent sense of inadequacy commonly known as imposter syndrome. Unlike ordinary moments of self-doubt, imposter syndrome is a pervasive belief that success is undeserved and that eventual exposure as a "fraud" is inevitable. Within academia, this experience is intensified by the culture of constant evaluation, peer comparison, and public visibility. Faculty are judged not only by students through evaluations, but also by colleagues, journal reviewers, funding agencies, and administrators. These overlapping systems of critique can reinforce feelings of unworthiness, even in the face of awards, publications, or strong teaching outcomes.

What makes imposter syndrome particularly significant in academia is its breadth and persistence across career stages. Graduate students may feel unqualified compared to their peers, early-career faculty may question whether they can meet tenure demands, and senior scholars may attribute decades of achievement to external factors such as timing, luck, or collaborators rather than personal merit. Far from being a problem of individual psychology alone, imposter syndrome is structurally reinforced by academic norms that elevate competition, emphasize flawless performance, and reward comparison over collaboration.

Defining Imposter Syndrome and Its Prevalence in Academia

Imposter syndrome is the ongoing perception one's accomplishments are undeserved or the result of luck rather than ability. Individuals experiencing it fear being exposed as a fraud despite clear evidence of competence and achievement. This internalized self-doubt persists even when external validation—such as awards, publications, or positive student outcomes—confirms their abilities [212].

In academia, imposter syndrome is not confined to a single stage of professional development. Graduate students often feel overwhelmed by the expertise of peers, questioning whether they were admitted by mistake. Early-career faculty may interpret the demands of tenure-track positions as proof that they do not belong in competitive environments. Even senior scholars with established reputations may quietly believe their success is tenuous, attributing achievements to fortunate timing, supportive collaborators, or institutional resources rather than personal merit. This broad distribution underscores how imposter syndrome is embedded in the culture of academia rather than isolated to individual psychology.

The academic culture intensifies these feelings. The profession is structured around constant evaluation and critique, from student evaluations and peer review to annual performance assessments and tenure dossiers. At the same time, academia fosters comparison with high-achieving peers, where publications, grants, and accolades are publicly visible markers of worth. The combination of relentless scrutiny and competitive benchmarking creates fertile ground for imposter syndrome to thrive.

Common Triggers

Several recurring experiences heighten imposter feelings among faculty, reinforcing the cycle of self-doubt:

- **Teaching evaluations**
  Anonymous student feedback, particularly when negative or inconsistent, can amplify insecurity. Faculty may fixate on a handful of critical comments while dismissing the majority of positive responses. Over time, this selective focus distorts self-perception, leading instructors to equate occasional dissatisfaction with overall incompetence.

- **Peer review**
  The manuscript and grant review process is deliberately rigorous and often critical, with rejection rates that remain high even for established scholars. Faculty may interpret these rejections as proof of inadequacy rather than recognizing them as structural features of an intensely competitive system. The repetitive cycle of rejection and revision can erode confidence and reinforce feelings of being unqualified.
- **Public presentations**
  Academic visibility—through conferences, invited lectures, or dissertation defenses—places faculty in vulnerable positions where their expertise is under scrutiny. The anticipation of challenging questions or public critique often triggers fears of being exposed as unprepared or intellectually deficient. This is particularly acute for early-career scholars presenting alongside seasoned experts.
- **Comparison culture**
  The highly visible nature of academic accomplishments—publications, awards, promotions, and grant announcements—creates an environment of constant benchmarking. Faculty frequently measure themselves against colleagues, sometimes overlooking their own achievements. This comparison culture fosters perceptions of falling short, even when accomplishments are equivalent or greater in scope.

Key Insight: Imposter syndrome in academia is not a fleeting sense of self-doubt but a systemically reinforced experience, triggered by structural practices of evaluation, critique, and comparison. Its prevalence across all career stages underscores the need for both individual coping strategies and institutional cultures that normalize vulnerability and recognize diverse forms of achievement.

Strategies for Reframing Self-Doubt and Building Authentic Confidence

Overcoming imposter syndrome does not mean eliminating self-doubt entirely. Doubt can serve a constructive role by encouraging reflection, humility, and continued growth. The challenge lies in reframing self-doubt into a balanced perspective that acknowledges achievements while recognizing areas for development. Several evidence-informed strategies help faculty transform imposter feelings into sources of resilience and authentic confidence.

Evidence-Based Self-Assessment
One of the most effective counterbalances to imposter thoughts is maintaining a tangible record of accomplishments. Faculty often remember criticism far more vividly than praise, creating a skewed self-image. By keeping teaching evaluations, thank-you notes from students, letters of support from colleagues, and records of publications or funded projects, faculty can revisit objective indicators of competence when self-doubt arises. Portfolios of achievements serve not only as reminders of ability but also as resources for promotion and tenure dossiers, reinforcing their dual value.

Normalizing Rejection
Rejection is a constant in academic life, from grant proposals to article submissions. Success rates for competitive funding often fall below 10–20 percent, making rejection the rule rather than the exception [213]. Faculty who internalize these outcomes as personal failures risk

reinforcing imposter beliefs. Reframing rejection as a structural feature of academia shifts the narrative: it reflects systemic scarcity, not individual inadequacy. Sharing rejection experiences in peer groups further normalizes the process, helping faculty see that even highly accomplished scholars face frequent setbacks.

Strength-Focused Reflection

Imposter feelings often stem from focusing on deficits rather than contributions. Faculty benefit from deliberately identifying their unique strengths and impact within the academic community. These may include innovative teaching practices that improve student engagement, interdisciplinary collaborations that bridge fields, or mentoring relationships that shape student trajectories. Reflecting on such contributions provides a more balanced self-assessment, highlighting dimensions of academic work not always captured in traditional metrics but essential to institutional and student success.

Mindset Shifts

A critical strategy involves moving from a performance mindset to a growth mindset. In a performance mindset, faculty frame each task as a test of belonging or competence: "I must prove I deserve this role." This perspective heightens pressure and magnifies failure. A growth mindset reframes experiences as opportunities for ongoing development: "I am continually learning and improving as a scholar and teacher." This shift reduces the burden of perfection, normalizes mistakes as part of intellectual growth, and fosters resilience in the face of setbacks.

Integrating Practices into Daily Routines

For these strategies to be effective, they must be woven into everyday academic routines rather than reserved for moments of crisis. Examples include setting aside time each semester to update an achievement portfolio, discussing rejection experiences openly in departmental meetings, or incorporating reflective journaling to track strengths and progress. Regular practice helps embed reframed perspectives into faculty identity, gradually reducing the intensity of imposter beliefs.

Key Insight: Authentic confidence emerges not from denying self-doubt but from balancing it with evidence, perspective, and intentional reflection. By normalizing rejection, recognizing strengths, and adopting growth-oriented mindsets, faculty can transform imposter feelings into motivation for continued scholarly and personal development.

Creating Supportive Peer Networks for Mutual Validation

Supportive academic communities are powerful buffers against imposter syndrome because they provide collective reassurance, normalize challenges, and affirm diverse pathways to success. Isolation often intensifies self-doubt, while shared dialogue reframes experiences as common rather than personal failings. Faculty at all stages benefit from intentional peer support structures that create safe spaces for candid discussion and mutual encouragement.

Forms of Peer Networks

- **Peer mentoring groups**: Small groups of faculty or graduate students who meet regularly to discuss professional progress, share feedback, and hold one another

accountable. These groups help reduce the sense of solitary struggle and provide practical strategies for navigating academic challenges.
- **Writing circles**: Collaborative spaces where participants share drafts, set writing goals, and provide constructive critique. Beyond productivity gains, these circles reinforce that struggles with rejection or revision are universal.
- **Informal discussion forums**: Departmental brown-bag lunches, online communities, or affinity groups create lower-stakes venues where faculty can share concerns and successes without the pressure of formal evaluation.

Functions of Supportive Networks

- **Sharing rejection narratives**: By openly discussing manuscript rejections, failed grant applications, or critical reviews, faculty normalize these experiences as part of academic life rather than as personal inadequacies.
- **Demystifying expectations**: Peer groups clarify opaque aspects of academia, such as promotion criteria, tenure processes, or conference etiquette, which often fuel uncertainty and imposter feelings.
- **Exchanging coping strategies**: Practical advice on managing workload, handling critical feedback, or preparing for presentations helps faculty build toolkits for resilience.
- **Celebrating successes**: Recognition of milestones—publishing an article, completing a project, or mentoring a student—reinforces self-worth and counters the tendency to discount accomplishments.

Role of Senior Faculty
Senior faculty can strengthen these networks by modeling vulnerability. When established scholars candidly share their own struggles with self-doubt, they validate the experiences of early-career colleagues and dismantle the myth of effortless success. Mentorship that acknowledges both achievements and challenges create a more authentic academic culture. Senior faculty also serve as advocates, ensuring that institutional recognition includes mentoring, teaching innovations, and service contributions alongside research productivity.

Long-Term Cultural Impact
Over time, supportive peer networks foster a culture of mutual recognition and inclusivity. Instead of reinforcing competition and comparison, these communities emphasize collaboration and shared growth. By reducing the isolation that fuels imposter beliefs, networks encourage faculty to view themselves as valued members of a broader scholarly community. Institutions that intentionally support such initiatives—through funding for writing groups, mentorship programs, or faculty learning communities—reinforce the message that psychological well-being is central to academic success.

Key Takeaways

- Imposter syndrome is pervasive in academia, affecting faculty across all career stages.
- Common triggers include teaching evaluations, peer review, public presentations, and comparison to peers.
- Reframing self-doubt into growth-oriented reflection helps build authentic confidence.

- Supportive peer networks foster validation, normalize challenges, and create long-term cultural change that reduces isolation and self-doubt.

Managing Rejection and Professional Setbacks

The Psychology of Academic Rejection

Rejection is woven into the fabric of academic life. It is not an exception but an expectation, occurring in nearly every professional domain: manuscripts declined by journals, grant proposals that fail to secure funding, conference submissions that are not accepted, and job applications that end without interviews. Because academia is built on competitive evaluation, these rejections are routine, yet their psychological impact is disproportionately heavy.

The weight of rejection stems from the profession's reliance on external validation. Faculty careers are often measured by publication records, grant success, and peer recognition. Each rejection challenges these markers of legitimacy and can feel like a verdict on intellectual worth. The impact is not simply professional but also deeply personal, as academic identity is often tightly bound to scholarly productivity.

For early-career scholars, the intensity of rejection can be especially acute. Graduate students and postdoctoral fellows, who are still building professional identity, may interpret rejection as confirmation that they lack the ability or intellect required to succeed. When a first manuscript is declined or a job application is unsuccessful, the experience can reinforce feelings of precarity and amplify imposter syndrome. The perception that one misstep could derail a career heightens the emotional toll of each rejection.

Mid-career faculty encounter rejection in different forms. After tenure, they may face the disappointment of unfunded projects, shelved book proposals, or unsuccessful bids for leadership positions. These setbacks can trigger doubts about stagnation, professional plateauing, or declining relevance. Rejection at this stage may feel like a challenge to long-term viability rather than initial belonging.

Even senior scholars are not immune. Established reputations can be unsettled by critical reviews, unfunded large-scale grants, or negative responses to high-profile publications. At this level, rejection may feel threatening to an entire body of work or legacy, raising fears that decades of scholarly contribution are being undermined or overlooked. The emotional sting is compounded when reputational standing is perceived to decline in highly competitive or fast-moving fields.

The structural realities of academia, however, are important to remember. Acceptance rates for leading journals can range from 5–15 percent, while funding rates for major research agencies may be equally low [214]. These numbers highlight that rejection is largely the product of scarcity and selectivity, not necessarily a reflection of individual inadequacy. Yet, because academia so often equates success with acceptance, the personal toll can be profound unless faculty deliberately adopt strategies to manage its impact.

Key Insight: Rejection in academia is systemic and predictable, but its emotional consequences are personal and often internalized. Understanding this dual reality—structural scarcity combined with personal vulnerability—is essential for reframing rejection as a common professional experience rather than an indictment of competence.

Developing Resilience Through Reframing and Growth Mindset

Resilience in the face of rejection requires a deliberate shift in perspective. Rather than interpreting setbacks as evidence of inadequacy, resilient faculty view them as temporary obstacles and opportunities for refinement. This process of reframing transforms rejection from a definitive end point into a stepping stone within the broader trajectory of academic development.

Reframing as a Developmental Tool

Reframing begins with challenging the binary of success versus failure. Instead of perceiving rejection as absolute, faculty can reinterpret it as part of the iterative process that defines scholarly work. A manuscript declined by a journal is not evidence of incompetence but rather an opportunity to revise arguments, clarify methodology, or target a more appropriate audience. Similarly, a grant rejection often provides detailed feedback that, when incorporated, increases the competitiveness of future submissions. By seeing rejection as part of an academic feedback loop, faculty can approach each attempt as an investment in growth rather than a final judgment.

The Growth Mindset in Academia

The concept of a growth mindset—the belief that ability and expertise are developed through effort, persistence, and learning—provides a powerful framework for resilience [215]. Faculty who embrace this perspective view intellectual challenges as opportunities to expand capacity rather than as threats to competence. For example:

- A rejected manuscript signals areas where clarity or evidence can be improved.
- A failed grant application marks the beginning of a longer funding journey, not the conclusion.
- Negative peer review feedback identifies blind spots that can sharpen research quality.

By reframing rejection as information rather than condemnation, faculty reinforce the idea that scholarly excellence emerges through iteration and perseverance.

Practical Applications of Reframing

- **Manuscripts**: Instead of focusing solely on the rejection notice, faculty can analyze reviewer feedback to identify patterns of critique. This approach shifts attention from "why the article was not accepted" to "how the article can be improved."
- **Grants**: Faculty who treat an unfunded grant as a draft for resubmission often succeed in subsequent rounds. Reframing transforms the proposal into a "living document" that evolves over time rather than a one-time effort.
- **Job Applications**: Rather than internalizing rejection as a lack of worth, candidates can reflect on alignment—recognizing that rejection may indicate institutional fit rather than individual failure.

Benefits of Reframing and Growth-Oriented Thinking

Faculty who develop resilience through reframing and growth mindset experience several benefits:

- Reduced emotional volatility: Setbacks are less likely to trigger intense self-doubt when framed as part of a long-term process.
- Sustained motivation: Recognizing that progress occurs incrementally fosters persistence across multiple cycles of rejection and revision.
- Improved performance: Constructive use of feedback results in stronger manuscripts, more competitive grants, and clearer professional narratives.

Key Insight: Resilience is not about avoiding rejection but about interpreting rejection differently. Faculty who adopt a growth mindset detach professional outcomes from personal worth and transform setbacks into actionable learning experiences that strengthen their long-term trajectory.

Work-Life Integration and Boundary Setting

Academic work is often framed as a vocation rather than a job. An identity blurring the line between professional obligation and personal meaning. Teaching, research, mentoring, and service are not tasks that end neatly at the close of a workday; they are cognitively and emotionally immersive roles that follow faculty into evenings, weekends, and personal life. In this context, traditional notions of work-life balance—implying a stable, equitable separation between work and non-work—fail to reflect the lived experience of academic professionals. The result is not merely time pressure, but a chronic erosion of boundaries that quietly reshapes how faculty relate to rest, relationships, and self-worth.

Work-life integration and boundary setting offer a more realistic and humane framework for navigating these demands. Rather than attempting to force artificial separations, integration acknowledges the fluidity of academic labor while emphasizing intentional limits that protect well-being and sustainability. Boundary setting, in this sense, is not an act of disengagement or reduced commitment, but a form of professional stewardship preserving intellectual vitality, emotional resilience, and long-term effectiveness. This section explores how faculty can move beyond the myth of balance toward deliberate integration, sustainable work rhythms, and clear boundaries that honor both professional responsibility and personal life.

The Myth of Work-Life Balance in Academia

The concept of *work-life balance* suggests a clear and stable division between professional responsibilities and personal life. In academia, this idealized balance is rarely achievable. Faculty navigate overlapping roles as teachers, researchers, advisors, committee members, and administrators, each with deadlines and demands that rarely align neatly with personal schedules. The academic calendar itself is unpredictable: grading piles up at semester's end, manuscript revisions arrive unexpectedly from journals, and grant submission deadlines often overlap with major family or personal events. These overlapping timelines create tension that cannot be resolved by simply allocating "equal" time to work and life.

A further complication is the cultural glorification of overwork. Within many academic environments, long hours, weekend productivity, and constant availability are interpreted as signs of dedication. Faculty who set boundaries or prioritize personal time may be perceived—by peers or even by themselves—as less committed or ambitious. This culture creates professional risk: declining committee work, delaying email responses, or refusing additional projects may carry implicit costs in terms of reputation or career advancement. As a result, many faculty internalize the expectation that balance is unattainable unless personal needs are consistently sacrificed.

The imbalance is exacerbated by the blurring of physical and temporal boundaries. With digital technologies, faculty are accessible to students and colleagues at all hours. The expectation to check email during evenings, weekends, or vacations further erodes distinctions between professional and personal domains. In practice, the "balance" becomes tilted heavily toward work, leaving recovery and personal relationships vulnerable.

Because of these systemic realities, *work-life integration* provides a more realistic framework than balance. Integration acknowledges that personal and professional roles are not separate compartments but interconnected aspects of life that require ongoing negotiation and intentional boundary-setting. For example, a faculty member may integrate professional and personal obligations by scheduling research writing during early mornings to free evenings for family time, or by aligning conference travel with personal opportunities for cultural exploration. Integration shifts the focus from achieving an unrealistic equilibrium to crafting flexible strategies that allow both professional responsibilities and personal well-being to coexist over the long term.

Key Insight: In academia, the pursuit of strict work-life balance often leads to frustration and guilt. A more sustainable approach is work-life integration, which reframes the relationship between professional and personal roles as dynamic, interconnected, and adaptable to shifting demands.

Creating Sustainable Work Rhythms and Honoring Rest Periods

Long-term success in academia requires more than hard work; it depends on creating sustainable rhythms that avoid cycles of overwork and collapse. The traditional pattern of pushing through intense bursts of productivity—such as meeting grant deadlines or completing grading marathons—often leads to exhaustion, reduced creativity, and declining health. Without deliberate planning, these peaks and crashes become normalized, leaving faculty vulnerable to chronic burnout.

Designing Work Rhythms Around Energy, Not Just Time
Sustainable rhythms begin with recognizing that productivity is not evenly distributed throughout the day. Faculty can improve efficiency by aligning tasks with natural energy cycles. For example:

- Mornings, when focus and mental clarity are often highest, can be reserved for research writing, data analysis, or manuscript revisions.

- Afternoons may be more suitable for teaching preparation, grading, or administrative responsibilities, which require concentration but less creative energy.
- Evenings may be intentionally protected for personal time, professional reading, or restorative activities.

At a broader level, faculty can design semester-based rhythms, anticipating predictable peaks such as midterms, finals, or conference seasons. By frontloading tasks such as syllabus design or grant drafting earlier in the term, faculty can reduce pressure during known high-demand periods.

The Role of Rest in Sustained Productivity

Rest is often mischaracterized as the absence of work, yet research in cognitive psychology and organizational studies confirms that recovery is essential to peak performance [216]. Breaks throughout the day prevent mental fatigue and allow for renewed concentration. Short, structured pauses—such as walking between classes, practicing mindfulness, or stepping away from screens—can restore focus for subsequent tasks.

On a larger scale, vacations and sabbaticals are not luxuries but integral components of academic careers. Time away from routine responsibilities allows faculty to recharge intellectually and emotionally. Sabbaticals, in particular, provide opportunities for deep reflection, research renewal, and creative breakthroughs that are difficult to achieve in the daily churn of teaching and service. Faculty who honor rest periods often return with fresh perspectives, improved problem-solving capacity, and greater teaching effectiveness.

Embedding Rest Into Academic Life

For rest to become part of sustainable rhythms, it must be intentionally scheduled and protected. Examples include:

- Blocking out non-negotiable downtime in calendars, just as one would for classes or meetings.
- Setting firm boundaries around weekends or evenings, dedicating them to personal or family activities.
- Treating restorative practices—exercise, meditation, hobbies, or social engagements—as priorities rather than optional add-ons.

Preventing Burnout Through Rhythmic Integration

By embedding cycles of effort and recovery into academic life, faculty can maintain long-term intellectual capacity rather than depleting it. Sustainable rhythms foster resilience, allowing scholars to navigate intense periods of work without compromising health, relationships, or creativity. In this sense, rest is not a retreat from productivity but an investment in sustained professional excellence.

Key Insight: Productivity in academia is not achieved by maximizing hours worked but by harmonizing effort with recovery. Faculty who create sustainable work rhythms and deliberately honor rest periods build the endurance necessary for long-term success.

Managing the "Always-On" Culture of Academic Life

The rapid growth of digital communication has transformed the academic workplace. Tools such as email, messaging platforms, video conferencing, and learning management systems (LMS) provide flexibility and efficiency but also create an "always-on" culture, where faculty feel compelled to be constantly accessible. The expectation of instant response—whether from students seeking clarification, colleagues coordinating projects, or administrators issuing requests—erodes the natural boundaries between professional and personal time.

The Impact of Constant Connectivity
The 24/7 availability enabled by technology contributes to chronic stress, disrupted rest, and diminished recovery. Faculty may check email before bed, respond to student questions during weekends, or carry work devices on vacations. This constant vigilance prevents psychological detachment from work, which research identifies as essential for mental health and long-term productivity. Over time, the inability to disconnect fuels burnout, reduces teaching effectiveness, and undermines overall well-being.

Drivers of the "Always-On" Mentality

- Student expectations: Many students, particularly in online or hybrid courses, expect near-immediate responses to emails or discussion posts, assuming faculty availability mirrors customer service models.
- Administrative demands: Requests for reports, data, or compliance documentation often arrive unexpectedly and with tight deadlines, reinforcing the pressure to remain constantly available.
- Collegial pressures: Collaborative projects and global networks may involve colleagues in different time zones, creating a sense of obligation to respond outside regular hours.
- Cultural norms: Academia frequently equates visibility and responsiveness with commitment, making faculty reluctant to set boundaries for fear of being perceived as disengaged.

Strategies for Faculty Boundary-Setting
Faculty can take deliberate steps to reclaim personal time while maintaining professionalism:

- Defining communication windows: Clearly communicating availability in syllabi, email signatures, or learning platforms (e.g., "Responses within 24 hours on weekdays") helps reset student expectations.
- Using technology intentionally: Delayed-send functions, scheduled office hours in LMS platforms, and auto-responses can maintain responsiveness while preventing intrusive notifications.
- Device management: Turning off push notifications, separating work and personal devices, or setting "do not disturb" hours reinforces healthy boundaries.
- Modeling consistency: Following personal policies—such as not answering emails at midnight—demonstrates reliability and normalizes reasonable turnaround times.

Institutional Responsibility
Individual strategies are essential but insufficient without institutional alignment. Institutions play a critical role in shaping norms:

- Policy development: Clear guidelines around expected response times for faculty and students reduce ambiguity.
- Leadership modeling: Administrators and department chairs who respect boundaries by avoiding after-hours requests set cultural standards for others.
- Professional development: Workshops on digital wellness, time management, and workload planning equip faculty with practical strategies for managing technology's demands.
- Cultural reinforcement: Recognizing and rewarding productivity achieved through sustainable practices, rather than overextension, shifts norms away from overwork.

Key Insight: The "always-on" culture is not simply a byproduct of technology but a reflection of expectations and norms within academic life. Faculty who set clear boundaries and institutions that support digital wellness create healthier, more sustainable environments that preserve both effectiveness and well-being.

Strategies for Protecting Personal Time and Relationships

Protecting personal time requires deliberate planning and consistent boundary-setting to prevent academic responsibilities from consuming every available hour. Faculty often experience "role spillover," where work obligations seep into evenings, weekends, or vacations, gradually eroding personal relationships and reducing opportunities for recovery. Over time, this imbalance not only harms individual well-being but also diminishes professional effectiveness, as creativity and resilience decline without adequate restoration. Effective strategies must address both the structural demands of academic life and the personal choices that shape daily routines.

Physical Boundaries
Establishing clear physical divisions between work and personal life is one of the simplest yet most powerful strategies. On campus, a designated office provides a contained space for academic tasks. At home, creating a specific workspace—whether a desk, a separate room, or even a defined corner—helps faculty mentally signal when they are "at work" versus "off duty." Closing a laptop at the end of the day or physically leaving a workspace reinforces the psychological transition between professional and personal roles. Without these boundaries, the temptation to let grading, emails, or research spill into personal spaces becomes overwhelming, leading to blurred identities and constant low-level stress.

Time Blocking
Faculty schedules are often fragmented, with competing obligations scattered across the day. Time blocking ensures that personal activities receive the same level of commitment as professional tasks. By scheduling family dinners, exercise sessions, or social engagements directly into calendars, faculty elevate these activities to non-negotiable priorities. For example, blocking out two evenings per week for family or reserving mornings for exercise establishes a

rhythm that protects personal well-being. Treating personal time as inviolable prevents it from being eroded by last-minute requests or creeping work obligations.

Prioritization

Not all academic tasks carry equal weight, yet many faculty treat every request as urgent. Effective prioritization involves distinguishing between essential duties—such as grading deadlines, course preparation, or grant submissions—and lower-priority commitments, such as optional committee service or additional administrative projects. Faculty who consciously focus on high-impact tasks preserve mental energy for both professional excellence and personal fulfillment. This approach also prevents overinvestment in activities that consume time without contributing meaningfully to career progression or institutional goals.

Support Systems

Faculty benefit from cultivating relationships outside academia that provide grounding perspectives and emotional support. Family, friends, and community networks offer a counterbalance to the insular nature of academic life, reminding faculty that their worth is not defined solely by publications, grants, or teaching evaluations. These external connections also provide outlets for stress relief, laughter, and belonging that cannot be replicated within professional environments. Maintaining these networks requires intentional effort, but they are critical for resilience and holistic well-being.

Saying No

Perhaps the most challenging but essential strategy is learning to decline additional commitments. Academia often rewards visibility and service, making it tempting to accept every invitation to join committees, collaborate on projects, or take on new teaching assignments. Yet constant acceptance leads to overextension, diminishing effectiveness across all roles. Saying no, even to prestigious opportunities, allows faculty to safeguard time for existing responsibilities and personal life. Practicing respectful but firm refusals—such as "I appreciate the invitation, but I am unable to take on additional commitments at this time"—builds a sustainable professional trajectory without sacrificing well-being.

Key Takeaways

- The traditional notion of work-life balance is a myth in academia; integration and negotiation provide more sustainable approaches.
- Sustainable work rhythms, paired with deliberate rest periods, enhance long-term productivity and prevent burnout.
- The "always-on" culture can be managed through consistent boundary-setting and institutional support.
- Protecting personal time and relationships requires intentional strategies: physical boundaries, time blocking, prioritization, external support networks, and the ability to say no.

Building Psychological Safety in Academic Environments

The health of academic institutions depends not only on intellectual rigor but also on the psychological safety of those who teach, learn, and lead within them. Faculty operate in environments defined by constant evaluation, layered hierarchies, and the competing demands of teaching, research, and service. While these conditions can foster excellence, they also create vulnerabilities that, if left unaddressed, erode confidence, collegiality, and long-term well-being.

This section explores the multi-dimensional nature of psychological safety in academia, beginning with the classroom and extending to departmental cultures and institutional structures. Classrooms must be spaces where both students and faculty feel free to take intellectual risks without fear of ridicule or retaliation. Yet even as faculty work to protect students, they themselves may encounter intimidation, particularly in the form of grade-related bullying. Beyond the classroom, toxic departmental cultures and microaggressions can undermine trust, while unresolved conflicts and opaque hierarchies leave faculty feeling voiceless.

Creating Emotionally Safe Classrooms for Both Students and Faculty

Psychological safety in academic settings begins in the classroom, where both students and faculty must feel free to engage without fear of judgment, ridicule, or retaliation. An emotionally safe classroom is one in which curiosity is encouraged, mistakes are treated as opportunities for growth, and differences of opinion are explored respectfully. Such environments not only improve learning outcomes but also contribute to long-term resilience by modeling how intellectual risk-taking can occur without personal harm [217].

For Students
Students thrive in classrooms where they feel respected, heard, and included. Emotional safety allows them to ask questions without worrying about embarrassment, share perspectives rooted in diverse backgrounds, and challenge ideas without personal risk. Faculty can cultivate this by:

- Setting clear ground rules: Establishing expectations for civil discourse, respectful listening, and inclusive participation from the first day.
- Encouraging diverse perspectives: Designing assignments and discussions that invite students to draw on cultural, social, or professional experiences.
- Responding constructively to mistakes: Treating errors as integral to the learning process by offering supportive feedback instead of punitive responses.
- Active facilitation: Ensuring that dominant voices do not overshadow quieter participants, thereby creating equitable opportunities for contribution.

When students perceive the classroom as emotionally safe, they are more likely to take intellectual risks, experiment with new ideas, and engage in critical inquiry. This deepens learning and fosters confidence that extends beyond academic contexts.

For Faculty
Emotional safety is equally critical for instructors. Faculty often teach under conditions of scrutiny, with student evaluations, peer observations, and administrative oversight shaping their

professional reputations. To feel safe, faculty need reassurance that experimentation in pedagogy or engagement with difficult topics will be supported rather than penalized. Key elements include:

- Institutional backing: Clear policies and administrative support when addressing disruptive classroom behavior or when navigating sensitive issues such as race, gender, or politics.
- Permission to innovate: Encouragement to try new teaching methods, technologies, or course designs without fear of negative consequences if results are imperfect.
- Recognition of vulnerability: Understanding that faculty, like students, benefit from environments where it is acceptable to say "I don't know" or to adjust course content in response to feedback.

Shared Benefits

Classrooms that normalize curiosity and imperfection benefit both students and faculty. For students, these environments reduce performance anxiety, encourage engagement, and validate their diverse contributions. For faculty, they foster professional growth, reduce fear of negative evaluations, and align teaching with the broader goals of inclusivity and equity. Together, emotionally safe classrooms become spaces of collaborative learning, where mutual respect and shared responsibility replace fear and defensiveness.

Key Insight: Psychological safety in the classroom is not simply about comfort; it is about creating conditions for intellectual risk-taking and growth. When both students and faculty feel secure in expressing vulnerability, the classroom becomes a site of authentic learning and professional development.

Student Bullying of Faculty for Better Grades

While much of the literature on classroom safety focuses on protecting students, faculty also face threats to psychological safety, particularly in the form of student-driven pressure and intimidation around grading. In some cases, students attempt to bully or manipulate instructors into awarding higher grades, using tactics such as persistent challenges to grading policies, hostile emails, public confrontations, or even leveraging course evaluations as retaliation. These behaviors can undermine faculty authority, erode confidence, and contribute to a hostile teaching environment.

Dynamics of Grade-Related Bullying

- Persistent pressure: Students may repeatedly request grade changes without substantive justification, framing the denial of such requests as unfair or unreasonable.
- Retaliation through evaluations: End-of-term student evaluations, often central to faculty reviews and promotion, may be weaponized by dissatisfied students to penalize instructors who enforce rigorous standards.
- Escalation to administration: Students sometimes bypass direct dialogue with faculty and appeal directly to department chairs or deans, framing grading disputes as misconduct rather than legitimate academic judgment.

- Collective pressure: In some instances, groups of students coordinate complaints or threats of formal grievance, further amplifying the sense of intimidation.

Cultural Considerations

Faculty working with diverse student populations must navigate cultural expectations that shape student behavior toward authority and education. For example:

- In cultures where education is strongly consumer-oriented, students may view tuition as a transactional investment and assume that higher grades are an entitlement rather than an earned outcome.
- In hierarchical educational traditions, students may struggle to accept critical feedback, interpreting it as disrespect rather than constructive guidance.
- International students may carry expectations from prior systems where grades were inflated or where negotiation with faculty was more normalized, leading to misaligned assumptions in U.S. or Western institutions.

These cultural dynamics highlight the importance of clear communication of standards and transparent grading policies to prevent misinterpretations that escalate into conflict.

The Role of Misperceptions from Previous Faculty Practices

A key factor fueling grade-related bullying is the false sense of skill mastery created by inconsistent or ineffective feedback in earlier courses. When students receive inflated grades or vague, non-critical evaluations, they may develop unrealistic beliefs about their abilities. Faculty who enforce rigorous standards are then perceived as unfairly harsh, even when their expectations align with disciplinary norms. This disconnect can lead to student frustration, entitlement, and at times, hostility. The result is a cycle in which strong pedagogical practices are challenged, while leniency reinforces poor academic habits.

Strategies for Faculty Protection and Response

- Transparent policies: Providing detailed grading rubrics, clear course objectives, and explicit explanations of evaluation criteria minimizes ambiguity and reduces opportunities for dispute.
- Consistent documentation: Keeping records of student performance, feedback, and communication protects faculty in cases where disputes escalate to formal complaints.
- Professional communication: Responding calmly and firmly to student pressure models professionalism and de-escalates conflict. Phrases such as, *"Grades reflect demonstrated performance, not negotiation"* reinforce academic standards without personalizing the dispute.
- Institutional support: Departments and administrators should back faculty when students challenge legitimate grading practices. Publicly affirming the principle of academic judgment strengthens faculty authority and discourages bullying behaviors.
- Feedback literacy for students: Embedding instruction on how to interpret and apply feedback within courses helps students recalibrate expectations and recognize that critique is a tool for development rather than punishment.

Key Insight: Student bullying of faculty over grades is often a symptom of misaligned expectations, shaped by cultural assumptions and reinforced by inconsistent feedback from prior instruction. Addressing this issue requires transparent standards, institutional backing, and proactive student education about the developmental purpose of feedback and the integrity of academic evaluation.

Addressing Toxic Department Cultures and Microaggressions

While classrooms are the most visible sites of academic interaction, the broader departmental and institutional culture plays a decisive role in determining psychological safety for faculty. Even when individual faculty members foster supportive learning environments, their efforts may be undermined by toxic departmental climates. These environments are marked by behaviors and norms that erode trust, silence dissent, and normalize hostility, making it difficult for faculty to thrive both personally and professionally.

Characteristics of Toxic Departmental Cultures

- Excessive competition: Faculty are pitted against one another for limited resources such as course releases, travel funds, or research support, fostering rivalry rather than collaboration.
- Favoritism: Unequal distribution of opportunities (e.g., committee assignments, promotions, or teaching schedules) creates resentment and perceptions of unfairness.
- Exclusion and marginalization: Certain voices—often women, junior faculty, or scholars from underrepresented backgrounds—may be systematically sidelined in decision-making processes.
- Unchecked incivility: Passive-aggressive communication, public disparagement, or chronic dismissiveness can become normalized, discouraging open dialogue and innovation.

The Impact of Microaggressions
Microaggressions are subtle, often unintentional, comments or actions that communicate derogatory assumptions about someone's identity [218]. In academic settings, these may include:

- Dismissing ideas until repeated by a male or senior colleague.
- Questioning a faculty member's qualifications based on accent, age, or appearance.
- Assuming faculty of color are responsible for diversity-related service while overlooking their research contributions.
- Jokes or offhand comments that perpetuate stereotypes.

While seemingly minor in isolation, the cumulative effect of microaggressions produces chronic stress, diminished confidence, and disengagement. Over time, these experiences undermine morale, weaken collegial bonds, and hinder productivity.

Strategies for Addressing Toxic Cultures and Microaggressions

1. Transparent Policies for Grievances and Misconduct
   Clear, accessible procedures are essential for addressing both overt misconduct and subtle patterns of exclusion. Policies should protect faculty from retaliation and ensure complaints are handled promptly and fairly. Institutions must also communicate that addressing toxicity is not optional but central to academic integrity.
2. Training to Recognize and Challenge Microaggressions
   Faculty and staff often fail to intervene when microaggressions occur, either due to lack of awareness or fear of conflict. Regular training in bias recognition, active bystander strategies, and inclusive communication equips community members to challenge harmful behaviors in real time.
3. Leadership Accountability
   Department chairs and administrators set the tone for workplace culture. Leaders must model respectful behavior, enforce accountability consistently, and avoid favoritism in workload distribution and recognition. Regular climate surveys and feedback mechanisms can hold leadership accountable for fostering equitable environments.
4. Peer Mentorship and Collaborative Projects
   Encouraging structures that promote cooperation rather than rivalry helps shift departmental culture. Peer mentorship programs support junior faculty, particularly those from underrepresented groups, in navigating professional challenges. Collaborative research and teaching initiatives build trust by aligning faculty interests toward shared goals instead of competition for recognition.

Long-Term Benefits of Cultural Change

Departments that address toxicity and microaggressions build psychologically safe environments where faculty feel respected, valued, and supported. This not only reduces attrition and burnout but also enhances creativity, collegiality, and institutional reputation. Faculty are more likely to innovate, mentor effectively, and engage in service when they trust that their contributions will be recognized and respected.

Key Insight: Toxic cultures and microaggressions are not simply interpersonal issues—they are systemic threats to academic well-being and productivity. Addressing them requires transparent policies, leadership accountability, faculty training, and intentional cultivation of collaboration over competition.

Developing Assertiveness Skills for Academic Conflicts

Academic environments are inherently collaborative yet resource-constrained, which makes conflict inevitable. Faculty regularly face disagreements over course assignments, research authorship, departmental budgets, committee responsibilities, and governance decisions. In healthy environments, conflict can serve as a catalyst for innovation and fairness. However, without psychological safety, conflict often escalates into hostility, power struggles, or silent withdrawal—outcomes that damage morale and stall progress. The ability to engage assertively provides faculty with a constructive middle ground between passivity and aggression, protecting both individual well-being and institutional relationships.

The Value of Assertiveness in Academia

Assertiveness is the skill of expressing one's needs, opinions, and boundaries clearly and respectfully while recognizing the legitimacy of others' perspectives. Unlike aggression, which seeks to dominate, or passivity, which avoids confrontation, assertiveness creates conditions for dialogue and equitable problem-solving. For faculty, assertiveness is especially critical because academic hierarchies, peer competition, and student evaluations often generate pressure to remain silent or deferential. By cultivating assertiveness, faculty can protect professional integrity without damaging collegiality.

Core Strategies for Academic Assertiveness

1. Using "I" Statements
   Framing concerns through personal experience reduces defensiveness and shifts the focus from blame to problem-solving. For example:
   - *Aggressive*: "You never distribute teaching loads fairly."
   - *Assertive*: "I feel overextended when my teaching load exceeds department norms, and I'd like to discuss how responsibilities can be balanced."

   This approach communicates needs without alienating colleagues or leadership.
2. Practicing Active Listening
   Assertiveness does not mean pushing one's perspective at the expense of others. Active listening—paraphrasing, summarizing, and validating others' points—builds trust and signals respect. Faculty who acknowledge a colleague's concerns before presenting their own demonstrate that they are invested in collaborative solutions rather than unilateral demands.
3. Seeking Win-Win Outcomes
   Academic conflicts often pit personal boundaries against institutional needs. Assertiveness requires reframing disputes as opportunities to negotiate solutions that meet both sets of interests. For example, a faculty member overwhelmed by service requests may propose an alternative—taking on one high-impact committee instead of multiple smaller ones—thus balancing institutional participation with personal sustainability.

Assertiveness Training in Faculty Development

Assertiveness is not an innate trait but a skill that can be learned and refined. Professional development programs can integrate assertiveness training through:

- Workshops and role-play scenarios that allow faculty to practice conflict dialogues in a safe environment.
- Mentorship programs where senior faculty model assertive communication in departmental discussions.
- Cross-cultural communication training to address the fact that assertiveness norms vary internationally, helping faculty adapt strategies for diverse academic communities.

Benefits of Assertiveness for Faculty and Institutions

- For individuals: Reduced stress, improved confidence, and greater alignment between workload and personal capacity.
- For departments: Healthier decision-making processes, increased trust, and fewer unresolved tensions that fester into long-term conflicts.
- For institutions: Stronger governance cultures where faculty feel empowered to contribute actively and responsibly.

Key Insight: Assertiveness equips faculty to navigate conflict without fear, hostility, or withdrawal. By expressing needs clearly and listening actively, faculty transform conflicts from stressors into opportunities for equitable solutions and stronger professional relationships.

Self-Advocacy Strategies in Hierarchical Academic Structures

Academia operates within layered hierarchies that shape nearly every aspect of professional life. Department chairs oversee teaching assignments and committee work, deans manage budgets and resource allocation, provosts set institutional priorities, and governing boards influence long-term strategy. While these structures provide necessary organization, they also concentrate decision-making power, often leaving faculty feeling peripheral to choices that directly impact their workload, recognition, and career advancement. Without the skills of self-advocacy, faculty may internalize feelings of disempowerment, hesitate to request support, or accept inequitable treatment as unchangeable.

The Importance of Self-Advocacy

Self-advocacy is the practice of assertively representing one's own needs, accomplishments, and boundaries within hierarchical systems. In academic settings, this means ensuring that contributions—whether in teaching, research, or service—are visible and valued. Far from being an act of rebellion, effective self-advocacy aligns with academic integrity by promoting transparency, equity, and fairness. When faculty articulate needs and highlight contributions, they not only advance individual well-being but also support the institution's mission by aligning resources with demonstrated value.

Core Elements of Effective Self-Advocacy

1. Preparation
   Successful advocacy begins with thorough preparation. Faculty should gather evidence-based documentation to support requests, including teaching evaluations, student success metrics, publication records, grant activity, and records of service contributions. Framing requests in terms of measurable outcomes and institutional benefits increases credibility. For instance, a faculty member seeking reduced teaching load for research can present data showing how prior research generated publications, student mentorship opportunities, or external funding.
2. Clarity
   Vague dissatisfaction rarely leads to change. Faculty should articulate specific needs and desired outcomes, such as requesting funding for a conference presentation, additional graduate assistant support, or transparent workload distribution. Clear communication shifts the conversation from complaint to actionable request. For example: *"I would like*

to request travel funding for the upcoming conference, as it directly supports our department's visibility and aligns with institutional goals."

3. Persistence
Advocacy is often a process, not a single interaction. Initial requests may be overlooked or delayed due to competing priorities. Following up respectfully and consistently reinforces the importance of the issue without escalating tension. Persistence communicates commitment and ensures that needs remain visible in decision-making cycles. Importantly, persistence should be paired with professionalism—firm reminders rather than adversarial confrontation.

4. Strategic Alliances
Individual voices can be strengthened through coalitions and mentorship networks. Faculty who align their requests with colleagues facing similar issues can amplify concerns, making them harder to dismiss. Mentors, particularly senior faculty with institutional credibility, can provide guidance on timing, framing, and strategy. Strategic alliances also reduce isolation, transforming self-advocacy into collective advocacy that benefits multiple stakeholders.

Institutional Role in Normalizing Self-Advocacy

For self-advocacy to flourish, institutions must destigmatize speaking up. Too often, faculty worry that requesting resources or negotiating workload will be perceived as resistance or entitlement. By explicitly affirming that self-advocacy is a professional responsibility, institutions foster a culture where transparency and fairness are the norm. Leadership training for chairs and deans can reinforce that faculty requests should be met with openness and seriousness, not defensiveness.

Key Takeaways

- Academic hierarchies can leave faculty feeling silenced unless they develop deliberate strategies for self-advocacy.
- Effective advocacy requires preparation, clarity, persistence, and strategic alliances.
- Self-advocacy is not defiance; it is a form of professional integrity that aligns faculty needs with institutional sustainability.
- When normalized, self-advocacy contributes to psychological safety, resilience, and equity across the academic community.

References

[1] Knowles, M., Robinson, P. A. & Caraccioli, C. (2025). *The Adult Learner: The Definitive Classic in Adult Education and Human Resource Development.* Routledge. https://www.routledge.com/The-Adult-Learner-The-Definitive-Classic-in-Adult-Education-and-Human-Resource-Development/Knowles-HoltonIII-Robinson-Caraccioli/p/book/9781032481562

[2] Blaschke, L. M. (2012). *Heutagogy and Lifelong Learning: A Review of Heutagogical Practice and Self-Determined Learning.* The International Review of Research in Open and Distributed Learning 13(1). https://doi.org/10.19173/irrodl.v13i1.1076

[3] (2018). *Faculty Beliefs about Intelligence Are Related to the Adoption of Active-Learning Practices.* CBE—Life Sciences Education 17(3). https://doi.org/10.1187/cbe.18-02-0031

[4] (2023). *Reflecting on their mission increases preservice teachers' growth mindsets.* Learning and Instruction 86. https://doi.org/10.1016/j.learninstruc.2023.101770

[5] (2020). *Faculty persistence with research-based instructional strategies: a case study of participation in a faculty online learning community.* International Journal of STEM Education 7(1). https://doi.org/10.1186/s40594-020-00221-8

[6] Chen, L., Chang, H., Rudoler, J. & al., e. (2022). *Cognitive training enhances growth mindset in children through plasticity of cortico-striatal circuits.* npj Science of Learning 7. https://doi.org/10.1038/s41539-022-00146-7

[7] Xu, K. M., Koorn, P., Koning, B. d., Skuballa, I. T., Lin, L., Henderikx, M., Marsh, H. W., Sweller, J. & Paas, F. (2021). *A Growth Mindset Lowers Perceived Cognitive Load and Improves Learning.* Journal of Educational Psychology 113(6), pp. 1177-1191. https://doi.org/10.1037/edu0000631

[8] (2024). *Criteria for Accreditation.* Higher Learning Commission. https://www.hlcommission.org/accreditation/policies/criteria/

[9] (n.d.). *Universal Design for Learning.* Denver Center for Teaching and Learning. https://inclusive-teaching.du.edu/inclusive-teaching/universal-design-learning

[10] (2023). *Rule 3335-6-02 - Ohio Administrative Code.* Ohio Administrative Code. https://codes.ohio.gov/ohio-administrative-code/rule-3335-6-02

[11] (2025). *WPI Faculty Handbook: Chapter Four - Promotions.* WPI Faculty Handbook. https://handbook.wpi.edu/chapter-4.html

[12]   (2025). *Faculty development for junior educators: advancing the Scholarship of Teaching and Learning (SoTL) Through Co-Teaching and Mentoring.* BMC Research Notes 18. https://doi.org/10.1186/s13104-025-07413-x

[13]   Bart, M. (2009). *Aligning Assessment Strategies with Institutional Goals.* Faculty Focus. https://www.facultyfocus.com/articles/educational-assessment/aligning-assessment-strategies-with-institutional-goals/

[14]   (2010). *The Socratic Dialogue and teacher education.* Teaching and Teacher Education 26(4), pp. 1104-1111. https://doi.org/10.1016/j.tate.2009.11.006

[15]   (2025). *Foundations of Modern Pedagogy.* educate.lgu-santol.gov.ph. https://educate.lgu-santol.gov.ph/teacher-training-and-pedagogy/foundations-of-modern-pedagogy/

[16]   Siebert, E. D. (1993). *Teaching and Research--A Dual Role for College Faculty at All Institutions of Higher Education.* Journal of College Science Teaching 22(5), pp. 283-285. https://eric.ed.gov/?id=EJ473529

[17]   Derouich, M. (2025). *Ensuring Outcome-Based Curriculum Coherence through Systematic CLO-PLO Alignment and Feedback Loops.* arXiv preprint. https://doi.org/10.48550/arXiv.2510.25905

[18]   Derouich, M. (2025). *Ensuring Outcome-Based Curriculum Coherence through Systematic CLO-PLO Alignment and Feedback Loops.* arXiv preprint. https://doi.org/10.48550/arXiv.2510.25905

[19]   Dickey, E. & Bejarano, A. (2023). *GAIDE: A Framework for Using Generative AI to Assist in Course Content Development.* arXiv preprint. https://doi.org/10.48550/arXiv.2308.12276

[20]   (2025). *The Link Between Faculty Development and Institutional Success.* National Center for Faculty Development & Diversity. https://www.ncfdd.org/resources/the-link-between-faculty-development-and-institutional-success/

[21]   Dolenc, N. R., Mitchell, C. & Tai, R. H. (2014). *Evidence of Self-Directed Learning on a High School Robotics Team.* Journal of Youth Development 9(1), pp. 1-15. https://doi.org/10.5195/jyd.2014.41

[22]   Edmondson, A. C. (2018). *The Fearless Organization: Creating Psychological Safety in the Workplace for Learning, Innovation, and Growth.* Wiley. https://www.wiley.com/en-us/The+Fearless+Organization%3A+Creating+Psychological+Safety+in+the+Workplace+for+Learning%2C+Innovation%2C+and+Growth-p-9781119477266

[23]   (2022). *Emotional Intelligence – The Daniel Goleman Model.* Reckon Talk. https://www.reckontalk.com/emotional-intelligence-daniel-goleman-model/

[24] (n.d.). *Carl Jung's Shadow: Understanding the Dark Side of the Psyche for Personal Growth and Integration*. A.Psi. https://apsiresearch.com/articles/shadow.html

[25] Mayes, C. (2005). *Jung and Education: Elements of an Archetypal Pedagogy*. R&L Education. https://www.bloomsbury.com/us/jung-and-education-9781578862542/

[26] (2025). *Individuation*. Quantum Drummer. https://quantumdrummer.com/2025/09/14/reflections-on-cg-jungs-the-development-of-personality-volume-17-of-the-collected-works/

[27] (n.d.). *Constructivism: A Philosophy of Active Learning and Self-Construction*. Knowway. https://www.knowway.org/en/constructivism-a-philosophy-of-active-learning-and-self-construction

[28] Ertmer, P. A. & Newby, T. J. (1993). *Behaviorism, Cognitivism, Constructivism: Comparing Critical Features from an Instructional Design Perspective*. Performance Improvement Quarterly 6(4), pp. 50-72. https://doi.org/10.1111/j.1937-8327.1993.tb00605.x

[29] (June 15, 2024). *Bloom's Taxonomy*. YouTube. https://www.youtube.com/watch?v=ve-Evb5bGoc

[30] (2025). *Mentoring for well-being, engagement and academic achievement in higher education students*. Frontiers in Education. https://doi.org/10.3389/feduc.2025.1606103

[31] Ngbabare, S. M. (2023). *Mentoring that matters: African graduate students' perceptions of faculty mentorship during transition*. Journal of International Students 13(1), pp. 1-20. https://doi.org/10.32674/dvhrcm67

[32] (n.d.). *Faculty Engagement*. AAUP Foundation. https://www.aaupfoundation.org/faculty-engagement

[33] Kumari, R., Tiwari, R., Akhtar, R. & Gupta, S. K. (2023). *Traditional Teaching Method Vs Modern Teaching Method*. GPH-International Journal of Educational Research 6(11), pp. 80-85. https://doi.org/10.5281/zenodo.10429275

[34] (2019). *Universal Design for Learning in postsecondary STEM education for students with disabilities: a systematic literature review*. International Journal of STEM Education 6(1). https://doi.org/10.1186/s40594-019-0161-8

[35] Serrano, D. R., Dea-Ayuela, M. A., Gonzalez-Burgos, E., Serrano-Gil, A. & Lalatsa, A. (2019). *Technology-Enhanced Learning in Higher Education: How to Enhance Student Engagement through Blended Learning*. European Journal of Education 54(2), pp. 273-286. https://doi.org/10.1111/ejed.12330

[36] D., F. & M., P. (2023). *The Role of Assessment in Improving Education and Promoting Educational Equity*. MDPI 15(2). https://doi.org/10.3390/education15020224

[37] (2023). *Authentic Assessments*. Middle States Commission on Higher Education. https://www.msche.org/2023/06/30/assessment-expectations-by-standard-guidelines/

[38] (n.d.). *Rubrics | University of Illinois Springfield*. University of Illinois Springfield. https://www.uis.edu/colrs/foundations-course-design/assessing-learners/rubrics

[39] (2026). *Guidance on technology tools for academic integrity*. Stanford Teaching Commons. https://teachingcommons.stanford.edu/news/guidance-technology-tools-academic-integrity

[40] (2021). *Accrediting Commissions' Standards on Faculty Governance*. American Association of University Professors. https://www.aaup.org/article/accrediting-commissions%E2%80%99-standards-faculty-governance

[41] (2021). *Accrediting Commissions' Standards on Faculty Governance*. American Association of University Professors. https://www.aaup.org/academe/issues/winter-2021/accrediting-commissions-standards-faculty-governance

[42] Derouich, M. (2025). *Ensuring Outcome-Based Curriculum Coherence through Systematic CLO-PLO Alignment and Feedback Loops*. arXiv preprint. https://doi.org/10.48550/arXiv.2510.25905

[43] (2020). *Policy on Grading, Assessment and Review*. American University, Washington, DC. https://www.american.edu/wcl/academics/academicservices/registrar/current-students/grading-policy.cfm

[44] (2025). *Research Brief: Higher Education and the ADA*. ADA National Network. https://adata.org/research_brief/higher-education-and-ada

[45] (2025). *Promotion Guidelines for Awarding Promotion to Research Professor*. Boise State University. https://www.boisestate.edu/sps/guidelines-promotion-research-professor/

[46] (n.d.). *Code of Federal Regulations Title 34 Department of Education PART 97 - Protection of Human Subjects*. U.S. Department of Education. https://www.ed.gov/grants-and-programs/manage-your-grant/human-subject-research/code-of-federal-regulations-title-34-department-of-education-part-97--protection-of-human-subjects

[47] (2024). *Harassment Based on Race, Color, or National Origin*. U.S. Department of Education. https://www.ed.gov/laws-and-policy/civil-rights-laws/race-color-and-national-origin-discrimination/race-color-and-national-origin-discrimination-key-issues/harassment-based-race-color-or

[48] (July 9, 2024). *Family Educational Rights and Privacy Act (FERPA)*. Centers for Disease Control and Prevention. https://www.cdc.gov/phlp/php/resources/family-educational-rights-and-privacy-act-ferpa.html

[49] (n.d.). *FAQs on Shared Governance*. American Association of University Professors (AAUP). https://www.aaup.org/programs/shared-governance/faqs-shared-governance

[50] (2025). *Shared Governance*. American Association of University Professors. https://www.aaup.org/shared-governance

[51] (n.d.). *Faculty Governance*. Rhodes College: Rhodes Handbook. https://handbook.rhodes.edu/book/export/html/1596

[52] (2024). *Accreditation Standards Overview*. Council for Higher Education Accreditation. https://www.chea.org/what-is-accreditation

[53] (n.d.). *Institutional Accreditation: A Call for Greater Faculty Involvement*. American Association of University Professors. https://www.aaup.org/report/call-for-greater-faculty-involvement

[54] (n.d.). *Faculty Roles and Expectations*. Montclair State University Faculty Handbook. https://www.montclair.edu/faculty-handbook/regulations/faculty-roles-and-expectations/

[55] (OECD), O. f. (2008). *Higher Education to 2030*. OECD Publishing. https://www.oecd.org/content/dam/oecd/en/publications/reports/2008/11/higher-education-to-2030-volume-1-demography_g1gh8814/9789264040663-en.pdf

[56] (2025). *Tailor Your Academic Job Search Materials*. Yale University Office of Career Strategy. https://ocs.yale.edu/tailor-your-materials-to-type-of-academic-institution/

[57] (n.d.). *Student Financial Wellness Survey*. https://tacc.org/sites/default/files/2024-04/trellis_strategies_building_bridges_04.11.24_sfws_report_texas_community_colleges.pdf

[58] (n.d.). *Discourse & Sensemaking Strategies in Large Lecture*. Center for Teaching & Learning, University of California, Berkeley. https://teaching.berkeley.edu/discourse-sensemaking-strategies-large-lecture

[59] Flash, P. (2019). *Teaching with Writing: A Practical Seminar for Faculty*. University of Minnesota. https://cla.umn.edu/language-center/news/teaching-writing-practical-seminar-faculty

[60] Monto, C. (2018). *Increasing Access with Intensive Hybridized Course Formats in a Community College Setting*. Community College Journal of Research and Practice. https://doi.org/10.1080/10668926.2018.1480190

[61] (n.d.). *Directory of Institutions*. Higher Learning Commission. https://www.hlcommission.org/directory-of-institutions/

[62] (n.d.). *Accreditation*. Pacifica Graduate Institute. https://www.pacifica.edu/about-pacifica/accreditation/

[63] (2025). *Standards for Accreditation - New England Commission Higher Education*. New England Commission of Higher Education. https://www.neche.org/standards-for-accreditation/

[64] Miller, V. D. (2020). *Faculty Unions*. In The SAGE Encyclopedia of Higher Education. https://sk.sagepub.com/ency/edvol/embed/the-sage-encyclopedia-of-higher-education/chpt/faculty-unions

[65] (n.d.). *Faculty Workload Report*. https://facultyaffairs.arizona.edu/sites/default/files/2023-10/FINAL_Faculty%20Workload%20Report.10.25.23.pdf

[66] (2021). *Guidelines for Faculty Evaluation*. Texas A&M University College of Liberal Arts. https://liberalarts.tamu.edu/wp-content/uploads/2021/09/College-of-Liberal-Arts-Faculty-Evaluation-Guidelines-FINAL-2021.pdf

[67] (n.d.). *Faculty Teaching Load and Responsibilities*. Reynolds Community College. https://www.reynolds.edu/policy/human_resources/3-02-faculty-teaching-load-and-responsibilities.html

[68] (n.d.). *Backward Design*. Eastern Illinois University. https://www.eiu.edu/instructional_design/backward_design.php

[69] Wiggins, G. & McTighe, J. (2005). *Understanding by Design*. Publisher: ASCD. https://www.ascd.org/books/understanding-by-design-2nd-edition

[70] Derouich, M. (2025). *Ensuring Outcome-Based Curriculum Coherence through Systematic CLO-PLO Alignment and Feedback Loops*. arXiv preprint. https://doi.org/10.48550/arXiv.2510.25905

[71] Bloom, B. (1956). *Bloom's Taxonomy*. Taxonomy of Educational Objectives: The Classification of Educational Goals. https://www.ou.edu/assessment/resources/blooms-taxonomy

[72] (n.d.). *Aligning Assessments with Outcomes*. Wilfrid Laurier University. https://researchcentres.wlu.ca/teaching-and-learning/planning/aligning-assessments-with-outcomes.html

[73] (n.d.). *Backward Course Design*. Indiana University Bloomington Center for Innovative Teaching & Learning. https://citl.indiana.edu/teaching-resources/course-design/backward-course-design/index.html

[74] (n.d.). *Backward Course Design*. Indiana University Bloomington Center for Innovative Teaching & Learning. https://citl.indiana.edu/teaching-resources/course-design/backward-course-design/index.html

[75] (n.d.). *Backwards Design – UAF Center for Teaching and Learning*. University of Alaska Fairbanks. https://ctl.uaf.edu/backwardsdesign/

[76] Biggs, J. (2014). *Constructive Alignment in Course Design*. Publisher: Springer. https://www.springer.com/gp/book/9789400776126

[77] (n.d.). *Backward Design*. University of Illinois Chicago. https://teaching.uic.edu/resources/teaching-guides/learning-principles-and-frameworks/backward-design/

[78] (n.d.). *Active Learning Exercises*. National Center for Principled Leadership & Research Ethics. https://ncpre.csl.illinois.edu/ethics/resources/educational-materials/active-learning-exercises

[79] Fuster-Barcelo, C., Rios-Munoz, G. R. & Munoz-Barrutia, A. (2025). *Scaffolding Collaborative Learning in STEM: A Two-Year Evaluation of a Tool-Integrated Project-Based Methodology*. arXiv preprint. https://doi.org/10.48550/arXiv.2509.02355

[80] El-Sabagh, H. A. (2021). *Adaptive e-learning environment based on learning styles and its impact on development students' engagement*. International Journal of Educational Technology in Higher Education 18. https://doi.org/10.1186/s41239-021-00289-4

[81] Derouich, M. (2025). *Ensuring Outcome-Based Curriculum Coherence through Systematic CLO-PLO Alignment and Feedback Loops*. arXiv preprint. https://doi.org/10.48550/arXiv.2510.25905

[82] Derouich, M. (2025). *Ensuring Outcome-Based Curriculum Coherence through Systematic CLO-PLO Alignment and Feedback Loops*. arXiv preprint. https://doi.org/10.48550/arXiv.2510.25905

[83] Harrington, C. & Thomas, M. (2018). *Designing a Motivational Syllabus: Creating a Learning Path for Student Engagement*. Routledge. https://www.routledge.com/Designing-a-Motivational-Syllabus-Creating-a-Learning-Path-for-Student-Engagement/Harrington-Thomas/p/book/9781620366257

[84] (n.d.). *Accreditation Criteria*. American Higher Education Accreditation Association. https://aheaa.org/accreditation-criteria/

[85] (2010). *Accreditation and the Federal Future of Higher Education*. American Association of University Professors. https://www.aaup.org/academe/issues/2010-issues-3/accreditation-and-federal-future-higher-education

[86] (2025). *Policy Implications of Curriculum Changes in Higher Education*. Pearson Center for Policy and Learning. https://pearsoncpl.com/policy-implications-of-curriculum-changes-in-higher-education/

[87] Derouich, M. (2025). *Ensuring Outcome-Based Curriculum Coherence through Systematic CLO-PLO Alignment and Feedback Loops*. arXiv preprint. https://doi.org/10.48550/arXiv.2510.25905

[88] Grauerholz, L., Lancey, P., Schellhase, K. & Watkins, C. (2020). *Linking Program Assessment to Institutional Goals*. Journal of Assessment in Higher Education 1(1). https://doi.org/10.32473/jahe.v1i1.117164

[89] Ewell, P. T. (2001). *Accreditation and Student Learning Outcomes: A Proposed Point of Departure*. Council for Higher Education Accreditation. https://www.chea.org/accreditation-and-student-learning-outcomes-proposed-point-departure

[90] (n.d.). *Accreditation Criteria*. American Higher Education Accreditation Association. https://aheaa.org/accreditation-criteria/

[91] (n.d.). *Racial and ethnic equity in US higher education*. https://www.mckinsey.com/industries/education/our-insights/racial-and-ethnic-equity-in-us-higher-education

[92] Henebery, B. (September 15, 2024). *Inclusive Teaching Boosts Student Engagement – Study*. The Educator K/12. https://www.theeducatoronline.com/k12/news/inclusive-teaching-boosts-student-engagement--study/285605

[93] Bavishi, P., Birnhak, A., Gaughan, J., Mitchell-Williams, J. & Phadtare, S. (2022). *Active Learning: A Shift from Passive Learning to Student Engagement Improves Understanding and Contextualization of Nutrition and Community Health*. Education Sciences 12(7). https://doi.org/10.3390/educsci12070430

[94] (2026). *Equitable and Inclusive Teaching and Learning*. University at Buffalo. https://www.buffalo.edu/catt/teach/develop/design/equitable-inclusive.html

[95] (November 30, 2025). *Open Educational Resources Reduce Financial Barriers*. EAB. https://eab.com/resources/research-report/use-open-educational-resources-to-reduce-financial-barriers-to-academic-success/

[96] Korp, A. (January 8, 2025). *Employers Seek Ethical, Adaptable Graduates in 2025 Job Market*. Drexel University's LeBow College of Business. https://drexel.edu/news/archive/2025/January/Employers-Seek-Ethical-Adaptable-Graduates-in-2025-Job-Market

[97] (2023). *Why Diverse Teams Drive Breakthrough Creativity*. Diversity Council Business Blog. https://diversitycouncil.org/why-diverse-teams-drive-breakthrough-creativity/

[98] Boor, I., Gerritsen, D., Greef, L. d. & Rodermans, J. (2021). *Meaningful Assessment in Interdisciplinary Education: A Practical Handbook for University Teachers*. Routledge. https://www.routledge.com/Meaningful-Assessment-in-Interdisciplinary-Education-A-Practical-Handbook-for-University-Teachers/Boor-Gerritsen-Greef-Rodermans/p/book/9789463729048

[99] Dallalfar, A., Kingston-Mann, E. & Sieber, T. (2011). *Transforming Classroom Culture: Inclusive Pedagogical Practices*. Springer. https://link.springer.com/book/10.1057/9780230370319

[100] (2000). *Dimensionality and Disciplinary Differences in Personal Epistemology*. Contemporary Educational Psychology 25(4), pp. 378-405. https://doi.org/10.1006/ceps.1999.1026

[101] (2006). *Cultural competence in interdisciplinary collaborations: a method for respecting diversity in research partnerships*. Journal of Nursing Education 45(1), pp. 19-25. https://doi.org/10.3928/01484834-20060101-08

[102] Joseph, M., Spencer, L. & Miranda, J. L. (2025). *Emerging Dialogues - Collaborative Rubric Development*. Emerging Dialogues in Assessment. https://www.aalhe.org/emerging-dialogues---collaborative-rubric-development

[103] (2025). *Resource sharing practices in academic research libraries – cancellations and tools*. The Journal of Academic Librarianship 51(5). https://doi.org/10.1016/j.acalib.2025.103105

[104] (2024). *Complexities of Interdisciplinary Learning in Higher Education: Insights and Strategies*. Interdisciplinary Education: Breaking Down Barriers and Overcoming Challenges (INTERD-BBC). https://blog.nus.edu.sg/interdbbc/2024/08/29/complexities-of-interdisciplinary-learning-in-higher-education-insights-and-strategies/

[105] (n.d.). *Bob Jensen's threads on Higher Education Controversies*. Bob Jensen's threads on Higher Education Controversies. http://faculty.trinity.edu/rjensen/HigherEdControversies.htm

[106] (2022). *Students' experiences of fairness in summative assessment: A study in a higher education context*. Studies in Educational Evaluation 72. https://doi.org/10.1016/j.stueduc.2021.101118

[107] Boor, I., Gerritsen, D., Greef, L. d. & Rodermans, J. (2021). *Meaningful Assessment in Interdisciplinary Education: A Practical Handbook for University Teachers*. Routledge. https://www.routledge.com/Meaningful-Assessment-in-Interdisciplinary-Education-A-Practical-Handbook-for-University-Teachers/Boor-Gerritsen-Greef-Rodermans/p/book/9789463729048

[108] (2025). *Active learning strategies in video learning: A meta-analysis*. Educational Research Review 48. https://doi.org/10.1016/j.edurev.2025.100708

[109] (2023). *Teaching presence promotes learner affective engagement: The roles of cognitive load and need for cognition.* Teaching and Teacher Education 129. https://doi.org/10.1016/j.tate.2023.104167

[110] Freeman, S., Eddy, S. L., McDonough, M., Smith, M. K., Okoroafor, N., Jordt, H. & Wenderoth, M. P. (2014). Active learning increases student performance in science, engineering, and mathematics. Proceedings of the National Academy of Sciences 111(23), pp. 8410-8415. https://doi.org/10.1073/pnas.131903011

[111] Deci, E. L. & Ryan, R. M. (2000). *Self-determination theory and the facilitation of intrinsic motivation, social development, and well-being.* American Psychologist 55(1), pp. 68-78. https://doi.org/10.1037/0003-066X.55.1.68

[112] (2025). *The influence of teacher leadership on student self-determination in higher education: The moderating role of institutional support and classroom climate.* Social Sciences & Humanities Open 12. https://doi.org/10.1016/j.ssaho.2025.102166

[113] (2021). *An Investigation of Instructors' Online Teaching Readiness.* Journal of Medical Education and Curricular Development 8, p. 238212052110303. https://doi.org/10.1177/23821205211030307

[114] (n.d.). *Section 504 of the Rehabilitation Act of 1973.* https://www.hhs.gov/civil-rights/for-individuals/disability/section-504-rehabilitation-act-of-1973/index.html

[115] Haywood, B. K., Boyd, D. E. & McArthur, J. A. (2023). *Purpose, place, and people: How the pandemic helped foster open and inclusive course design.* To Improve the Academy: A Journal of Educational Development 42(1), pp. 5-20. https://doi.org/10.3998/tia.1680

[116] (2026). *FERPA Compliance Guidelines.* University of Maine System. https://www.maine.edu/information-technology/ferpa-compliance-guidelines/

[117] Harrison, B. (2023). *An Educators Handbook Promotes Compliance in Higher Ed.* ComplianceBridge. https://compliancebridge.com/educators-handbook/

[118] (n.d.). *The Impact of Belonging on Student Growth.* ASCD. https://www.ascd.org/el/articles/the-impact-of-belonging-on-student-growth

[119] Services, S. A. (n.d.). *Universal Design for Learning: Assessment.* Portland State University. https://www.pdx.edu/student-academic-support-services/testing-services/faculty/universal-design-for-learning-assessment

[120] (2025). *Growth Mindset in the Higher Education Classroom.* University of North Texas. https://digitalstrategy.unt.edu/clear/files/growthmindsettipsheet.pdf

[121] (2025). *Growth Mindset in the Higher Education Classroom*. University of North Texas. https://digitalstrategy.unt.edu/clear/files/growthmindsettipsheet.pd

[122] Tadulako, M. U., Tadulako, D. U., Tadulako, W. U. & Tadulako, M. M. (2020). *Factors Contributing to Student Anxiety during Classroom Presentation: A Qualitative Study*. ELS Journal on Interdisciplinary Studies in Humanities 8(2), pp. 442-450. https://doi.org/10.34050/els-jish.v8i2.44297

[123] (2025). *Game-Based Learning Enhances Engagement and Comprehension in Undergraduate Architecture and Biology Education*. MDPI 16(1). https://doi.org/10.3390/educsci16010009

[124] Sajja, R., Sermet, Y., Cikmaz, M., Cwiertny, D. & Demir, I. (2023). *Artificial Intelligence-Enabled Intelligent Assistant for Personalized and Adaptive Learning in Higher Education*. arXiv preprint. https://doi.org/10.48550/arXiv.2309.10892

[125] (2025). *The Use of Extended Reality (XR) in Higher Education: A Systematic Review*. TechTrends 69. https://doi.org/10.1007/s11528-025-01092-y

[126] (2020). *Quality of Feedback in Higher Education: A Review of Literature*. Educ. Sci. 2020. https://doi.org/10.3390/educsci10030060

[127] Chisum, R. (October 15, 2024). *The Poltergeist of Poor Feedback: How Inadequate or Delayed Feedback Can Haunt Student Success*. Sam Houston State University Online. https://online.shsu.edu/publications/news/2024/october/the-poltergeist-of-poor-feedback.html

[128] (2025). *Feedback that improves Student Performance*. University of New Brunswick. https://www.unb.ca/fredericton/cetl/services/teaching-tips/instructional-methods/feedback-that-improves-student-performance.html

[129] (2025). The Impact of Timely Formative Feedback on University Student Motivation. International Journal of Academic Research in Progressive Education and Development 14, pp. 1-12. https://kwpublications.com/papers_submitted/17528/the-role-of-effective-feedback-in-enhancing-student-academic-achievement-a-comprehensive-study.pdf

[130] Maille, P. (2021). *The Competing Impacts of Negative Feedback on Academic Performance*. Journal of Applied Business and Economics 23(2). https://doi.org/10.33423/jabe.v23i2.4102

[131] Maille, P. (2021). *The Competing Impacts of Negative Feedback on Academic Performance*. Journal of Applied Business and Economics 23(2). https://doi.org/10.33423/jabe.v23i2.4102

[132] Mulenga, R. & Shilongo, H. (2024). *Academic Integrity in Higher Education: Understanding and Addressing Plagiarism*. Acta Pedagogia Asiana 3(1). https://doi.org/10.53623/apga.v3i1.337

[133] T., B., S., M., M., M., J., M., S., E. & B., S. (2024). *Fabricating Citations: The Policies of New Jersey Public Institutions of Higher Education*. Journal of Academic Ethics. https://doi.org/10.1007/s10805-024-09564-1

[134] Brown, S. J. & Hammond, K. (2022). *Plagiarism in Higher Education: Navigating a Perfect Storm*. European Journal of Education and Pedagogy 3(5). https://doi.org/10.24018/ejedu.2022.3.5.452

[135] Weber-Wulff, D., Anohina-Naumeca, A., Bjelobaba, S., Foltýnek, T., Guerrero-Dib, J., Popoola, O., Šigut, P. & Waddington, L. (2023). *Testing of Detection Tools for AI-Generated Text*. International Journal for Educational Integrity. https://doi.org/10.1007/s40940-023-00185-0

[136] (2025). *Misrepresentation: Copying and Pasting – Academic Integrity at East Central University*. East Central University. https://open.ocolearnok.org/ecuacademicintegrity/chapter/misrepresentation-copying/

[137] Oliveira, E. A., Mohoni, M., López-Pernas, S. & Saqr, M. (2025). *Human-AI Collaboration or Academic Misconduct? Measuring AI Use in Student Writing Through Stylometric Evidence*. arXiv preprint. https://doi.org/10.48550/arXiv.2505.08828

[138] (2025). Benefits and Challenges of Alternative Assessment Methods in Higher Education. International Journal of Social Impact. https://ijsi.in/wp-content/uploads/2025/02/18.02.009.20251001.pd

[139] kizi, K. B. (2025). THE IMPACT OF LEARNING STYLES ON MEMORY AND INFORMATION RETENTION. American Journal of Education and Learning. https://advancedscienti.com/index.php/AJEL/article/view/1401

[140] Bassner, P., Frankford, E. & Krusche, S. (2024). *Iris: An AI-Driven Virtual Tutor For Computer Science Education*. arXiv preprint arXiv:2405.08008. https://doi.org/10.48550/arXiv.2405.08008

[141] Sajja, R., Sermet, Y., Cikmaz, M., Cwiertny, D. & Demir, I. (2023). *Artificial Intelligence-Enabled Intelligent Assistant for Personalized and Adaptive Learning in Higher Education*. arXiv preprint. https://doi.org/10.48550/arXiv.2309.10892

[142] Delianidi, M., Diamantaras, K., Moras, I. & Sidiropoulos, A. (2024). *DK-PRACTICE: An Intelligent Educational Platform for Personalized Learning Content Recommendations Based on Students Knowledge State*. arXiv preprint. https://doi.org/10.48550/arXiv.2501.10373

[143] Hamadi, R., Rezgui, A. & Darejeh, A. (2025). *From Service-Oriented Computing to Metaverse Services: A Framework for Inclusive and Immersive Learning for Neurodivergent Students*. arXiv preprint arXiv:2509.15545. https://doi.org/10.48550/arXiv.2509.15545

[144] Hamadi, R., Rezgui, A. & Darejeh, A. (2025). *From Service-Oriented Computing to Metaverse Services: A Framework for Inclusive and Immersive Learning for Neurodivergent Students.* arXiv preprint arXiv:2509.15545. https://doi.org/10.48550/arXiv.2509.15545

[145] Yang, L., Chang, I. & Ritz, S. (2022). *Research experiences for Canadian aspiring physicians: a descriptive analysis of medical school admission policies concerning research involvement in Canada.* BMC Medical Education 22. https://doi.org/10.1186/s12909-022-03207-y

[146] Colclasure, B. C., Alai, A., Quinn, K., Granberry, T., Doyle, E. L. & Brooks, T. D. (2024). *Voices from Graduate School and the Workforce: Identified Student Outcomes from Completing a Multi-Semester Undergraduate Research Experience Capstone.* Education Sciences. https://doi.org/10.3390/educsci14060598

[147] Walter, H. & Wade, E. (2024). *STEM Persistence Among Women, Non-Binary, and Students of Color: A Longitudinal Study of the Impact of a Residential Science-Oriented Summer Bridge Program.* Journal of STEM Education: Innovations and Research 25(2). https://doi.org/10.63504/jstem.v25i2.2647

[148] Barr, C. A., Brodeur, D. R., Kumar, U. & Heilman, D. W. (2022). *Integrating Authentic Research, Peer Learning, and High-Impact Project Work into the General Chemistry Laboratory.* Journal of Chemical Education 99(12). https://doi.org/10.1021/acs.jchemed.2c00346

[149] (2025). *The Role of Accreditation in Enhancing Academic Quality.* International Accrediting Commission for Digital Education. https://iacde.org/iacde-insights/digital-accreditation-standards-what-makes-a-school-high-quality/

[150] (n.d.). *State of Student 2024 Report.* https://www.ncuk.ac.uk/ncuk-updates/transforming-student-futures-2nd-insights-report/

[151] Bi, X. (2025). *Fostering inclusive learning environments through culturally responsive pedagogy for international students in U.S. higher education.* Journal of International Students 156, pp. 21-38. https://doi.org/10.32674/bd7brj48

[152] (2025). Student Evaluations of Teaching: Impact of Faculty Race, Ethnicity, and Accent. Journal of the PA Education Association. https://doi.org/10.17077/2158-199X.1003

[153] Greenwald, A. G., Poehlman, T. A., Uhlmann, E. L. & Banaji, M. R. (2009). *Understanding and Using the Implicit Association Test: III. Meta-Analysis of Predictive Validity.* Journal of Personality and Social Psychology 97(1). https://doi.org/10.1037/a0015575

[154] Dragoo, K. E. & Graber, A. A. (n.d.). *The Rights of Students with Disabilities Under the IDEA, Section 504, and the ADA.* https://www.congress.gov/crs-product/R48068

[155] (n.d.). *Confidentiality of Disability Documentation and Status*. Cambridge College. https://www.cambridgecollege.edu/policies-procedures/student-affairs/confidentiality-of-disability-documentation-status

[156] (2025). *Universal Design for Learning as an Equity Framework: Addressing Educational Barriers and Enablers for Diverse Non-Traditional Learners*. MDPI 15(9). https://doi.org/10.3390/educsci15091265

[157] (2023). *Inclusive and active pedagogies reduce academic outcome gaps and improve long-term performance*. PLOS Biology 21(6). https://doi.org/10.1371/journal.pbio.3001950

[158] (n.d.). *Teaching Professional Communication: A Practical Approach*. https://link.springer.com/chapter/10.1007/978-3-031-51038-0_10

[159] Kausar, F. N. (2023). *Role of Communication Styles between University Instructors and Students in Fostering a Positive Learning Environment and Enhancing Academic Success*. The Critical Review of Social Sciences Studies 4(1), pp. 1-10. https://doi.org/10.59075/psv4y717

[160] Ghafar, Z. N. (2023). *Understanding the Importance of Email Etiquette and Addressing Email Communication Challenges Among BTVI Students*. Journal of Digital Learning and Distance Education 3(5). https://doi.org/10.56778/jdlde.v3i5.353

[161] Akolgo, D. R. (2025). *The effect of professor feedback emails on student classroom participation*. Cardinal Scholar. https://doi.org/10.31274/204488

[162] O'Meara, K., Culpepper, D., Misra, J. & Jaeger, A. (2021). *The Faculty Workload and Rewards Project*. University of Maryland. https://advance.umd.edu/fwrp/home/

[163] Hesli, V. L. & Lee, J. M. (2011). *Faculty Research Productivity: Why Do Some of Our Colleagues Publish More than Others?*. PS: Political Science & Politics. https://doi.org/10.1017/S1049096511000420

[164] (2023). *Faculty Time Expenditure Across Research, Teaching, and Service: Do Gender Differences Persist?*. J Higher Educ 94(4), pp. 537-554. https://doi.org/10.1080/00221546.2023.2200190

[165] (2025). *Student Academic Grievance Procedures*. University of South Carolina. https://sc.edu/study/colleges_schools/artsandsciences/internal/documents/faculty_staff/policies/cas_policy_student_academic_grievance_procedures_august2025.pdf

[166] Andersen, G. & Team, M. R. (2024). *The Importance of Recommendation Letters in University Admission*. MoldStud. https://moldstud.com/articles/p-the-role-of-letters-of-recommendation-in-university-admissions

[167] (2025). *Grad student applicants: Avoid these common mistakes*. Achievable. https://achievable.me/exams/gre/resources/avoid-recommender-pitfalls-on-your-graduate-school-applications/

[168] (2025). *Grad student applicants: Avoid these common mistakes*. Achievable. https://achievable.me/exams/gre/resources/avoid-recommender-pitfalls-on-your-graduate-school-applications/

[169] (2025). *FERPA and Education Research - Colorado College*. Colorado College. https://www.coloradocollege.edu/other/irb/ferpa.html

[170] (2024). *Prohibited Relationships with Students*. University of Southern California. https://policy.usc.edu/prohibited-relationships-with-students/

[171] (2021). *Teaching Evaluations: Peer and Administrative Evaluations for Promotion*. Penn State College of Earth and Mineral Sciences. https://www-d9.ems.psu.edu/teaching-evaluations-peer-and-administrative-evaluations-promotion

[172] Chávez, K. & Mitchell, K. M. (2020). *Exploring Bias in Student Evaluations: Gender, Race, and Ethnicity*. PS: Political Science & Politics 53(2), pp. 270-274. https://doi.org/10.1017/S1049096519001744

[173] (n.d.). *Leveraging Self-Reflection to Improve your Teaching*. UCLA Teaching & Learning Center. https://teaching.ucla.edu/resources/teaching-guides/leveraging-self-reflection-to-improve-your-teaching/

[174] Innovation, U. o. (n.d.). *Peer Observation of Teaching*. University of California. https://dtei.uci.edu/peer-observation-of-teaching/

[175] (November 30, 2023). *Peer Observation and Professional Development in Higher Education*. Nature Research Intelligence. https://www.nature.com/research-intelligence/nri-topic-summaries/peer-observation-and-professional-development-in-higher-education-micro-167416

[176] Development, C. S. (2025). *Guidelines and Best Practices for Peer Observations of Teaching*. California State University. https://www.csuchico.edu/faaf/_assets/documents/guidelines-peer-observations.pdf

[177] Development, C. S. (2025). *Guidelines and Best Practices for Peer Observations of Teaching*. California State University. https://www.csuchico.edu/faaf/_assets/documents/guidelines-peer-observations.pdf

[178] Diversity, O. o. (n.d.). *Best Practices in Faculty Mentoring*. Cornell University. https://facultydevelopment.cornell.edu/faculty-development/mentorship/best-practices-in-faculty-mentoring/

[179] (2024). *FACULTY HANDBOOK*. Walsh University. https://www.walsh.edu/_files/WU-Faculty-Handbook-v35-Final_December-2024.pdf

[180] (n.d.). *Teaching Portfolios*. DePaul University Teaching Commons. https://resources.depaul.edu/teaching-commons/teaching-guides/reflective-practice/Pages/teaching-portfolios.aspx

[181] Dee, K., Livesay, G. & Williams, J. (n.d.). *Preparing Your Teaching Portfolio*. https://peer.asee.org/preparing-your-teaching-portfolio

[182] (April 21, 2025). *Reconsidering Student Evaluations of Teaching*. American Sociological Association. https://www.asanet.org/for-press/press-releases/reconsidering-student-evaluations-of-teaching/

[183] (2025). *The Link Between Faculty Development and Institutional Success*. National Center for Faculty Development and Diversity. https://www.ncfdd.org/resources/the-link-between-faculty-development-and-institutional-success/

[184] (2025). *Evidence of Teaching Effectiveness*. Center for Teaching Excellence Resources. https://cteresources.bc.edu/documentation/teaching-portfolios/evidence-of-teaching-effectiveness/

[185] Bachmann, J., Espín-Noboa, L., Iñiguez, G. & Karimi, F. (2024). *Cumulative Advantage of Brokerage in Academia*. arXiv preprint. https://doi.org/10.48550/arXiv.2407.11909

[186] (2025). *Faculty as Partners in Assurance of Learning*. AACSB International. https://www.aacsb.edu/insights/articles/2025/05/faculty-as-partners-in-assurance-of-learning

[187] (n.d.). *FAQs on Shared Governance*. American Association of University Professors (AAUP). https://www.aaup.org/programs/shared-governance/faqs-shared-governance

[188] (n.d.). *Seven principles for effective change management*. Deloitte US. https://www.deloitte.com/us/en/Industries/government-public/articles/effective-change-management-higher-education.html

[189] Eickholt, J. (2018). *Barriers to Active Learning for Computer Science Faculty*. arXiv preprint arXiv:1808.02426. https://doi.org/10.48550/arXiv.1808.02426

[190] Eickholt, J. (2018). *Barriers to Active Learning for Computer Science Faculty*. arXiv preprint arXiv:1808.02426. https://doi.org/10.48550/arXiv.1808.02426

[191] (October 23, 2024). *Advising appointments correlated with higher student retention*. Penn State University. https://www.psu.edu/news/office-undergraduate-education/story/advising-appointments-correlated-higher-student-retention

[192] (2013). *Best Practices in Faculty Mentoring*. Penn State College of Earth and Mineral Sciences. https://www.ems.psu.edu/resources-faculty-and-staff/mentoring-best-practices

[193] (2025). *Mentorship Effects on Stress and Practice Readiness for Nurse Practitioner Students*. The Journal for Nurse Practitioners 21(10). https://doi.org/10.1016/j.nurpra.2025.105560

[194] Diversity, C. U. (n.d.). *Best Practices in Faculty Mentoring*. Cornell University. https://facultydevelopment.cornell.edu/faculty-development/mentorship/best-practices-in-faculty-mentoring/

[195] (September 23, 2024). *Survey: Gaps persist in college student resource awareness*. Inside Higher Ed. https://www.insidehighered.com/news/student-success/academic-life/2024/09/24/survey-gaps-persist-college-student-resource

[196] Alcivar, D., Flositz, E., Garib, V. & Savidakis, J. (2021). *Fostering Faculty Champions for Student Career Readiness*. NACE Journal. https://www.naceweb.org/research/reports/the-integration-of-career-readiness-into-experiential-learning-and-high-impact-practices/5870e224-1377-4662-8a96-cb6e37235652

[197] (May 13, 2025). *Internships, Experiential Learning Impact Early Career Success*. National Association of Colleges and Employers. https://naceweb.org/about-us/press/internships-experiential-learning-impact-early-career-success

[198] Collins, M. (April 21, 2024). *Collaborating With Faculty for Successful Student Outcomes, Institutional Effectiveness*. National Association of Colleges and Employers. https://www.naceweb.org/diversity-equity-and-inclusion/individuals-with-disabilities/ready-willing-but-still-underemployed/89f1fbd2-6163-4270-9ff7-3775f1e9e3e6

[199] Vitae, I. (2024). *Alumni Engagement Strategies That Work*. Vitae. https://www.vitaeready.org/learning-hub/alumni-engagement-strategies-that-work/

[200] Washaya, S. (2025). *Plagiarism and its effects on the quality, credibility and integrity of student research at GZU*. DZIMBAHWE JOURNAL OF MULTIDISCIPLINARY RESEARCH 3(1). https://gzuscholar.gzu.ac.zw/index.php/DJMR/article/view/86

[201] (n.d.). *The Importance of Citing Sources in Academic Writing*. Knowway.org. https://www.knowway.org/en/the-importance-of-citing-sources-in-academic-writing

[202] (2025). *AI Plagiarism Detection Tool for Educators – Packback*. Packback. https://packback.co/product/originality

[203] Weber-Wulff, D. (2023). *Testing of detection tools for AI-generated text*. International Journal for Educational Integrity. https://doi.org/10.1007/s40979-023-00146-z

[204] Reddy, R. G., Lee, D., Fung, Y. R., Nguyen, K. D., Zeng, Q., Li, M., Wang, Z., Voss, C. & Ji, H. (2023). *SmartBook: AI-Assisted Situation Report Generation for Intelligence Analysts*. arXiv preprint. https://doi.org/10.48550/arXiv.2303.14337

[205] Mazaheriyan, A. & Nourbakhsh, E. (2025). *Beyond the Hype: Critical Analysis of Student Motivations and Ethical Boundaries in Educational AI Use in Higher Education*. arXiv preprint. https://doi.org/10.48550/arXiv.2511.11369

[206] (2026). *Guidance for Faculty on Addressing AI-Related Academic Integrity Issues*. Harvard University. https://bokcenter.harvard.edu/guidance-faculty-addressing-ai-related-academic-integrity-issues

[207] (2022). *Striking a Balance between Work and Play: The Effects of Work–Life Interference and Burnout on Faculty Turnover Intentions and Career Satisfaction*. International Journal of Environmental Research and Public Health 19(2). https://doi.org/10.3390/ijerph19020809

[208] (2024). *Tabulating NIAID's R01 and R21 Application and Award Counts for FY 2024*. NIAID: National Institute of Allergy and Infectious Diseases. https://www.niaid.nih.gov/grants-contracts/r01-and-r21-application-and-award-counts-2024

[209] Hanson, M. A., Barreiro, P. G., Crosetto, P. & Brockington, D. (2023). *The strain on scientific publishing*. arXiv preprint. https://doi.org/10.48550/arXiv.2309.15884

[210] (n.d.). *BARRIERS TO ADVANCEMENT*. https://transforms.sfsu.edu/sites/default/files/documents/IT_Catalyst_Brief_FINAL_EE2%203.pdf

[211] (2022). *Striking a Balance between Work and Play: The Effects of Work–Life Interference and Burnout on Faculty Turnover Intentions and Career Satisfaction*. International Journal of Environmental Research and Public Health 19(2). https://doi.org/10.3390/ijerph19020809

[212] (n.d.). *Imposter Syndrome | Center for Teaching and Learning*. Stanford University Center for Teaching and Learning. https://ctl.stanford.edu/imposter-syndrome

[213] (2024). *EDU Funding Rates - Directorate for STEM Education (EDU) | NSF*. National Science Foundation. https://www.nsf.gov/edu/funding-rates

[214] (2025). *Journal Acceptance Rates and Publishing Timelines*. Human Guide. https://premierdissertations.com/journal-acceptance-rates/

[215] (2024). *Maximizing opportunities for success as an early career STEM faculty: a growth mindset approach*. BMC Proceedings 18. https://doi.org/10.1186/s12919-025-00356-y

[216] (2022). *A systematic review of at-work recovery and a framework for future research*. Journal of Vocational Behavior 137. https://doi.org/10.1016/j.jvb.2022.103747

[217] Jauregui, J. & McClintock, A. (2021). *Creating Psychological Safety in the Learning Environment: Straightforward Answers to a Longstanding Challenge*. Academic Medicine 96. https://doi.org/10.1097/ACM.0000000000004319

[218] (2025). *Microaggression*. Wikipedia. https://en.wikipedia.org/wiki/Microaggression

[219] "Dall-E," OpenAI, [Online]. Available: https://chatgpt.com/g/g-2fkFE8rbu-dall-e. [Accessed 2026].

About the Author

Dr. David A. Schippers, Sc.D., CISSP, is not a theorist of higher education—he is a systems builder who has lived inside its pressure points.

A scholar-practitioner with deep roots in cybersecurity, organizational leadership, and academic governance, Dr. Schippers has spent decades working at the intersection of industry, technology, and higher education. As a Chief Academic Officer, dean, department chair, and faculty mentor, he has redesigned academic programs, rebuilt faculty development models, and helped institutions move from inertia to intentional excellence.

The Faculty Keystone emerges from a hard truth he has witnessed repeatedly across many institutions: brilliant professionals are hired into academia with little preparation for the psychological, pedagogical, and ethical demands of teaching—and then left to survive by imitation rather than mastery.

This book is not about checking boxes or surviving probationary years. It is about forming faculty identity.

Drawing from adult learning theory, Jungian psychology, assessment science, accreditation realities, and real-world classroom experience, Dr. Schippers equips new and transitioning faculty to move beyond content delivery toward intentional, student-centered, and resilient teaching practice. He challenges the myth that rigor requires rigidity, that authority demands distance, or that burnout is simply the price of belonging.

His writing blends practical frameworks with deep reflection—connecting course design to identity, assessment to ethics, technology to human judgment, and mentorship to long-term institutional health. At the core of his philosophy is a simple but disruptive belief:

Faculty are not interchangeable parts in a system.
They are keystones.
And when they fracture, the structure collapses.

Dr. Schippers continues his work mentoring faculty and academic leaders who are ready to stop replicating inherited dysfunction and start building learning environments grounded in clarity, courage, and professional integrity.

This book does not offer shortcuts. It offers foundations. And for those entrusted with shaping minds, foundations are everything.

Continue the Conversation with Dr. David A. Schippers

If *The Faculty Keystone* resonated with you, your journey does not end here.

Dr. David A. Schippers writes at the intersection of leadership, higher education, cybersecurity, and artificial intelligence, challenging conventional thinking while equipping professionals with practical frameworks for real-world impact. His books confront complexity directly, offering clarity where institutions, systems, and leaders often fall short.

Explore other titles by Dr. Schippers:

Burn the Script: Kill the Leadership Theater, Lead for Real
A direct challenge to performative leadership culture. Built from decades of executive and academic experience, this book equips leaders to make difficult decisions, build trust under pressure, and lead with clarity rather than slogans.

The Force of Technology
A comprehensive examination of innovation, cybersecurity, and risk management in a rapidly evolving digital landscape. Designed for leaders and professionals navigating technological disruption with strategic discipline.

The Scholar's Key: Hidden Knowledge for Doctoral Achievement
A structured, principled roadmap for doctoral candidates seeking clarity, momentum, and resilience in advanced academic work.

Across disciplines and industries, Dr. Schippers' work shares a common thread: formation over performance, integrity over appearance, and leadership grounded in responsibility.

Whether you serve in higher education, industry, government, or executive leadership, his books provide frameworks that endure beyond trends and tactics.

To discover more titles, speaking engagements, and academic resources, search for **Dr. David A. Schippers** wherever books are sold.

Lead intentionally. Build wisely. Strengthen what holds everything together.